SOCIAL COMMUNICATIC
DEVELOPMENT AND DISORDERS

This new standout volume is the first to describe developmental areas associated with social competence and social communication, as well as provide evidence-based information on effective assessment and intervention for children who have problems with social communication and social interactions. Expertly crafted, the volume offers both theory and practice within one comprehensive, yet manageable resource for busy professionals. The first section covers social communication theory and associated developmental domains. Case studies are provided to exemplify how different variables may affect social communication development. The second section covers evidence-based practices for social communication disorders and includes case studies, incidence and prevalence estimates, the current *DSM-5* definition of the disorder, referral guidelines, recommended practices of assessment and intervention, and a list of clinical resources.

Social Communication Development and Disorders is an ideal text for a range of courses in Communication Sciences and Disorders or Speech-Language Pathology, and a must-have reference for professionals working with children with social competence or social communication problems, including speech-language pathologists (SLPs), regular and special educators, psychologists, and support personnel such as social workers, counselors, and occupational therapists.

Deborah A. Hwa-Froelich, PhD, Professor at Saint Louis University, conducts research on sociocultural, socioeconomic, and social-emotional factors influencing communication development and disorders. She has received several awards, including Fellow of the American Speech-Language-Hearing Association and the Angel in Adoption award from the Congressional Coalition for Adoption Institute.

LANGUAGE AND SPEECH DISORDERS
BOOK SERIES
Series Editors
Martin J. Ball, Linköping University, Sweden
Jack S. Damico, University of Louisiana at Lafayette

This new series brings together course material and new research for students, practitioners, and researchers in the various areas of language and speech disorders. Textbooks covering the basics of the discipline will be designed for courses within communication disorders programs in the English-speaking world, and monographs and edited collections will present cutting-edge research from leading scholars in the field.

PUBLISHED

Recovery from Stuttering, Howell

Handbook of Vowels and Vowel Disorders, Ball & Gibbon (Eds.)

Handbook of Qualitative Research in Communication Disorders, Ball, Müller & Nelson (Eds.)

Dialogue and Dementia, Schrauf & Müller (Eds.)

Understanding Individual Differences in Language Development Across the School Years, Tomblin and Nippold (Eds.)

Unusual Productions in Phonology: Universals and Language-Specific Considerations, Yavaş (Ed.)

Social Communication Development and Disorders, Hwa-Froelich (Ed.)

For continually updated information about published and forthcoming titles in the *Language and Speech Disorders* book series, please visit **www.psypress.com/language-and-speech-disorders**

SOCIAL COMMUNICATION DEVELOPMENT AND DISORDERS

Edited by
Deborah A. Hwa-Froelich

Psychology Press
Taylor & Francis Group

NEW YORK AND LONDON

KH

First published 2015
by Psychology Press
711 Third Avenue, New York, NY 10017

and by Psychology Press
27 Church Road, Hove, East Sussex BN3 2FA

Psychology Press is an imprint of the Taylor & Francis Group, an informa business

Library of Congress Cataloging in Publication Data

Social communication development and disorders / edited by Deborah A. Hwa-Froelich.
     pages cm — (Language and Speech Disorders)
     Includes bibliographical references and index.
  1. Children with social disabilities.   2. Child development.   3. Child psychology.
  I. Hwa-Froelich, Deborah A., editor.
     HV713.S617   2014
     362.7—dc23
     2014026524

ISBN: 978-1-84872-534-8 (hbk)
ISBN: 978-1-84872-535-5 (pbk)
ISBN: 978-1-315-73562-7 (ebk)

Typeset in Minion
by Apex CoVantage, LLC

Printed and bound in the United States of America by Publishers Graphics, LLC on sustainably sourced paper.

7/15/15

For my children and grandchildren who taught me much about social-emotional and social communication development.

CONTENTS

CONTRIBUTORS

Catherine Adams, PhD, is a clinical senior lecturer in Speech and Language Therapy at the University of Manchester in the UK. She has previously worked in health care and schools services with a range of children who have communication needs. Dr. Adams's research interests lie in understanding pragmatic language impairments and comprehension difficulties in children and obtaining evidence to support interventions. She is still a practicing speech and language pathologist.

Bonnie Brinton, PhD, is a professor of Communication Disorders at Brigham Young University (BYU), Provo, Utah. Her work focuses on assessment and intervention with children who experience difficulty with social communication. Dr. Brinton has been a professor at the University of Nevada; a research scientist at the Schiefelbusch Institute for Lifespan Studies, University of Kansas; and Dean of Graduate Studies at BYU. She is a fellow of the American Speech-Language-Hearing Association.

Danai K. Fannin, PhD, is an assistant professor of Communicative Disorders at Northern Illinois University. She received her PhD from the University of North Carolina at Chapel Hill and was a postdoctoral fellow in the lab of Connie Kasari, PhD, at the Neuropsychiatric Institute at University of California, Los Angeles. Her research interests include the development of evidence-based autism treatment, with a focus on providing appropriate evaluation and intervention for culturally and linguistically diverse families.

Martin Fujiki, PhD, is a professor of Communication Disorders at Brigham Young University (BYU), Provo, Utah. He has authored numerous publications in the area of social and emotional competence in children with language impairment. Dr. Fujiki has been a professor at the University of Nevada and BYU, and a research scientist at the Schiefelbusch Institute for Lifespan Studies, University of Kansas. He is currently serving as an associate editor for *Language Speech and Hearing Services in Schools*. He is a fellow of the American Speech-Language-Hearing Association.

Deborah A. Hwa-Froelich, PhD, is professor in the department of Communication Sciences and Disorders at Saint Louis University. Her research focuses on sociocultural, socioeconomic, and social-emotional factors influencing communication development and disorders. She is the Founder of and a consultant for the International Adoption Clinic at Saint Louis University. Some of the awards she has received for her work include Louis M. Di Carlo Award, Diversity Champion, and Fellow of the American Speech-Language-Hearing Association. She also received the Angel in Adoption award from the Congressional Coalition for Adoption Institute for her work with children adopted from abroad.

Geralyn R. Timler, PhD, is an assistant professor and Director of the Child Language and Social Communication Lab in the Department of Speech Pathology and Audiology at Miami University. Her clinical and research interests focus on social communication and pragmatic skills in preschoolers and school-age children with Fetal Alcohol Spectrum Disorders, Specific Language Impairment, Attention Deficit Hyperactivity Disorder (ADHD), and Autism Spectrum Disorders. She has developed a hypothetical peer conflict task to examine children's knowledge about goals and strategies for resolving conflicts with peers. She has also examined the accuracy of parent report measures, norm-referenced language tests, and conversational language samples to identify language impairment and pragmatic deficits in children with ADHD. Her work has been funded by the American Speech, Language, and Hearing Foundation. Dr. Timler is currently serving on the coordinating committee for the American Speech-Language-Hearing Association's Special Interest Group 1, "Language, Learning, and Education."

Linda R. Watson, EdD, CCC-SLP, is a professor in the Division of Speech & Hearing Sciences at UNC–Chapel Hill. She has extensive clinical and research expertise in development of and interventions for young children with ASD. She currently engages in interdisciplinary autism research, graduate teaching related to autism and other aspects of translational research, and extensive mentoring of undergraduate and graduate students with interests in autism research. Ongoing collaborative research includes efficacy studies of a parent-mediated intervention for infants at risk for autism and a classroom-based social-communication intervention for preschoolers with ASD, a longitudinal study of prelinguistic predictors of later language outcomes in children with ASD, and a study of sensory processing patterns of children with autism or other developmental disabilities.

Carol E. Westby, PhD, CCC-SLP, has received the Honors of ASHA, Fellow, and the Certificate of Recognition for Special Contributions to Multicultural Affairs awards. She has published extensively and presents nationally and internationally on a variety of topics related to child language, literacy, and social-emotional development. She is currently a consultant/supervisor for Bilingual Multicultural Services where she is piloting a program to promote social-emotional development in preschool/elementary school children.

Katherine E. White, BS, will be completing her Master's degree in speech-language pathology at Miami University in Oxford, Ohio. Her contribution to this book includes excerpts from her undergraduate senior honor's thesis, titled "Fetal Alcohol Spectrum Disorder (FASD): What Clinicians Need to Know." This undergraduate project was supported by a Dean's Scholar Award from Miami University's College of Arts and Sciences.

FIGURES

TABLES

ACKNOWLEDGMENTS

Several individuals made significant contributions to this book. I would especially like to thank the contributing authors, without whom this book would not have been possible: Catherine Adams, Bonnie Brinton, Danai Fannin, Martin Fujiki, Geralyn Timler, Linda Watson, Carol Westby, and Katherine E. White. I have had the pleasure of working with many graduate students who also helped with literature searches and with reviewing and editing the book chapters: Mary Clare Becker, Lindsey Boville, Kelsey Rosenquist, and Rebecca Odegard.

Section I

SOCIAL COMMUNICATION THEORY AND
ASSOCIATED DEVELOPMENTAL DOMAINS

1

SOCIAL COMMUNICATION THEORETICAL FOUNDATIONS AND INTRODUCTION

Deborah A. Hwa-Froelich

These children [children with pragmatic disorder] spoke aloud to no one in particular, displayed inadequate conversational skills, exhibited poor maintenance of topic and verbosity and answered besides the point of a question in the presence of unimpaired phonology and syntax.

—Cummings (2009, p. 47)

LEARNING OBJECTIVES

Readers will be able to

1. Define *social competence, pragmatic language,* and *social communication disorder.*
2. Describe the heterogeneity of social communication disorders.
3. Discuss theories related to social communication.

Oliver was initially seen at a Child Find screening at the age of 3.5 years. He was the firstborn son of a two-parent Caucasian family from a working-class background that included a younger sister who was 15 months old. Although Oliver passed the hearing, motor, and cognitive sections of the screener, he demonstrated difficulty answering questions and retelling a story. His parents reported that he had difficulty playing with his cousins and neighborhood children because he interrupted their play, interrupted their conversations, and talked nonstop about topics unrelated to what everyone else had been talking about.

During a more thorough evaluation, Oliver demonstrated low average receptive and expressive language skills. In particular, Oliver often answered wh-questions inappropriately, including questions asking who, what, where, when, or why. His language sample consisted of several utterances covering a variety of unrelated topics. When asked to retell a story, he included few details about the original story and added extraneous information. He was observed to interrupt the examiner and often expressed off-topic comments. Oliver demonstrated appropriate functional and symbolic play, but his symbolic play appeared to involve fewer objects and linked steps as well as fewer instances of goal-directed play. For example, he often loaded blocks and miniature animals into a truck, drove the truck to another location, and dumped the animals and blocks without a goal as to where the animals were going or what the blocks were to be used for at the new location.

Oliver demonstrated a pragmatic language impairment that was associated with a mild receptive and expressive language impairment. These weaknesses were also reflected in his symbolic play development. The early childhood team recommended that Oliver enroll into a special education preschool program to improve his receptive and expressive language, play skills, and social communication.

Oliver's profile of behaviors and development provides an example of how pragmatic language impairment can affect one's social and communicative competence across contexts and interactions. Although Oliver's language performance and play development were in the average range, he exhibited specific weaknesses that were related to social communication skills necessary for interactions and appropriate pragmatic language. It is difficult to know which developmental weakness—play or language delays—occurred first or whether these relationships are causal in nature. Yet, it is clear that Oliver was not able to interact with others successfully and needed assistance to become more socially competent. The purpose of this book is to describe developmental areas associated with social competence and social communication, and to provide evidence-based information to guide professionals working with children who have problems with social competence or social communication. This chapter includes (a) definitions of social competence, social communication, and pragmatic language; (b) descriptions of theories associated with these skills; and (c) an outline of the chapters for this book.

DEFINITIONS AND SIGNIFICANCE

What do I mean by social competence? Simply put, social competence consists of having the knowledge, skills, and behaviors to fulfill one's needs and meet his or her expectations in social interactions (Goldstein, Kaczmarek, & English, 2002). Social communicative competence includes the knowledge and appropriate use of social behaviors, competent communication, and pragmatic rules. Thus, persons with a social communication disorder have difficulty with social communication nonverbal and verbal behaviors and pragmatics. Oliver's unsuccessful interactions with peers and adults reveal his poorly developed social competence. He also struggled with social communication when he did not understand or effectively use communication in socially expected ways, such as answering questions, maintaining topics, taking turns in conversation, making accurate inferences from nonverbal behaviors or ambiguous language and repairing his communication when others did not understand him. All social interactions are contextually based and dynamic in that when involved in social interaction, individuals simultaneously access and process their knowledge and experiences with others and the world. Knowledge about people and the world is acquired through active internal and external experiences and includes facts, concepts, and social cognition of one's own feelings and intentions as well as the feelings and intentions of others. Social cognition includes understanding not only one's own knowledge of how one feels and how these feelings cause one to act in certain ways, but also how emotions cause people to act and how events or people's behavior can elicit emotions, which may be explicitly or implicitly communicated (Muma, 1991).

Social communication involves not only competent oral communication but knowledge of what communicative behaviors mean and effective sociocultural communication of intentions or needs (Crago & Eriks-Brophy, 1994; T. Gallagher, 1991; Müller, 2000). Communicative competence involves comprehension and expression of the language-specific phonology, syntax, semantics, and pragmatics. Pragmatic rules are culturally influenced rules for interaction and talk. Internal and external experiences can be shared with others both nonverbally (facial expressions, tone of voice, postures, and gestures) and verbally, which are influenced by sociocultural values that are modeled, taught, and passed down from generation to generation. These values are reflected in pragmatic rules for talking. Ninio and Snow (1996) defined pragmatic language as "the acquisition of knowledge necessary for the appropriate, effective, rule-governed employment of speech in interpersonal situations" (p. 4). Although Oliver demonstrated competent phonology, he had low average receptive and expressive language development, which affected his responses to questions and his discourse skills. Oliver had not learned how to attend to and interpret others' social communication; respond appropriately to questions; initiate, maintain, and organize discourse for conversations; or communicate his intentions appropriately. Oliver demonstrated a primary pragmatic language disorder or, according to the *Diagnostic and Statistical Manual of Mental Disorders* (5th ed.; *DSM-5*; American Psychiatric Association [APA], 2013), a social communication disorder (Müller, 2000). In other words, Oliver did not understand or use pragmatic language rules effectively, resulting in poor social communication and social competence.

Why is social competence important? Without social competence, individuals have difficulty relating to and connecting with other people. This may result in poor relationships with family, friends, teachers, coworkers, or supervisors. Without successful relationships, individuals who have poor social competence lead isolated, lonely lives. They may also struggle in the classroom, which can make attaining and maintaining employment a challenge.

The challenges faced by socially incompetent individuals are not just anecdotal. Research has provided evidence of negative outcomes for children with poor social competence (for a review see Ladd, 1999). Reviewing research on social competence, Ladd reported several studies in which children's social competence was correlated with later school adjustment problems such as truancy, discipline problems, and higher dropout rates. Several variables may affect social competence and result in myriad social outcomes. These include parental factors such as attachment, parental sensitivity, or attunement; friendship variables such as behaviors that affect acceptance and rejection of peers or facilitate friendships; and individual factors such as temperament, gender, and cultural differences.

With as many variables that play into and affect social competence, it is not surprising that there is great heterogeneity across individuals with social competence and social communication disorders. Oliver represents an example of a child with pragmatic language impairment that resulted in a mild social competence problem. However, pragmatic language impairment can be a defining characteristic of a disorder, such as Autism Spectrum Disorder (ASD) and can co-occur with language impairment (LI), and with disorders of social competence such as Attention Deficit Disorder with or without the Hyperactivity component (ADD/ADHD), disruptive behavior disorder (DBD) and children who have experienced maltreatment.

THEORETICAL FOUNDATIONS

Several theoretical perspectives provide different explanations for how social competence, communicative competence, and social communication competence are acquired. Because social competence includes culturally influenced social cognition and world knowledge, constructionist and social learning or social interaction theories may be involved. Theories explaining communicative competence in form, content, and use, include these constructivist and social learning theories as well as pragmatic theories. Social communication competence is a coalescence of the two. It accesses and compares prior world and social knowledge as well as sociocultural and linguistic rules of form, content, and use with the current interaction. Theories of information processing, connectionism, and dynamic systems may help to explain within-culture variability in social communication development and disorders.

Cognitive Constructivist and Social Learning Theories

Cognitive constructivist and social interaction theorists believe that interaction with one's world facilitates cognitive, social and communication learning and development (Hobson, 2004; Vygotsky, 1934/1986). According to Piaget's theory of cognitive development (Piaget, 1983), cognitive development precedes children's language development, and certain cognitive stages need to be attained in order for language stages to be achieved. For example, during the sensory motor stage of development, it is after children use sensory motor schema to learn about and act upon their physical environment that children learn labels associated with objects and actions.

Some theorists believe that learning occurs within social and cultural contexts (Bandura, 1986; Hobson, 2004; Vygotsky, 1934/1986). Bandura proposed a social learning theory in that when children are motivated to learn, they learn by observing and imitating others, and they expect similar outcomes for themselves following their imitation of others. Although Vygotsky also believed learning involved social interaction, it was his view that caregivers mediate children's learning to create a zone of proximal development, that is, what a child can do with adult facilitation and what a child can do independently. In other words, children's interaction with the environment is socially facilitated and provides children developmentally supported learning experiences. Vygotsky described language as a means for self-regulation. He believed that language was internalized and was a means by which children regulated their emotions and behaviors. Thus, children learn how to interact through adult-mediated social and communicative interactions.

Another social interaction theory is the Transactional model or Inter-action theory (Gallagher, S., 2013; Sameroff, 1987; Sameroff & Chandler, 1975). In this model, social interaction is bidirectional. The child interacts with and influences caregivers' responses, which, in turn, affect the child's development. In other words, the transaction of the child with his or her social environment determines developmental outcomes. The transactional nature of social interaction is varied among individuals. Both internal variables (i.e., gender, temperament, neurological devel-opment) and external variables (i.e., maternal sensitivity, parental input, birth order) can affect transactional learning, resulting in great develop-mental variability (Gallagher, S., 2013; Wetherby, 1991).

Friendship theory is related to social learning and interaction with peers. These relationships normally include familial interactions, but peer friendships, collaborative learning groups, and group member-ships are also vital (Sullivan, 1953). Children develop social skills spe-cific to the different interpersonal contexts they experience to achieve successful relationships. Initially, children learn how to coexist and play side by side, then play cooperatively by negotiating and taking on roles in dramatic play, and eventually develop friendships in which children prefer and care about another person (Goldstein & Morgan, 2002). As children mature and become more socially competent, they develop social and communication skills to participate in cooperative learning groups. These groups facilitate sharing of ideas, resources, information, encouragement, and constructive criticism toward the achievement of group goals or outcomes. These social skills eventually enable adoles-cents and adults to become functional, contributing members of a wide variety of social groups.

These theories help to explain how individuals learn and acquire social competence and acquire communication skills including lin-guistic form and content. There are additional theories that address the functions of language or pragmatic language. Communicative compe-tence involves not only form and content but also knowledge of appro-priate use of pragmatic language rules.

Pragmatic Theories

Several theorists have described theories associated with the acquisi-tion of pragmatic rules as well as different types of language use. These theories include language use, commonly referred to as speech acts, and conversational implicature or relevance. Pragmatics has been studied in relation to (a) the use of deixis, (b) the context of the interaction, and (c) comprehension and use of nonliteral language, discourse, and conversa-tion (for a review see Cummings, 2009).

Early theories formulated by Austin (1962) and Searle (1969) described how expressive language is used for more than merely reporting facts or events. Speech acts use language as a means to make promises, declarations, directions, questions, comments, threats, warnings, suggestions, and many other purposes (Searle, 1969). Individuals can differ in terms of the range of speech acts they use, as well as the range of incorrect comprehension and/or expression of speech acts.

Grice (1975) proposed a theory of conversational implicature, which was later simplified to a theory of relevance by Sperber and Wilson (1986). Grice believed there were four maxims that speakers expect during conversations with others. These include (a) quality—individuals should not give false information or unproven information; (b) quantity—individual contributions should provide just enough information, to make a point; (c) relation—contributions should retain the topic of the conversation; and (d) manner—contributions should be brief, orderly, and clear (Cummings, 2009). These four maxis were simplified to one theory of relevance in that speakers should try "to be as relevant as possible" (Wilson & Sperber, 1991, p. 381). Individuals who have problems with relevance may have difficulty making truthful statements or statements based on fact. They may not give enough information to be understood or may give too much information by talking incessantly. They may digress from the original topic, forgetting what the topic was, give irrelevant information, or add information that is unclear. For example, Oliver would often add information unrelated to the topic during conversation and story retell.

These pragmatic theories focused on language use and assumed competence in other communication areas (form and content). In order to become competent in social communication, individuals must acquire knowledge and skills in social competence and communicative competence. They need to be able to process social and communication stimuli while accessing past experiences and knowledge to determine and successfully execute an appropriate response.

Information Processing, Connectionism, and Dynamic Systems Theories

Social communication competence involves the ability to interpret both nonverbal and verbal messages, the context of the interaction, and the sociocultural interaction rules while planning and managing one's behavior during the interaction. This complex skill involves the processing of incoming information, retrieval of cognitive, social, and linguistic knowledge, working memory, and executive function skills to compare and contrast knowledge while attending to the current situation and selecting, planning, and monitoring one's response (Crick & Dodge, 1994). Two theories that help explain this process are information processing and connectionism theories. A third theory, dynamic systems theory (DST) provides an explanation for the variability across individuals' social competence, social cognition, and social communication development along with associated disorders.

According to the information processing theory, three stages are involved when appraising information: (a) a sensory memory stage, (b) a short-term or working memory stage, and (c) a long-term memory stage (Atkinson & Shiffrin, 1968). According to this theory, individuals may process stimuli bidirectionally using both bottom-up and top-down processing during the sensory memory stage. Bottom-up processing involves an individual's initial awareness and appraisal of the stimulus's emotional value. In top-down processing, individuals perceive, attend, appraise, and compare stimuli with long-term memories that are associated with or similar to the stimuli.

From information processing theory, other theories such as parallel-distributed processing, connectionist, and social information processing theories have developed. According to parallel-distributed theory, information from social communicative interactions is processed by different memory sections of the brain at the same time (Rumelhart & McClelland, 1986). In other words, processing is not sequential but simultaneous involving multiple parts of the brain. Building upon this theory, connectionist theorists believe that memory is stored in neural networks across multiple brain locations. Neural networks are formed when patterns of neural synapses (neural pathways receiving and simultaneously sending information) are activated. When neural networks are activated often, the network pattern becomes stronger and facilitates memory retrieval and generalization of information.

Social information processing theorists agree that processing is often simultaneous and can occur along parallel pathways. However, they focus their theory on "conscious rule interpretation" as opposed to having an "intuitive processor," and apply social information processing to social adjustment development (Crick & Dodge, 1994, p. 77). Crick and Dodge (1994) described the steps of social information processing when individuals interact with others. First, individuals encode the cues of the situation internally and externally. The second step involves an interpretation process during which the cues are interpreted and evaluated across causes, intentions, and personal and interpersonal goals. These are compared to memories of past experiences and social rules. Next, individuals regulate themselves to clarify their own personal goals as well as the goals of others. Clarification of goals enables them to begin the process of selecting a response by searching for and evaluating choices of behavioral responses, possible outcomes, and their ability to execute the behavioral choice in order to select and construct a response. Finally, individuals employ the response while monitoring and regulating their behavior. The partner in the social interaction responds, and the process begins again.

These processing and connectionist theories are generally founded on four assumptions: (a) the brain has capacity limitations constraining the amount, speed, and efficiency for processing; (b) there is a process manager or executive function that manages information processing to encode, transform, process, store, retrieve, and use information; (c) processing is bidirectional as described earlier; and (d) there are genetic predispositions to process information in specific ways.

Dynamic Systems Theory

While social learning and social interaction theories help to explain how learning is socially mediated, information processing and connectionism help to explain the complex neurological processes involved in interpreting and participating in social interactions. However, none of these theories explains the individual developmental variability in social communication outcomes. DST provides a model of dynamic interaction among multiple systems that helps explain the heterogeneity of social communication disorders.

DST is closely related to connectionist theory and grew from studies of complex systems in biology, physics, and psychology (Thelen & Bates, 2003). Recently, DST has been discussed as a theory to explain emotion development and self-organization (Lewis & Granic, 2000), language development and disorders (De Bot, Lowie, & Verspoor, 2007), and bilingual and disrupted language development and disorders (Hwa-Froelich, 2012; Kohnert, 2008). DST describes humans as complex systems in which complex interactions with elements of the system can result in a variety of different developmental patterns and outcomes. Through developmental processes, each individual experiences transitions during which internal systems destabilize and reorganize in systematic ways. Variables affecting transitions or changes are interrelated with other variables. Some of the constraining factors in dynamic systems may include initial system structures, such as neurobiological development, exposure to expected experiences, such as developmentally appropriate interactions with a caring adult; dependent experiences, such as sensitive nurturing interactions with the environment; and early emerging foundations of self-organization (Lewis, 1997). Human development is viewed as a nonlinear emergent process in which an individual may organize systems around *attractor states* that were formed by previous experiences or knowledge. Unstable systems require less energy to change whereas stable systems need more energy to change. For example, children diagnosed with ASD may demonstrate consistent repetitive behaviors at home, which may be an indication of a stable system with attractor states drawn toward a static, familiar, and less structured daily life. Consequently they will need more energy (attention, memory, motivation, and processing speed) to transition and function within a structured environment (such as school) with structured routines, rules, and increased novelty. Because variables and constraints can freely vary among each other, these variations can result in a mix of indeterminism and determinism resulting in large differences in developmental outcomes. Thus, development is not always predictable in a linear or simple way (Fogel, Lyra, & Valsiner, 1997).

The principles of general systems theory include (a) complex systems consist of many interdependent parts that dynamically influence each other; (b) complex systems organize in such a way that behavior of the system cannot be described in terms of the parts and relationships of the parts; (c) the unique transactions between the individual and its relationships create self-organization and stabilization over time; (d) many different processes can lead to a similar system organization or equifinality; and (e) systems dynamically create independent but related hierarchical patterns (Fogel, 1993). The more flexible the system, the greater the opportunity to make use of available resources to adjust to changes.

DST helps explain the heterogeneity and highly varied range of social behaviors and social communication performance across social communication disorders. The many involved variables as well as the multiple ways humans may self-organize may explain the variability in individual developmental outcomes. In Oliver's case, he possessed adequate cognitive and communication skills to help him learn and apply social communication strategies with peers and family members. Early intervention focused on learning the meaning and intention of questions, explicitly teaching pragmatic strategies for initiating interactions, maintaining topics in conversations, and taking turns during play with peers and conversations with adults. Sequential pictures and visual cues were used and later faded to help Oliver learn how to organize his discourse in retelling stories. After a year of early intervention, Oliver learned how to answer questions, initiate social and communicative interactions, take turns, initiate, change, and maintain topics in conversation and was able to organize his discourse in storytelling and conversations in a logical sequence.

Early intervention enabled Oliver to develop the necessary skills to achieve social communicative competence. Other children may demonstrate a more complex picture of social competence and social communication, which may be challenging for professionals working with individuals with social communication disorders. The purpose of this book is to provide information about developmental areas related to social competence and social communication as well as individual chapters devoted to evidence-based assessment and intervention practices for children with social communication disorders.

BOOK ORGANIZATION

The purpose of this book is to provide two perspectives of social communication. One perspective is that of a developmental nature. To understand atypical development, it is important to understand typical social communication development. The second perspective is a clinical one. The second section of this book focuses on a review of evidence-based practices for assessment and treatment of social communication disorders.

Evidence-Based Practice

What is evidence-based practice (EBP)? EBP has been defined as "the integration of best research evidence with clinical expertise and patient values" (Sackett, Strauss, Richardson, Rosenberg, & Haynes, 2000, p.1). Based on this definition, to provide EBP, professionals must integrate clinical expertise and/or expert opinion with the best available scientific evidence while considering the values of the client, patient, and/or caregiver. By doing so, it is more likely that practitioners will provide high-quality services that also reflect the individual interests, values, and needs of their clients and families. The American Speech-Language-Hearing Association (ASHA; 2013) describes the clinical process of providing EBP as consisting of four steps: (1) framing the clinical question, (2) finding the evidence, (3) assessing the evidence, and (4) making a clinical decision (ASHA, 2013). To frame the clinical question, practitioners consider the population, interventions, comparisons, and outcomes (PICO). The clinical question is based on the particular individual factors associated with a client or group of clients. These factors may include but are certainly not limited to such factors as age, gender, socioeconomic status, language history, and type of communication disorder. The interventions may include different therapeutic strategies or models and comparisons of these strategies or models across populations or types and severity levels of disorders. The outcome would be the effectiveness of the particular treatment strategy or model on the particular disorder or clinical question. Assessing outcomes involves the level of evidence available to answer the clinical question (ASHA, 2013).

The second step of EBP is finding the evidence to answer the clinical question. There are two kinds of evidence, systematic reviews, and individual studies. Systematic reviews are formal studies, such as meta-analyses that review high-quality evidence. High-quality evidence can include meta-analyses of randomized controlled studies, quasi-experimental design studies, and single-subject design studies. ASHA (2013) provides several websites where systematic reviews of studies on communication sciences and disorders can be found. However, sometimes, these systematic reviews are not available for all clinical questions. In this case, practitioners may search for individual studies of high quality. The levels of evidence from highest quality to lowest quality include (1) randomized control trial study; (2) well-designed, controlled study without randomization; (3) well-designed, quasi-experimental design study; (4) well-designed non-experimental correlational or case/single-subject design study; and (5) expert committee report, consensus conference, or clinical experience of respected authorities (ASHA, 2013).

Once the evidence has been located, the practitioner must assess the evidence. It is important to check that the evidence is relevant to the particular clinical question. In addition, the practitioner should review the authors of the research to assess to what extent potential for investigator bias is possible. Sometimes advocacy groups or groups who may receive financial benefit are the authors of research, which may affect their collection and interpretation of the data. Subsequent to this review, the practitioner should complete a critical review of the study design and efficacy of the interventions.

The fourth and final step in EBP is make a clinical decision. Clinical decision making involves integrating the research evidence, clinical expertise, and the client's values, goals, and needs to provide individualized services of high quality. Taking the best research evidence available and interpreting this evidence through a research lens of efficacy, a clinical lens of effectiveness, and clinical applicability in accordance with the client's preferences and needs is pulling all the components and EBP steps together. By implementing this practice, the practitioner is more likely to provide high-quality interventions and see more positive outcomes. However, the practitioner must also measure client outcomes prior to, during and following application of EBP to insure the effectiveness of their clinical intervention. This process ensures that clinical application is truly effective with their client's particular values, goals, and needs.

Book Organization

Several developmental areas form the foundations for social competence. These include neurological, social-emotional, cognitive processing, and social communication development. The first section of this book includes chapters on social neuroscience, social and emotional development, development of related cognitive processes, and social communication development. Carol Westby, PhD, is a Board-Certified Child Language Specialist and an ASHA Honors recipient, who has published and presented extensively on social communication development and disorders. She is currently a consultant/supervisor for Bilingual Multicultural Services and is designing a program to facilitate social-emotional development. She wrote Chapter 2, which describes the neurological science associated with social processing, learning, and communication. Deborah Hwa-Froelich is a professor in the Department of Communication Sciences and Disorders at Saint Louis University, and her research focuses on sociocultural, socioeconomic, and social-emotional factors influencing communication development and disorders. She is also the founder and consultant for the International Adoption Clinic at Saint Louis University. Dr. Hwa-Froelich, PhD, wrote Chapter 3, which describes social and emotional development; Chapter 4, which focuses on the development of cognitive processes; and Chapter 5, which explains social communication development. The chapter on social-emotional development includes such topics as attachment, attunement, emotion development, and self-regulation. The chapter on cognitive processes involved with social communication development discusses attention, social cognition, memory, and executive function development. Finally Chapter 5 focuses on social communication development including intersubjectivity, nonverbal communication, verbal communication, and pragmatic language development. The chapters in Section I include a case study and a description of variables that may affect social communication development.

Each chapter in the second section of the book includes a case study, incidence, and prevalence estimates, the current *DSM*-5 definition of the disorder, referral guidelines, recommended practices of assessment and intervention, and a list of clinical resources. Specialists with clinical and research experience specific to social communication disorders have written these chapters. Catherine Adams, PhD, is a senior lecturer at the University of Manchester with extensive research and clinical experience with children who have a Pragmatic Language Impairment. Currently she is completing a randomized controlled trial study studying intervention efficacy for children with pragmatic language impairment. Dr. Adams wrote Chapter 6, Assessment and intervention for children with Pragmatic Language Impairment. Chapter 7 was coauthored by Danai Kasambira Fannin, PhD, an assistant professor in communicative disorders at Northern Illinois University, and Linda Watson, EdD, a professor at the University of North Carolina. Dr. Fannin was a postdoctoral fellow who worked with Connie Kasari, PhD, at the Neuropsychiatric Institute at University of California, Los Angeles. Her research interests include the development of evidence-based autism treatment, with a focus on providing appropriate evaluation and intervention for culturally and linguistically diverse children and their families. Dr. Watson has published and presented extensively on ASD and currently is a co-investigator on a federally funded project studying intervention efficacy of social programs and children with ASD. Chapter 7, Social communication assessment and intervention for children on the Autism Spectrum, focuses on children with ASD. Bonnie Brinton, PhD, and Martin Fujiki, PhD, are professors in the department of communicative disorders at the University of Brigham Young. Dr. Brinton specializes in assessment and intervention with children with social communication disorders and Dr. Fujiki conducts research in social-emotional competence in children with language impairment. They coauthored the chapter Social communication assessment and intervention for children with language impairment (Chapter 8). Geralyn Timler, PhD, an assistant professor and Katherine E. White, a graduate student and director of the Child Language and Social Communication Lab at Miami University wrote Chapter 9, which describes evidence-based practice for children with attention disorders. Dr. Timler has research and clinical interests focusing on social communication and pragmatic skills in children with Fetal Alcohol Spectrum Disorders, Specific Language Impairment, Attention Deficit Hyperactivity Disorder (ADHD), and ASD. Dr. Hwa-Froelich wrote Chapter 10, which describes social communication assessments and interventions for children exposed to maltreatment, and Dr. Westby wrote Chapter 11, which focuses on social communication assessment and treatment for children with Disruptive Behavior Disorders (DBD).

DISCUSSION QUESTIONS

1. What skills and knowledge does one need to have competent social communication?
2. Why are social communication and social competence important?
3. What theories help to explain social communication?

4. Which theory offers the best explanation for the heterogeneity of social communication disorders, and why?

REFERENCES

American Psychiatric Association (2013). *Diagnostic and statistical manual of mental disorders* (5th ed.). Arlington, VA: Author.

American Speech-Language-Hearing Association (2013). Evidence-based practice. Retrieved from www.asha.org/members/ebp/

Atkinson, R., & Shiffrin, R. (1968). Human memory: A proposed system and its control processes. In K. Spence & J. Spence (Eds.), *The psychology of learning and motivation: Advances in research and theory* (Vol. 2, pp. 89–195). New York, NY: Academic Press.

Austin, J. L. (1962). *How to do things with words*. New York, NY: Oxford University Press.

Bandura, A. (1986). *Social foundations of thought and action. A social cognitive theory*. Englewood Cliffs, NJ: Prentice Hall.

Crago, M. B., & Eriks-Brophy, A. (1994). Culture, conversation, and interaction. In. J. F. Duchan, L. Hewitt, & R. M. Sonnenmeier (Eds.), *Pragmatics from theory to practice* (pp. 43–58). Englewoods Cliff, NJ: Prentice Hall.

Crick, N. R., & Dodge, K. A. (1994). A review and reformulation of social information processing mechanisms in children's social adjustment. *Psychological Bulletin, 115*, 74–101.

Cummings, L. (2009). *Clinical pragmatics*. Cambridge, UK: Cambridge University Press.

De Bot, K., Lowie, W., & Verspoor, M. (2007). A dynamic systems approach to second language acquisition. *Bilingualism: Language and Cognition, 10*(1), 7–21. doi:10.1017/S1366728906002732

Fogel, A. (1993). *Developing through relationships. Origins of communication, self, and culture*. Chicago, IL: University of Chicago Press.

Fogel, A., Lyra, M. C. D. P., & Valsiner, J. (1997). Introduction: Perspectives on indeterminism and development. In. A. Fogel, M. C. D. P. Lyra, & J. Valsiner (Eds.), *Dynamics and indeterminism in developmental and social processes* (pp. 1–10). Mahwah, NJ: Erlbaum.

Gallagher, S. (2013). When the problem of intersubjectivity becomes the solution. In M. Legerstee, D. W. Haley, & M. Bornstein, (Eds.), *The infant mind, origins of the social brain.* (pp. 48–74). New York, NY: Guilford Press.

Gallagher, T. (Ed.). (1991). *Pragmatics of language: Clinical practice issues*. San Diego, CA: Singular.

Goldstein, H., Kaczmarek, L. A., & English, K. M. (2002). *Promoting social communication: Children with developmental disabilities from birth to adolescence*. Baltimore, MD: Brookes.

Goldstein, H., & Morgan, L. (2002). Social interaction and models of friendship development. In H. Goldstein, L. A. Kaczmarek, & K. M. English (Eds.), *Promoting social communication children with developmental disabilities from birth to adolescence* (pp. 5–25). Baltimore, MD: Brookes.

Grice, H. P. (1975). Logic and Conversation. In P. Cole & J. L. Morgan (Eds.), *Syntax and Semantics Vol. 3. Speech acts* (pp. 41–58). New York, NY: Academic Press.

Hobson, P. (2004). *The cradle of thought. Exploring the origins of thinking.* Oxford, UK: Oxford University Press.

Hwa-Froelich, D. A. (2012). Theoretical foundations for the development of internationally adopted children. In *Supporting development of internationally adopted children* (pp. 1–19). Baltimore, MD: Brookes.

Kohnert, K. (2008). *Language disorders in bilingual children and adults.* San Diego, CA: Plural.

Ladd, G. W. (1999). Peer relationships and social competence during early and middle childhood. *Annual Review of Psychology, 50,* 333–359. Retrieved from http://mltei.org/cqn/Adolescent%20Development/Resources/Peers/Ladd,%20Peer%20relationships%20and%20social%20competence%20during%20early%20and%20middle%20childhood.pdf

Lewis, M. D. (1997). Personality self-organization: Cascading constraints on cognition-emotion interaction. In A. Fogel, M. C. D. P. Lyra, & J. Valsiner (Eds.), *Dynamics and indeterminism in developmental and social processes* (pp. 193–216). Mahwah, NJ: Erlbaum.

Lewis, M. D., & Granic, I. (2000). Emotion development and self-organization: Dynamic systems approaches to emotional development. In M. I. Hoffman & C. Shantz (Series Eds.), *Cambridge studies in social emotional development.* New York, NY: Cambridge University Press.

Müller, N. (Ed.). (2000). *Pragmatics in speech and language pathology.* Philadelphia, PA: John Benjamins.

Muma, J. R. (1991). Experiential realism: Clinical implications. In T. Gallagher (Ed.), *Pragmatics of language: Clinical practice issues* (pp. 229–247). San Diego, CA: Singular.

Ninio, A., & Snow, C. E. (1996). *Pragmatic development.* Boulder, CO: Westview Press.

Piaget, J. (1983). Piaget's theory. In P. Mussen (ed.), *Handbook of child psychology* (4th ed., Vol. 1, pp. 103–128). New York, NY: Wiley.

Rumelhart, D., & McClelland, J. (Eds.). (1986). *Parallel distributed processing: Explorations in the microstructure of cognition.* Cambridge, MA: MIT Press.

Sackett, D. L., Strauss, S. E., Richardson, W. S., Rosenberg, W., & Haynes, R. B. (2000). *Evidence-Based medicine: How to practice and teach EBM* (2nd ed.). Edinburgh: Churchill Livingstone.

Sameroff, A. J. (1987). The social context of development. In N. Eisenberg (Ed.), *Contemporary topics in developmental psychology* (pp. 273–291). New York, NY: Wiley.

Sameroff, A.J., & Chandler, M.J. (1975). Reproductive risk and the continuum of caretaking causality. In F.D. Horowitz, M. Hetherington, S. Scarr-Salaparek & G. Siegel (Eds.), *Review of child development research* (Vol. 4, pp. 187–244). Chicago, IL: University of Chicago Press.

Searle, J.R. (1969). *Speech acts.* Cambridge, UK: Cambridge University Press.

Sperber, D., & Wilson, D. (1986). *Relevance: Communication and cognition.* Oxford, UK: Basil Blackwell.

Sullivan, H. S. (1953). *The interpersonal theory of psychiatry.* New York, NY: W.W. Norton.

Thelen, E., & Bates, E. (2003). Connectionism and dynamic systems: Are they really different? *Developmental Science, 6*(4), 378–391. www.wiley.com/bw/journal.asp?ref=1363-755x

Vygotsky, L. (1986). *Thought and language* (A. Kozulin, Trans.). London, UK: MIT Press. (Original work published 1934)

Wetherby, A. M. (1991). Profiling pragmatic abilities in the emerging language of young children. In T. Gallagher (Ed.), *Pragmatics of language: Clinical practice issues* (pp. 249–281). San Diego, CA: Singular.

Wilson, D., & Sperber, D. (1991). Inference and implicature [Reprint of Wilson & Sperber 1986]. In S. Davis (Ed.), *Pragmatics: A reader* (pp. 377–392). Oxford, UK: Oxford University Press.

2

SOCIAL NEUROSCIENCE

Carol E. Westby

And yet what are we to do about this terribly significant business of
"other people," so ill-equipped are we all to envision one another's inte-
rior workings and invisible aims?

—Philip Roth, in *American Pastoral*

I know you think you understand what you thought I said but I'm not
sure you realize that what you heard is not what I meant.

—Alan Greenspan

LEARNING OBJECTIVES

Readers will be able to

1. Describe the dimensions or types of theory of mind.
2. Identify the neuroanatomical areas associated with the different
   dimensions of theory of mind.
3. Explain the ways the environment and genetics influence neu-
   roanatomical/neurochemical functioning.

In the chapter-opening quotations, Philip Roth, the American novelist
noted for his characterizations, asks how we are to understand the intents
of others. Alan Greenspan, the American economist who was the chair-
man of the US Federal Reserve, questions our ability to understand his
intent and meaning. Processing Roth's and Greenspan's statements requires
social understanding and what has been termed a "theory of mind."

The term *theory of mind* (ToM) was introduced by Premack and Woodruff (1978) when they asked, "Does the chimpanzee have a theory of mind?" They defined ToM as the ability to impute mental states to oneself and others. This began a new direction in psychology—from an emphasis on cognition to an emerging investigation of social skill. Current research in neuroscience is explaining how the brain functions when processing cognitive and social information. This chapter reviews current research in social neuroscience, particularly the research in the neuroanatomical and neurochemical underpinnings for ToM and related behaviors.

WHAT IS SOCIAL NEUROSCIENCE?

History of Social Neuroscience

The technologies of the 1970s and 1980s made possible the fields of cognitive and social science as we now know them. Cognitive neuroscience focused on the neural substrates of memory, language, and spatial perception and their behavioral manifestations. The emphasis was on nonsocial aspects of cognition. Social neuroscience is a term applied to an emerging field of study concerned with identifying the neuroanatomy, neurochemistry, and neural processes underlying social behavior or social cognition. Using methods and theories of neuroscience, social neuroscience seeks to better understand the relationship between the brain and social behavior (Decety & Keenan, 2006; Waldrop, 1993). This relationship is reciprocal: the brain affects social cognition and behavior, and social cognition/behavior affects the brain (Insel & Dernald, 2004). The field of social neuroscience has emerged in just the last few years. The first issues of the journals *Social Neuroscience* and *Social Cognitive and Affective Neuroscience* were published in 2006. The international, interdisciplinary Society for Social Neuroscience was launched in January 2010. The term *social neuroscience* first appeared in an article by Cacioppo and Bertson (1992) who proposed that social psychology and neuroscience represent two ends of a continuum of levels of organization studied in psychology. Understanding social behaviors must acknowledge research demonstrating both that (a) neuroanatomical/neurochemical events influence social processes and (b) social processes influence neuroanatomical/neurochemical events. Recent work in epigenetics is demonstrating how environmental factors influence gene expression which can influence social behavior. Epigenetics is the study of heritable changes in gene activity that are not caused by changes in the DNA sequence. The first issue of *Epigenetics and Chromatin* was published in 2008. Epigenetic discoveries reveal that social factors such as environmental, dietary, behavioral, and medical experiences can significantly affect the development of an individual (including ToM understanding) and sometimes his or her offspring.

Social Neuroscience Methods

A number of methods are used in cognitive and social neuroscience to investigate the confluence of neural, cognitive, and social processes. These methods draw from behavioral techniques developed in social psychology, cognitive psychology, and neuropsychology and are associated with a variety of neurobiological techniques including functional magnetic resonance imaging (fMRI), magnetoencephalography (MEG), positron emission tomography (PET), facial electromyography (EMG), transcranial magnetic stimulation (TMS), electroencephalography (EEG), event-related potentials (ERPs), electrocardiograms, electromyograms, endocrinology, immunology, galvanic skin response (GSR), single-cell recording, and studies of focal brain lesion patients. These neurobiological methods can be grouped together into ones that measure more external bodily responses, electrophysiological methods, hemodynamic measures, and lesion methods. Bodily response methods include GSR (also known as skin conductance response [SCR]), facial EMG, and the eyeblink startle response. Electrophysiological methods include single-cell recordings, EEG, and ERPs. Hemodynamic measures, which, instead of directly measuring neural activity, measure changes in blood flow, include PET and fMRI. Lesion methods traditionally study brains that have been damaged via natural causes, such as strokes, traumatic injuries, tumors, neurosurgery, infection, or neurodegenerative disorders. In its ability to create a type of "virtual lesion" that is temporary, TMS may also be included in this category (Ward, 2012).

Assessing Theory of Mind

Deficits in ToM are characteristic of nearly all, if not all, social-emotional difficulties including deficits in social communication. Once Premack and Woodruff (1978) introduced the term *theory of mind*, it was rapidly adopted by developmental psychologists. By the late 1980s and early 1990s, deficits in ToM became associated with autism spectrum disorder (ASD; e.g., Baron-Cohen, 1995). But ToM deficits and delays in developing ToM are not limited to those with ASD. Deficits in ToM underlie many of the social communication difficulties exhibited not only by persons with ASD but also by persons with other communication disorders (e.g., language impairment, deafness, attention-deficit hyperactivity disorder, traumatic brain injury, Parkinson's disease, dementia), behavioral disorders, and psychiatric conditions, as well as children who have experienced abuse and neglect (Baron-Cohen, 2011; Perry, 2011).

Until the early 2000s, most of the research on ToM was at the behavioral psychological or cognitive level—how persons performed when given tasks that required them to reflect on the knowledge, thoughts, and beliefs of others. ToM, however, extends beyond mentalizing about cognitive processes of knowing, thinking, and believing. ToM also involves reflecting on the emotions of oneself and others and appropriately responding to or empathizing with the emotions of others. With the advent of social neuroscience and epigenetics, an increasing number of studies have investigated the neuroanatomical and neurochemical functions associated with these behavioral activities and how environmental factors may influence neuroanatomical and chemical functioning. This research has revealed that ToM is not a unitary construct; there are several different dimensions or types of ToM, each having differing neuroanatomical and neurochemical underpinnings (Abu-Akel & Shamay-Tsoory, 2011; Frith & Frith, 2003; Northoff et al., 2006; Shamay-Tsoory, 2011). Although there can be overlap in regions of the brain involved in the different types of ToM, specific brain areas are critical for performance of particular dimensions of ToM. In investigating ToM, researchers have studied how differing individuals perform a variety of ToM tasks—neurotypical individuals, individuals who have had circumscribed brain insults (strokes, tumors, penetrating wounds), individuals with different diagnoses (autism, schizophrenia, behavioral disorders), and persons of different ages. This research provides evidence for the distinctions among several types of ToM:

- Cognitive ToM: The ability to attribute mental states—beliefs, intents, desires, pretending, knowledge, and so on—to oneself and others and to understand that others have beliefs, desires, and intentions that are different from one's own.
- Affective ToM: Process of recognizing one's own emotions or inferring the affective states of others by sharing their emotions and by understanding the other's emotions. Affective ToM can be subdivided into the following:
  - Affective cognitive ToM or cognitive empathy: Recognition/identification one's own emotions and the emotions of others
  - Affective empathy: The capacity to respond with an appropriate emotion to another's emotion.
- Interpersonal ToM: Cognitive and affective ToM for others (recognizing thoughts and emotions of others and making inferences about them).
- Intrapersonal ToM: Cognitive and affective ToM for oneself (a sense of self and reflecting on one's own thoughts and emotions and using this information to learn and plan).

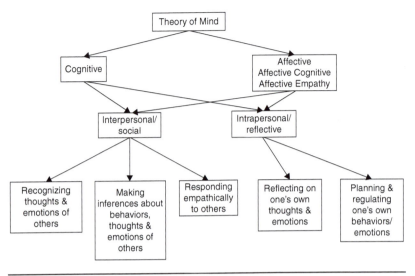

Figure 2.1 Dimensions of Theory of Mind

See Figure 2.1, which shows the dimensions of ToM.

Evidence for the neural bases of cognitive and affective ToM has come from two sources: functional imaging studies of normal participants and patients with brain injuries. Shamay-Toorsy and colleagues (Abu-Akel & Shamay-Tsoory, 2011; Shamay-Tsoory, & Aharon-Peretz, 2007; Shamay-Tsoory, Hararib, Aharon-Peretz, & Levkovitzbet, 2010; Shamay-Tsoory, Tibi-Elhanany, & Aharon-Peretz, 2007) have probably the most extensive set of studies on the neuroanatomical bases of cognitive and affective ToM. In several studies they have asked participants to judge mental or emotional states based on verbal and eye gaze cues of a cartoon figure. The task consists of 64 trials, each showing a cartoon outline of a face (named "Yoni") and four colored pictures of objects belonging to a single category (e.g., fruits, chairs), one in each corner of the computer screen. (View the materials at http://sans.haifa.ac.il/Downloads.html). The participant's task is to point to the image to which Yoni is referring, based on a sentence that appears at the top of the screen and available cues, such as Yoni's eye gaze, Yoni's facial expression, or the eye gaze and facial expression of the face to which Yoni is referring. There are two main conditions: "cognitive" and "affective," requiring either a first-order (what someone is thinking/feeling) or a second-order (what someone is thinking/feeling someone else is thinking/feeling) inference. In the cognitive conditions, both Yoni's facial expression and the verbal cue are emotionally neutral, whereas in the affective conditions, both cues provide affective information (i.e., Yoni is thinking of [cognitive condition] versus Yoni loves [affective condition]). Whereas the cognitive condition requires understanding beliefs about others' beliefs and desires (Yoni is thinking of the toy that ___ wants), the affective condition involves understanding of one's emotions in regard to the others' emotions (Yoni loves the toy that ___ loves).

Neuroscience studies have shown that attributing emotional states to oneself and others involves some different neuroanatomical areas than attributing mental states to oneself and others. Attributing emotional states to oneself and others is termed affective ToM. Affective ToM has two components: an affective cognitive component (sometimes termed cognitive empathy) that involves an awareness or recognition of one's own feelings or the feelings of others and an affective empathy (emotional empathy) component that involves the ability to experience the emotions of others. Affective empathy is elicited by the perceived, imagined, or inferred affective state of another and includes some cognitive appreciation of the other's affective state comprising perspective taking, self–other distinction, and knowledge of the causal relation between the self and the other's affective state (Walter, 2012). Affective empathy includes some meta-knowledge about self and the other that distinguishes it from emotional mimicry and emotional contagion. Emotional mimicry is defined as automatic synchronization of emotional behavior, for example, affective expressions, vocalizations, postures, and movements with those of another person—one yawns when seeing another yawn. Emotional contagion occurs when people experience emotions similar to those of others by mere association. Emotional mimicry and contagion require neither perspective taking nor an explicit self–other distinction. It can be difficult to know whether a person is really experiencing affective empathy or is instead displaying emotional mimicry or emotion contagion.

Over the years, the majority of studies on ToM have focused on performance on cognitive ToM tasks. These have investigated persons' ability to attribute *mental states*—beliefs, intents, desires, pretending, knowledge, and so on—to oneself and others and to understand that others have beliefs, desires, and intentions that are different from one's own. The term *theory of mind* has typically been applied to passing of cognitive ToM tasks involving false belief about contents (e.g., M&Ms in a crayon box) or locations (a toy is moved to a new location). In a false-belief-contents task, children are shown a crayon box and asked what they think is with inside. After the children guess, they are shown that their prediction was wrong—the crayon box contains candy. The experimenter then recloses the bag or box and asks the children what they think another person, who has not been shown the true contents of the box, will think is inside. The children pass the task if they respond that another person will think that there are crayons in the crayon in the box but fail the task if they respond that another person will think that the crayon box contains candy (Gopnik & Astington, 1988).

In the most common version of the false-belief-locations task (often called the Sally–Anne task), children are shown two dolls, Sally and Anne, who have a basket and a box, respectively. Sally also has a marble, which she places in her basket, and then leaves the room. While she is out of the room, Anne takes the marble from the basket and puts it in the box. Sally returns, and the child is then asked where Sally will look for the marble. Children pass the task if they answer that Sally will look in the basket, where she put the marble; children fail the task if they answer that Sally will look in the box, where the children know the marble is hidden, even though Sally cannot know this, because she did not see it hidden there. For both of these tasks, children must be able to understand that another's mental representation of the situation is different from their own, and the child must be able to predict behavior based on that understanding. Typically developing children pass these tasks between ages 4 or 5.

Shamay-Toorsy and colleagues (Shamay-Tsoory, Aharon-Pretz, & Perry, 2007; Shamay-Tsoory, Tomer, & Aharon-Peretz, 2005) have also developed a variety of vignettes that require participants to employ first-order and second-order cognitive or affective ToM. For example,

> Joe and Anna are setting the table for a festive dinner in the dining room. Anna pours Joe a glass of water, but some water spills on his new shirt. Joe says: "It's nothing, I will change the shirt later." Anna puts the glass on the table and goes to look for a paper towel to dry Joe's shirt. When she leaves the dining room, Joe takes his handkerchief and dries the shirt and the table. Anna peeks into the dining room, sees what Joe is doing, and so she doesn't bring a paper towel. Anna returns to the dining room.

The participants were then asked,

1. What does Joe think that Anna thinks about the shirt's condition, when she returns to the dining room? (second order)
2. What does Anna think of the shirt's condition? (first order)

In the affective false-belief task, the setting is the same, but this time when Anna leaves the dining room, Joe gets furious about the wet shirt and kicks the table. Anna peeks into the dining room, sees what Joe is doing and feels guilty.

This time participants are asked,

1. What does Joe think that Anna feels about the wet shirt, when she returns? (second order)
2. What does Anna think Joe feels about the wet shirt? (second order)
3. How does Joe feel? (first order)

Participants also responded to questions about vignettes that required them to interpret higher order ToM involving lies and sarcasm, for example,

- a cognitive lie—stealing someone's iPad, then telling him you haven't seen it and have no idea where it is;
- an affective lie—telling your grandmother that her meatloaf is delicious, even though you hate it;
- a cognitive sarcasm ToM—a man walks into a very messy office and says, "You're office is so tidy";
- an affective sarcasm ToM—a father forgets to pick up his son after school, leaving him in the rain for some time. When the father and son finally get home, the mother says to the father, "You are such a good father."

Performing tasks that require participants to mentalize about people's thoughts and beliefs (cognitive ToM) consistently result in activation of the temporal parietal junction (TPJ; bilaterally, but especially the right), the dorsal lateral prefrontal (dLPFC) and dorsal medial prefrontal (dMPFC) cortex, and the dorsal anterior cingulate cortex (dACC). When mentalizing about people's emotions (affective cognitive ToM), the TPJ is also involved, but in addition, the orbital frontal cortex (OFC), the inferior lateral frontal cortex (ILFC), the ventral medial prefrontal cortex (vMPFC), and the ventral anterior cingulate cortex (vACC) are activated. (See Figure 2.2.) These areas have direct connections into the insula cortex (which is folded deeply within the lateral sulcus), the midcingulate cortex, and the amygdala, which are involved in affective or emotional empathy. Because of its multiple connections to other brain areas, the vMPFC is an important relay station between cognitive and affective processing. It is connected to and receives input from the ventral tegmental area in the midbrain, the amygdala, the temporal lobe, the olfactory system, and the dorsomedial thalamus and, in turn, sends signals to the temporal lobe, the amygdala, the lateral hypothalamus, the hippocampal formation, the cingulate cortex, and the other regions of the prefrontal cortex. This network of connections enables the vMPFC to receive and monitor large amounts of sensory data and to influence many other brain regions, particularly the amygdala, which is highly

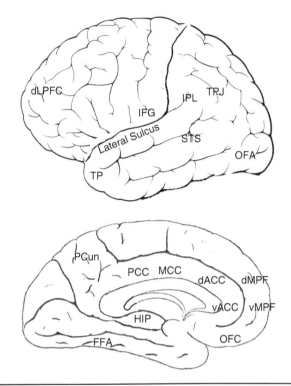

Figure 2.2 Brain areas involved with Theory of Mind. Cognitive ToM: dACC (dorsal anterior cingulate cortex); LPF (dorsal lateral prefrontal cortex); dMPF (dorsal medial prefrontal cortex); STS (superior temporal sulcus); TPJ (temporal pariental junction). Affective ToM: IFG (inferior frontal gyrus); OFA (occipital facial area); OFC (orbital frontal cortex); vMPF (ventromedial prefrontal cortex). Intrapersonal ToM: PCun (precuneus); PCC (posterior cingulate cortex); middle cingulate cortex (MCC); vMPF (ventromedial prefrontal cortex); vACC (ventral anterior cingulate cortex). Facial processing: occipital facial area (OFA); fusiform facial area (FFA); superior temporal sulcus (STS). Episodic memory: hippocampus (HIP), posterior cingulate cortex (PCC), inferior parietal lobule (IFP), & medial frontal (MPF)

involved in emotional processing (Abu-Akel, & Shamay-Tsoory, 2011; Shamay-Tsoory et al., 2005; Shamay-Tsoory & Aharon-Pretz, et al., 2009; Shamay-Tsoory, Tibi-Elhanany, et al., 2007). By integrating this range of information, the vMPFC plays a role in the inhibition of emotional responses and the process of decision making, particularly social and moral decision making (Bechara, Tranel, & Damasio, 2000). Persons with damage to the vMPFC can make hypothetical moral judgments without error but cannot apply the same moral principles to similar situations in their own lives. Social moral decision making requires an integration of cognitive and affective ToM for others and for oneself.

THEORY OF MIND PROCESSING

Affective Cognitive ToM and Affective Empathy

When typically developing persons witness another person in physical or psychological pain, they have an empathic response—they feel the sadness, anger, or pain of the person they are observing. It is possible to have a cognitive awareness of the emotions of others (affective cognitive ToM) without having an empathic response to their emotions (affective empathy). For example, one might recognize that persons are sad or feeling pain but not feel sadness with them. Neurotypical persons are also likely to experience empathic responses when watching a well-acted film or reading a book with vivid characters. Deficits in affective empathy are a primary diagnostic characteristic of persons with psychiatric personality disorders (e.g., antisocial personality disorder and conduct disorders with callous-unemotional traits) (American Psychiatric Association [APA], 2013; Baron-Cohen, 2011). Deficits in empathy are characteristic of persons with autism, even those with Asperger's syndrome who typically develop some degree of cognitive ToM.

Shamay-Tsoory and colleagues (Shamay-Tsoory et al., 2009) explored the neurological foundations for affective cognitive ToM versus affective empathy ToM. They compared the performance of persons with lesions in the vMPF cortex or the inferior frontal gyrus with two control groups—a healthy group and a group with lesions outside the frontal lobes on tasks measuring emotion recognition, second-order false belief, and affective cognitive and emotional empathy. The researchers administered the Interpersonal Reactivity Index (Davis, 1983) which measures both components of empathy. The affective cognitive items involve perspective taking or the ability to transpose oneself into fictional situations. The affective empathy items tap persons' feelings of warmth, compassion, or concern for others or feelings of anxiety or discomfort from tense interpersonal settings. Participants rated each item of the Index in terms of how well it described them. An affective cognitive item is "I try to look at everybody's side of a disagreement before I make a decision." An affective empathy item is "When I see someone being taken advantage of, I feel kind of protective towards them." The researchers found that subjects with lesions in the vMPFC to be specifically impaired in affective cognitive ToM (cognitive empathy), whereas patients with IFG lesions were specifically impaired in affective empathy and emotion recognition.

Experimental evidence suggests that motor simulation may be a trigger for the simulation of associated feeling states or affective empathy. The discovery of mirror neurons in the inferior frontal and inferior parietal regions of the brain (Rizzolatti, Fadiga, Gallese, & Fogassi, 1996) provided new insights into possible explanations for the ability to imitate and to empathize. A mirror neuron is a neuron that fires both when an animal acts and when the animal observes or hears the same action performed by another; hence, they act as a bridge between the self and the other. Mirror neurons respond not just to the motor properties of an action but also to the goal of the action. Thus, the neuron "mirrors" the behavior or intent of the other, as though the observer were itself acting.

Researchers who support a simulation theory explanation of ToM maintain that mirror neurons can explain the early development of affective ToM and are involved in empathy (Decety & Jackson, 2004; Keysers, 2011). According to simulation theory, ToM is activated because we subconsciously empathize with the person we're observing and imagine what we would desire and believe in that scenario. The mirror neurons may account for the emergence of the precursors to affective ToM when the infant demonstrates emotional contagion (crying when other infants cry) and emotional mimicry or emotional sharing (imitating the emotional expressions of others). Keysers and Gazzola (2006, 2007) have shown that people who are more empathic according to self-report questionnaires have stronger activations both in the mirror system for hand actions and in the mirror system for emotions, providing more direct support for the idea that the mirror system is linked to empathy. Walter (2012) suggested that there are two possible roads to affective empathy: a low road and a high road. For the low road, features indicating affective states or suffering (facial expressions, body movements, blood, or injuries) might trigger emotional contagion and mimicry (via the mirror neurons) and lead more or less to automatic empathic responding in a bottom-up manner. With the high road to empathy, empathic responses are induced top-down by higher cognitive processes. The observer draws inferences about the thoughts and feelings of another based on contextual or situational information, for example, knowing that a friend wrecked his new car or that your brother just won a scholarship.

Facial Processing

Interpersonal ToM, particularly affective ToM, makes use of reading faces and bodies when making inferences about others. Precursors to affective cognitive ToM emerge when joint attention behaviors begin to appear by 6 months (Mundy & Newell, 2007). Processing of faces can be divided into perceptual processing which involves distinguishing different facial configurations and conceptual processing which involves understanding the meaning linked to particular facial expressions. These processes involve subcortical and cortical pathways. A subcortical pathway is involved in detecting faces and directing visual attention to them; and a cortical pathway is involved in the detailed visual-perceptual analysis of faces. Both of these components interact in the conscious processing of the emotions and intentions of others (Gobbini & Haxby, 2007).

Three regions in both the left and right hemispheres of the cortex are critical in facial processing: the occipital face area (OFA), the fusiform face area (FFA), and the superior temporal sulcus (STS; Haxby, Hoffman, & Gobbini, 2000). The OFA is located in the inferior occipital gyrus. (See Figure 2.2.) It is an early stage in perceptual analysis of faces that sends inputs to the fusiform and superior temporal regions. It shows greater fMRI response to faces relative to other categories. The OFA activity is sensitive to any physical change in the stimulus. The FFA area responds to faces more than other stimuli and is particularly important for recognizing familiar faces. The STS responds to changeable aspects of a face, particularly poses and gaze directions, whereas the FFA responds to stable aspects of the face (the person's identity). These changeable aspects are particularly important for extracting social cues that are likely to be fleeting (Allison, Puce, & McCarthy, 2000). Recognizing invariant facial features is critical for identifying persons and noting dynamic facial features provides information regarding the mental and emotional states of others. Lesions in these areas disrupt facial processing. In young children and illiterate persons, more of the facial processing is done by these areas in the left hemisphere. As persons become literate, these areas are activated by processing print and facial processing moves more to the right hemisphere (Dehaene, 2013; Dundas, Plaut, & Behrmann, 2013).

There is some evidence that newborns' orientation to faces is mediated by the subcortical visual pathway (Tomalski, Csibra, & Johnson, 2009). The eyes carry considerable information about persons' emotional states. One must be looking at eyes if one is to interpret eye information. Several studies have shown that adults and young children with ASD look more at the mouth, other body parts, or objects in the environment rather than at the eyes (Klin & Jones, 2008; Rice, Moriuchi, Jones, & Klin, 2012). A recent study conducted eye-tracking measures of infants/toddlers who were low or high risk for autism between 2 and 24 months of age (Jones & Klin, 2013). Children with siblings diagnosed with autism were considered high risk. All children showed similar patterns of eye fixation in the first 2 months, but for those children later diagnosed with ASD they began to exhibit a decline in eye fixation from 2 to 6 months, a pattern that was not observed in children who did not develop autism. Perhaps this change in eye tracking in neurotypical infants after 2 months may be related to a switch from subcortical to cortical processing of visual stimuli.

The deficits in face and emotion recognition reported in people with ASD do not appear to be due to functioning of the cortical visual areas (Weigelt, Koldewyn, & Kanwisher, 2012). Instead, these facial processing deficits seem more likely to be due to underconnectivity between the posterior facial recognition areas and anterior frontal areas, particularly the medial prefrontal area responsible for interpretation of the facial information. There is evidence from diffusion tensor imaging that children with ASD show areas of decreased white matter integrity (Schipul, Keller, & Just, 2011). Specifically, reduced white matter connectivity has been found between the fusiform face area and frontal area and the posterior superior temporal area and medial frontal cortex (Just, Keller, & Kana, 2013). Thus, persons with ASD perceive the visual information similarly to those without ASD, but they fail to interpret the information appropriately.

Interpersonal and Intrapersonal ToM

Cognitive and affective ToM can be either interpersonal, which involves recognizing thoughts and emotions of others and making inferences about them or intrapersonal which involves having a sense of self, and reflecting on one's own thoughts and emotions, regulating one's emotions, and using this information to learn and plan. Lucariello and colleagues (Lucariello, Le Donne, Durand, & Yarnell, 2006) compared development of interpersonal and intrapersonal ToM by asking children to respond to vignettes that required cognitive and affective reflection on others or on oneself. See Table 2.1.

Researchers have used neural imaging to investigate neural functioning for a variety of self-referential tasks involving verbal, spatial, social, emotional, or memory processing (Northoff et al., 2006). Kana and colleagues (Kana, Klein, Klinger, Travers, & Klinger, 2013) had high-functioning adults with autism and neurotypical adults make yes–no decisions about whether visually presented adjectives (e.g., smart,

Table 2.1 Interpersonal and Intrapersonal Theory of Mind

	Interpersonal	Intrapersonal
Cognitive	• Mary plays a trick on Sam, whose favorite snack is M&Ms. Mary puts M&Ms in toothpaste box and puts box on Sam's table. What will another kid think is in the box before opening it? What did Sam think was inside the toothpaste box before opening it?	• Ask child if he/she prefers M&Ms or toothpaste. C says M&Ms and is then handed a wrapped box. C unwraps and sees toothpaste box. C opens box and finds M&Ms. • What does it look like is in the box? What is really in the box? • What did you think was inside the toothpaste box before opening it?
Affective	• How did Sam feel about what was inside the box before opening it?	• How did you feel about what was inside the box before opening it?

unhappy) described themselves (self-judgment) or their favorite teacher (other-judgment). British researcher Lombardo and colleagues (2009) had neurotypical adults make mental reflections about themselves or the Queen. On the self task, participants judged on a scale from 1 (*not at all likely*) to 4 (*very likely*) how likely they themselves would personally agree with opinion questions (e.g., "How likely are you to think that keeping a diary is important"). On the other task, the same mentalizing judgments were made, except this time they were in reference to how likely the British queen would agree with the opinion questions (e.g., "How likely is the Queen to think that keeping a diary is important"). Vogeley and colleagues (2004) asked participants to count the number of balls seen from the perspective of an avatar in a scene or from their own perspective.

There is considerable overlap of neural areas that process both self- and other-reflection, but there is also some specificity. A review of imaging studies on self-reflection provides significant support that cortical midline structures (CMS), a set of regions in the midline of the cortex arching around the corpus callosum are involved in intrapersonal ToM activities (self-referential processing). The CMS (constituting the medial prefrontal cortex, the anterior, middle, and posterior cingulate cortices; and the precuneus) are thought to functionally integrate self-related thought and planning (Northoff et al., 2006). The CMS may mediate the evaluative and self-reflective aspects of the self, ToM may help understand the mental states of oneself and others, and the mirror neuron system (MNS) may help the self simulate the actions of the other to understand goals and intentions. Ramachandran (2009) speculates that mirror neurons may provide the neurological basis of human self-awareness or intrapersonal ToM. He hypothesizes that these neurons can not only help simulate other people's behavior but can also be turned inward to create meta-representations of one's own earlier brain processes. This could be the neural basis of introspection and of the reciprocity of self-awareness and other awareness.

METACOGNITION, EXECUTIVE FUNCTIONS, AND ToM

Neural Foundations for Metacognition and Executive Functions

The study of metacognition emerged at the same time as the study of ToM (Flavell, 1979), but while researchers investigating ToM focused on its development in young children, researchers investigating metacognition focused on school-age children and adolescents. Metacognition is thinking about one's thinking and, hence, is an aspect of intrapersonal cognitive ToM. Metacognition consists of both knowledge and use of this knowledge to regulate or control one's cognitive processes. Metacognition, as a critical component of executive functions (EFs), is not easily, or always, separated from EF. And EF has been defined in multiple ways. Most definitions of EF view it as deliberate, top-down processes involved in the conscious, goal-directed control of thought, action, and emotion. Three processes are viewed as the foundations for EF: cognitive flexibility, inhibitory control, and working memory (Miyake et al., 2000). Metacognitive awareness of these processes is used to regulate and plan behavior. Some researchers and educators consider planning and regulating behaviors as part of EF, while others consider them part of metacognition. EF requires intrapersonal and interpersonal theory of mind. One must reflect on one's knowledge, recognizing one's knowledge and skills (metacognition or intrapersonal ToM), and in some situations, one must consider the impact one's choices and behaviors will have on others (intrapersonal ToM). Simultaneously, one must have sufficient EF to inhibit irrelevant, off-task thoughts or attention to distractions in the environment to employ ToM (one's metacognition knowledge; Doherty, 2009).

The frontal lobes are known to be necessary, but not sufficient, for EF (Alvarez & Emory, 2006). The frontal lobes have multiple connections to cortical, subcortical, and brain stem sites that likely give rise to higher level cognitive functions such as inhibition, flexibility of thinking, problem solving, planning, impulse control, concept formation, and abstract thinking. Neuroimaging and lesion studies have identified the functions that are most often associated with the particular regions of the prefrontal cortex. These same areas are activated in ToM processing:

- The dorsolateral prefrontal cortex (dlPFC) is associated with verbal fluency, ability to maintain and shift set, planning, response inhibition, working memory, organizational skills, reasoning, problem solving, and abstract thinking (Clark et al., 2008).
- The anterior cingulate cortex (ACC) is associated with inhibition of inappropriate responses, decision making, and motivated behaviors (Allman, Hakeem, Erwin, Nimchinsky, & Hof, 2001).
- The orbitofrontal cortex (OFC) plays a key role in impulse control, maintenance of set, monitoring ongoing behavior and socially appropriate behaviors. The OFC also has roles in representing the value of rewards based on sensory stimuli and evaluating subjective emotional experiences (Rolls & Grabenhorst, 2008).

Until recently, EF was assumed to be a unitary construct with interrelated components. Although it is recognized that EF encompasses a variety of subfunctions (cognitive flexibility, inhibitory control, and working memory) that work together in the service of goal-directed problem solving, it is generally assumed that these subfunctions operate in a consistent fashion across contexts or content domains (Hongwanishkul, Happaney, Lee, & Zelazo, 2005). In contrast to a domain general view of EF, recent neuroscience research had indicated that EF operates differently in different contexts. In light of this research, two types of EF have been distinguished— "cool" EF involved in tasks requiring cognitive or abstract reasoning and a "hot" EF involved tasks that have an affective/emotional, motivational, or incentive/reward (Zelazo & Cunningham, 2007). Like early research assessing ToM, which focused on cognitive ToM to the exclusion of affective ToM, until recently, most studies of EF have focused on tasks assessing cool (cognitive) EF skills such as the following:

- Attention: selective attention, sustained attention, and inhibiting a response to distractions.
- Goal setting: initiating, planning, problem solving, and strategic behaviors to reach goals.
- Cognitive flexibility: working memory, attention shifting (stopping one task and starting another), and conceptual transfer (learning something in one setting and using the knowledge in a different setting).

Measuring these cognitive aspects of EF has employed tasks that have no obvious rewards or punishments for completing the activity. In contrast, hot (or affective/emotional) EF tasks trigger an effective response often because of associated rewards or punishments. They are related to social or communication skills and are not easily measured, because they depend on a person's use of current input and his or her interaction with the environment. Table 2.2 shows types of cold and hot EF tasks.

Neuroimaging studies have confirmed that cool and hot EF tasks activate different neuroanatomical structures (Rubia, 2011). Cool EF processes are subsumed primarily by the dorsolateral and ventrolateral prefrontal cortex. Hot EF processes are subsumed by ventromedial pathways connecting mesolimbic reward circuitry, including the amygdala and striatum, to the ventromedial prefrontal and orbital frontal cortex. These neuroanatomical foundations are similar to those involved in cognitive and affective ToM. And, just as there is a dissociation between cognitive and affective ToM, there is a dissociation between cool and hot EF. Performance on one type of EF task does not predict performance on the other type.

Hot and cool EFs are very similar in that they both require future-oriented cognitive skills; however, hot EFs generally encompass

Table 2.2 Examples of Cold and Hot EF Tasks

EF cool tasks or assessments	Description
Reverse digit span	Repeating digits in reverse order
Wisconsin Card Sorting Test	Sort cards by color, shape, number rules quickly and flexibly (Heaton, 1981)
Color word Stroop	Name the color of the ink and ignore the written color name ("red" is printed in green ink; say "green" rather than "red"; Stroop, 1935)
Tower of London	Moving 3 to 5 different sized beads following rules measured by time and number of moves (Shallice, 1982)

EF hot tasks	
Delay of gratification	Given a cookie and explain choice of eating one cookie now or if child waits until examiner returns, will receive 2 cookies.
Gambling	Participants select cards from 4 decks, winning or losing money each time 2 "good" decks, 2 "bad" decks. Scores based on good choices—bad choices. By elementary school, students develop an awareness of which decks will give them better rewards (Garon, Moore, & Waschblusch, 2006).

situations that involve higher risks or more stakes and provoke emotional arousal (Hongwanishkul et al., 2005). Both cool and hot EFs have been associated with *mental time travel* that includes episodic autobiographical memory and episodic future thinking. Autobiographical memory for past experiences involves remembering, which is different from knowing. I know that I have ridden most of the rides at Disney World (semantic memory), but I have an autobiographical memory for only some of them, for example, my first time on the Space Mountain roller coaster—the sounds, darkness, flashing lights, and dizziness when I got off. Autobiographical memory involves an awareness of oneself (intrapersonal ToM) in the past (Fivush, 2011). Similar to autobiographic memory, which allows an individual to reexperience an event, episodic future thinking allows an individual to pre-experience an event (Atance & O'Neill, 2001). Episodic future thinking (or mental time travel) involves intrapersonal ToM because it requires that one imagine oneself in the future; it also involves developing a plan that takes into account one's specific situation; hence, it involves EFs. Autobiographical past memory and episodic future thinking skills emerge around age 4, the same time that children become able to think about the perceptions and beliefs of others (Atance & O'Neill, 2005).

Neuroimaging has revealed that remembering and simulating the future depend on common neural substrates; the core network activated in both cases includes the hippocampus, the posterior cingulate gyrus, the medial frontal cortices, and the TPJ (inferior parietal lobule and lateral temporal cortices; Botzung, Denkova, & Manning, 2008; Mullally & Maguire, 2013). It is possible to form new semantic memories, but not episodic memories, without the hippocampus. Activity in this network is greater during simulation of future events than during remembering. Remembering past events and simulating future ones activates overlapping regions of the core network of brain structures, but past and future time travel is associated with a distinct subsystem within the network. For example, extensive regions of the medial prefrontal cortex, the parietal lobe, and the anterior portion of the hippocampus are activated during the imagining of future events, but not during the retrieval of memories. On the other hand, remembering, but not imagining, leads to activation of parts of the visual cortex, likely reflecting the imagery associated with memory retrieval.

Individuals who have deficits in ToM abilities—as is the case with ASD—are likely to show similar deficits in autobiographical memory and episodic future thinking (Powell & Jordan, 1993; Terrett et al., 2013). Deficits in future thinking may explain some of the repetitive and stereotyped behaviors and the lack of behavioral flexibility seen in persons with ASD. It is plausible that such inflexibility stems from underlying difficulties with planning and future thinking (Suddendorf & Corballis, 1997). These episodic memory deficits may be due to the inability to form a relationship between one's past and present self and to dissociate from one's own current state.

NEUROCHEMISTRY

Genetic Factors Influencing Neurochemistry

Neuroanatomical models for ToM cannot fully explain how various pathologies that present with differing neurobiological abnormalities such as autism or reactive attachment disorder exhibit similar ToM dysfunctions or how persons with a single disease such as Parkinson's disease exhibit differing profiles of ToM impairments. To explain these variations, Abu-Akel and Shamay-Tsoory (2011) suggest considering the neurochemical basis of ToM. There is some evidence that the dopaminergic-serotonergic (DS) system has a role in ToM. This is based on the observations that ToM dysfunctions are frequent consequences of disorders that are associated with deficits in the DS system such as autism (Chugani, 2012; Folsom & Fatemi, 2011) and schizophrenia (Bosia et al., 2010) and that the DS system innervates the PFC, the TPJ, and the ACC, regions critical to ToM. Genetic variations influence production and metabolism of neurotransmitters, such as dopamine, which in turn, affect ToM performance. Furthermore, there exists a rather complex interaction of genotype and environment related to differential susceptibility and biological sensitivity to context—the differential-sensitivity hypothesis (Pluess, Stevens, & Belsky, 2013). This hypothesis states that persons differ in their susceptibility to environmental influence—both the adverse effects of unsupportive contextual conditions and beneficial effects of supportive ones. Several genotypes are known to affect production or metabolism of neurotransmitters that have been associated with variations in social skills, aggression, and ToM.

Monoamine oxidases (MAOs) are enzymes that are involved in the breakdown or inactivation of neurotransmitters such as serotonin and dopamine and are, therefore, capable of influencing feelings, mood, and behavior of individuals. The monoamine oxidase A gene (MAOA) is involved in neural circuitry between the ventromedial frontal cortex and the amygdala, regions implicated in social behavior, theory of mind, and empathy. The low-activity MAOA genotype has been associated with antisocial behavior, particularly in persons who have experienced abuse during childhood (Fergusson, Boden, Howood, Miller, & Kennedy, 2011). Maltreated children with genotypes causing high levels of MAOA are less likely to develop antisocial behavior (Caspi et al., 2002). An interesting finding of this study was that those more vulnerable to the adverse effects of maltreatment actually scored lowest in antisocial behavior when not exposed to maltreatment, suggesting perhaps greater plasticity rather than just greater vulnerability. Other research has supported this hypothesis. For example, Kim-Cohen and colleagues (2006) found that boys with the low-MAOA-activity variant were rated by mothers and teachers as having mental health problems, and specifically attention-deficit/hyperactivity disorder symptoms, if they had been victims of abuse, but fewer problems if they had not, compared with the high-MAOA activity genotype. Foley and colleagues (2004) also observed that twin boys with the low-activity allele were more likely to be diagnosed with conduct disorder if they were exposed to higher levels of childhood adversity and less likely if exposed to lower levels of adversity compared with boys with the high-MAOA-activity allele. Figure 2.3 shows the effects of genotype-environment interactions on social skills and ToM.

A similar pattern has been found between the dopamine receptor *DRD4* gene and environment. The dopamine receptor *DRD4* gene variation predicts preschoolers' developing theory of mind (Lackner, Sabbagh, Hallinan, Liu, & Holden, 2012) and it moderates infants sensitivity to maternal affective communications (Gervai et al., 2007). In supportive environments, neurotypical children with the short allele variant of the *DRD4* gene perform better on ToM tasks than children with the long allele variant. However, infants with the short variant of the DRD4 gene are more affected by disrupted maternal communication, having more disorganized attachments that could potentially later result in lower ToM.

The long 7-repeat allele of *DRD4* has been associated with hyperactivity. But several studies have suggested that parenting may affect the cognitive development of children with the 7-repeat allele of *DRD4*. Parenting that has maternal sensitivity, mindfulness, and autonomy-support at 15 months was found to alter children's executive functions at 18 to 20 months (Bakermans-Kranenburg & Van IJzendoorn, 2006). Children with poorer quality parenting exhibited more hyperactivity—they were more impulsive and sensation seeking than were those with higher quality parenting. Yet 4-year-old children with the long *DRD4* allele who experienced higher quality parenting actually exhibited better effortful control than did children who did not have this allele (Sheese, Voelker, Rothbart, & Posner, 2007). Children with the *DRD4* long allele and secure attachment with their mothers exhibited more prosocial, altruistic

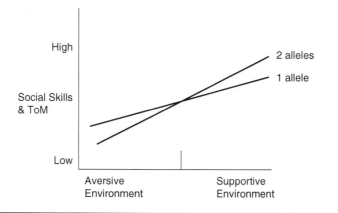

Figure 2.3 Effects of genotype–environment interactions on social skills and ToM

behavior than did children with the *DRD4* long allele and insecure attachment. Children with the *DRD4* short allele exhibited no difference in altruism regardless of their attachment (Bakermans-Kranenburg & Van IJzendoorn, 2011).

Oxytocin plays a role in how we perceive our own and other's emotional states. Oxytocin increases sociability and emotional empathy (Hurlemann et al., 2010). In contrast to persons with one or two copies of the G allele for the oxytocin receptor gene (*OXTR*), persons with one or two copies of the A allele have exhibited lower dispositional empathy as measured by their ratings on the Interpersonal Reactivity Index (Davis, 1983) and lower behavioral empathy as measured by their scores on "Reading the Mind in the Eyes" test that required them to interpret emotions from eyes (Rodrigues, Saslow, Garcia, Johna, & Keltnercet, 2009). Variants of the *OXTR* gene have been associated with autism (Hammock et al., 2012; Wermter et al., 2010).

Environmental/Genetic Factor Interactions

Environmental factors can affect neuroanatomical development and neurochemical functioning. Children who have been reared in institutions in their early years have significantly smaller cortical gray matter volume (Sheridan, Fox, Zeanah, McLaughlin, & Nelson, 2012). Maltreated children have been found to have smaller brain volumes in the OFC, the area critically important in affective ToM (de Brito et al., 2013; Hanson et al., 2010), as well as in the middle temporal gyrus (de Brito et al. 2013), which is implicated in autobiographical memory, emotion regulation, and decision making. Many of the brain changes in institutionalized and maltreated children have been found to be related to the brain's response to stress. Stress produces long-lasting alternations to the hypothalamic–pituitary–adrenal (HPA) axis. When persons experience ongoing toxic stress, the adrenals continue to produce high levels of cortisol. This long-term exposure to cortisol results in reduced dendritic growth and atrophy of neurons in the hippocampus, dendritic shortening in the medial prefrontal cortex, increased dendritic growth, and neuronal hypertrophy in the amygdala. These brain changes result in poorer memory and ToM, while at the same time more intense fear and anger responses. The *FKBP5* gene is involved in regulation of the HPA axis. The HPA axis is less regulated in children with several allele variations of the *FKBP5* gene who have experienced early abuse or neglect, and as a result such children are exposed to higher cortisol levels associated with stress (White, Bogdan, Fisher, Munoz, & Hariri, 2012). Variations in the *FKBP5* gene alleles contribute to risk or resilience in response to difficult environments (Gillespie, Phifer, Bradley, & Ressler, 2009).

Recent work in developmental neuroscience and epigenetics is offering suggestions for how early-life experiences and environmental influences interact directly with genes in the developing brain. Studies are showing how epigenetic mechanisms that regulate gene activity in the central nervous system are modified by experiences, particularly those occurring within the context of caregiving (Roth & Sweatt, 2011). Environmental experiences can result in special chemicals called tags (epigenomes) becoming attached to our genes, and, depending on the nature of these tags, specific genes can either be silenced (prevented from being expressed as protein) or pushed to become more active. These epigenetic changes may last through cell divisions for the duration of the cell's life and may be inherited for multiple generations. When these epigenomic chemicals become attached to genes controlling neurotransmitters, ToM abilities can be disrupted. These epigenetic changes in combination with particular genotypes may explain why some children reared in abusive or neglectful backgrounds appear to develop relatively well, while others exhibit deficits in theory of mind and social skills and are at greater risk for a variety of health problems. Children with the short variant of the *DRD4* dopamine receptor gene, the low-activity *MAOA* gene, the AA or AG allele of the oxytocin gene, or variants of the *FKBP5* gene are likely to have significant social and behavioral difficulties if they experience maltreatment in early childhood but not if they are reared in healthy, supportive environments.

CULTURAL NEUROSCIENCE

Cultural neuroscience is the study of how cultural values, practices, and beliefs shape and are shaped by the mind, brain, and genes. The first issue of *Culture and Neuroscience* was published in 2013. ToM is a primary factor that separates humans from other primates. Human social interactions require ToM, but people in different cultures have differing theories regarding what the mind is (Luhrmann, 2011), and they hold differing views of their relationships with one another. Interpersonal and intrapersonal ToM abilities develop in a relatively similar time frame across cultures, but there are some variations in just how these abilities are manifested. For example, children in the United States develop understanding that people can have different beliefs or opinions before an understanding that people can be knowledgeable or ignorant. This order of development is reversed in Chinese and Iranian children (Shahaeian, Peterson, Slaughter, & Wellman, 2011). Wellman, Fang, Liu, Zhu, and Liu (2006) suggested that some cultures, such as the

Chinese, value knowing and children acquiring practical knowledge, whereas other cultures, such as the United States, give more emphasis to truth, falsity, and differences in belief. Because of these different values or emphases, knowing may be more salient and important in some cultures and thinking and believing may be more salient and important in other cultures.

Cultural neuroscience is interested in how these and other differences in values might be reflected in differences in brain functioning. Cultures have often been contrasted in terms of value systems oriented either to individualism or to collectivism. Individualist cultures, such as those of the United States and Western Europe, view the self as autonomous from others; collectivist cultures, such as China, Korea, and Japan, view the self as connected to or defined by others or the social situation (Triandis, 1995). fMRI studies of persons from individualistic and collective cultures performing ToM tasks show many similarities in the areas of the brain that are activated, but there are some variations that could be explained by these differences in cultural orientations. Particularly, there are neural differences when persons from individualistic and collective cultures make judgments about themselves. Researchers have suggested this may be because persons from collective cultures have a reduced sense of self–other distinction than persons from individualistic cultures do (Chaio et al., 2009; Sul, Choi, & Kang, 2012). When processing emotional expressions, persons from collective cultures show greater amygdala response than do persons from individualistic cultures. At this time, the clinical significance of these differences in neural functioning among cultural groups is uncertain.

DISCUSSION QUESTIONS

1. Describe the different dimensions of ToM and their neuroanatomical foundations.
2. How can the different dimensions of ToM be assessed?
3. Explain why some children may be less affected by poor environments than other children.
4. Discuss the relationships among metacognition, EF, and ToM.
5. How are cognitive and affective ToM related to hot and cold EF tasks?
6. What behavioral precursors should be observed in children before they pass the typical ToM tasks?
7. Describe the neural components of facial processing.

INSTRUCTIONAL RESOURCES

Websites

Child Maltreatment and Brain Consequences: www.youtube.com/watch?v=r6_ nindqsTs

Epigenetics: www.pbs.org/wgbh/nova/body/epigenetics.html

Nova Science Now Mirror Neurons: www.youtube.com/watch?v=Xmx1qPyo8Ks

TED Talks Epigenetics: www.youtube.com/watch?v=JTBg6hqeuTg

TED Talks Rebecca Sax, How We Read Each Other's Minds: www.youtube. com/watch?v=GOCUH7TxHRI

TED Talks: VS Ramachandran: The Neurons That Shaped Civilization: www. youtube.com/watch?v=t0pwKzTRG5E

The Human Spark DVD: www.pbs.org/wnet/humanspark/episodes/program-three-brain-matters/video-full-episode/418/

Simon Baron-Cohen, Zero Degrees of Empathy: www.youtube.com/ watch?v=Aq_nCTGSfWE

REFERENCES

Abu-Akel, A., & Shamay-Tsoory, S. (2011). Neuroanatomical and neurochemical bases of theory of mind. *Neuropsychologia, 49*, 2971–2984.

Allison, T., Puce, A., & McCarthy, G. (2000). Social perception from visual cues: Role of the STS region. *Trends in Cognitive Science, 4*, 267–278.

Allman, J. M., Hakeem, A., Erwin, J. M., Nimchinsky, E., & Hof, P. (2001). The anterior cingulate cortex: The evolution of an interface between emotion and cognition. *Annals of the New York Academy of Sciences, 935*, 107–117.

Alvarez, J. A., & Emory, E. (2006). Executive function and the frontal lobes: A meta-analytic review. *Neuropsychology Review, 16*, 17–42.

American Psychiatric Association. (2013). *Diagnostic and statistical manual of mental disorders* (5th ed.). Arlington VA: Author.

Atance, C. M., & O'Neill, D. K. (2001). Episodic future thinking. *Trends in Cognitive Sciences, 5*, 533–539.

Atance, C. M., & O'Neill, D. K. (2005). The emergence of episodic future thinking in humans. *Learning and Motivation, 26*, 126–144.

Bakermans-Kranenburg, M. J., & Van IJzendoorn, M. H. (2006). Gene–environment interaction of the dopamine D4 receptor (DRD4) and observed maternal insensitivity predicting externalizing behavior in preschoolers. *Developmental Psychobiology, 48*, 406–409.

Bakermans-Kranenburg, M. J., & Van IJzendoorn, M. H. (2011). Differential susceptibility to rearing environment depending on dopamine-related genes: New evidence and a meta-analysis. *Development and Psychopathology, 23*, 39–52.

Baron-Cohen, S. (1995). *Mindblindness: An essay on autism and theory of mind.* Cambridge, MA: MIT Press.

Baron-Cohen, S. (2011). *The science of evil.* New York, NY: Basic Book.

Bechara, A., Tranel, D., & Damasio, H. (2000). Characterization of the decision-making deficit of patients with ventromedial prefrontal cortex lesions. *Brain, 123,* 2189–2202.

Bosia, M., Anselmetti, S., Bechi, M., Lorenzi, C., Pirovano, A., Cocchi, F., . . . Cavallaro, R. (2010). Effect of 5-HT1A-receptor functional polymorphism on theory of mind performances in schizophrenia. *Psychiatry Research, 188,* 187–190.

Botzung, A., Denkova, E., & Manning, L. (2008). Experiencing past and future personal events: Functional neuroimaging evidence on the neural bases of mental time travel. *Brain and Cognition, 66,* 202–212.

Cacioppo, J. T., & Bertson, G. G. (1992). Social psychological contributions to the decade of the brain: Doctrine of multi-level analysis. *American Psychologist, 47,* 1019–1028.

Caspi, A., McClay, J., Moffitt, T. E., Mill, J., Martin, J., Craig, I. W., . . . Pulton, R. (2002). Role of genotype in the cycle of violence in maltreated children. *Science, 297,* 851–854.

Chaio, J. Y., Harada, T., Komeda, J., Li, Z., Mano, Y., Saito, D., . . . Iidka, T. (2009). Neural basis of individualistic and collectivistic views of self. *Human Brain Mapping, 30,* 2813–2820.

Chugani, D. C. (2012). Neuroimaging and neurochemistry in autism. *Pediatric Clinics of North America, 59,* 63–73.

Clark, L., Bechara, A., Damasio, H., Aitken, M.R.F., Sahakian, B. J., & Robbins, T.W.L. (2008). Differential effects of insular and ventromedial prefrontal cortex lesions on risky decision making. *Brain, 131,* 1311–1322.

Davis, M. H. (1983). Measuring individual differences in empathy: Evidence for a multidimensional approach. *Journal of Personal Social Psychology, 44,* 113–126.

de Brito, S., Viding, E., Sebastian, C. L., Kelly, P. A., Mechelli, A., Maris, H., & McCrory, E. J. (2013). Reduced orbitofrontal and temporal grey matter in a community sample of maltreated children. *Journal of Child Psychology and Psychiatry, 54,* 105–112.

Decety, J., & Jackson, P. L. (2004). The functional architecture of human empathy. *Behavioral and Cognitive Neuroscience Reviews, 3,* 71–100.

Decety, J., & Keenan, J. P. (2006). Social neuroscience: A new journal. *Social Neuroscience, 1,* 1–4.

Dehaene, S. S. (2013). Inside the letterbox: How literacy transforms the human brain. *Cerebrum.* Retrieved from https://www.dana.org/Cerebrum/2013/Inside_the_Letterbox__How_Literacy_Transforms_the_Human_Brain/

Doherty, M. J. (2009). *Theory of mind: How children understand others' thoughts and feelings.* New York, NY: Psychology Press.

Dundas, E. M., Plaut, D. C., & Behrmann, M. (2013). The joint development of hemispheric lateralization for words and faces. *Journal of Experimental Psychology: General, PMID, 142,* 348–358.

Fergusson, D., Boden, J. M., Howood, L. J., Miller, A. L., & Kennedy, M. A. (2011). MAOA, abuse exposure and antisocial behavior: 30-year longitudinal study. *British Journal of Psychiatry, 198,* 457–463.

Fivush, R. (2011). The development of autobiographical memory. *Annual Review of Psychology, 2,* 559–582.

Flavell, J. H. (1979). Metacognition and cognitive monitoring: A new area of cognitive-developmental inquiry. *American Psychologist, 34,* 906–911.

Foley, D. L., Eaves, L. J., Wormley, B., Silberg, J. L., Maes, H. H., . . . Riley, B. (2004). Childhood adversity, monomine oxidase A genotype, and risk for conduct disorder. *Archives of General Psychiatry, 61,* 738–744.

Folsom, T. D., & Fatemi, S. H. (2011). Neurochemical mechanisms in disease. *Advances in Neurobiology, 1,* 383–398.

Frith, U., & Frith, C. D. (2003). Development and neurophysiology of mentalizing. *Philosophical Transactions of the Royal Society of London, Series B, 358,* 459–473.

Garon, N., Moore, C., & Waaschbusch, D. A. (2006). Decision making in children with ADHD only, ADHD-anxious/depressed, and control children using a child version of the Iowa gambling task. *Journal of Attention Disorders, 9,* 607–619.

Gervai, J., Novak, A., Lakatos, K., Toth, I., Denis, D., Ronai, Z., . . . Sasvari-Szkekely, M. (2007). Infant genotype may moderate sensitivity to maternal affective communications: Attachment disorganization, quality of care, and the DRD4 polymorphism. *Social Neuroscience, 2,* 307–319.

Gillespie, C. F., Phifer, J., Bradley, B., & Ressler, K. J. (2009). Risk and resilience: Genetic and environmental influences on development of the stress response. *Depression and Anxiety, 26,* 984–992.

Gobbini, M. I., & Haxby, J. V. (2007). Neural systems for recognition of familiar faces. *Neuropsychologia, 45,* 32–41.

Gopnik, A., & Astington, J. W. (1988). Children's understanding of representational change and its relation to the understanding of false belief and the appearance-reality distinction. *Child Development, 59,* 26–37.

Hammock, E., Veenstra-VanderWeele, J., Yan, Z., Kerr, T. M., Morris, M., Anderson, G. M., . . . Jacob, S. (2012). Examining autism spectrum disorders by biomarkers: Example from the oxytocin and serotonin systems. *Journal of the American Academy of Child and Adolescent Psychiatry, 51,* 712–721.

Hanson, J. L., Chung, M. K., Avants, B. B., Shirtcliff, E. A., Gee, J. C., Davison, R. J., & Pollak, S. D. (2010). Early stress is associated with alterations in the orbitofrontal cortex: A tensor-based morphometry investigation of brain structure and behavioral risk. *Journal of Neuroscience, 30,* 7466–7472.

Haxby, J. V., Hoffman, E. A., & Gobbini, M. I. (2000). The distributed human neural system for face perception. *Trends in Cognitive Sciences, 4*, 223–233.

Heaton, R. K. (1981). *A manual for the Wisconsin Card Sorting Test*. Odessa, FL: Psychological Assessment Resources.

Hongwanishkul, D., Happaney, K. R., Lee, W. S. C., & Zelazo, P. D. (2005). Assessment of hot and cool executive function in young children: Age-related changes and individual differences. *Developmental Neuropsychology, 28*, 617–644.

Hurlemann, R., Patin, A., Onur, O. A., Cohen, M. X., Baumgartner, T., Metzler, S., . . . Kendrick, K. M. (2010). Oxytocin enhances amygdala-dependent, socially-reinforced learning and emotional empathy in humans. *Journal of Neuroscience, 30*, 4999–5007.

Insel, T. R., & Dernald, R. D. (2004). How the brain processes social information: Searching for the social brain. *Annual Review of Neuroscience, 72*, 697–722.

Jones, W., & Klin, A. (2013). Attention to eyes is present but in decline in 2–6-month-old infants later diagnosed with autism. *Nature, 504*, 427–431.

Just, M. A., Keller, T. A., & Kana, R. K. (2013). A theory of autism based on frontal-posterior underconnectivity. In M. A. Just & K. A. Pelphrey (Eds.), *Development and brain systems in autism* (pp. 35–63). New York, NY: Psychology Press.

Kana, R. K., Klein, C. L., Klinger, L. G., Travers, B. G., & Klinger, M. R. (2013). Neural representations of self versus other: Lessons from autism. In M. A. Just & K. A. Pelphry (Eds.), *Development and brain systems in autism* (pp. 179–201). New York, NY: Psychology Press.

Keysers, C. (2011). *The empathetic brain*. Retrieved from http://www.empathic brain.com/#

Keysers, C., & Gazzola, V. (2006). Towards a unifying neural theory of social cognition. *Progress in Brain Research, 156*, 379–401.

Keysers, C., & Gazzola, V. (2007). Integrating simulation and theory of mind: From self to social cognition. *Trends in Cognitive Sciences, 11*, 194–196.

Kim-Cohen, J., Caspi, A., Taylor, A., Williams, B., Newcombe, R., Craig, I. W., & Moffitt, T. E. (2006). MAOA, maltreatment, and gene–environment interaction predicting children's mental health: New evidence and a meta-analysis. *Molecular Psychiatry, 11*, 903–913.

Klin, A., & Jones, W., (2008). Altered face scanning and impaired recognition of biological motion in a 15-month-old infant with autism. *Developmental Science, 11*, 40–46.

Lackner, C., Sabbagh, M. A., Hallinan, E., Liu, X., & Holden, J. (2012). Dopamine receptor D4 gene variation predicts preschoolers' developing theory of mind. *Developmental Science, 15*, 272–280.

Lombardo, M. V., Chakrabarti, B., Bullmore, E. T., Wheelwright, S. J., Sadek, S. A., Suckling, J., . . . Baron-Cohen, S. (2009). Shared neural circuits for mentalizing about the self and others. *Journal of Cognitive Neuroscience, 22*, 1623–1635.

Lucariello, J., Le Donne, M., Durand, T., & Yarnell, L. (2006). Social and intrapersonal theories of mind "I interact therefore I am." In A. Antonietti, O. Liverta-Sempio, & A. Marchetti (Eds.), *Theory of mind in developmental contexts* (pp. 149–171). New York, NY: Springer.

Luhrmann, T. M. (2011). Toward an anthropological theory of mind. *Suomen Antropologi: Journal of the Finnish Anthropological Society, 36,* 5–69. Retrieved from http://groups.psych.northwestern.edu/gentner/papers/gentner_2012.pdf

Miyake, A., Friedman, N. P., Emerson, M. J., Witzki, A. H., Howerter, A., & Wager, T. D. (2000). The unity and diversity of executive functions and their contributions to complex "frontal lobe" tasks: A latent variable analysis. *Cognitive Psychology, 41,* 49–100.

Mullally, S. L., & Maguire, E. A. (2013). Memory, imagination, and predicting the future: A common brain mechanism? *The Neuroscientist, 19,* 1–15.

Mundy, P., & Newell, L. (2007). Attention, joint attention, and social cognition. *Current Directions in Psychological Science, 16*(5), 269–274.

Northoff, G., Heinzel, A., de Greck, M., Felix, B., Dobrowolny, H., & Panksepp, J. (2006). Self-referential processing in our brain—a meta-analysis of imaging studies on the self. *NeuroImage, 31,* 440–457.

Perry, B. (2011). *Born for love: Why empathy is essential—and endangered.* New York, NY: William Morrow.

Pluess, M., Stevens, S. E., & Belsky, J. (2013). Differential susceptibility: Developmental and rvolutionary mechanisms of gene-environment interactions. In M. Legerstee, D. W. Haley, M. H. Bornstein (Eds.), *The infant mind: Origins of the social brain* (pp. 77–120). New York, NY: Guilford.

Powell, S. D., & Jordan, R. R. (1993). Being subjective about autistic thinking and learning to learn. *Educational Psychology, 13,* 359–370.

Premack, D. G., & Woodruff, G. (1978). "Does the chimpanzee have a theory of mind?" *Behavioral and Brain Sciences, 1,* 515–526.

Ramachandran, V. S. (2009, January 1). *Self awareness: The last frontier* [Edge Foundation web essay]. Retrieved from http:// www.edge.org/3rd_culture/rama08/rama08_index.html

Rice, K., Moriuchi, J. M, Jones, W., & Klin, A. (2012). Parsing heterogeneity in autism spectrum disorders: Visual scanning of dynamic social scenes in school-aged children. *Journal of the American Academy of Child & Adolescent Psychiatry, 51,* 238–248.

Rizzolatti, G., Fadiga, L., Gallese, V., & Fogassi, L. (1996). Premotor cortex and the recognition of motor actions. *Cognitive Brain Research, 3,* 131–141.

Rodrigues, S. M., Saslow, L. R., Garcia, N., Johna, O. P., & Keltnercet, D. (2009). Ocytocin genetic variation relates to empathy and stress reactivity in humans. *Proceedings of the National Academy of Sciences, 106,* 21437–21441.

Rolls, E. T., & Grabenhorst, F. (2008). The orbitofrontal cortex and beyond: From affect to decision-making. *Progress in Neurobiology, 86,* 216–244.

Roth, T. L., & Sweatt, J. D. (2011). Annual research review: Epigenetic mechanisms and environmental shaping of the brain during sensitive periods of development. *Journal of Child Psychology and Psychiatry, 52,* 398–408.

Rubia, K. (2011). "Cool" inferior frontostriatal dysfunction in attention-deficit/hyperactivity disorder versus "hot" ventromedial orbitofrontal-limbic dysfunction in conduct disorder: A review. *Biological Psychiatry, 69,* 69–87.

Schipul, S. E., Keller, T. A., & Just, M. A. (2011). Inter-regional brain communication and its disturbance in autism. *Frontiers of Systems Neuroscience, 5,* 1–11.

Shahaeian, A., Peterson, C. C., Slaughter, V., & Wellman, H. W. (2011). Culture and the sequence of steps in theory of mind development. *Developmental Psychology, 47,* 1239–1247.

Shallice, T. (1982). Specific impairments of planning. *Philosophical Transactions of the Royal Society of London, Series B, Biological Sciences, 298,* 199–209.

Shamay-Tsoory, S. (2011). The neural bases of empathy. *The Neuroscientist, 17,* 18–24.

Shamay-Tsoory, S., & Aharon-Peretz, J. (2007). Dissociable prefrontal networks for cognitive and affective theory of mind. A lesion study. *Neuropsychologia, 45,* 3054–3067.

Shamay-Tsoory, S., Aharon-Peretz, J., & Perry, D. (2009). Two systems for empathy: A double dissociation between emotional and cognitive empathy in inferior frontal gyrus versus ventromedial prefrontal lesions. *Brain, 132,* 617–627.

Shamay-Tsoory, S., Hararib, H., Aharon-Peretzc, J., & Levkovitzbet, Y. (2010). The role of the orbitofrontal cortext in affective theory of mind deficits in criminal offenders with psychopathic tendencies. *Cortex, 46,* 668–677.

Shamay-Tsoory, S., Tibi-Elhanany, Y., & Aharon-Peretz, J. (2007). The ventromedial prefrontal cortex is involved in understanding affective but not cognitive theory of mind stories. *Social Neuroscience, 1,* 149–166.

Shamay-Tsoory, S., Tomer, R., & Aharon-Peretz, J. (2005). The neuroanatomical basis of understanding sarcasm and its relationship to social cognition. *Neuropsychology, 19,* 288–300.

Sheese, B. E., Voelker, P. M., Rothbart, M. K., & Posner, M. I. (2007). Parenting quality interacts with genetic variation in dopamine receptor DRD4 to influence temperament in early childhood. *Development and Psychopathology, 19,* 1039–1046.

Sheridan, M. A., Fox, N. A., Zeanah, C. H., McLaughlin, K. A., & Nelson, C. A. (2012). Variation in neural development as a result of exposure to institutionalization early in childhood. *Proceedings of the National Academy of Science USA, 109,* 12927–12932.

Stroop, J. R. (1935). Studies of interference in serial verbal reactions. *Journal of Experimental Psychology: General, 106,* 404–426.

Suddendorf, T., & Corballis, M. C. (1997). Mental time travel and the evolution of the human mind. *Genetic, Social, & General Psychology Monographs, 123*, 133–167.

Sul, S., Choi, I., & Kang, P. (2012). Cultural difference in neural mechanisms of self-recognition. *Social Neuroscience, 4*, 402–411.

Terrett, G., Rendell, P. G., Raponi-Saunders, S., Henry, J. D., Bailey, P. E., & Altgassen, M. (2013). Episodic future thinking in children with autism spectrum disorder. *Journal of Autism and Developmental Disorders, 43*, 2558–2568.

Tomalski, P., Csibra, G., & Johnson, M. H. (2009). Rapid orienting toward face-like stimuli with gaze-relevant contrast information. *Perception, 38*, 569–578.

Triandis, H. C. (1995). *Individualism & collectivism*. Boulder, CO: Westview Press.

Vogeley, K., May, M., Ritz, A., Falkai, P., Zilles, K., & Fink, G. R., (2004). Neural correlates of first-person perspective as one constituent of human self-consciousness. *Journal of Cognitive Neuroscience, 16*, 817–827.

Waldrop, M. M. (1993). Cognitive neuroscience: A world with a future. *Science, 261*, 1805–1806.

Walter, H. (2012). Social cognitive neuroscience of empathy: Concepts, circuits, and genes. *Emotion Review, 4*, 9–17.

Ward, J. (2012). *The student's guide to social neuroscience*. New York, NY: Psychology Press.

Weigelt, S., Koldewyn, K., & Kanwisher, N. (2012). Face identify recognition in spectrum disorders: A review of behavioral studies. *Neuroscience and Biobehavior Reviews, 36*, 1060–1084.

Wellman, H. M., Fang, F., Liu, D., Zhu, L., & Liu, L. (2006). Scaling theory of mind understandings in Chinese children. *Psychological Science, 17*, 1075–1081.

Wermter, A. K., Kamp-Becker, I., Hesse, P., Schulte-Körne, G., Strauch, K., & Remschmidt, H. (2010). Evidence for the involvement of genetic variation in the oxytocin receptor gene (OXTR) in the etiology of autistic disorders on high-functioning level. *American Journal of Medicine Genetics B Neuropsychiatric Genetics, 153B*, 629–639.

White, M. G., Bogdan, R., Fisher, P. M., Munoz, K. E., Williamson, D. E., & Hariri, A. R. (2012). FKBP5 and emotional neglect interact to predict individual differences in amygdala reactivity. *Genes, Brain and Behavior, 11*, 869–878.

Zelazo, P. D., & Cunningham, W. (2007). Executive function: Mechanisms underlying emotion regulation. In J. Gross (Ed.), *Handbook of emotion regulation* (pp. 135–158). New York, NY: Guilford.

3

SOCIAL-EMOTIONAL DEVELOPMENT ASSOCIATED WITH SOCIAL COMMUNICATION

Deborah A. Hwa-Froelich

[E]motions represent the dynamic processes created within the socially influenced, value-appraising processes of the brain. . . . Emotional processing prepares the brain and rest of the body for action.
—Siegel (1999, pp. 123–124)

From the beginning of life, emotion constitutes both the process and the content of communication between infant and caregiver . . . parents use words to talk about feeling and direct a shared attention to the infant's state of mind. The parents may state directly that the baby is feeling sad or happy or scared, giving the infant the interactive verbal experience of being able both to identify and to share an emotional experience.
—Siegel (1999, p. 270)

LEARNING OBJECTIVES

Readers will

1. Be able to define attachment, attunement, and attachment relationships.
2. Be able to describe the development of emotion regulation and self-regulation.
3. Gain knowledge about how cultural differences in values and beliefs may affect social emotional development.

4. Learn how environmental and socioeconomic variables may influence social emotional development.
5. Be able to describe how different cultural caregiving habits may influence children's social emotional development.

Anthony was referred to the special education cooperative by his grandparents, Mr. and Mrs. Lopez. They were concerned that he was not talking at the age of 3. Mr. and Mrs. Lopez were business leaders in the small community and often provided child care for their two grandchildren during the day until Mrs. Barber, Anthony's mother, was able to pick them up after work. Mrs. Barber had siblings living in the area who also provided support for her and her children. During an interview with the speech-language pathologist (SLP), Mrs. Barber shared that she and her husband were alcoholics but recently she had stopped drinking and was attending Alcoholics Anonymous (AA). Her husband continued to drink, and for this reason, she was seeking a divorce and full custody of her children. She reported that she stopped drinking when she learned that she was pregnant with Anthony but had struggled to stay sober during the first 2 years of Anthony's life. After Anthony turned 2, she decided to stop drinking and has been sober for the past year.

As part of an ecological assessment, the early childhood team collected medical reports and conducted several assessments. Anthony's pediatrician reported that Anthony did not show characteristics of Fetal Alcohol Syndrome. Prior to administration of behavioral measures, Anthony passed a hearing screening. The SLP and the school psychologist interviewed Mrs. Barber, Anthony's mother, and observed Anthony following his brother's lead and taking turns during pretend play. A behavioral assessment took place at the early childhood preschool with the early childhood special educator (ECSE), SLP, mother and grandmother. A play-based assessment and the Preschool Language Scale-4 (PLS-4; Zimmerman, Steiner, & Pond, 2002) were administered. Anthony displayed strengths in understanding language, attention, solving problems, and demonstrating complex thematic play without language expression. He did not express himself during play or testing which affected measures of memory, emotional expression, sense of self, emotional themes and social interactions. Although Anthony scored within normal range on the receptive language portion of the PLS-4, he did not respond during the expressive language section. He also demonstrated freezing behaviors when voice or sound levels increased in volume. In conclusion, Anthony was delayed in socio-emotional and communication development and demonstrated some anxious and insecure behaviors.

Anthony exhibited social, emotional, and expressive language delays that were influenced by his exposure to negative experiences such as his parents' alcohol abuse and possibly contentious disagreements during his parents' marriage, as well as the process of separation and divorce. Loud voices or noises resulted in a fight or flight response of freezing behaviors often observed in children who have experienced traumatic events or children who are insecurely attached to their caregivers. To help Anthony overcome his fears and insecurity, he needed to repair his relationship with his mother and build trusting relationships with other adults such as his grandparents.

When infants are born, they are completely dependent on the care of others to provide safety, nurturance, affection, and stimulation. It is because of this dependency to meet their needs that infants need and seek a social and emotional connection with their caregivers. While it is outside the scope of this chapter to describe in rich detail all aspects of social and emotional development, the purpose of this chapter is to summarize the stages of socio-emotional and regulation development (attachment, attunement, empathy, interpersonal regulation to intrapersonal regulation, self-regulation, and inhibition), and relate these developmental areas to social communication development and disorders.

ATTACHMENT AND ATTUNEMENT

Over time, infants develop an emotionally based relationship or *attachment* to persons who provide for their needs by interpreting their nonverbal behaviors and verbal cries for help and through the caregivers' attempts to make infants feel safe, secure, and satisfied (Ainsworth, 1973; Bowlby, 1969). Attachment develops during infants' early years to create an enduring emotional relationship between the infant and a nurturing adult caregiver(s) who provides comfort and a sense of safety by providing routinized care in a predictable environment. Greenspan (1985) describes the stages of this socio-emotional development as (a) falling in love with the caregiver around 3 to 4 months of age, (b) knowing the caregiver is permanent at 9 months, and (c) feeling securely attached by 2 years of age. Over time, infants develop a mental representation of their attachment relationship and infants refer to these mental representations as a "secure base" or a source of comfort during times of separation or distress (Siegel, 1999, p. 71). For example, during object permanence the infant has a mental representation of his or her mother or primary caregiver and calls out when this person is not in sight. By

1 year of age when the infant seeks comfort or interaction, the infant anticipates the caregivers' responses and calms down when the caregiver approaches (Wilson, 2012). From the foundation of this secure attached relationship, the infant views the world as predictable and manageable which allows them to venture out to explore the environment, interacting with novel objects, events, and other persons. This parent–infant relationship also provides a framework for later relationships with others (Eagle, 1995; Siegel, 1999). Through the infinite interactions infants have with their caregivers and the nurturing attuned effect of caregivers' responses on infants' physiological state, caregivers influence how infants view the world and how they interact with their environment. Small and large differences in these parent–infant interactions can result in uniquely different socio-emotional developmental outcomes (Wilson, 2012). These variations are in alignment with dynamic systems theory as described in Chapter 1.

When caregivers respond consistently, appropriately, and contingently to their infants' cries for comfort or assistance over time, a *secure* attachment is more likely to develop. This requires sensitivity, in that the caregiver must be able to read infants' cues to figure out what is causing their distress as well as which kinds of responses will calm them. As caregivers are consistently successful in calming an infant or *attuned* to the infant, their infants will prefer and seek assistance from them as a means to resolve their distressed state and achieve a state of calm (Greenspan, 1985; Wilson, 2012). Through attunement a secure attachment develops, and from this foundation, infants feel safe enough to explore because they have learned that their caregiver will assist or care for them if they become scared or hurt. If during their exploration of the world, infants are uncertain, they may interact with their caregiver through eye contact or physically moving closer to the caregiver to observe the caregiver's response to the object or situation. If the caregiver smiles, comments that it is safe, or models how to interact with the novel object, event, or person, the infant borrows the calm emotional state from the caregiver to regulate his or her initial uncertainty or fear. Only when infants feel safe can they explore their environment so that learning can take place (Greenspan, 1985; Wilson, 2012).

Over time, infants develop a mental representation not only of the caregiver but also of the kind of relationship they expect with their caregiver. If the majority of the interactions result in attunement, in that the caregiver is successful in comforting, calming, and meeting the infant's needs, then the infant expects the caregiver to be emotionally and physically available and interact in positive and supportive ways. This type of caregiver–child relationship is often judged to be a secure attachment

(Bernier, Carlson, & Whipple, 2010; Stams, Juffer, & Van IJzensoorn, 2002). As Samantha Wilson (2012) described,

> caregivers are not perfectly accurate in deciphering their children's needs at *all* times, nor should they be expected to be; there are many expectable (and appropriate) missteps in dyadic communication. These missteps, in and of themselves, are not inherently problematic, and in fact provide the child with mild, tolerable frustrations that allow him to increase regulatory coping. In most cases, a competent (i.e., 'good enough') caregiver recognizes the miscues and works to repair them quickly. (p. 62)

In other words, it is through more consistent and competent social interactions that children feel they have a strong, secure foundation from which to explore the world allowing them to better manage and/or predict outcomes. It also helps children to view interactions with other people as positive and enjoyable promoting future relationships with peers and other adults. Through attuned caregiving, children receive face-to-face contact with their caregivers, enabling them to process facial expressions, tone of voice, and body postures (nurturing, flexible versus stiff and distant postures). This type of interaction helps children also develop skills to process, determine the value of, and interpret emotions of others, which are discussed in Chapter 4.

What happens when caregivers are not successful at reading their infants' cues, respond inconsistently, negatively, or inappropriately to their infants' cries for comfort or safety? Infants are born expecting and dependent upon developmentally appropriate care and stimulation (Fox, Levitt, & Nelson, 2010). Thus, when the majority of the infant–caregiver interactions are inappropriate, inconsistent, and/ or negative, then infants may feel insecure, unsafe, or unsure about their safety even when the caregiver is present (Cicchetti & Toth, 1995; Siegel, 1999). They perceive the environment as unpredictable, chaotic, overwhelming, and/or unsafe. In these kinds of cases, children demonstrate a type of *insecure* attachment relationship. Typically, three different types of insecure attachment have been described in the literature (Siegel, 1999; Wilson, 2012). An *avoidant* type of insecure attachment is demonstrated when the child avoids the caregiver, does not appear to share or exchange emotions with the caregiver, and does not show stress behaviors on separation, novel, or fearful situations. The parents may appear emotionally unavailable, to have low affect, insensitive to their child's needs, or developmentally inappropriate. A caregiver–child relationship is judged to be a *resistant* insecure attachment when the child tends to inhibit play or exploration and/or appears to be ambivalent when stressed. For example, a child continues to cry regardless of whether the parent is present or not or s/he appears to be focused on his or her distress. The parent or parents are inconsistently available, sensitive, or successful and thus seem to be unpredictable. Finally, perhaps the most impaired attachment relationship that is most often associated with psychopathology is a *disorganized* attachment (Wilson, 2012). Children who demonstrate a disorganized type of attachment may display contradictory behaviors such as seeking caregiver proximity and comfort while trying to strike the caregiver, an inconsistent approach pattern in which the child walks toward the parent and then stops or backs up or has uninhibited, impulsive, frantic behavior with little to no emotional connection to the caregiver during a free-play situation (Siegel, 1999; Wilson, 2012). Parents may be abusive, may be emotionally frightening, or display sudden unpredictable shifts in their mental states, such as rapid shifts from happy and loving to sad, distant, or angry.

In insecure attachment relationships, a child is unable to cope with stress either because the parent is the cause of the stress or because the child experienced such negative early experiences that when a stressful event occurs, the child has not developed coping behaviors or a secure relationship with the caregiver or caregivers. Instead of having a caregiver help children cope, a secure attachment relationship representation to refer to or coping behaviors to employ for stressful events, children may develop reflexive behavioral patterns such as a fight or flight response to all stressful stimuli. This fight-or-flight reflex is associated with the primitive part of the brain, the limbic system, and serves as a primitive, unconscious, survival behavior (refer to Chapter 2). As Siegel (1999) describes, "emotions are primarily nonconscious mental processes. In their essence they create a readiness for action, . . . disposing us to behave in particular ways within the environment" (p. 132). When stressed, infants may activate the sympathetic-adrenomedullary (SAM) system responsible for activation of the fight-or-flight response (Ladage, 2009). Long-term exposure to stress may result in an overactive hypothalamic-pituitary-adrenal (HPA) stress axis resulting in higher than normal levels of the growth hormone, cortisol. The lasting effect of high cortisol levels is *psycho-social short stature* (growth disorder associated with stress or emotional deprivation), as well as lower cognitive and motor performance scores (Ladage, 2009; Mason & Narad, 2005, p. 5). The limbic–hypothalamic–pituitary–adrenocortical axis may also be affected which is associated with the production of glucocorticoids. This hormone has a negative impact on processes involved in learning and memory (for a review see Gunnar & Quevedo, 2007). Children who are exposed to adverse care for long periods may maintain high stress levels resulting in over-pruning of synaptic connections and less than optimal neurological development such as in the right hemisphere and frontal lobes. These neurological structures are important for processing emotions and behaviors, attachment, empathy, regulation of affect, problem solving, and cognitive flexibility (Fox et al., 2010; Gunnar & Quevedo, 2007; Nelson, 2007; Sánchez & Pollak, 2009; Schore, 2001; Siegel, 1999). Emotions may be psychologically separated from consciousness or be repressed, and therefore, these emotions may not be expressed verbally. In some cases children may not appraise or reflect on these emotions (Saarni, 1999). Children who have a fight-or-flight response often display heightened vigilance, flighty, active, aggressive, passive withdrawal, or freezing behaviors in response to stimuli they perceive as a threat. With this kind of response, learning becomes secondary to survival and these learning patterns persist unless children experience significant changes in the maltreating environment. Overall, when children endure high levels of stress for long periods, their physical, social, emotional, cognitive, and overall learning are adversely affected. Because of their negative relational experiences, children who are insecurely attached tend to have more difficulty regulating and understanding their own and others' emotions, which may negatively affect their social competence.

Regardless of culturally diverse parenting practices, similar estimates of secure and insecure attachment have been reported across countries (Van IJzendoorn & Sagi-Schwartz, 2008). For example, the US Department of Health and Human Services (DHHS) estimates that approximately 65% of infants have a secure attachment relationship and 35% have an insecure attachment (DHHS, 1991). Emery, Paquette, and Bigras (2008) reported approximately 59% of 138 Canadian teen mothers had a secure attachment with their infants. As far as insecure attachment relationships, approximately 20% of infant attachment relationships are avoidant, and 10% to 15% were reported to be ambivalent in the United States (DHHS, 1991). Similarly, Taylor, Marshall, Mann, and Goldberg (2012) reported a rate of 28% insecure attachment in cases with medically unexplained symptoms across 10 general medicine practices in the United Kingdom, and Emery and colleagues (2008) reported a rate of 9% avoidant and 5% resistant or ambivalent attachment in Canadian parent–infant samples (Taylor et al., 2012). Approximately 10% to 15% of US caregiver–infant relationships and 26% of Canadian teen mother–infant relationships were reported to be disorganized (Emery et al., 2008; DHHS, 1991).

TRANSITION FROM INTERPERSONAL REGULATION TO INTRAPERSONAL EMOTION REGULATION

Before emotion regulation can be discussed, it is important to define what emotion is and outline the stages of emotional development. Holodynski (2013) reviewed the historical and cultural literature on emotion and emotional development and defined emotions as

> a functional psychological system involving the synchronic interplay of general components and serving to regulate actions within the macrostructure of activity in line with a person's motives. . . . An emotion is made up of four components: appraisal, expression, body regulation, and subjective feeling. (p. 11)

Emotions are important intrapersonally and interpersonally. Knowing how one feels about objects or events helps one determine an individually appropriate response. During interpersonal interactions, emotions help each participant by adding information to the interchange. Accurate interpersonal interpretation of other people's emotions helps to guide one's behavior during the interaction (Denham, 1998). Denham (1998) describes emotions as a process during which each individual orients to a change in their environment or in themselves that alerts the Autonomic Nervous System (ANS) and the lower primitive brain. Orientation and alertness moves to an appraisal process during which the stimulus is judged along a continuum of intensity, familiarity, and expectedness and is compared with past memories of similar stimuli or situations. If the appraisal does not match internal expectations of the stimulus or situation, then the infant becomes aroused by this dissonance and is more alert and energized (Siegel, 1999). If the stimulus is appraised as positive or interesting, the infant may move from a calm state to a heightened arousal or alertness. However, if the stimulus triggers a negative emotion or uncertainty, the infant may move to a heightened stress reaction for which the caregiver is needed to help the infant achieve a state of calm. These changes in mental states may involve lower level emotions such as fear, frustration, surprise, or joy (Siegel, 1999). As the infant develops and has more experiences mediated by a caring adult, changes in the environment and the ANS result in sympathetic and parasympathetic physiological changes associated with stress, excitement, or calm, such as increased/decreased blood pressure, respiration, and heart rate (Siegel, 1999). Changes in the environment and the ANS also trigger cognitive appraisal of the stimulus or stimuli such as conscious tendencies to behave in certain ways (crying, clinging, increased movement, exploration;

Denham, 1998). Over time, in a secure attachment relationship, infants eventually remember and learn which stimuli are safe or how to seek and read their caregivers' cues as to whether they should engage with the stimulus. They also learn coping strategies to achieve a calmer state when confronted with situations that are stressful or exciting or in the absence of the caregiver (sucking on thumb, cuddling with a blanket).

Emotions provide meaning and motivation for activity and participation, help organize the brain, and are linked to one's memories. As explained in Chapter 2, the right and left hemispheres are differentiated in emotion processing. The right tends to process nonverbal communication and positive emotions while the left tends to process verbal communication and negative emotions (Siegel, 1999). Emotional understanding of self and others helps individuals understand and connect with others (Siegel, 1999). It is through socio-emotional interactions with caregivers that children learn about their emotions and learn to regulate them independently from their caregivers. The more secure and attuned the attachment relationship, the more caregivers help infants achieve a calm, positive emotional state when they experience physiological stressors such as hunger, pain, fear, or discomfort. Caregivers model through face-to-face interactions, a calm, loving face and tone of voice as well as nurturing postures and touch. At the same time, nurturing caregivers provide labels for the infant's mental states and emotions to help the infant begin to identify their own internal states. In other words, the infant borrows the emotional and mental states of their caregivers to help regulate their stress and negative emotions (Bronson, 2000; Legerstee, 2005; Schore, 2001, Sroufe, 1997). Table 3.1 provides the sequence of emotional development.

As the child begins to encounter novel objects, events, and people, he or she emotionally engages with his or her caregiver to check the caregiver's emotional state or opinion regarding the exploration of these uncertain contexts (Mundy & Sigman, 2006). From these interchanges, the child learns how to interpret different emotions from facial expressions and vocal tones, which objects or events should be avoided or treated with caution and which ones are safe, and how to minimize their stress or uncertainty in stressful situations (Legerstee, 2005; Moses, Baldwin, Rosicky, & Tidbell, 2001). As children and caregivers interact and experience joint attention, children gain knowledge about their internal feelings, about how their caregiver calms them, about how to deal with stressful events, and about how other people feel and act. At the same time, children are acquiring a symbol system to associate labels to feelings, mental states, and beliefs.

There are differences in frequency of different emotions displayed and expressed. Denham (1998) reviewed research in which toddlers

Table 3.1 Development of Emotions

0–3 months	Aware of self-interest in world
5 months	Aware/responds to familiar others
7 months	Discriminates between facial expressions
9 months	Intentionality
13 months	Complex emotions (love, curiosity, protest)
18 months	Shows joy, fear, and anger
2 years	Mental models of feelings, can link emotions to situations, can deceive and understand deception
3 years	Emotional talking, can understand people may feel differently about same event
4 years	Bridges emotion to beliefs to causality, time, space; shows empathy toward peers
5–6 years	Knows beliefs can result in specific emotions, can predict emotions
7–8 years	Understands a person can feel several emotions at the same time, morally bad behavior results in negative emotions and morally praiseworthy acts result in positive emotions

Source:
Denham (1998); Holodynski (2013); Pons, Harris, and de Rosnay (2004); and Timler (2003).

display more happy and angry emotions than sad, painful, or distressful ones. By preschool age, children's negative emotions tend to decrease in frequency. During the first 3 years, children consistently demonstrate the emotions of anger, fearfulness, interest, and joy. Denham also reported in her literature review that boys tended to express more anger, less shame, and less pride, whereas girls tended to express more sadness, shame, and pride (for a review, see Denham, 1998). Gender differences may be influenced by parents' differentiated interactions with their sons and daughters. Carpendale and Lewis (2006) reviewed studies in which parents expressed more emotional words to their daughters than to their sons, which, over time, was associated with girls expressing more emotion words than did boys.

As children mature, they increase their understanding and expression of emotions. As Denham (1998) described, over 75% of 3-year-old children use terms for feeling good, happy, sad, afraid, angry, loving, mean, and surprised (Ridgeway & Kuczaj, 1985). By the end of the preschool period, over 75% of 6-year-olds also use terms for feeling comfortable, excited, upset, glad, unhappy, relaxed, bored, lonely, annoyed, disappointed, shy, pleased, worried, calm, embarrassed, hating, nervous, and cheerful (Ridgeway & Kucaj, 1985). (p. 77)

The secure relationship, socio-emotional knowledge, and language development work together to enable the child to regulate negative emotions, develop empathy (affective empathy as described by Westby in Chapter 2), think and problem solve in language or develop what Vygotsky (1934/1986) termed *internal speech*. When caregivers accurately interpret their children's emotions and explain the emotions of others, these children not only learn the emotional labels linked to emotional events, they learn how emotions cause people to act in certain ways and that certain kinds of events cause people to feel particular emotions (for a review see Cole, Armstrong, & Pemberton, 2010; Denham, 1998). This social knowledge and understanding builds their social cognition and understanding about the world and people as well as helps them predict and plan for future interactions (discussed in Chapter 4). In other words, these experiences help the child gradually move from an interpersonal (caregiver–child) system of emotion regulation, that is, depending on the caregiver to help them regulate stressful situations, to an intrapersonal regulation system where children begin to independently calm themselves and eventually learn to care for others (Holodynski, 2013).

Understanding of emotions is also affected by parenting strategies. When parents express more anger, tension, or sadness, their children demonstrate more anger, confusion, or pain (Denham, 1998). In addition, when caregivers arbitrarily set limits and consistently enforce those limits, they tend to have children who have less understanding of emotion, whereas caregivers who were inconsistent in setting limits and enforcement had children with more emotion understanding. This was not true for the caregivers who were more indulgent and set fewer limits. These indulgent caregivers tended to have children with less emotion understanding. In other words, families whose discipline is less arbitrary, more empathetic, and rational may use a situation-by-situation approach considering negative and positive emotional experiences. This approach allows children to more effectively learn about emotions (Denham, 1998).

Because children's knowledge of self and others' emotions is dependent on their caregivers' view of the world, when caregivers are inaccurate in interpreting their children's emotions or inappropriate in social interactions with their children, their children may demonstrate delays or different patterns of development and expression of emotions and affective ToM. If parents are inaccurate in reading and labeling their children's emotions, their children may have difficulty identifying their own feelings as well as the feelings of others. Children who are insecurely attached may not know how they feel, or they may mask their feelings to other people (Siegel, 1999). There may be a disconnect between the right and left hemispheres when nonverbal and verbal expressions of emotions contradict each other. For example in the case of children with an avoidant attachment, they may have parents who are rejecting or uninvolved. These children may avoid social interactions and reduce emotional expression to avoid their frustration of interacting with an unavailable or negative parent. As adults, they may suppress their own emotions and prefer to not emotionally engage with others (Siegel, 1999). In the case of an ambivalent attachment relationship, children may feel shame, anxiety, and fear about their ability to regulate their emotions during separation and demonstrate strong reactions associated with separation. This type of response may occur when parents prolong the separation or angrily initiate and threaten to use separation as a type of punishment. When these children mature, they may attempt to avoid rejection by mirroring others' emotions instead of sharing their own feelings. They may either suppress or not be able to identify their own emotions (Siegel, 1999). As adults, they may demonstrate separation anxiety and may cling to or try to maintain favor or connection with others. In a disorganized attachment relationship, the child experiences separation associated with their parents' rage. Thus, the child not only experiences the separation as loss of comfort and safety; they also experience fear for their own safety with no support to regulate or understand their emotions. In these cases, children develop mental states that are unregulated and somewhat chaotic, linked to ingrained behavioral patterns in reaction to associated stimuli, such as freezing, fighting, or fleeing. As adults, they may demonstrate disorganized narratives about their past relationships and inconsistent behaviors that promote, dismiss, or avoid closeness in relationships. These behavioral attachment patterns often vary across individuals and their unique history of trauma and/ or abuse (Siegel, 1999).

In contrast to infants with an insecure attachment pattern, infants in a secure attachment relationship develop an effective intrapersonal regulation system. Thus, the ability to regulate oneself is learned from many social interactions and social contexts with nurturing caregivers.

Through these attuned experiences and over time, children's neurological and nervous systems develop a tolerance for and an ability to regulate strong arousal and emotional reactions and achieve a mentally and physiologically calm state (Egeland, Weinfield, Bosquet, & Cheng, 2000; Schore, 2001; Sroufe, 1997). Thus, developing a secure attachment relationship enables children to initially use the caregiver as a means to interpersonally regulate stress and negative emotions while they explore the world. As children develop a mental model of their caregiver, as well as social cognition and world knowledge, they learn strategies for independently and intrapersonally regulating their stress and negative emotions in the absence of the caregiver.

As in Anthony's case, he developed an insecure attachment relationship in which his caregivers were the source of stress or negative emotions and were unable or failed to provide attuned care. Children in these situations may be unable to regulate strong arousal and negative emotions and may demonstrate unusual behavior patterns in the face of stressful situations (Wilson, 2012). Caregivers may have provided inconsistent, intrusive, abusive, passive, or disconnected care. As a result, their infants may be over- or under-aroused and may have a poorly organized ANS (Egeland et al., 2000). Infants may not be able to reach a calm state and may be inconsolable, withdrawn, or angry. Over time, the inconsistent, ineffective, or abusive interactions leave children in a chronic hypersensitive or hyposensitive state of arousal resulting in persistent neurological stress patterns. These patterns of inappropriate and ineffective regulatory systems become the default pattern for processing and dealing with stress and negative emotions (refer to Chapter 1 for theoretical explanations). Children may display strong reactions to external stressors (aggression, flight, or withdrawal) and are unable to regulate themselves when stressed. For example, Anthony's default pattern when he felt scared or threatened was to become motionless and freeze. By not talking to others, he demonstrated a passive, disconnected interactional pattern with his family and others. Anthony did not have external or internal sources to assist him in regulating his negative emotional states. Children with insecure attachment relationships may be reluctant to or may inappropriately explore their environment resulting in learning delays. They may demonstrate physical growth deficiencies because of persistent neuroendocrine stimulation in reaction to stress. And they may have difficulty relating to others because they do not have a close trusting relationship with their caregivers (Wilson, 2012). These children may not be able to develop interpersonal or intrapersonal regulation systems.

DEVELOPMENT OF EMPATHY

There is little research documenting the development of empathy. In a discussion about variables involved in the development of empathy, Knafo and Uzefovsky (2013) describe hypothetically how empathy develops. From their perspective, empathy develops similar to, and is associated with, other cognitive functions, such as self- and emotion regulation and social understanding. They state that the infant must first differentiate themselves from others, which typically occurs during the first year of life. During this stage of "global empathy," the infant feels what others feel (becoming stressed when others are stressed) but does not discriminate between their own feelings separate from others' feelings (Knafo & Uzefovsky, 2013, p. 100). For example Anthony remained in a state of global empathy in which he felt the distress of others but was unable to cope with others' distress. After approximately 1 year, the infant moves to a stage of "egocentric empathic distress," in which he or she desires to be comforted when another person is upset (Knafo & Uzefovsky, 2013, p. 100). At the age of 2 years, children demonstrate "quasi-egocentric empathic distress," when they recognize someone else is distressed and offer solutions that would help alleviate their own distress, not realizing that someone else may desire a different solution (Knafo & Uzefovsky, 2013, p. 100). Later in the second year of life, children begin to understand that other people may have different feelings than their own or the state of "veridical empathic distress" (Knafo & Uzefovsky, 2013, p. 100). There is emerging evidence showing an increase in empathic concern during 14 to 20 months, 2 years, and 3 years of age (Knafo & Uzefovsky, 2013).

SELF-REGULATION AND INHIBITION

Self-regulation involves learning how to manage affect, attention, and behavior by inhibiting impulses (Barkley, 1997; Raffaelli, Crockett, & Shen, 2005). As infants learn to move from interpersonal to intrapersonal regulation, they learn coping strategies to inhibit negative emotions. Initially, infants are able to stop or reduce their crying when their caregiver attends to their physiological needs of hunger, distress, or fatigue. As they mature, infants have a mental representation of their caregiver or develop coping strategies to calm themselves in the absence of their caregiver (Bronson, 2000). For example, infants may use a stuffed animal or pacifier to calm themselves. Table 3.2 describes the developmental changes in self-regulation.

Table 3.2 Developmental Changes in Self-Regulation

Age	Developmental changes	Integrated developmental areas	Outcomes
2 months	Moves from internal control Develops sleep/wakecycles Inhibits primitive reflexes	Demonstrates biological regulation Attention/alertness increases	Awake more often Increased interaction
7–9 months	Develops specific attachments Connects emotion and behavior Self-soothing behaviors develop Beginning mobility	Mobility Has shared meanings Intimate with others	Position/place in environment changes Changes expectations of self/others Displays negative reactions Shows fear of strangers
12 months	Develops symbolic behaviors Expresses affect Increases mobility	Increased mobility Attached to parents Shares emotions	Explores world Has a secure base Expresses feelings
18–21 months	Uses language Increases autonomy Aware of obstacles	Words, verbal expression Aware of separation Declarative knowledge/schemas	Strong sense of self Resists control Behavioral self-control
30–48 months	Thinks in emotions Knows social rules Develops self-concept Delays gratification	Sense of self Differentiates between fantasy/reality Understands cause and effect	Understands mistakes Follows rules Has new expectations and standards
48–96 months	Ability to shift attention Increase in inhibitory control Decrease in impulsivity	Increase in abstract thinking Flexibility in attention and thought Increased social understanding	Predicts outcomes and alters behavior Dynamic thinking reflected in problem solving

Source:
Adapted from Bronson (2000); Emde, Gaensbauer, and Harmon (1976); Mischel, Shoda, and Rodriguez (1989); Murphy, Eisenberg, Fabes, Shepard, and Guthrie (1999); and Raffaelli et al. (2005).

During the toddler and preschool ages, children learn to inhibit three different kinds of impulses: (a) reflexes or unconscious impulses,

(b) ineffective actions, and (c) interfering or damaging actions affecting task completion (Barkley, 1997). An example of inhibition of reflexive or unconscious impulses is when they learn to inhibit a startle reflex for repetitive and familiar sounds such as doorbells and telephone rings. They learn to stop an ineffective action, for example, when they learn to inhibit their desire to crawl down stairs face-first and turn around to decline the stairs without seeing where they are going. Finally, they learn how to interact with objects and to avoid sources that may damage or interfere with completion of a task. For example, children learn that parents do not want them to play with car keys or cell phones; they inhibit playing with these forbidden objects in the presence of their parents and run or hide when trying to operate or play with these objects.

As described earlier, some inhibition and regulation of emotions, attention, and behavior develop prior to learning language. Infants learn to attend to their caregivers' facial expressions to determine whether they should engage with an object (Mundy & Sigman, 2006). As caregivers model and express directions and social rules in simple language to their children, children initially learn to regulate their behavior in the presence of the caregiver (Bronson, 2000). As children learn to understand and express language, they begin to inhibit their impulses and follow directions and social rules when their caregivers are not present (Bronson, 2000; Vygotsky, 1934/1986). Over time, they begin to use language or self-talk as a way to inhibit and regulate their behavior. For example, children may talk aloud to inhibit touching something, saying, "Mommy said, 'Don't touch.' "

Inhibition and self-regulation are related to caregivers' sensitivity in interacting with their children (Bernier et al., 2010). Measures of maternal sensitivity, parent talk about mental states, and support for autonomy when children were 15 months old were related to children's working memory development at 18 months of age and their executive function abilities at 26 months of age more than children's cognitive ability and mothers' education (Bernier et al., 2010). Parental support of autonomy was defined as scaffolding, respect of individual differences in rate of learning, and encouragement of child participation and role in successful task completion. Over time, children are able to motivate themselves and monitor their progress by independently analyzing and synthesizing their behavior prior to, during, and after completion of a task. In other words, the development of self-regulation allows children to inhibit attention on distractions and focus their attention to complete tasks successfully and competently (Welsh, Pennington, & Groisser, 1991; Zelazo, Carter, Reznick, & Frye, 1997). These sensitive parenting behaviors, mental state talk, and support for their children's autonomy (scaffolding, respect, and encouragement) facilitated and promoted executive function development, which are discussed further in Chapter 4.

After language develops, self-regulation development continues to develop, and is integrated with, other developmental areas. For example, Murphy and colleagues (1999) followed 4- to 6-year-old children for 6 years longitudinally and found improvements in shifting attention and inhibitory control with no change in focused attention and behavior regulation. In a cross-sectional study of children between 6 and 12 years of age, improvements in self-regulation behaviors were related to children's improved ability in abstract thinking (Mischel et al., 1989). Additionally, Raffaelli and colleagues (2005) compared parental report measures of regulation of emotion, behavior, and attention when 646 children were between 4 and 5, 8 and 9, and 12 and 13 years of age. They found significant improvement in self-regulation during the period between early and middle childhood but not between middle-childhood and adolescent ages. Gender differences were also reported at each period (early childhood, middle childhood, and adolescence) with girls demonstrating more regulation than boys (Raffaelli et al., 2005).

FACTORS AFFECTING SOCIO-EMOTIONAL DEVELOPMENT

Cultural differences in beliefs and values have been documented extensively in the literature. Most cultural factors affecting socio-emotional development can be organized into three categories: (a) the mind-set of the caregivers, (b) the physical and social environment, and (c) cultural habits in caring for and rearing children (Lewis, 2000).

Mind-Set of Caregivers

The importance of caregiver sensitivity on the development of the caregiver–infant relationship affects attachment and a child's closeness in future relationships. According to mainstream and Western definitions of caregiver sensitivity, sensitive caregiving includes responding promptly, consistently, and appropriately. However, these interactions may also be influenced by cultural preferences for independence or interdependence (for a review see Lewis, 2000).

Some cultures prefer infant behaviors that promote child dependence on the caregiver while other cultures may prefer caregiving behaviors that encourage infant exploration and separation from parents to promote independence. For example, Puerto Rican mothers were found to physically and verbally restrain their children's exploration in contrast to US mothers who encouraged more independent exploration and gave more suggestions and fewer directions (Harwood, Schölmerich, & Schulze, 2000). On the other hand, Vietnamese parents talked about using the threat of separation or shunning as methods to facilitate dependence, filial obligation, and obedience (Hwa-Froelich & Westby, 2003). Each group of parents may view children's reactions to separation differently. If children cry on separation and desire to be reunited with their parents, Asian parents may view this behavior as a sign of successful parenting in that their child needs to renew their interdependence with them. Consequently, Asian mothers expect and willingly provide soothing assurances that they are still connected. On the other hand, Western parents may view crying behavior and drive to reunite as confrontational, insecure behavior. Thus, to foster independence, Western mothers may desire to eliminate this dependent behavior and apply strategies and experiences to help their children separate from them without crying (Harkness, Super, & Mavridis, 2011; Rothbaum & Rusk, 2011). Given these cultural variations on how parents socialize and discipline their children in exploration, separation, obedience, and behavior, children may demonstrate differences in social and emotional behaviors such as attachment.

Cultural differences in parent-infant attachment with more insecure attachments were reported by Van IJzendoorn and Sagi-Schwartz (2008). Children with insecure attachments were overrepresented in some African countries as well as Japan, Indonesia, and Israel. However, they found more intracultural variation than inter-cultural variation (Van IJzendoorn & Sagi-Schwartz, 2008). Chen and Rubin (2011a) reviewed the literature on children's reactions to stressful situations and found cultural differences. They reported that Korean and Chinese toddlers appeared more fearful and anxious than Italian and Australian children did in experimental situations. In another study, Chinese toddlers demonstrated more vigilant and reactive behaviors than Canadian toddlers did (Chen & Rubin, 2011a).

Differences in attunement may also be due to cultural differences in values. In a study of 796 mother–infant dyads from 11 countries, the majority of the mothers and infants demonstrated attuned behaviors. Behaviors varied based on what value the mothers stressed; that is, if physical development was stressed, the infants had more advanced physical development, or if mothers stressed social interaction, the infants demonstrated more social attention (Bornstein, 2013).

In spite of these cultural variations, the basic patterns of attachment described in this chapter have been found in every culture (Stevenson-Hinde, 2011). Because of the intracultural variation as well as intercultural differences, it is important for all professionals to be aware that cultural beliefs and values influence caregiving and infant behaviors and that these variances may not indicate a clinically relevant insecure relationship. Professionals may need to gather information from a local sample of parent–infant interactions to understand cultural variances in parental beliefs and values and parent–infant interactions before determining whether a clinically relevant insecure attachment exists.

Physical and Social Environments

Physical and social environments include the settings where children and their families live and interact, such as neighborhoods, schools, parks, and the community at large. The social environment involves the people who are responsible for the care of children and people with whom children interact on a regular basis (Lewis, 2000). Poverty or low socioeconomic status (SES) may have a detrimental influence on social and emotional development particularly in the domain of physical and social environments. Children from low-income backgrounds are more likely to live with a single mother who did not finish high school and may not be employed (for a review see Aber, Jones, & Cohen, 2000).

Single adolescent mothers may have had an insecure relationship with their own parents and consequently their children may be at greater risk of developing an insecure attachment relationship. Van IJzendoorn and Bakermans-Kranenburg (2010) conducted a meta-analysis of studies employing the Adult Attachment Interview (Cassidy & Shaver, 2008) across gender, SES, and culture. Adult attachment interviews are structured interviews gathering narrative information about an adult's perspective of their childhood relationships with their parents. Based on the coherence of these narratives, trained psychologists can derive one of three attachment classifications: (a) Secure–Autonomous, (b) Insecure–Dismissing, or (c) Insecure–Preoccupied. Adults who are secure appreciate the importance of attachment relationships. Adults with a dismissive insecure attachment may view the parent–child relationship idealistically but are unable to describe relationships in concrete terms or dismiss the importance of this relationship in their lives. The preoccupied, insecure adult focuses on the negative impact their previous attachment relationship had on their lives displaying anger or passivity toward these relationships (Cassidy & Shaver, 2008). From this meta-analysis, more adolescents, in particular adolescent mothers from low-income backgrounds, were judged to have a dismissive insecure attachment with their parents (Van Ijzendoorn & Bakermans-Kranenburg, 2010). With this kind of socio-emotional background, young adolescent mothers are at risk of replicating this type of attachment relationship with their infants. In addition to the history of an insecure relationship, the risk of developing an insecure relationship with their children, because of their low-income status, these families often reside in poor neighborhoods with poor-quality schools, little or no access to health or public services, and more risk of exposure to environmental toxins, such as lead.

The health and the development of children born into impoverished environments are at risk. First, poverty is associated with poorer birth outcomes. Infants born into poverty are more often associated with low birth weight and at risk of high infant mortality (Aber et al., 2000). Once they leave the hospital, these infants are also more likely to be exposed to environmental lead and have elevated blood lead levels. Small or low levels of lead have been shown to have negative effects on brain development (Aber et al., 2000). Poverty has also been associated with poorer health outcomes including a higher incidence of asthma, upper respiratory infections, tuberculosis, and pediatric AIDS (for a review, see Aber et al., 2000).

In addition to environmental toxins, poor neighborhoods are often unsafe and violent. Exposure to violence or experiencing violence can have traumatic effects on children and their family. Long-term exposure or experiencing a traumatic event can increase the stress on children and their families resulting in a state of hypervigilence (Aber et al., 2000).

Cultural Habits in Child Rearing

Cultural habits in rearing children may develop from the beliefs and values of a particular culture. Differences in display and regulation of emotions have been reported in the literature (for a review see Chen & Rubin, 2011b). Differences in smiling and laughing, differences in sociodramatic or symbolic play (discussed in chapter 4), as well as cultural differences in parenting behaviors have been reported (Chen, 2011; Chen & Rubin, 2011a; Hwa-Froelich, 2004; Hwa-Froelich & Vigil, 2004; Vigil & Hwa-Froelich, 2004). Some of these differences may be explained by differences in values of independence and interdependence or individualism versus collectivism (Hwa-Froelich & Vigil, 2004). Chen (2011) describes these differences "while individuals in Western societies attempt to maintain a balance between prosocial concerns and individual freedom of choice, individuals in group-oriented societies regard responsiveness to the needs of others as a fundamental commitment" (p. 32). For example, in Ugandan and Kenyan African cultures, a value of social responsibility is associated with being more intelligent. Mothers will share taking care of infants with other mothers and older children. The ability to care for others is valued as a developmental skill. Social skills are also viewed as an important developmental skill by parents in Latin America. Latin American parents described their goal of having children who were socially competent (e.g., respectful, cooperative, fulfilling family obligations; Chen, 2011).

Cultures differ in their preferences for aggressive, assertive, shy, inhibited, attentive, self-focused, or other-focused behavior (Chen, 2011). For example, Korean children prefer to exclude aggressive peers, whereas in the United States, some peer groups support and approve of aggressive behaviors. A shy, inhibited demeanor is often associated with insecurity in Western societies, but in Asian ones, it is viewed as a positive behavior and is associated with social maturity. US parents described their infants in terms of intelligence and independent and rebellious behaviors, whereas European parents (specifically parents from Italy, the Netherlands, Spain, and Sweden) talked about their children's social and emotional characteristics in that they were "happy, well-balanced or even-tempered" (Chen, 2011, p. 89).

Often these behaviors are taught or modeled by children's parents. Chen (2011) described literature in which Asian parent goals are to teach children to be obedient and harmonious with others. Because of these values, research has found that children from East Asian countries such as Japan and China tend to have better perspective taking and show more concern for others than children from Western countries do. Individuals from East Asian societies also use strategies to engage in active, attentive listening instead of expressing individual ideas or feelings and their emotions often reflect the emotions of others (Chen, 2011). Independent and interdependent differences in beliefs, goals, and strategies for problem solving are compared in Table 3.3.

Different cultures also socialize children to display or suppress different emotions. In interdependent cultures in which the goal for children is to achieve harmony, it is more likely that children may suppress individual expressions of emotions and attend more to other people's emotions, whereas children from independent cultures are more likely to express their individual positive emotions, while suppressing individual negative emotions (Rothbaum & Rusk, 2011). Rothbaum and Rusk (2011) describe several studies that contrast the cultural parenting differences in promoting emotional regulation. For example, East Asian parents were found to promote "low-arousal positive emotions of calm and peaceful" and "self-effacement" whereas European American parents reinforced more "high-arousal positive emotions of excitement and elation" and "self-esteem" (pp. 109, 110). Trommsdorf and Cole (2011) reported some emotions are valued differently across cultures.

Table 3.3 Independent and Interdependent Views and Goals

	Independence	Interdependence
Self-concept	Individualistic	Collective
Control	To control oneself	To allow others to control oneself
Social goals	To achieve autonomy	To achieve harmony
Emotion goals	To be happy	To be calm
Situational strategies	To solve a problem by changing the situation through initiation or determination of outcomes (self goals)	To solve a problem by attending and adjusting to a larger context (group goals) and accepting the situation
Regulation strategies	To achieve happiness through expression of emotions, redirection of attention from negative to positive emotions	To achieve a sense of calm by suppression of emotions, redirection of attention from self to others' emotions

Source:
Adapted from Table 5.1 in Rothbaum and Rusk (2011, p. 103).

For example, joy, happiness, and pride are often valued as positive emotions in many Western cultures. However, Asian cultures tend to place less value on these emotions, which may be viewed as being less sensitive toward others and placing a child at odds with achieving calmness. Another example is the negative emotion of shame. In most Western cultures, shame is often associated with psychological disorders (insecure attachment, depression) and viewed as a particularly negative and harmful emotion in terms of harming one's self-esteem. However, some Asian cultures believe shame is an acceptable emotion because it assists children in learning their place in a hierarchical society, to regret an inappropriate behavior, and to learn how to maintain or achieve interpersonal harmony (Trommsdorf & Cole, 2011).

For example, to support a collective family as in Anthony's case, intervention focused on creating safe environments, building a positive, loving relationship with his mother and grandparents as well as his uncle who interacted with Anthony on a regular basis. Anthony attended the early childhood special education program and received in-class speech-language therapy following a relationship- and play-based approach. The grandparents and occasionally the uncle provided child care for Anthony when he was not attending preschool and while his mother was working. Both the ECSE and the SLP worked with Mrs. Barber and Mr. and Mrs. Lopez on building a close, positive relationship with

Anthony by learning communication strategies to talk about emotions, mental states, and perspectives and adapted play-based activities in culturally appropriate ways. The social worker also gave them strategies for positive discipline, resources for counseling support, and economic resources for the mother who was trying to care for her sons while divorcing her husband. As Anthony developed trusting relationships, he slowly began to express himself and his feelings through nonverbal communication and eventually began to express himself verbally at preschool. Over time, he felt safe enough to verbalize his thoughts with his grandparents and his mother.

DISCUSSION QUESTIONS

1. How does an insecure attachment affect children's learning?
2. If children have an insecure attachment relationship with their parents, how does this affect their adult relationships?
3. How is caregiving related to the development of emotion regulation?
4. How is emotion regulation related to self-regulation?
5. In what ways do caregiver beliefs and values affect emotional development? Emotion regulation?
6. In what ways does the physical environment influence social and emotional development?
7. In what ways do cultures differ in caregiving habits?
8. In what ways do cultural caregiving habits influence the social and emotional development of children?

INSTRUCTIONAL RESOURCES

Websites

Association for Treatment and Training in the Attachment of Children: www.attach.org/

Attachment Parenting International: www.attachmentparenting.org/

Center on Social and Emotional Foundations for Early Learning at Vanderbilt University: http://csefel.vanderbilt.edu/

Department of Economic and Social Affairs (DESA): http://undesadspd.org/CommissionforSocialDevelopment.aspx

Smith, M., Saisan, J., & Segal, J. (2013, June). Attachment disorders and reactive attachment. Retrieved from www.helpguide.org/mental/parenting_bonding_reactive_attachment_disorder.htm

This Emotional Life. (n.d.). Retrieved from www.pbs.org/thisemotionallife/topic/attachment

WebMD. (2012). Preschool emotional development. Retrieved from www.webmd.com/parenting/guide/preschooler-emotional-development

WebMD. (2013). What is attachment parenting? Retrieved from www.webmd.com/parenting/what-is-attachment-parenting

Zero to Three (2012). Development of social emotional skills. Retrieved from www.zerotothree.org/child-development/social-emotional-development/social-emotional-development.html

Video Resources

Arredondo, D. E. (2009). Attunement and why it matters [Video]. Retrieved from www.youtube.com/watch?v=URpuKgKt9kg&list=PL2A0CF58E2C7D0AC3

Barkley, R. A. (1997). Behavioral inhibition, sustained attention, and executive functions: Constructing a unifying theory of ADHD. *Psychological Bulletin*, *121*, 65–94. Retrieved from www.apa.org/pubs/journals/bul/

Baumeister, R. (2013). Experts in emotion 18.3—Roy Baumeister on self-regulation and emotion. Retrieved from Schore, A. (2009). Allan Schore and attachment. Retrieved from: www.youtube.com/watch?v=6IC7Vwi69XQ

Bergman, N. (2010). Dr. Nils Bergman on the social emotional intelligence of infants. Retrieved from www.youtube.com/watch?v=51xmkaj8dOg

Bergman, N. (2010). Skin to skin contact—Dr. Nils Bergman. Retrieved from www.youtube.com/watch?v=2IYtFrgbDUo

Damasio, A. (2011). Antonio Damasio: The quest to understand consciousness. Retrieved from www.ted.com/talks/antonio_damasio_the_quest_to_understand_consciousness.html

Davidson, R. (2013). The heart-brain connection: The neuroscience of social, emotional, and academic learning. Retrieved from www.youtube.com/watch?v=o9fVvsR-CqM

Schore, A. (2009). Allan Schore and attachment. Retrieved from www.youtube.com/watch?v=43t5cww4NZk

Schore, A. (2011). Dr. Allan Schore. Retrieved from www.youtube.com/watch?v=aybKnSZ26Sw

Schore, A. (2013). Allan Schore neurobiology of secure attachment. Retrieved from www.youtube.com/watch?v=WVuJ5KhpL34

Siegel, D. J. (2011). Dr. Dan Siegel—on ambivalent attachment. Retrieved from www.youtube.com/watch?v=nGhZtUrpCuc

Siegel, D. J. (2011). Dr. Dan Siegel—on avoidant attachment. Retrieved from www.youtube.com/watch?v=qgYJ82kQIyg

Siegel, D. J. (2011). Dr. Dan Siegel—on disorganized attachment. Retrieved from www.youtube.com/watch?v=rpQtPsuhLzc

Siegel, D. J. (2009). Dr. Dan Siegel—on integrating the two hemispheres of our brains. Retrieved from www.youtube.com/watch?v=xPjhfUVgvOQ

Siegel, D. J. (2012). Dr Daniel Siegel, MD—we feel, therefore we learn: The neuroscience of social emotion Retrieved from www.youtube.com/ watch?v=iPkaAevFHWU

Siegel, D. J. (2012). Dr. Dan Siegel—on optimal attachment. Retrieved from www.youtube.com/watch?v=_XjXv6zseA0

Tronick (2010). Still face experiment. Retrieved from www.youtube.com/ watch?v=Btg9PiT0sZg

Waters, E. (2011). Secure, insecure, avoidant, & ambivalent attachment in mothers and children. Retrieved from www.youtube.com/watch?v=DH1m_ ZMO7GU

REFERENCES

Aber, J. L., Jones, S., & Cohen, J. (2000). The impact of poverty on the mental health and development of very young children. In C. H. Zeanah (Ed.), *Handbook of infant mental health* (pp. 113–128). New York, NY: Guilford Press.

Ainsworth, M. D. (1973). The development of infant-mother attachment. In B. M. Caldwell & H. N. Ricciuti (Eds.), *Review of child development research* (Vol. 3, pp. 1–94). Chicago, IL: University of Chicago Press.

Barkley, R. A. (1997). Behavioral inhibition, sustained attention, and executive functions: Constructing a unifying theory of ADHD. *Psychological Bulletin, 121*, 65–94. Retrieved from www.apa.org/pubs/journals/bul/

Bernier, A., Carlson, S. M., & Whipple, N. (2010). From external regulation to self-regulation: Early parenting precursors of young children's executive functioning. *Child Development, 81*(1), 326–339.

Bornstein, M. H. (2013). Mother-infant attunement. A multilevel approach via body, brain, and behavior. In M. Legerstee, D. W. Haley, & M. Bornstein (Eds.), *The infant mind, origins of the social brain* (pp. 266–298). New York, NY: Guilford Press.

Bowlby, J. (1969). *Attachment.* London, UK: Penguin.

Bronson, M. B. (2000). *Self-regulation in early childhood.* New York, NY: Guilford Press.

Carpendale, J., & Lewis, C. (2006). *How children develop social understanding.* Malden, MA: Blackwell Publishing.

Cassidy, J., & Shaver, P. R. (Eds.). (2008). *Handbook of attachment: Theory, research and clinical applications* (2nd ed.). New York, NY: Guilford Press.

Chen, X. (2011). Culture and children's socioemotional functioning: A con textual-developmental perspective. In X. Chen & K. H. Rubin (Eds.), *Socioemotional development in cultural context* (pp. 29–52). New York, NY: Guilford Press.

Chen, X., & Rubin, K. H. (2011a). Culture and socioemotional development: An introduction. In X. Chen & K. H. Rubin (Eds.), *Socioemotional development in cultural context* (pp. 1–8). New York, NY: Guilford Press.

Chen, X., & Rubin, K. H. (Eds.). (2011b). *Socioemotional development in cultural context*. New York, NY: Guilford Press.

Cicchetti, D., & Toth, S. L. (1995). Child maltreatment and attachment organization. In S. Goldberg, R. Muir, & J. Kerr (Eds.), *Attachment theory social, developmental and clinical perspectives* (pp. 279–308). Hillsdale, NJ: The Analytic Press.

Cole, P., Armstrong, L. M., & Pemberton, C. K. (2010). The role of language in the development of emotion regulation. In S. D. Calkins & M. A. Bell (Eds.), *Child development at the intersection of emotion and cognition* (pp. 59–77). Washington, DC: American Psychological Association.

Denham, S. A. (1998). *Emotional development in young children*. New York, NY: Guilford Press.

Eagle, M. (1995). The developmental perspectives of attachment and psychoanalytic theory. In S. Goldberg, R. Muir, & J. Kerr (Eds.), *Attachment theory social, developmental and clinical perspectives* (pp. 123–150). Hillsdale, NJ: The Analytic Press.

Egeland, B., Weinfield, N. S., Bosquet, M., & Cheng, V. (2000). Remembering, repeating, and working through: Lessons from attachment-based intervention. In J. Osofsky & H. Fitzgerald (Eds.), *WAIMH Handbook of Infant Mental Health, Volume 4. Infant mental health in groups at high risk* (pp. 37–89). New York, NY: Wiley.

Emde, R. N., Gaensbauer, T. J., & Harmon, R. J. (1976). *Emotional expression in infancy: A biobehavioral study* (Psychological Issues, Monograph, No. 37). New York, NY: International Universities Press.

Emery, J., Paquette, D. & Bigras, M. (2008). Factors predicting attachment patterns in infants of adolescent mothers. *Journal of Family Studies, 14*, 65–90.

Fox, S. E., Levitt, P., & Nelson, C. A., III. (2010). How timing and quality of early experiences influence the development of brain architecture. *Child Development, 81*(1), 28–40. doi:10.1111/j.1467-8624.2009.01380.x

Greenspan, S. E. (1985). *First feelings*. New York, NY: Penguin Books.

Gunnar, M., & Quevedo, K. (2007). The neurobiology of stress and development. *Annual Review of Psychology, 58*, 145–173. doi:10.1146/annurev.psych.58.110-405.085605

Harkness, S., Super, C. M., & Mavridis, C. (2011). Parental ethnotheories about children's socioemotional development. In X. Chen & K. H. Rubin (Eds.), *Socioemotional development in cultural context* (pp. 73–98). New York, NY: Guilford Press.

Harwood, R. L., Schölmerich, A., & Schulze, P. A. (2000). Homogeneity and heterogeneity in cultural belief systems. *New Directions for Child and Adolescent Development, 87*, 41–57.

Holodynski, M. (2013). The internalization theory of emotions: A cultural historical approach to the development of emotions. *Mind, Culture, and Activity, 20*, 4–38. doi:10.1080/10749039.2012.74.5571

Hwa-Froelich, D. A. (2004). Play assessment for children from culturally and linguistically diverse backgrounds. *Perspectives on Language, Learning* and Education and on Communication Disorders and Sciences in Culturally and Linguistically Diverse Populations, 11(2), 6–10. doi:10.1044/cds11.2.5

Hwa-Froelich, D. A., & Vigil, D. C. (2004). Three aspects of cultural influence on communication: A literature review. Communication Disorders Quarterly, 25(3), 110–118. doi:10.1177/15257401040250030201

Hwa-Froelich, D. A., & Westby, C. E. (2003). Frameworks of education: Perspectives of Southeast Asian parents and Head Start staff. Language, Speech, and Hearing Services in the Schools, 34, 299–319. doi: 10.1044/0161-1461(2003/025)

Knafo, A., & Uzefovsky, F. (2013). Variation in empathy. The interplay of genetic and environmental factors. In M. Legerstee, D. W. Haley, & M. Bornstein (Eds.), The infant mind, origins of the social brain (pp. 97–120). New York, NY: Guilford Press.

Ladage, J. S. (2009). Medical issues in international adoption and their influence on language development. Topics in Language Disorders, 29(1), 6–17. doi:10.1097/TLD.0b013e3181974ac0

Legerstee, M. (2005). Infants' sense of people. New York, NY: Cambridge University Press.

Lewis, M. L. (2000). The cultural context of infant mental health: The developmental niche of infant-caregiver relationships. In C. H. Zeanah (Ed.), Handbook of infant mental health (pp. 91–107). New York, NY: Guilford Press.

Mason, P., & Narad, C. (2005). International adoption: A health and developmental perspective. Seminars in Speech and Language, 26(1), 1–9. Retrieved from www.ovid.com/site/catalog/Journal/1176.jsp

Mischel, W., Shoda, Y., & Rodriguez, M. I. (1989). Delay of gratification in children. Science, 244, 933–938.

Moses, L. J., Baldwin, D., Rosicky, J. G., & Tidball, G. (2001). Evidence for referential understanding in the emotions domain at twelve and eighteen months. Child Development, 72(3), 718–735. Retrieved from www.jstor.org/pss/1132451

Mundy, P., & Sigman, M. (2006). Joint attention, social competence, and developmental psychopathology. In D. Cicchetti & D. J. Cohen (Eds.), Developmental psychopathology (pp. 293–332). Hoboken, NJ: Wiley.

Murphy, B., Eisenberg, N., Fabes, R. A., Shepard, S., & Guthrie, I. K. (1999). Consistency and change in children's emotionality and regulation: A longitudinal study. Merrill-Palmer Quarterly, 45, 413–444.

Nelson, C. A. (2007). A neurobiological perspective on early human deprivation. Child Development Perspectives, 1(1), 13–18. doi:10.1111/j.1750-8606.2007.00004.x

Pons, F., Harris, P. L., & de Rosnay, M. (2004). Emotion comprehension between 3 and 11 years: Developmental periods and hierarchical organization. *European Journal of Developmental Psychology, 1*(2), 127–152. doi:10.1080/17405620344000022

Raffaelli, M., Crockett, L. J., & Shen, Y.-L. (2005). Developmental stability and change in self-regulation from childhood to adolescence. *The Journal of Genetic Psychology, 166*(1), 54–75.

Rothbaum, F., & Rusk, N. (2011). Pathways to emotion regulation: Cultural differences in internalization. In X. Chen & K. H. Rubin (Eds.), *Socioemotional development in cultural context* (pp. 99–127). New York, NY: Guilford Press.

Saarni, C. (1999). *The development of emotional competence.* New York, NY: Guilford Press.

Sánchez, M., & Pollak, S. D. (2009). Socioemotional development following early abuse and neglect. Challenges and insights from translational research. In M. de Hoon & M. R. Gunnar (Eds.), *Handbook of developmental social neuroscience* (pp. 497–520). New York, NY: Guilford Press.

Schore, A. N. (2001). The effects of secure attachment relationship on right brain development, affect regulation, and infant mental health. *Infant Mental Health Journal, 22*, 7–66. doi:10.1002/1097–0355(200101/04)22: 1<7::AID-IMHJ2>3.0.CO;2-N

Siegel, D. (1999). *The developing mind.* New York, NY: Guilford Press.

Sroufe, L. A. (1997). *Emotional development: The organization of emotional life in the early years.* Cambridge, UK: Cambridge University Press.

Stams, G. J. M., Juffer, F., & Van Ijzendoorn, M. H. (2002). Maternal sensitivity, infant attachment, and temperament in early childhood predict adjustment in middle childhood: The case of adopted children and their biologically unrelated parents. *Developmental Psychology, 18*(5), 806–821.

Stevenson-Hinde, J. (2011). Culture and socioemotional development, with a focus on fearfulness and attachment. In X. Chen & K. H. Rubin (Eds.), *Socioemotional development in cultural context* (pp. 11–28). New York, NY: Guilford Press.

Taylor, R. E., Marshall, T., Mann, A., & Goldberg, D. P. (2012). Insecure attachment and frequent attendance in primary care: a longitudinal cohort study of medically unexplained symptom presentations in the ten UK general practices. *Psychological Medicine, 42*(2), 855–864. doi: 10.1017/S0033291711001589

Timler, G. (2003). Reading emotion cues: Social communication difficulties in pediatric populations. *Seminars in Speech and Language, 24*(2), 121–130.

Trommsdorf, G., & Cole, P.M. (2011). Emotion, self-regulation, and social behavior in cultural contexts. In X. Chen & K.H. Rubin (Eds.), *Socioemotional development in cultural context* (pp. 131–163). New York, NY: Guilford Press.

US Department of Health and Human Services (1991). Infant attachment: What we know now. Retrieved from http://aspe.hhs.gov/daltcp/reports/inatrpt.htm

Van IJzendoorn, M. H., & Bakermans-Kranenburg, M. J. (2010). Invariance of adult attachment across gender, age, culture, and socioeconomic status? *Journal of Social and Personal Relationships, 27*, 200–208. doi:19.1177/0265407509360908

Van IJzendoorn, M. H., & Sagi-Schwartz, A. (2008). Cross-cultural patterns of attachment: Universal and contextual dimensions. In J. Cassidy & P. R. Shaver (Eds.), *Handbook of attachment: Theory, research, and clinical applications* (2nd ed., pp. 880–905). New York, NY: Guilford Press.

Vigil, D. C., & Hwa-Froelich, D. A. (2004). Interaction styles in minority caregivers: Implications for intervention. *Communication Disorders Quarterly, 25*(3), 119–126. doi:10.1177/15257401040250030301

Vygotsky, L. (1986). *Thought and language* (A. Kozulin, Trans.). London, UK: MIT Press. (Original work published 1934).

Welsh, M. C., Pennington, B. F., & Groisser, D. B. (1991). A normative-developmental study of executive function: A window on prefrontal function in children. *Developmental Neuropsychology, 7*(2), 1331–1349. doi:10.1080/87565649109540483

Wilson, S. L. (2012). Socio-emotional and relationship development. In D. A. Hwa-Froelich (Ed.), *Supporting development in internationally adopted children* (pp. 59–84). Baltimore, MD: Brookes.

Zelazo, P. D., Carter, A., Reznick, J. S., & Frye, D. (1997). Early development of executive function: A problem-solving framework. *Review of General Psychology, 1*(2), 198–226. doi:10.1037/1089-2680.1.2.198

Zimmerman, I. L., Steiner, V. G., & Pond, R. E. (2002). *Preschool Language Scale-4* (4th ed.). San Antonio, TX: Psychological Corporation.

4

DEVELOPMENT OF COGNITIVE PROCESSES ASSOCIATED WITH SOCIAL COMMUNICATION

Deborah A. Hwa-Froelich

We all need contingent communication. Our history of being close with others, having affective attunements and resonating states of mind, allows us to connect with others and to have a sense of coherence within our own internal processes. Adaptations to patterns of misattunements without repair, and to the subsequent dreaded states of shame and humiliation, shape our subjective experience of self, others, and the world. These patterns of relationships can lead to a large disparity between our adaptive, public selves and our inner, private selves. The attachment models that reflect these early, pre-explicit-memory experiences influence our emotions and their regulation, response flexibility, consciousness, self-knowledge, narrative, and openness to and drive toward interpersonal intimacy.

—Siegel (1999, p. 298)

LEARNING OBJECTIVES

Readers will

1. Be able to describe the development of attention, social cognition, memory, and their relationship to executive function.
2. Be able to discuss how intersubjectivity and inhibition are related to the development of attention.
3. Gain knowledge about how social cognition, memory, play, and social interaction are neurologically represented and developmentally intertwined.

4. Be exposed to how culture affects the brain, specifically attention, memory, and executive function.

Natalya was born in Russia and spent approximately 1 year in a Russian orphanage until she was adopted into the US. The orphanage staff reported that Natalya was healthy with the exception of a few respiratory infections and had no history of ear infections. Natalya lives with her mother, her father, and a younger sister, who was also adopted from Russia. Her mother is a Mexican native whose dominant language is Spanish. Her father is Caucasian and monolingual, speaking American English. The mother reported that she spoke mostly Spanish to Natalya; Natalya spent summers in Mexico visiting family members and had recently been exposed to English when she started preschool at age 3. Natalya was slow to learn English and was demonstrating inattention, impulsivity, and inappropriate behaviors at preschool.

Prior to seeking an evaluation from an international adoption clinic, Natalya was evaluated by an adoption medical clinic and the local early childhood special education team. A pediatrician with training in Adoption Medicine and experience assessing children adopted from abroad evaluated Natalya at age 3. The doctor reported a history of immaturity, lack of handedness, auditory hypersensitivity to noise, drooling, hyperactivity, and short attention span as well as loss of focus. Natalya did not meet criteria for fetal alcohol syndrome. Thus, the physician suggested that these behaviors may be related to an immature or atypical nervous system. The early childhood special education team completed an evaluation of Natalya when she was 4 years old. All assessments were administered in English with the assistance of a Spanish interpreter. Natalya performed within one standard deviation (*SD*) of the mean on an intelligence, articulation, and general language tests. Her verbal intelligence quotient (IQ) and performance on another standardized English language test were slightly more than 1 *SD* below the mean with specific difficulty in English expressive vocabulary, morphology/syntax, word retrieval, and answering questions. The team observed that Natalya tended to seek sensory input, had difficulty attending in noise, lacked persistence to complete tasks, and improved her performance when reinforcement and redirection were provided. Based on these findings, Natalya did not qualify for special education services but instead received English as a Second Language (ESL) and emergent literacy intervention in the kindergarten classroom.

An international adoption clinic team conducted a developmental assessment when Natalya was 5 years, 6 months old. While Natalya scored within 1 *SD* of the mean on general Spanish and English standardized assessments, she demonstrated significant delays in phonological short-term memory and attention on Spanish and English nonword repetition tasks, a selective attention go/no-go task, and forward and backward digit span tasks. She also demonstrated these same areas of difficulty during a play assessment. During administration of Theory of Mind tasks in Spanish and English, she demonstrated a lack of understanding of her own and others' perspectives. Auditory processing of English stimuli was also delayed, particularly in auditory figure-ground tasks, word discrimination, and word memory. These results indicated that Natalya demonstrated significant delays in attention, memory, linguistic processing, and social cognition, which may be affecting her executive functioning and her performance in the classroom.

Children such as Natalya have been exposed to a variety of caregiver inputs, making it challenging to determine whether her behaviors and learning problems are due to the variability in her care and language exposure or due to a true learning disorder. In order to make this determination, practitioners must understand how attention, social cognition, memory, and executive function develop in children raised in environments that provide the nurturing care and experiences children depend on and expect. The purpose of this chapter is to describe typical development of attention, social cognition, memory, and executive function.

DEVELOPMENT OF ATTENTION, SOCIAL COGNITION, MEMORY, AND EXECUTIVE FUNCTION

A complete and in-depth description of typical development in each area is beyond the scope of this book. Instead, an abbreviated description of typical development in each area is provided to enable readers to understand how these areas develop simultaneously and relate to social communication development.

Growth and physical development of the brain is critical during the early years of infancy and toddlerhood. The brain develops from back to front and thus, the frontal lobes (important for executive function abilities) develop later and are the last part of the brain to be myelinated (Dunbar, 2013). Genetics, uterine environment, and postpartum environment have a great impact on this development. Both maternal nutrition and exposure to toxins have significant effects on infant development in utero (Ladage & Harris, 2012; Wilson, 2012). Most of the neurons are present at birth and begin to develop synaptic connections, which often operate in functional ways. In other words, neurons that fire together are connected, and the frequency of firing strengthens those connections. After this neurological development, a stage of pruning occurs in which connections that are used more frequently are maintained and those that are less frequently used are pruned (Ladage & Harris, 2012; Wilson, 2012). It is the type and frequency of early childhood experiences that influence which connections are saved and which ones are lost. What this means is that children exposed to early adverse care, such as poor prenatal care, toxins, and/or poor nutrition, are at risk of poor neurological development, which may result in poorer cognitive development, such as poorer attention, social understanding, memory, and executive function skills.

Development of Attention

Three systems devoted to attention develop within the first year of life: (a) the reticular activating system, (b) the posterior attentional system, and (c) anterior attentional system (Calkins & Marcovitch, 2010). The reticular activating system is hypothetically responsible for focusing on stimuli and inhibiting distractions. The posterior attentional system is thought to allow shifting of attention from one stimulus to another. The anterior attentional system develops during the end of the first year and is responsible for sensory regulation.

As soon as infants are born, they begin attending to objects and people in their environments. During the first 6 months, they focus on people's faces and respond to eye gaze and facial expressions (Mundy, 2013). Trevarthen (1979, 1992) termed this face-to-face sharing of feelings and mental states as *primary intersubjectivity*. The sharing of emotions and mental states helps children learn about emotions communicated through facial expressions, tone of voice, and postures. Through this face-to-face interaction, infants between 5 and 8 months of age also discriminate, attend to, and imitate mouth and tongue movements, as well as sounds from their native language (Legerstee, 2005; Moon, Cooper, & Fifer, 1993; Mundy, 2013; Nazzi, Jusczyk, & Johnson, 2000). Infants begin to switch their attention from one stimulus to another and alternate gaze around 4 to 6 months of age (Mundy, 2013). This shift in attention requires some development of self-regulation (i.e., inhibition of attention from one stimulus to focus attention on another). In other words, attention and self-regulation seem to develop concurrently and lead to the development of *secondary intersubjectivity*.

Secondary intersubjectivity occurs around 5 to 6 months of age when infants are able to share their attention between another person and an object or event (Legerstee, 2005; Mundy & Sigman, 2006). Infants begin to follow their caregivers' directed gaze, gesture, or head turn toward an object or event around 8 to 10 months of age (Corkum & Moore, 1998; Morales, Mundy, & Rojas, 1998; Mundy & Sigman, 2006). Around 10 months of age, infants will react to and communicate their feelings about an object or event to others in two different ways. First, they initiate joint attention, which involves looking at the object and then looking back at the adult. Infants also regulate the other person's behavior by gazing at, shaking, or pointing to an object to direct the adult's eye gaze and to check to see if the adult is looking at the object (Mundy & Sigman, 2006). Through these actions, the infant is asking the other person if he or she sees what the infant sees and whether the infant should engage with this object. Over the next 8 months, infants refine and develop their intentional nonverbal communication abilities by initiating joint attention and regulating others' behaviors to achieve joint attention. The infants' desires to share experiences, socially engage, and interact with others are what drive these attention-seeking behaviors. These behaviors tend to occur prior to and simultaneously with infants' social communication of wants and needs (Legerstee, 2005; Moses, Baldwin, Rosicky, & Tidball, 2001; Mundy & Sigman, 2006). Secondary intersubjectivity, initiated joint attention, and response to joint attention are related to inhibition, self-regulation, interpretation of nonverbal expression of emotions, and social cognitive development (for a review see Mundy & Sigman, 2006; Shin, 2012). Thus, joint attention is necessary for social competence and communication.

Attention and inhibition skills enable children to solve problems, persist at a task until it is mastered and take on a role during symbolic play (attention and inhibition related to emotion and self-regulation are discussed in Chapter 3). When solving a problem, negative emotions such as frustration can occur and children must inhibit their frustration to selectively attend, focus, and persist in order to be successful. When initially confronted with a novel toy that requires specific behavioral responses for activation, children may use trial-and-error problem-solving techniques. While trying different approaches, they must inhibit methods that are ineffective and refine their behaviors to effectively manipulate the toy. Their attention must be focused on the parts and characteristics of the toy that are essential for operating the toy. For example, some pop-up toys require five different movements to successfully open all the boxes, sometimes pushing and other times turning or sliding different knobs and buttons. Other toys may require putting an object in a slot and pressing a button or a lever to cause the object to slide down a ramp. Children must inhibit ineffective strategies such as pushing the object or shaking the ramp, focus their attention, and learn the appropriate behavioral sequence to successfully operate the toy. When engaged in symbolic or pretend play, they must also inhibit their actions and way of talking to pretend to be someone else. For example if they are pretending to be a doctor, they must regulate themselves to take on the persona of a pretend doctor. By pretending that an object represents something else, such as pretending that a rope is a snake or a fire hose, they have to inhibit using a rope for typical purposes and use it as a hose or treat it like a live snake.

Inhibition and focused attention are important components of working memory and executive function (Brocki, Eninger, Thorell, & Bohlin, 2010; Kofler, Rapport, Bolden, Sarver, & Raiker, 2010). For example, inhibition and selective attention skills at 5 years of age predicted working memory skills at 6 years of age (Brocki et al., 2010). Focused, as opposed to divided, attention was important for working memory capacity (Kofler et al., 2010). Poor behavioral inhibition and negative behaviors measured at 2 years of age were correlated with poorer Theory of Mind (ToM) performance, a measure of social understanding, at 3 years of age (Suway, Degman, Sussman, & Fox, 2011). Thus, inhibition and selective, focused attention are important skills for later working memory and ToM, which are important for solving problems, social understanding, and interpersonal communication at older ages.

Social Understanding

It is primarily through consistent and contingent face-to-face interactions or intersubjectivity that infants learn to share emotional states with their caregiver, identify and regulate their own emotional states, and draw inferences about their own and others' mental states from their caregivers' nonverbal and verbal communication (Baldwin & Moses, 1994; Butterworth, 1994; Legerstee, 2005; Moses et al., 2001; Smith, 2005; Trevarthen, 1979, 1992). Nonverbal aspects of the communicated message include facial expressions, tone of voice, and physical movements associated with the social context. Perceptions of these face-to-face interactions help infants' access and use adult mental states to facilitate emotional understanding, resolve infant's uncertainty about their own emotional states, and help infants begin to identify their own feelings (Smith, 2005). These child–caregiver social, emotional, and communicative interactions facilitate infants' abilities to develop social understanding and knowledge about their own emotions, desires, and intentions (Perner, 1991; Zeedyk, 1996). As self-awareness of feelings and intentions develop during the first 4 to 6 months of life, infants begin to have an emerging sense of self and intra-ToM (Legerstee, 2005). "Intra-ToM is the ability to identify one's own thoughts and feelings, knowing what one knows and does not know and determining how to access what one does not know" (Hwa-Froelich, 2012, p. 180). Initially infants develop a sense of animacy. Infants as young as 5- and 8-weeks-old imitated gestures, and by 2 to 4 months of age, they imitated mouth movements demonstrated by a person but not gestures or mouth movements of an inanimate object (for a review see Legerstee, 2013). This emerging social knowledge reflects the development of cognitive and affective cognitive ToM as defined in Chapter 2. Refer to Table 4.1 for developmental stages of ToM.

They begin to learn inter-ToM through primary and secondary intersubjectivity. Inter-ToM is the awareness that other people have thoughts and feelings that may be different from one's own thoughts and feelings, may be caused by certain events, or their feelings and thoughts may cause them to act in certain ways (Baron-Cohen, 1997). This social cognition about the relationship between people's emotions, behaviors, and causative events allows children to predict what others are thinking from what the children know about them and the world (social cognition), and to use this social cognition to understand or respond to a

Table 4.1 Stages of Theory of Mind Development (Miller, 2012; Westby, 1999)

4–6 months	Has an emerging sense of self and enjoys primary intersubjectivity
5–6 months	Responds to joint attention with objects and begins to follow line of regard
9–15 months	Initiates joint attention and behavioral requests with others often involving an object, event, or person (secondary intersubjectivity)
18–24 months	Engages in pretend; understands desires Has implicit ToM, understands relations between line of sight and behavior
3 years	Understands people see world differently; understands imaginary objects are different from real
4–5 years	Has explicit ToM: Knows different viewpoints lead others to different interpretations Understands beliefs cause people to act in certain ways Understands someone will act differently because of a false belief Understands deception is a means of creating false beliefs
6–8 years	Appropriately judges situations when one remembers, knows, forgets, or guesses, thinks about what someone else is thinking about (second-order ToM)
8–12 years	Understands strategies to hide and detect deceit, higher levels of affective and cognitive ToM in inferential language (lies, sarcasm, puns, idioms, etc.)

Sources:
Miller, 2012; Westby, 1999.

particular social situation (Garfield, Peterson, & Perry, 2001; Wellman, Phillips, & Rodriguez, 2000; Zeedyk, 1996). Infants between the ages of 3 and 8 months begin to understand the actions of others before they can interpret the goals associated with these actions (for a review see Mundy, 2013). By 9 months of age, they begin to understand behavior to achieve a goal such as sharing action and attention during ball play. Children who are approximately 12 to 15 months old understand people's choices and demonstrate the understanding that that others may make different decisions (through joint attention) about interacting with an object or during an event (Mundy, 2013). During the first 2 years of life, infants know how people behave before they begin to understand how they think (Legerstee, 2013).

Typically developing children implicitly acquire intra- and inter-ToM, which involves an understanding of self and others' mental states; the ability to draw inferences about others' mental states, intentions, and perspectives; and an understanding of deception and false beliefs or first-order ToM. This social understanding has frequently been measured through the administration of false belief tasks (for a review see Miller, 2012). Having a false belief is when persons behave a certain way when they believe something is true while being unaware that the reality of their belief has changed. For example, children can observe their sibling moving their mother's car keys from the table to the couch when the mother is not in the room. When the mother looks for her car keys, children may point to the couch (implicit social understanding) because they know their mother believes she left the keys on the table (false belief) and did not see their sibling who moved the keys to the couch (Hwa-Froelich, 2012; Miller, 2012). Implicit social understanding of mistaken beliefs develops prior to explicit social understanding, which is the ability to explain why someone has a false belief and how that false belief affects his or her actions. Implicit social knowledge underlies children's ability to communicate about this knowledge (Low, 2010). Several studies have documented that implicit false belief performance is present in children between the ages of 14 and 24 months by measuring the eye gaze of 2 year-old children during tasks involving a relocation of specific objects (Low, 2010; for a review see Sabbagh, Benson, & Kuhlmeier, 2013).

Children's explicit communication about false beliefs in children develops between 3 and 4 years of age and is correlated with and predicted by communicative competence (Astington & Jenkins, 1999; Legerstee, 2005; Lewis & Osborne, 1990; Low, 2010; Perner & Lang, 1999). As children gain knowledge through social experiences with others and social talk about emotions, their social understanding and communicative competence improve simultaneously. Jill de Villiers and Peter de Villiers (2000) proposed that children must develop linguistic complementation in order to pass false belief tasks. For example, expression of mental states in the English language requires the use of dependent clauses such as *The wolf knew* **where Granny lived**. The de Villiers' research has provided much evidence that general language ability and complex grammatical knowledge are correlated with performance on false belief tasks (for a review see Carpendale & Lewis, 2006, p. 172). However, this theory has come into question when children whose language (e.g., Cantonese, Mandarin, German) allows them to talk about desire and belief using less complex grammatical structures developed social understanding at about the same age as US children (for a review see Carpendale & Lewis, 2006, pp. 171–172). In these cases, understanding of false belief was not dependent on complementation or complex grammatical structures. Rather, false belief may be related to the knowledge and use of mental state words. For example, in cultures and languages in which there are few mental state words, social understanding develops later than in cultures and languages that include words for emotions and mental states. These differences are discussed in a later section of this chapter.

Social understanding of emotions improves with age (Miller, 2012; Pons, Harris, & de Rosnay, 2004). In a cross-sectional study of 100 children between the ages of 3 and 11 years, Pons and colleagues documented that emotional understanding developed in three stages and that there were no statistically significant differences between boys and girls. Three- to 5-year-olds are able to recognize emotions displayed in facial expressions, understand how external causes affect emotion, and the relationship between memory and emotion (i.e., how intensity of emotion diminishes over time). Five- to 7-year-olds understand that a person's belief will affect their actions, regardless of whether their belief is false or true (first-order ToM). They also understand that persons' desires are related to their emotional reactions and that people may display one emotion while feeling another (Pons et al., 2004). Knowing what another person is thinking or feeling about what someone else is thinking or feeling is second-order ToM, which develops around the age of 7 years (Miller, 2012). Later, 9- to 11-year-olds may use psychological strategies (distraction) to regulate their emotions, understand that people can have multiple or mixed emotions about a particular event, and begin to relate moral judgments with emotions (negative emotions are related to amoral actions such as bullying and positive emotions are related to moral actions such as sacrifice for the greater good). ToM abilities higher than second order that enable children to understand figurative language, idioms, lies, and sarcasm develop between 8 and 12 years of age (for a review see Miller, 2012).

Social understanding of false beliefs has been found to be related to metalinguistic abilities such as rhyming but not inhibitory control (Farrar & Ashwell, 2012). Four-year-old children completed a vocabulary measure; three ToM tasks, (a) an unexpected location task, (b) an unexpected contents task, and (c) an unexpected identity task; and a color-sorting task that switched to a shape-sorting task using the same stimuli as a measure of inhibitory control. The rhyming tasks involved 20 sets of three words. Ten sets included a foil that was semantically associated with one of the rhyming words and a set of 10 words that did not have a semantic foil. ToM scores were positively correlated with the vocabulary score and both sets of rhyming words, but not with the measure of inhibitory control (Farrar & Ashwell, 2012). In other words, social understanding appears to be strongly associated with vocabulary and metalinguistic knowledge.

Development of Memory

Although attention, emotion, and memory are mental actions we can describe, little is known about how neurological activity is related to or results in mental experiences. Therefore, this section describes the current state of scientific and theoretical knowledge. Memory can be described as the process of how past experiences affect the brain's future responses (Siegel, 1999). It is theorized that memories are built from repeated and systematic neuronal firing patterns that encode, store, and retrieve previous experiences (Siegel, 1999). Thus, infant neurological development is dependent on and expecting to be exposed to care and experiences that accelerate neurological growth, neural connectivity, coherence, and integration. Infants must be exposed to the process of encoding, storing, and retrieving memories to develop, use, and maintain neuronal memory connections (Siegel & Hartsell, 2003). This neural stimulation and growth forms the foundations for higher and more complex and dynamic cognitive thought. For example, Siegel (1999) hypothesizes that short-term memory may be represented as transient neuronal changes, whereas long-term memory may involve structural changes that form the foundations for higher level cognitive processes.

While many different theories about memory exist, for the purposes of this chapter, memory will be described generally as two major components; implicit (sometimes referred to as nondeclarative memory) and explicit (declarative) memory. These components involve additional different, overlapping, and dynamically integrated neurological systems (Fivush, 2011). Implicit memories can be described as unconscious summaries of mental or perceptual models of an experience and is associated with such brain structures as the amygdala and the limbic system. The limbic system includes the basal ganglia and the motor cortex for behavioral memory and the perceptual cortex for perceptual memory (Siegel, 1999). From repeated experiences, the brain processes experience similarities and differences to create mental models of these experiences. These mental or perceptual models include procedural memories (emotional, behavioral, sensory, or physical body models), such as implicit procedural memories for the actions of sitting, walking, or standing (Fivush, 2011; Hwa-Froelich, 2012). Implicit memories can be represented in the developing sense of self in that infants begin to sense who is most like them through early interactions with caregivers. This developing sense of self can be seen in 2- to 3-month-old infants' early preferences for human interaction or interest, extended attention on humanlike stimuli such as pictures or drawings of faces, and discrimination between humans and objects (Legerstee, 2005). This implicit memory is also evident after approximately 1 to 3 months of age, when infants imitate mouth and tongue movements of other humans but not those of an inanimate object (Legerstee, 2005). Implicit memories include visual and sensory memories associated with facial expressions, tone of voice, body postures, tactile, and olfactory memories.

Explicit memory can be described as conscious summaries of events (episodic memory), words, or concepts (semantic memory; Siegel & Hartsell, 2003). As infants respond to their environment, they collect information about objects, humans and other animate beings, actions, emotions or mental states, routines or events. Research with infants has provided evidence of event recall in 3- and 9-month-old infants (for a review see Fivush, 2011). If their caretakers provide nonverbal and verbal communication in association with the infants' interactions, infants begin to develop an associated explicit memory of abstract symbols (vocabulary, categories, concepts, gestures, or semantic memory) with which to interpret or imitate during social interactions. These conscious nonverbal and verbal explicit memories are the building blocks for future internal and external narratives about their experiences (Siegel, 1999). Around 9 months of age, children develop object permanence; that is, they recognize something continues to exist, even when it is out of sight, and they will look for a hidden or missing object (Siegel & Hartsell, 2003). Infants demonstrate the emerging representation (object permanence) of their parents by crying when the parents are not visible. By 12 to 15 months of age, infants also begin to use words to represent their caregivers and express a label (mama or dada) to gain their caregivers' attention or regulate their caregivers' behaviors (Siegel & Hartsell, 2003).

Around 18 months of age as the hippocampus matures, it is thought that toddlers' explicit memory development involves the encoding processes of implicit memory through the hippocampus (Siegel & Hartsell, 2003). Experiences are contextualized beyond unconscious mental models to form mental representations of experiences. In order to build mental representations, it is thought that children must move explicit memory from short-term storage to long-term storage or cortical consolidation (Siegel, 1999). Although the consolidation process is not fully understood, it seems to involve Rapid Eye Movement (REM) sleep and continued maturation of the frontal lobes (Siegel, 1999; Siegel & Hartsell, 2003). Children may also process past experiences through pretend play allowing them to replay experiences to encode and retrieve the experience over and over, which may be another process of cortical consolidation.

Maturation between 1 and 5 years of age brings the development of expressive language and a more individualized sense of self. The interaction of these two developmental domains facilitates growth of semantic memory (knowledge of facts) and episodic memory (recall for previous situations, events, or personal experiences) and autonoetic consciousness or autobiographical memory (the sense of oneself currently and one's associated feelings at the time of the event, currently and how one would feel about the same event in the future; Carpendale & Lewis, 2006; Fivush, 2011). For example, I have knowledge about a surgery I had but do not have an episodic memory of what transpired during the surgery except for what the doctor shared (semantic memory). In contrast, I remember implicitly and explicitly my feelings and thoughts associated with the birth of my children (episodic and autobiographical memory). One must develop a sense of self or intra-theory of mind to develop a sense of self across time or autobiographical memory (Fivush, 2011). Measuring the development of autobiographical memory is linked with the development of verbal language and narratives, the vehicle through which one can share their experiences and feelings with others. Thus, the development of episodic and autobiographical memory is important for the development of social understanding of self and others.

Research has shown that mothers who provide elaborative discourse with rich descriptions and extensions about the topic as well as engage with the child during interactions with an object or an event have children who are more engaged and demonstrate better recall of the event or interaction (Bauer, 2013; Fivush, 2011). When caregivers have conversations about the child's experiences, they create for the child a self-narrative or declarative memory about those experiences and the child's feelings associated with the event. An elaborative style includes open-ended questions that provide some information and facilitate children's recall of the event. This style also involves the parent including the child's responses into the narrative (Fivush, 2011; Siegel, 1999). For example, 3- and 4-year-old children are able to plan based on internal goals and desires. Thus, they can plan future events from current self-awareness of desires. However, it is not until they are 5 years old, that they are able to link past experiences with the present. It is thought that cortical consolidation of the child's sense of self and expressive language is complete by the age of 5, which allows for the expression of autobiographical memory (Fivush, 2011; Siegel & Hartsell, 2003). The ability to link time concepts and causality with past, present and future events does not develop until the age of 12 years, and these skills develop in complexity through adolescence.

Stress and trauma can have negative effects on memory. Small and moderate amounts have less effect than do large or consistent stress and trauma, which can result in the destructive pruning of neuronal growth (Siegel, 1999). Research with children adopted from institutional care has provided evidence that these children were able to encode information in immediate recall tasks but were less skilled for a delayed memory task. These differences may indicate problems with initial consolidation of information for long-term memory (Kroupina, Bauer, Gunnar, & Johnson, 2010). In addition, children who have been exposed to trauma or stress may have implicit memories that remain intact, while explicit memories may be blocked. In other words, individuals may demonstrate unconscious behavioral reactions to associated stimuli of past experiences but may not be able to describe their feelings or thoughts. There may be a disconnect between their implicit and explicit memories (Siegel, 1999).

Representations

Mental representations are an individual's perspective or image of reality (Siegel, 1999). Children often demonstrate mental representations through play and eventually share their representations with others through verbal communication. Representative or play development can be described across four dimensions: (a) decontextualization, (b), themes, (c) theme organization, and (d) self and other relationships (Westby, 2000). Development of decontextualization involves knowledge and understanding of objects' functions and of how one uses these objects. Around 5 to 9 months of age, infants develop models of object function called schemas. These schemas typically include exploratory behaviors such as hitting, banging, mouthing, and throwing (Linder, 2008). By approximately 8 to 12 months, infants interact with life-like objects and imitate functions they have experienced or observed such as using a spoon to feed themselves (Linder, 2008; Westby, 2000). Children begin to decontextualize their play around 2 to 3 years of age by pretending to eat and drink with child-size replicas, miniature pretend food, or nonexistent food. By approximately 3.5 and 4 years of age, children understand knowledge as a representation for reality and share their perception of reality through language (Carpendale & Lewis, 2006; Siegel, 1999). They use language to describe the scene ("I'm talking to the police") with pretend props to substitute for the real object such as a bowl as a hat or a hand gesture as if they are holding an imaginary set of keys to start a car or open a locked door (Linder, 2008; Westby, 2000). Children use short-term and long-term memory of objects, object functions, and ways to play with objects that may not be present or available in the play context using their memory of the size, shape, and function of the object.

Themes of life or mental scripts of activities, both experienced and not experienced by children are also represented in children's play (Lillard, 1994; Westby, 2000). Between 15 and 24 months of age, children pretend to carry out typical daily routines such as sleeping or eating. Then around 2 and 3 years of age, children's play themes include events that occur often but perhaps not every day, such as shopping at a store or going to the doctor. Around 3 to 5 years of age, children's play will include pretend or fantasy themes they have observed but not experienced, such as putting out a fire like a firefighter or pretending to be an astronaut flying to the moon (D. Singer, Golinkoff, Hirsh-Pasek, 2006; Westby, 2000).

These representational themes become more complex as children mature (Westby, 2000). Prior to 2 years of age, 17- to 22-month-old children may use two or three objects and demonstrate two or three steps in their play. For example, they may use a bottle to feed a doll. As memory of routines, objects, and functions increase, children mentally plan and sequence events, which requires the use of self-regulation, working memory, and executive function skills. For example, 2- to 3-year-old children may set the table and fix food on a stove to put on the plates on the table before they sit down to pretend to eat and then clear the table and wash the dishes. This level of play facilitates the executive function to plan complex play episodes by combining multiple objects and themes, such as combining the theme of cooking breakfast with a theme of starting a fire and adding a third theme of the baby getting hurt and needing to go to the hospital. This play complexity typically develops between 4 and 6 years of age.

The last dimension of play development, self and other relationships, integrates social and cognitive knowledge with decontextualization, themes, and thematic organization (Westby, 2000). Initially infants and toddlers pretend on themselves, such as pretending to eat or sleep. By the time they are between 17 and 22 months old, children may pretend to feed, bathe, or operate on their dolls or stuffed animals. After 2 to 3 years of age, they begin to have conversations with their doll or stuffed animals and their dolls/animals can talk back to them. Children also begin to act out episodes in which their dolls or stuffed animals have false beliefs, play tricks on others, and have emotions. Eventually around 4 to 6 years of age, children learn to pretend to be other people and their play reflects the perspective, voice, actions, and beliefs of the character they represent (Diamond, 2000; Westby, 2000). To take on a role of someone else means children have to inhibit their own personality traits, focus their attention to pretend to be someone else, plan and set goals, and organize props and behavior while also monitoring their own behavior (Berk, Mann, & Ogan, 2006; Perner, 1991). Through these dimensions of play development, children refine their skills of inhibition, self-regulation, attention, social understanding, and memory.

Executive Function

Singer and Bashir (1999) describe executive function as a set of mental processes which involves "inhibiting actions, restraining and delaying responses, attending selectively, setting goals, planning, and organizing, as well as maintaining and shifting set" (B. Singer & Bashir, 1999, p. 266). Because executive function is integrally related to selective/focused attention and working memory, these mental processes are often activated simultaneously (Barkley, 1996, 1997; Cowan & Alloway, 2009; Cowan & Courage, 2009; National Center for Learning Disabilities, 2005; Pennington & Ozonoff, 1996; B. Singer & Bashir, 1999). Executive function has been related to mathematical ability, reading ability, verbal and nonverbal reasoning, academic achievement, communication, social skills, social understanding, and emotion regulation (for a review see Bernier, Carlson, & Whipple, 2010, Carpendale & Lewis, 2006). Processes related to executive function emerge prior to age 3 such as attentional and cognitive control between 1 to 3 months of age. However, significant development in executive function occurs between the ages of 3 and 5 years (Calkins & Marcovitch, 2010). For example, Müller and colleagues (2012) found that executive function performance at age 2 and 3 predicted social understanding at age 3 and 4. Language performance at age 3 was found to mediate the relationship between social understanding and executive function when the children were 4 years old (Müller, Liebermann-Finestone, Carpendale, Hammond, & Bibok, 2012). In other words, executive function is integrally involved and important in the development of social understanding and language.

For executive function to be fully effective, children need to develop selective attention, working memory, self-regulation, and inhibition skills. Selective attention requires regulation of emotions such as excitement, fear, or frustration and inhibition of attention to nonessential information or distractions in order to monitor oneself, focus, persist, and think flexibly to complete the task at hand. Flexible thinking involves working memory. Baddeley (1992) defined working memory as "a brain system that provides temporary storage and manipulation of the information necessary for such complex cognitive tasks as language comprehension, learning, and reasoning" (p. 556). Working memory can be described as *online* processing of both long-term and short-term memories. It flexibly manipulates this information, which allows children to outline possible solutions as well as plan and organize the steps and materials needed to solve a problem or finish a task. Some components of executive function, such as attention and self-regulation, begin to develop in infancy (Bernier et al., 2010; Diamond, 2000; Reznick, 2009). Executive skills in young children can be measured through discrimination of error, delay of gratification, or Simon Says (go/no-go) tasks. Children as young as 18- to 24-months-old were able to identify errors in block constructions, 4-year-old children were able to delay gratification (inhibiting eating one food to wait for a larger amount of food), and 4- to 5-year-old children were successful at inhibiting actions and following directions when Simon says them (for a review see Zelazo, Carlson, & Kesek, 2008).

Most of these skills continue to develop and are refined as children interact with different people, contexts, and problems. In a study with participants ranging from 8 to 64 years of age, De Luca and colleagues (2003) found that different executive function skills are stronger at different age levels. For example, the ability to shift attention reached adult levels in 8- to 10-year-old children, strategic planning and organization of goal-directed behavior peaked between 20 and 29 years of age, but effective planning and problem-solving improved from 12 to 14 years of age and declined in the 50 to 64 age group.

FACTORS AFFECTING ATTENTION, SOCIAL UNDERSTANDING, MEMORY, AND EXECUTIVE FUNCTION

Contextual and Relationship Factors

Culture is passed from generation to generation through implicit and explicit socialization and preferred ways of teaching. Children become socialized to learn in certain ways (Hall, 1976; Hofstede, 2001). Some cultures promote teaching that is within and dependent on the context. Consequently, children become accustomed to learning that is linked to contextual information. In contrast, some cultures teach with less dependence on the context or a decontextualized instructional style. Western cultures tend to support low-context learning, and Eastern cultures tend to support high-context learning (for a review see Park & Huang, 2010).

Hofstede (2001) studied cultures around the world and documented differences along several different dimensions, such as individualistic or collective tendencies. When cultures are more focused on self-goals and motivations, they are judged to be more individualistic. In contrast, when cultures pay more attention to group goals and interests, they are more collective. Western cultures tend to be more individualistic and Eastern cultures tend to be more collective (Park & Huang, 2010). These differences in values have been found to affect executive functioning performance as well as how persons process and organize information and what types of things individuals attend to and remember.

Cultural Differences in Attention

Several behavioral studies have compared East Asian and American participants. East Asian adults were found to demonstrate a bias toward attending to and processing context, encoding information holistically, relying less on categories and using more intuitive reasoning (Boduroglu, Shah, & Nisbett, 2009; Park & Huang, 2010). Park and Huang (2010) reviewed studies on eye gaze and found that when presented with embedded objects in pictures, adult Westerners fixated their gaze on the objects while East Asian adults tended to gaze less at the object and focus more on the background scenes. However, in some contexts, East Asians will focus more centrally and Westerners will attend to stimuli more holistically. They also reported on research in which East Asians attended longer on a focal face region while Westerners scan the face and research showing cultural differences in interpretation of facial expressions, such as facial displays of fear and disgust. Thus, cultural experiences may affect interpretation of social context and facial expressions.

Cultural Differences in Social Understanding

Social understanding appears to be related to many familial factors across several countries including Australia, Canada, England, Greece, and Japan. Children from these countries, who lived close to older children or lived with older siblings demonstrated better social understanding than children who did not live near or with older children (for a review see Carpendale & Lewis, 2006, p. 136). Children demonstrated greater social understanding when they had parents, who explicitly talked about mental states and displayed sensitivity during interactions with their children. On the other hand, having authoritarian parents who used criticism, yelling, or spanking was negatively correlated with social understanding (Carpendale & Lewis, 2006). For example, in a study with 5-year-old children, a higher socioeconomic status and mothers employed in skilled jobs who provided their children with social context and support, space to play, positive discipline, and quality child care predicted a higher level of ToM performance (Galende, Sánchez de Miguel, & Arranz, 2011).

Children from hierarchical cultures where elders have more power and authoritarian parenting styles are preferred may demonstrate poorer performance on false belief tasks. In contrast, in cultures where individualism and equality are promoted, children may demonstrate better performance. For example, Carpendale and Lewis (2006, p. 144) reviewed the literature and found that a higher percentage of 44-month-old children in Australia correctly performed the false belief task than did children in the US and children in Japan. The Australian culture may value more individualism, independence, and equality, whereas Japanese children of the same age, who are from a more collective and hierarchical society, were less often correct than were US children.

Linguistic differences among cultures may also affect acquisition of social understanding. In studies of cultures whose language does not typically refer to mental states (Quechuan of Peru, Mofu of Cameroon, Tolai and Tainae of Papua, New Guinea) children's ToM performance lagged behind Western cultures, whose language includes explicit references for mental states (for a review see Carpendale & Lewis, 2006, pp. 144–145).

Cultural Differences in Memory Development

Culture also affects memory, memory development, and skills. Based on a culture's values, memory is shaped by what is explicitly taught or repeatedly modeled. For example, Aboriginal children had better visual memory skills in comparison to White Australian children (Ross & Wang, 2010). Exemplifying a high contextual learning style, the Aboriginal children's increased visual memory skills were presumably influenced by being taught to track beetles and animals in the desert. Moreover, individualism and collectivism were found to affect autobiographical memory recall. Chinese adults, who are members of a collectivist culture, not only rated autobiographical memories as less important than did their American peers; they also recalled fewer personal events (Ross & Wang, 2010). Additionally, Asian participants asked to describe memories, provided more memories involving other people, whereas Australian participants provided more personal memories that did not involve other people. In other words, persons from diverse cultural backgrounds may attend to, focus on, and recall unique but culturally relevant information. This cultural bias may influence eye gaze, social cognition, and learning styles.

Children from different cultures also display different types of sociodramatic play (Hwa-Froelich, 2004). Children from Western and more technologically advanced countries tend to demonstrate sociodramatic play along fantasy themes (Chen, 2011). For example, Anglo-American and Korean preschool children were observed during play. The Anglo-American children demonstrated more social and pretend play, whereas the Korean children exhibited more educational activity, had more unoccupied time, or tended to play beside, not with, other children (Farver, Kim, & Lee, 1995). Farver and Shinn (1997) hypothesized that different play styles may be due to the presence of different kinds of play stimuli in that the Anglo-American preschool had more toys and the Korean preschool had more educational materials. They videotaped dyads of Korean and Anglo-American children playing with the same stimuli (castle, dolls representing a royal family, horses, a carriage, furniture, and a dragon). In spite of playing with the same stimuli, the children demonstrated culturally different play behaviors and pragmatic language. Anglo-American children's play themes involved a sense of danger and fantasy, whereas, Korean children's play included more everyday activities and family themes. The Anglo-American children described their own actions, often rejected their partner's ideas, and directions. In contrast, the Korean children described their partner's actions, used more tag questions, and tended to agree or make polite requests. Because play assessments may list fantasy play as a higher developmental skill, it is important for practitioners to be aware that cultural preferences or beliefs may facilitate more everyday themes than fantasy themes (Linder, 2008; Westby, 2000).

Farver and colleagues also investigated cultural differences in mother–child play interactions (Farver & Howes, 1993; Farver & Wimbarti, 1995). There were differences in beliefs about the value of play. The Anglo-American mothers felt play was important for children's education and development, but the Mexican mothers believed the purpose of play was to occupy children's time. Because of these different play beliefs, Mexican mothers gave more explicit directions than did the American mothers. Consequently, the Mexican mothers were less involved in their children's play, and their children demonstrated less cooperative pretend and symbolic play. Indonesian mothers also believed that play was a way to occupy children's time (Farver & Wimbarti, 1995). However, these mothers made more suggestions to facilitate pretend play as a strategy to keep their children occupied for longer periods. In contrast, Indonesian mothers, who valued play as an intellectual and social pursuit, gave explicit directions for task completion. In other words, how play was valued in each culture affected the ways parents interacted with children during play. It is important for practitioners to be aware and respectful of these differences when working with families from diverse cultural backgrounds. In these situations it may be better to work with parents on giving explicit directions for more structured or academic play activities and more suggestions to extend sociodramatic play.

Cultural Differences in Executive Function Development

Cultural preferences for inhibited and regulated behavior may also affect executive function development. For example, in a comparison of three preschools across the three cultures of Japan, China, and the US, Tobin, Wu and Davidson (1989) found that Chinese preschoolers were expected to inhibit impulses at earlier ages than Western preschoolers. The Japanese preschoolers were socialized to help regulate each others' behavior as a way of learning how to cooperate within a large group. These differences in cultural expectations of preschool behavior may help children develop the attention, inhibition, regulation, and memory required for executive function. In a study of preschoolers from Beijing, China and the US, Chinese children had significantly better executive function performance than US children on a battery of executive function tasks (Sabbagh, Xu, Carlson, Moses, & Lee, 2006). The investigators also measured ToM ability and found no group differences. However, executive function performance was predictive of ToM performance. The authors concluded that cultural differences in social rearing influenced executive function development, and because ToM tasks require children to use their executive function skills, executive function is related to ToM tasks. The findings support the hypothesis that cultural socialization differences strongly influence differences in attention, inhibition, regulation, and working memory. Because the Chinese children are socialized to inhibit impulses at earlier ages, their regulation and inhibition may help them perform at higher levels of executive function. Executive function is important for ToM skills because one must attend to nonverbal, verbal, and pragmatic information to comprehend social communication. However, linguistic competence and social cognition also predict ToM abilities. Thus, while no differences were found in social understanding or ToM performance, executive function skills predicted higher ToM performance (Sabbagh et al., 2006).

There is some evidence showing that bilingual children have better executive function skills than monolingual children. In a study comparing three language groups: native bilinguals; English-speaking, monolingual children; and English speakers enrolled in a second-language immersion class, the native bilingual children had significantly better executive function performance than the other two groups (Carlson & Metzloff, 2008). Their performance was better in spite of having lower language scores and parents who had received less education and less income. The authors argued that the bilingual children were "doing more with less" and that the task of attending to and thinking in two languages gives bilingual children an advantage in executive function development (Carlson & Meltzoff, 2008, p. 293). Carlson and Metzloff (2008) also suggested that bilingual skills may need to be at a high enough level to enhance metalinguistic and cognitive abilities.

To summarize, cultural values and experiences may affect the development of attention, social understanding, memory, and executive function. Cultural differences in adult-mediated interactions, such as high- or low-context instructional strategies and values of individualism and collectivism, can influence what children attend to, remember, and inhibit. In the case of Natalya, although her general language development appeared to be similar across both languages, she may not have achieved an advanced bilingual level to allow her to develop metalinguistic or cognitive skills to assist her executive function development. While her processing skills were significantly better in Spanish, her dominant language, her phonological processing in Spanish was significantly lower than other Spanish–English bilinguals of the same age. In addition, she demonstrated weak selective attention, inhibition, and working memory skills in both languages, regardless of whether the session took place in quiet or noise, one-to-one individual settings, or large or small groups. Because of her difficulty with attention and working memory, she was unable to solve problems, organize her play, or relate in socially appropriate ways with her peers and her teachers. In other words, her executive function and social understanding were negatively affected. Natalya needed medication to improve her attention as well as support services to assist her memory and executive function in order for her to learn effectively. With medical intervention, Natalya was able to inhibit distractions and focus on attending in class. The SLP worked with Natalya during individual sessions in a quiet room to facilitate English vocabulary learning, processing of complex directions and questions, and interpretation of nonverbal and verbal communication of emotions and mental states.

The classroom teacher moved Natalya to a seat that was closer to the front, reduced the noise level in the classroom, increased visual supports for large-group instruction, and provided more opportunities for Natalya to receive new information through small-group instruction. The parents continued to facilitate Natalya's Spanish-language development through shared storybooks. The SLP and teacher provided examples of different levels of questions that increased in complexity to help the parents facilitate inferential language and perspective taking relative to the story characters. Natalya was able to attend during classroom instruction and to interpret nonverbal and verbal communication more accurately at school. The parents reported that Natalya was able to answer more complex questions about the stories they read at home and were pleased with her progress at school.

DISCUSSION QUESTIONS

1. How does neurological development relate to attention and memory development?
2. In what ways does inhibition or self-regulation affect attention?
3. What is memory?
4. How do explicit and implicit memories differ?
5. Compare and contrast autobiographical, semantic, procedural, and episodic memory.
6. How do children demonstrate memory recall initially?
7. Why are attention and memory important for executive function?
8. How does culture affect children's attention and memory?

INSTRUCTIONAL RESOURCES

Videos

A Selective Attention Test: www.youtube.com/watch?v=vJG698U2Mvo

Brown, S. (2008). Stuart Brown: Playing is more than just having fun. Retrieved from www.ted.com/talks/stuart_brown_says_play_is_more_than_fun_it_s_vital.html

Compare and Contrast Implicit and Explicit Memory: www.youtube.com/watch?v=o-W6TDYi0Cw

Dr. Siegel—On How You Can Change the Brain: www.youtube.com/watch?v=i4tR5Ebc4Mw

Executive Function: www.youtube.com/watch?v=efCq_vHUMqs

Types of Memory: www.youtube.com/watch?v=mjzhcNeL0G0

Unexpected Contents video. Retrieved from www.youtube.com/watch?v=8h Lubgp Y2_w

Unseen displacement and explaining action, Sally-Anne story. Retrieved from www.youtube.com/watch?v=QjkTQtggLH4

Websites

Brain Rules: www.brainrules.net/attention

Brain Tools: www.mindtools.com/memory.html

Center on the Developing Child, Harvard University: http://developingchild. harvard.edu/resources/multimedia/videos/inbrief_series/inbrief_execu tive_function/

Human Memory: www.human-memory.net/

National Center for Learning Disabilities: www.ncld.org/types-learning-dis abilities/executive-function-disorders/what-is-executive-function

Psychology Today: www.psychologytoday.com/basics/memory

REFERENCES

Astington, J. W., & Jenkins, J. M. (1999). A longitudinal study of the relation between language and theory-of-mind development. *Developmental Psychology, 35*(5), 1311–1320. Retrieved from www.apa.org/pubs/journals/dev/

Baddeley, A. (1992). Working memory. *Science, 255*, 556–559. doi:10.1126/science.1736359

Baldwin, D. A., & Moses, L. J. (1994). Early understanding of referential intent and attentional focus: Evidence from language and emotion. In C. Lewis & P. Mitchell (Eds.), *Children's early understanding of mind. Origins and development* (pp. 133–156). Hillsdale, NJ: Erlbaum.

Barkley, R. A. (1996). Linkages between attention and executive functions. In G. R. Lyon & N. A. Krasnegor (Eds.), *Attention, memory, and executive function* (pp. 307–325). Baltimore, MD: Brookes.

Barkley, R. A. (1997). Behavioral inhibition, sustained attention, and executive functions: Constructing a unifying theory of ADHD. *Psychological Bulletin, 121*, 65–94. Retrieved from www.apa.org/pubs/journals/bul/

Baron-Cohen, S. (1997). *Mindblindness. An essay on autism and theory of mind.* Cambridge, MA: MIT Press.

Bauer, P. (2013). Event memory. Neural, cognitive, and social influences on early development. In M. Legerstee, D. W. Haley, & M. H. Bornstein (Eds.), *The infant mind, origins of the social brain* (pp. 146–166). New York, NY: Guilford Press.

Berk, L. E., Mann, T. D., & Ogan, A. T. (2006). Make-believe play: Wellspring for development of self-regulation. In D. G. Singer, R. M. Golinkoff, & K. Hirsh-Pasek (Eds.), *Play=learning.* Oxford, UK: Oxford University Press.

Bernier, A., Carlson, S. M., & Whipple, N. (2010). From external regulation to self-regulation: Early parenting precursors of young children's executive functioning. *Child Development, 81*(1), 326–339. doi:10.1111/j.1467-8624.2009.01397.x

Boduroglu, A., Shah, P., & Nisbett, R. E. (2009). Cultural differences in allocation of attention in visual information processing. *Journal of Cross-Cultural Psychology, 40*, 349–360. doi:10.1177/0022022108331005

Brocki, K. C., Eninger, L., Thorell, L. B., & Bohlin, G. (2010). Interrelations between executive function and symptoms of hyperactivity/impulsivity and inattention in preschoolers: A two year longitudinal study. *Journal of Abnormal Child Psychology, 38*, 163–171. doi:10.1007/s10802-009-9354-9

Butterworth, G. (1994). Theory of mind and the facts of embodiment. In C. Lewis & P. Mitchell (Eds.), *Children's early understanding of mind. Origins and development* (pp. 115–132). Hillsdale, NJ: Erlbaum.

Calkins, S. D., & Marcovitch, S. (2010). Emotion regulation and executive functioning in early development: Integrated mechanisms of control supporting adaptive functioning. In S. D. Calkins & M. A. Bell (Eds.), *Child development of the intersection of emotion and cognition* (pp. 37–57). Washington, DC: American Psychological Association.

Carlson, S. M., & Meltzoff, A. N. (2008). Bilingual experience and executive functioning in young children. *Developmental Science, 11*(2), 282–298. doi:10.1111/j.1467-7687.2008.00675.x

Carpendale, J., & Lewis, C. (2006). *How children develop social understanding.* Malden, MA: Blackwell Publishing.

Chen, X. (2011). Culture and children's socioemotional functioning: A contextual-developmental perspective. In X. Chen & K. H. Rubin (Eds.), *Socioemotional development in cultural context* (pp. 29–52). New York, NY: Guilford Press.

Corkum, V., & Moore, C. (1998). The origins of joint visual attention in infants. *Developmental Psychology, 34*(1), 28–38. Retrieved from: www.apa.org/pubs/journals/dev/

Cowan, N., & Alloway, T. (2009). Development of working memory in childhood. In N. Cowan & M. L. Courage (Eds.), *The development of memory in infancy and childhood* (pp. 303–341). New York, NY: Psychology Press.

Cowan, N., & Courage, M. L. (Eds.). (2009). *The development of memory in infancy and childhood.* New York, NY: Psychology Press.

De Luca, C. R., Wood, S. J., Anderson, V., Buchanan, J. A., Proffitt, T. M., Mahoney, K., & Pantelis, C. (2003). Normative data from the Cantab I: Development of executive function over the lifespan. *Journal of Clinical and Experimental Neuropsychology, 25*(2), 242–254.

de Villiers, J. G., & de Villiers, P. A. (2000). Linguistic determinism and the understanding of false beliefs. In P. Mitchell & K. J. Riggs (Eds.),

Children's reasoning and the mind (pp. 191–228). Hove, UK: Psychology Press.

Diamond, A. (2000). The early development of executive functions. In E. Bialystok, & F. I. M. Craik (Eds.), *Lifespan cognition: Mechanisms of change* (pp. 70–95). New York, NY: Oxford University Press.

Dunbar, R. I. M. (2013). An evolutionary basis for social cognition. In M. Legerstee, D. W. Haley, & M. H. Bornstein (Eds.), *The infant mind, origins of the social brain* (pp. 3–18). New York, NY: Guilford Press.

Farrar, M. J., & Ashwell, S. (2012). Phonological awareness, executive functioning, and theory of mind. *Cognitive Development, 27*, 77–89. doi:10.1016/j.cogdev.2011.08.002

Farver, J. M. & Howes, C. (1993). Cultural differences in American and Mexican mother-child pretend play. *Merrill-Palmer Quarterly, 39*(3), 344–358.

Farver, J. M., Kim, Y. K., & Lee, Y. (1995). Cultural differences in Korean- and Anglo-American preschoolers' social interaction and play behaviors. *Child Development, 66*, 1088–1099.

Farver, J. M. & Shinn, Y. L. (1997). Social pretend play in Korean- and Anglo-American preschoolers. *Child Development, 68*(3), 544–556.

Farver, J. M., & Wimbarti, S. (1995). Indonesian children's play with their mothers and older siblings. *Child Development, 66*, 1493–1503.

Fivush, R. (2011). The development of autobiographical memory. *The Annual Review of Psychology, 62*, 559–582. doi:10.1146/annurev.psych.121208.131702

Galende, N., Sánchez de Miguel, M., & Arranz, E. (2011). The role of physical context, verbal skills, non-parental care, social support, and type of parental discipline in the development of ToM capacity in five-year-old children. *Social Development, 20*, 845–861. doi:10.1111/j.1467-9507.2011.00625.x

Garfield, J. L., Peterson, C. C., & Perry, T. (2001). Social cognition, language acquisition, and the development of theory of mind. *Mind & Language, 16*, 494–541. doi:10.1111/1468-0017.00180

Hall, E. T. (1976). *Beyond culture*. New York: Anchor Books of Random House.

Hofstede, G. (2001). *Culture's consequences: Comparing values, behaviors, institutions and organizations across nations* (2nd ed.). Thousand Oaks, CA: Sage.

Hwa-Froelich, D. A. (2004). Play assessment for children from culturally and linguistically diverse backgrounds. *Perspectives on Language, Learning and Education and on Communication Disorders and Sciences in Culturally and Linguistically Diverse Populations, 11*(2), 6–10. doi:10.1044/cds11.2.5

Hwa-Froelich, D. A. (2012). *Supporting development in internationally adopted children*. Baltimore, MD: Brookes.

Kofler, M. J., Rapport, M. D., Bolden, J., Sarver, D. E., & Raiker, J. S. (2010). ADHD and working memory: The impact of central executive deficits and exceeding storage/rehearsal capacity on observed inattentive behavior. *Journal of Abnormal Child Psychology, 38,* 149–161. doi:10.1007/s10802-009-9357-6

Kroupina, M. G., Bauer, P. J., Gunnar, M. R., & Johnson, D. E. (2010). Institutional care as a risk for declarative memory development. In P. J. Bauer (Ed.), *Advances in child development and behavior, Vol. 18. Variations of early experience: Implications for the development of declarative memory in infancy* (pp. 138–160). London, UK: Elsevier.

Ladage, J. S., & Harris, S. E. (2012). Physical growth, health and motor development. In D. A. Hwa-Froelich (Ed.), *Supporting development in internationally adopted children* (pp. 21–57). Baltimore, MD: Brookes.

Legerstee, M. (2005). *Infants' sense of people.* New York, NY: Cambridge University Press.

Legerstee, M. (2013). The developing social brain. Social connections and social bonds, social loss, and jealousy in infancy. In M. Legerstee, D. W. Haley, & M. H. Bornstein (Eds.). *The infant mind, origins of the social brain* (pp. 223–247). New York, NY: Guilford Press.

Lewis, C., & Osborne, A. (1990). Three-year-old's problems with false belief: Conceptual deficit or linguistic artifact? *Child Development, 61,* 1514–1519. doi:10.1111/j.14678624.1990.tb02879.x

Lillard, A. (1994). Making sense of pretense. In C. Lewis, & P. Mitchell (Eds.), *Children's early understanding of mind. Origins and development* (pp. 211–234). Hillsdale, NJ: Erlbaum.

Linder, T. (2008). *Transdisciplinary play-based assessment* (2nd ed.). Baltimore, MD: Brookes.

Low, J. (2010). Preschoolers' implicit and explicit false-belief understanding: Relations with complex syntactical mastery. *Child Development, 81*(2), 597–615. doi:10.1111/j.1467–8624.2009.01418.x

Miller, S. A. (2012). *Theory of mind: Beyond the preschool years.* New York, NY: Psychology Press.

Moon, C., Cooper, R. P., & Fifer, W. P. (1993). Two-day-olds prefer their native language. *Infant Behavior and Development, 16,* 495–500. doi:10.101 6/0163–6383(93)80007-U

Morales, M., Mundy, P., & Rojas, J. (1998). Following the direction of gaze and language development in 6-month-olds. *Infant Behavior & Development, 21*(2), 373–377. doi:10.1016/S0163–6383(98)90014–5

Moses, L. J., Baldwin, D., Rosicky, J. G., & Tidball, G. (2001). Evidence for referential understanding in the emotions domain at twelve and eighteen months. *Child Development, 72*(3), 718–735. Retrieved from www.jstor.org/pss/1132451

Müller, U., Liebermann-Finestone, D. P., Carpendale, J. I. M., Hammond, S., & Bibok, M. B. (2012). Knowing minds, controlling actions: The developmental relations between theory of mind and executive function from 2 to 4 years of age. *Journal of Experimental Child Psychology, 111*, 331–348. doi:10.1016/j.jecp.2011.08.014

Mundy, P. (2013). Neural connectivity, joint attention, and the social-cognitive deficits of autism. In M. Legerstee, D. W. Haley, & M. H. Bornstein (Eds.). *The infant mind, origins of the social brain* (pp. 324–352). New York, NY: Guilford Press.

Mundy, P., & Sigman, M. (2006). Joint attention, social competence, and developmental psychopathology. In. D. Cicchetti & D. J. Cohen (Eds.), *Developmental psychopathology* (pp. 293–332). Hoboken, NJ: Wiley & Sons.

National Center for Learning Disabilities (2005). Executive function fact sheet. Retrieved from www.nldline.com/xf_fact_sheet.htm.

Nazzi, T., Jusczyk, P. W., & Johnson, E. K. (2000). Language discrimination by English-learning 5-month-olds: Effects of rhythm and familiarity. *Journal of Memory and Language, 43*, 1–19. doi:10.1006/jmla.20000.2698

Park, D. C., & Huang, C.-M. (2010). Culture wires the brain: A cognitive neuroscience perspective. *Perspectives in Psychological Science, 5*(4), 391–400. doi:10.1177/1745691610374591

Pennington, B. F., & Ozonoff, S. (1996). Executive functions and developmental psychopathology. *Journal of Child Psychology and Psychiatry, 37*, 51–87. doi:10.1111/j.1469-7610.1996.tb01380.x

Perner, J. (1991). *Understanding the representational mind*. Cambridge, MA: MIT Press.

Perner, J., & Lang, B. (1999). Development of theory of mind and executive control. *Trends in Cognitive Sciences, 3*(9), 337–344. doi:10.1016/S1364-6613(99)01362-5

Pons, F., Harris, P. L., & de Rosnay, M. (2004). Emotion comprehension between 3 and 11 years: Developmental periods and hierarchical organization. *European Journal of Developmental Psychology, 1*(2), 127–152. doi:10.1080/17405620344000022

Reznick, J. S. (2009). Working memory in infants and toddlers. In N. Cowan & M. L. Courage (Eds.), *The development of memory in infancy and childhood* (pp. 303–341). New York, NY: Psychology Press.

Ross, M., & Wang, Q. (2010). Why we remember and what we remember: Culture and autobiographical memory. *Perspectives on Psychological Science, 5*(4), 401–409. doi:10.1177/1745691610375555

Sabbagh, M. A., Benson, J. E., & Kuhlmeier, V. A. (2013). False-belief understanding in infants and preschoolers. In M. Legerstee, D. W. Haley, & M. H. Bornstein (Eds.), *The infant mind, origins of the social brain* (pp. 301–323). New York, NY: Guilford Press.

Sabbagh, M. A., Xu, F., Carlson, S. M., Moses, L. J., & Lee, K. (2006). The development of executive functioning and theory of mind. *Psychological Science, 17*, 74–81. doi:10.1111/j.1467-9280.2005.01667.x

Shin, M. (2012). The role of joint attention in social communication and play among infants. *Journal of Early Childhood Research, 10*(3), 309–317. doi:10.1177/1476718X12443023

Siegel, D. J. (1999). *The developing mind.* New York, NY: Guilford Press.

Siegel, D. J., & Hartsell, M. (2003). *Parenting from the inside out.* New York, NY: Tarcher/Penguin.

Singer, B. D., & Bashir, A. S. (1999). What are executive functions and self-regulation and what do they have to do with language-learning disorders? *Language, Speech, and Hearing Services in Schools, 30,* 265–273. Retrieved from http://lshss.asha.org/cgi/content/abstract/30/3/265#othe rarticles

Singer, D. G., Golinkoff, R. M., & Hirsh-Pasek, K. (2006). *Play=Learning.* Oxford, UK: Oxford University Press.

Smith, A. D. (2005). The inferential transmission of language. *Adaptive Behavior, 13*(4), 311–324. doi:10.1177/105971230501300402

Suway, J. G., Degnan, K. A., Sussman, A. L., & Fox, N. A. (2011). The relations among theory of mind, behavioral inhibition, and peer interactions in early childhood. *Social Development, 21,* 331–342. doi:10.1111/ j.1467-9507.2011.00634.x

Tobin, J. J., Wu, D. Y. H., & Davidson, D. H. (1989). *Preschool in three cultures: Japan, China, and the United States.* New Haven, CT: Yale University Press.

Trevarthen, C. (1979). Communication and cooperation in early infancy. A description of primary intersubjectivity. In M. Bullowa (Ed.), *Before speech: The beginning of human communication* (pp. 321–347). Cambridge, UK: Cambridge University Press.

Trevarthen, C. (1992). An infant's motives for speaking and thinking in the culture. In A. H. Wold (Ed.), *The dialogical alternative: Towards a theory of language and mind* (pp. 99–137). Oslo, Norway: Scandinavian University Press.

Wellman, H. M., Phillips, A. T., & Rodriguez, T. (2000). Young children's understanding of perception, desire, and emotion. *Child Development, 71,* 895–912. doi:10.1111/1467-8624.00198

Westby, C. E. (1998). Assessment of communicative competence in children with psychiatric disorders. In D. Rogers-Adkinson & P. L. Griffith (Eds.), *Communication disorders and children with psychiatric and behavioral disorders* (pp. 177–258). San Diego, CA: Singular.

Westby, C. E. (2000). A scale for assessing development of children's play. In K. Gitlin-Weiner, A. Sandgund, & C. Schaefer (Eds.), *Play diagnosis and assessment* (pp. 15–57). New York, NY: Wiley.

Wilson, S. L. (2012). Cognitive development. In D. A. Hwa-Froelich (Ed.), *Supporting development in internationally adopted children* (pp. 85–105). Baltimore, MD: Brookes.

Zeedyk, M. S. (1996). Developmental accounts of intentionality: Toward integration. *Developmental Review, 16,* 416–461. doi:10.1006/drev.1996.0018

Zelazo, P. D., Carlson, S. M., & Kesek, A. (2008). The development of executive function in childhood. In M. L. Collins & C. A. Nelson (Eds.). *Handbook of developmental cognitive neuroscience* (pp. 553–574). Cambridge, MA: MIT Press.

5

SOCIAL COMMUNICATION DEVELOPMENT

Deborah A. Hwa-Froelich

The child's behavior influences the caregiver's responsiveness which influences the child's development. The child's developmental outcome is determined by the mutual interaction or transaction of the child and the environment.

—Wetherby (1991, p. 255)

The values of a culture influence the communicative interactions that caregivers have with their children. Children are socialized into their culture by the ways in which caregivers and peers talk to them and guide them to participate in conversations.

—Crago and Eriks-Brophy (1994, p. 44)

LEARNING OBJECTIVES

Readers will

1. Be able to describe developmental skills that are related to social communication development.
2. Be able to define primary and secondary intersubjectivity and how these skills relate to the social communication development.
3. Gain knowledge about nonverbal, verbal, and pragmatic communication development and their relationship to social communication development.

4. Be exposed to how sociocultural factors such as poverty, the hierarchy of dependence and interpersonal relationships, and linguistic diversity, affect social communication development.

Shelly lived in a two-parent family from a low-income background. Both parents were Caucasian and had not graduated from high school. Her mother suffered from diabetes as well as limited vision and was the primary caregiver. The father worked long hours during the week as a laborer and rarely interacted with Shelly.

The county health department had referred Shelly and her mother for early intervention services with concerns about failure to thrive due to Shelly's overall developmental delays and lack of weight gain. During the initial home visit, the early intervention team observed a home environment that limited Shelly's stimulation and exploration. The furniture and floor space were covered with objects or papers, the curtains were closed, and the lighting was poor. Shelly spent most of the day in a playpen in a darkened room with no toys and little social interaction with adults. The mother reported feeling afraid to pick up or hold her daughter. She felt the only safe place for her daughter was in the playpen. She was concerned about her daughter's loss of weight and wanted to know how to feed her so that she would be healthy.

The initial assessment occurred at 9 months of age at which time Shelly avoided or did not initiate eye contact, her interests were directed toward objects more than toward people, and she did not respond to her name being called. Cognitively, Shelly demonstrated curiosity, fleeting attention with toys, and few schemas when interacting with objects. Although her play skills were developmentally delayed in terms of focused attention, play complexity, and functional use of toys, she demonstrated some cognitive flexibility when trying to manipulate cause-and-effect toys. Expressively, Shelly used limited gestures such as reaching for objects, but no other symbolic gestures were observed. The only intentional communication observed was protesting. Shelly's mother reported that Shelly had made some sounds earlier but stopped making these sounds and now was quiet most of the time. Few vocalizations were observed during the assessment, and the interaction between Shelly and her mother involved little face-to-face eye gaze or verbal communication.

The team concluded that Shelly was at risk of failure to thrive because of the lack of social interaction she was receiving from her parents. While her parents loved her, they lacked the knowledge and confidence to provide collaborative, contingent social and communicative interactions. Shelly needed these kinds of social interactions to develop a close, secure relationship with her parents to enable her to be socially motivated to interact and communicate and to be able to regulate her emotions to develop sustained and focused attention. Her parents needed support to help them develop a positive relationship with Shelly and learn how to mediate and facilitate Shelly's social, emotional, communication, and cognitive learning potential.

Shelly's case demonstrates the importance of early face-to-face communicative interactions in infants' survival and development. Although Shelly was born without any health problems or concerns, she was at risk of failure to thrive and developing significant delays across multiple developmental domains because of her parents' lack of confidence and knowledge in caring for her. Her profile is an example of how environmental variables can result in unique and dynamic developmental outcomes. Dynamic systems theory, as explained in Chapter 1, helps provide a theoretical understanding for such diversity in the development of social communication competence.

As defined in Chapter 1, social competence consists of having the knowledge, skills and behaviors to fulfill one's needs and meet his or her expectations in social interactions (Goldstein, Kaczmarek, & English, 2002). To be a competent communicator during social interactions, one must know, interpret, and demonstrate socially appropriate behaviors as well as have adequate oral language skills (Kaczmarek, 2002). As discussed in Chapters 3 and 4, social competence is influenced by (a) attachment, (b) the ability and desire to share experiences with others, (c) regulation of emotions and attention, and (d) the ability to recall past events and social knowledge to predict, plan, and guide behavior during social interactions (Hwa-Froelich, 2012a). When caregivers are sensitive and accurate in reading their infants' behaviors and meeting their needs, a close, trusting relationship develops. Through socially mediated conversations with their parents, infants learn communication behaviors and refine their communication to facilitate the likelihood in achieving their goals. For example, infant crying results in a caregiver coming to intervene or infant cooing results in caregivers smiling and attending to the infant. Infants learn to trust and depend on persons who most reliably meet their needs, forming a secure attachment with them.

These relationships between communication and outcomes are learned in specific culturally influenced contexts in which certain behaviors may be expected and associated with consequences in particular places and times. The communicative functions and social rules of communication that children learn are dependent upon social interactions with adults as explained by social interaction theorists in Chapter 1. Initially, infants are exposed to and share emotions and experiences with their caregivers and siblings. Needs, emotions, intentions, and the desire to share experiences motivate infants to communicate. These early social communication skills are associated with later language competence and academic achievement (Greenwood, Walker, & Utley, 2002; Hart & Risley, 1995). In Shelly's case, she had not developed a secure attachment to her parents, and with the limited social interaction she had little opportunity to share emotions and experiences or learn how to communicate socially. Using communication instrumentally to share emotions, needs, wants, and experiences and developing knowledge about mental states and mental actions are the major components of social communication competence. This chapter includes discussions about the development of social communication. Attachment and social and emotional development are discussed in Chapter 3.

The necessary skills needed for effective social interactions include the ability to (a) process, interpret, and express nonverbal and verbal communication; (b) use communication for a variety of functions; (c) predict and plan communication for future social interactions and contexts; and (d) flexibly respond to a dynamically changing communicative interaction (Hwa-Froelich, 2012a). In other words, one must be able to interpret and express through facial expressions, gestures, posture, proximity, tone of voice, and vocal intensity, using appropriate verbal content and pragmatic conventions. To be able to demonstrate these skills, one must have a strong foundation in receptive and expressive language competence, and pragmatic language competence, defined by Ninio and Snow (1996) as "the appropriate, effective, rule-governed employment of speech in interpersonal situations" (p. 4).

Other cognitive skills are also involved such as executive function, working memory, selective attention, and the ability to switch attention. In addition, one must develop social cognition (the knowledge that events cause people to feel particular emotions and emotions cause people to act in certain ways), and social understanding which involves what many refer to as Theory of Mind (ToM), the perception of and understanding of one's and others' mental states (for a review of the history of theoretical terminology see Carpendale & Lewis, 2006). These cognitive skills are described in Chapter 4. This chapter focuses on typical social communication development of (a) intersubjectivity and nonverbal communication development, (b) speech and language development, and (c) pragmatic language development. The final section of this chapter describes factors affecting social communication competence.

INTERSUBJECTIVITY AND NONVERBAL COMMUNICATION

Infants expect developmentally appropriate care and depend upon their caregivers to sensitively read their behaviors and respond contingently and accurately to their cries for help (Lewis, 1997). To share their emotions, needs, and wants with others, infants must learn how to initiate and maintain interaction with another person. This process begins during face-to-face interactions sharing feelings and mental states. As described in Chapter 4, this process involves primary intersubjectivity (Trevarthen, 1979, 1992). This drive for social interaction and intentionality facilitates the sharing of emotions and communication between a caregiver and an infant so that the infant feels *felt*. If the caregiver accurately reads and interprets an infant's emotions, amplifies positive emotional states, and assists the infant in regulating or reducing negative emotional states, the caregiver is successful in interpreting and facilitating the infant's communicative intentions. Through primary intersubjectivity, caregivers help children learn to identify their own emotions and eventually how to identify and predict others' emotions. This ability to recognize or predict self and other people's emotions, intentions, or thought is called the development of social understanding or Theory of Mind (ToM) as discussed in Chapter 4 (Baldwin & Moses, 1994; Baron-Cohen, 1997; Butterworth, 1994; Carpendale & Lewis, 2006).

Social competence and socially competent communication behaviors emerge from the developmental foundations of social understanding and intersubjectivity and are affected by individual (endogenous) and environmental (exogenous) factors (for a review see Hwa-Froelich, 2012b). Initially infants are motivated by egocentric desires and needs. Although infants are largely egocentric, they typically prefer interactions with people rather than objects, which may indicate a human proclivity to perceive the mental/emotional states of others (Legerstee, 2005). To meet their infants' biological needs of hunger and discomfort, caregivers interact through primary intersubjectivity, communicating through positive facial expressions, nurturing touch, and a soothing tone of voice, which helps infants begin to interpret facial expressions and vocal tones associated with different emotions.

Caregivers communicate about their own and others' emotions, expectations, and intentions. They describe their and others' social cognition about objects, actions, and emotions. By 5 to 6 months of age, infants develop joint attention (e.g., look at what others look at and get others to look at what they are looking at) by following the gaze of others to see what others see and follow a line of regard when others point. This stage is called secondary intersubjectivity or sharing mental/emotional states involving an object (Legerstee, 2005). Infants and toddlers, between 9 and 15 months of age, learn to co-regulate their interactions with others by sharing mental/emotional states and social referencing, and directing and sharing joint attention with caregivers (Baron-Cohen, 1997; Bruner, 1999; Legerstee, 2005). Children begin to perceive and infer what object, event, or being, someone else sees, and eventually they learn that other people may have different thoughts, perspective, and knowledge than they do about the same objects and events, or what was described as inter-ToM in Chapter 4.

Nonverbal Communication Development

In addition to developing intersubjectivity and social understanding, social communicative competence is dependent upon the development of communicative competence. For typical communication development, mothers must have received adequate prenatal and postpartum treatment. Healthy prenatal care includes adequate nutrition and no exposure to or intake of chemical substances that would harm the fetus (toxins, drugs, alcohol, or nicotine). Healthy infants would have no neurological symptoms, hearing loss or recurrent ear infections, or oral motor anomalies such as cleft palate, all of which would affect communication development. However, not only is it important for infants to have received adequate prenatal care and be neurologically and physically intact; social interaction theorists also believe infants must be exposed to language-rich social interactions to develop perception, processing, and accurate phonological processing and expression, as well as receptive and expressive language competence (Vygotsky, 1934/1986). When children receive inconsistent or inappropriate social interactions or their communication is misinterpreted, they are at risk of exhibiting dysfunctional or delayed communication development and social-emotional relationships (Beck, 1996; Coh, Matias, Tronick, Connell, & Lyons-Ruth, 1986; Solantus-Simlua, Punamaki, & Beardslee, 2002; Sroufe, 1997). The amount and quality of caregiver verbal stimulation are strongly correlated with children's communication abilities in children being raised by their biological parents and for children attending a child care center (Clarke-Stewart, 1973; National Institute of Child Health and Human Development Early Child Care Research Network [NICHD], 2000; Stafford & Bayer, 1993).

Communication involves not only comprehension and expression of verbal messages, but also includes nonverbal components such as facial expressions, tone of voice, gestures, and postures (Anderson, 1998; Nowicki & Duke, 1994). For interpretation of mental and emotional states during social interactions, it is important to accurately interpret and express facial expressions, gestures, and tone of voice (Chiat & Roy, 2008). Facial expressions and tone of voice make up approximately 55% and 38%, respectively, of all nonverbal communication, which is about 93% of all nonverbal communication (Koneya & Barbour, 1976).

It is through face-to-face interactions that children learn to associate nonverbal aspects of communication with social and emotional meaning (Beer & Ochsner, 2006). For example, infants associate and interpret facial expressions and tone of voice to determine how they should react to ambiguous situations or stimuli (Siegel, 1999; Walden & Ogan, 1988). Interpretation of facial expressions and tone of voice develop at about the same time. Caron, Caron, and Myers (1982) studied 108 infants between 18 and 30 weeks old and found that 30-week-old infants discriminated between happy and surprised facial expressions. Later, at about 1 year of age, infants altered their behavior toward a false visual cliff based on their mothers' facial expressions of joy or fear. This change in behavior indicates the infants inferred different meanings from different facial expressions and adjusted their behavior accordingly (Sorce, Emde, Campos, & Klinnert, 1985).

After children develop language to label emotions, their discrimination and understanding can be measured through receptive and expressive language. Camras and Allison (1985) asked 109 children between the ages of 3 to 8 years to identify characters' emotions in short stories by selecting an emotional label or facial expression for happy, sad, disgust, and fear. The 3-year-olds were able to identify emotions at an average level of 82% accuracy using labels or selecting facial expressions, and the 8-year-old children were more accurate than were younger children. Thus, accuracy improved with age. Similar to facial expressions, discrimination and recognition of vocal emotions begin to develop by 5 months of age (for a review see Campanella & Belin, 2007) and accuracy improves with age. Rothman and Nowicki (2004) recruited 81 children between the ages of 4 and 12 years and asked them to identify the emotion expressed by adults and children stating the same sentence in happy, sad, angry or frightened voices. The 4-year-old children had an average error score of 12.1 of a total 24 responses, with a standard deviation (SD) of 5.9, whereas the 8-year-old children had an average error score of 7.1 (SD = 5.3; Rothman & Nowicki, 2004, p. 76). Thus, the 8-year-old-children made fewer errors than did the 4-year-old-children when interpreting different emotional vocal tones.

There may also be gender differences in nonverbal communication performance. McClure (2000) conducted a meta-analysis of 104 studies that used identification of facial expressions including infants, children, or adolescents up to the age of 18 years. McClure reported that females were more accurate than were males and that older subjects performed better than did younger subjects. The female advantage was found across all age groups regardless of the measures administered, the age reflected in the face stimuli, and the gender of the investigators. Gender differences were also found with 50 second-born children between the ages of 33 and 40 months who were asked to label emotions expressed by puppets acting out stories (Dunn, Brown, Slomkousky, Tesla, & Youngblade, 1991). Girls were better able to label emotions than were boys. Because all children were second-born children, gender and birth order may influence reading of facial expressions and tone of voice. A younger sibling has the advantage of watching emotional interactions of their older sibling and their parents, an advantage the oldest sibling does not experience.

Gesture comprehension and expression occurs about the same time in development. Deictic gestures such as reaching, giving, pointing, and showing, develop between 10 and 12 months of age (Capone & McGregor, 2004). Representational gestures, such as using a cupped hand to represent a glass or cup for drinking, develop around 12 to 15 months of age (Capone & McGregor, 2004; Crais, Watson, & Baranek, 2009). These gestures develop at approximately the same time that early communicative functions develop, which is discussed in the subsection on pragmatic language development. Table 5.1 depicts the parallel development of nonverbal and pragmatic communication.

SPEECH AND LANGUAGE DEVELOPMENT

This section does not include specific developmental milestones but provides a brief general overview of speech and language development. Speech and language development follow a predictable pattern. Several studies have documented monolingual English developmental milestones for vowel, consonant, and consonant cluster productions. Before infants are able to talk, their prelinguistic development moves from reflexive crying and vegetative sounds at birth to 2 months, to cooing and laughter from 2 to 4 months of age, vocal play from 4 to 6 months, canonical babbling around 6 months of age or older, and eventually to jargon and meaningful speech from 10 to 18 months of age (Bauman-Waengler, 2009; Ferguson, Menn, & Stoel-Gammon, 1992).

Production of phonemes begins with vowel then consonant production. Labial consonants /m, b/ are the first to develop followed by front

Table 5.1 Nonverbal and Pragmatic Language Development

	Nonverbal Development	Pragmatic Development
0–8 months	Discriminates facial expressions and vocal tones	Perlocutionary stage: attends/responds to stimuli, anticipation, initiates behavior to continue activity, shows self, changes behavior to achieve goal
6–12 months	Interprets facial expressions to alter behavior	Illocutionary stage (proto-imperatives and protodeclaratives) Referencing
10–12 months	Develops deictic gestures	
13–24 months	Develops representational and symbolic gestures	Locutionary stage, speech acts develop
3–4 years	Labels emotions in facial expressions/vocal tones	

Source:
Adapted from Westby (2012).

and back plosives, such as /p, t, k/. More plosives are articulated followed by fricatives such as /f, s/ (Bauman-Waengler, 2009). By the age of 6 years, most children accurately produce more than 90% of all vowels, consonants, and consonant cluster productions (James, van Doorn, & McLeod, 2002). Children who are 4 years old and older typically demonstrate at least 90% intelligibility in all productions (Gordon-Brannan, 1994).

Predictable simplification processes are evident in children's speech but inhibition of these processes develops over time. For example, syllable reduplication, such as *dada* for *daddy*, occurs before 1 year of age but is no longer used by 1.6 to 1.9 years of age (Bauman-Waengler, 2009). Deletion of final consonants (*two car* for *two cars*) is no longer present by age 3, and weak or unstressed syllable deletion (*ocpus* for *octopus*) disappears by age 4. Cluster reduction (*srong* for *strong*) and epenthesis (insertion of sounds such as *athulete* for *athlete* may continue to be evident in 8-year-old children (Bauman-Waengler, 2009). Adultlike phonological development tends to appear between 5 to 8 years of age (Bauman-Waengler, 2009; James, 2001).

Comprehension begins at the single word level and progresses rapidly to three and four word sentences. Initially around 8 to 12 months of age, infants understand a few single words in the context of daily routines

(Chapman, 1978; Edmonston, & Thane, 1992). These would include words like *mama, bottle,* or *binkie.* By 1 to 1.5 years of age, children begin to understand words outside of the context with some contextual support. After 18 months of age, children begin to understand words for objects that are not in the immediate context and some two-word combinations. Then by age 2 to 3, children begin understanding three- or four-word sentences based on past experiences and the context of the situation (Chapman, 1978; Edmonston & Thane, 1992).

Meaningful linguistic productions begin around 10 to 18 months of age with the consistent use of words to represent objects. Nouns, pronouns (*me, you*), function words (*that*), and relational words (*all gone*) are acquired earlier and in larger numbers than are verbs (Banajee, DiCarlo, & Stricklin, 2003; Nelson, 1973). Children typically develop a 20 or more word vocabulary by approximately 18 to 24 months of age, at which time they begin to use multi-word utterances and decontextualized language that is talking about objects, persons, and events not in the present context (for a review see Owens, 2012). Mean length of utterance increases with vocabulary knowledge and usage. Utterance complexity develops over time as well with the expression of noun and verb phrases and dependent clauses. Explicit verbal talk about means–end or problem solving occurs at 4 years of age and becomes internalized at later ages (Winsler, Carlton, & Barry, 2000). Adultlike oral language competency is typically achieved by age 5 years (Owens, 2012).

Inflectional morpheme acquisition follows a typical progression. Initially children learn morphemes in the following order:

1. present progressive *–ing*
2–3. prepositions *in* and *on*
4. plural *–s*
5. irregular past tense (came, broke)
6. possessive *–s*
7. uncontractible *Be* verb (Dogs *are* nice)
8. articles *a* and *the*
9. regular past tense *–ed*
10. regular third-person noun–verb agreement *–s* (The dog walk*s*)
11. irregular third-person noun–verb agreement (he *has, does*)
12. uncontractible auxiliary *Be* verb, (Who is here? I *am*)
13. contractible copula (It'*s* my car)
14. contractible auxiliary *Be* verb (Daddy'*s* going too) (Brown, 1973).

All are typically acquired by 50 months of age. Refer to Table 5.2 for operations of reference and semantic relations.

Table 5.2 Operations of Reference and Semantic Relations

Operations of Reference	Examples	Intent
Nomination	There dog	There's a dog.
Recurrence	More cookie	I want more cookie.
Negation		
Denial	No hit	I don't hit.
Rejection	No bed	I don't want to go to bed.
Nonexistent	All gone	The food is gone.

Semantic Relations	Examples	Intent
Action + agent	Doggie run	The dog is running.
Action + object	Eat food	I am eating food.
Action + locative	Go in	I go in.
Agent + object	Mommy hat	Mommy is wearing a hat.
Entity + locative	Bear chair	The bear is in the chair.
Possessor + Possession	Baby shoe	This is the baby's shoe.
Entity + attributive	Big shoe	The shoe is big.
Demonstrative + Entity	That chair	Not this chair, that chair.

Source:
Adapted from Brown (1973).

Brown (1973) also described semantic and syntactical development in stages of sentence types and structure. Stages coincide with morphological development and the mean length of the number of morphemes in utterances (MLU_m). Stage I typically occurs between the ages of 15 and 30 months when children have a 50- to 60-word vocabulary and are just beginning to link words together. These two-word utterances could be operations of reference and/or demonstrate semantic relations. During Stage II, which occurs between 28 and 36 months of age, the first four morphemes (*-ing, in, on*, plural *–s*) are acquired and the children's average MLU_m is 2.25 (Brown, 1973). Stage III, which occurs around 36 to 42 months of age, involves the acquisition of the next three morphemes (irregular past tense, possessive *–s*, uncontractible *Be*) and a MLU_m of approximately 2.75. During Stage IV, children, typically between 40 and 46 months of age, express an average MLU_m of 3.5 and acquire morphemes 8, 9 and 10 (articles *a* and *the*, regular past tense, third-person noun–verb agreement *–s*). Finally, Stage V occurs approximately between 42 and 52 months of age, during which the children acquire the last morphemes (irregular noun–verb agreement, uncontractible auxiliary *Be* verb, contractible *Be* copula, and auxiliary *Be* verb) and achieve an average MLU_m of 4.0 (Brown, 1973).

PRAGMATIC LANGUAGE DEVELOPMENT

Pragmatic development and refinement continues across the lifespan. However, in this section, development of pragmatic language during a child's early years through school age is the focus. Emergence of pragmatic language development occurs in three stages: (a) perlocutionary, (b) illocutionary, and (c) locutionary (Bates, 1976). Research in pragmatic development has covered several topics. The purpose of this chapter is to focus on the skills that develop during childhood, not all aspects of pragmatic language. These include (a) intentionality, (b) speech acts, (c) politeness rules, and (d) rules associated with conversational exchanges.

Intentionality

The perlocutionary stage may range from the ages of 0 to about 9 months of age. During this stage, the infant's behavior, such as crying or smiling, may or may not be intentional or goal directed. However, some parents may interpret and verbally react to their vocalizations or behavior as intentional (Westby, 2012).

Following the perlocutionary stage, the illocutionary stage tends to occur between 9 to 13 months of age. During this stage, infants begin to demonstrate behaviors that are goal directed or intentional. These behaviors include attention-seeking behaviors such as showing, reaching, pointing, and vocalizations as well as using eye gaze to check for parent attention. Bates (1976) describes some of these early attempts as protoimperatives (attempts to get an adult to do something) and proto-declaratives (attempts to direct an adult's attention). Protoimperatives are behaviors that infants use to initiate a behavioral request and proto-declaratives are behaviors infants use to initiate joint attention (Bates, 1976).

To move from a perlocutionary stage to the illocutionary and locutionary stages, children must learn how to reference persons, objects, or actions (Westby, 2012). Referencing is used to direct or hold another person's attention. For example, parents often place objects within their infant's field of vision and talk about the object. Around 8 months of age, infants begin to look for the object and check and follow the adult's line of regard. By 12 months of age, if infants cannot see the object, they will check the parent's line of regard and search for the object. About the same time, referential gestures, such as pointing and reaching, develop concurrent with word use in emerging pragmatic language development (Capone & McGregor, 2004). During this developmental stage, parents begin to ask what and where questions such as "What is it?" or "Where is it?" This transactional interaction reinforces children's bids for joint attention and behavioral requests, and facilitates turn taking and longer conversational exchanges.

Infants begin to demonstrate prelinguistic behaviors of self-regulation, social interaction and joint attention (Wetherby & Prizant, 2002). Table 5.3 lists the types of behaviors for each category and includes gestures, movements, and vocalizations that communicate intention. These behaviors are influenced by the caregivers or by family members' responses, which are culturally influenced. These cultural factors are discussed in the subsequent section on factors affecting social communication development.

Speech Acts

Speech acts, or using speech for specific functions, can be organized according to developmental stages. Speech can be used functionally for personal or interpersonal functions. Halliday (1975) suggested that speech can be used internally for memory, problem solving, or development of ideas. Interpersonal functions are *speech acts* in which individuals use words to cause action (Austin, 1962). Speech acts include using language to make promises, declarations, directions, questions, comments, threats, warnings, suggestions, and many other actions

Table 5.3 Early Prelinguistic Communication of Intention

Behavioral Regulation	Social Interaction	Joint Attention
Request specific object	Greet (notes initiation or termination of activity)	Transfer (gives object)
Request object	Request social routine (initiates game or routine)	Comment on object
Request action	Show off (for attention)	Comment on action or event
Protest action	Call (attract attention)	*Request information
	Acknowledgment (indication communication was received)	*Clarification
	Request permission (seeks approval to do something)	
	Personal (shows mood or feelings)	

*Typically appears in locutionary stage.

(Searle, 1969). For example, saying "help" can cause an adult to help a child complete an action like procuring a desired object that is out of the child's reach. To effectively use speech for action, the speaker must have certain kinds of knowledge:

- Knowledge of the linguistic structures used for specific functions.
- Social knowledge of appropriate contexts for different speech acts.
- Social cognition of the most appropriate linguistic speech act form to use with a particular speaker based on the speaker's personal characteristics (i.e., register; McTear & Conti-Ramsden, 1992).

Following the perlocutionary and illocutionary stages and prelinguistic intentional communication, toddlers, around 13 to 18 months of age, begin to understand and express words. Bates (1976) called this the locutionary stage. During this stage, children learn to use words to represent objects, attributes, and actions. They also begin to use words as a tool to get their wants and needs met. Initially, infants and toddlers view the world from an egocentric viewpoint, and as their linguistic skills mature, they develop more refined and advanced functions that are culturally influenced. Each culture defines what behaviors are appropriate or inappropriate and what is polite or impolite for speech acts and conversational exchanges.

One of the first speech acts children learn is requesting (Bruner, 1983). Bruner described three kinds of responses in emerging pragmatic language development: (a) requests for objects, (b) requests for others' participation in an interaction, and (c) requests for help to achieve a goal. The success of the interaction is dependent on the caregiver's ability to accurately interpret the child's request in order to respond in the way the child expects or desires. Requests for objects that are within sight or close to the child develop prior to 12 months of age. Requests for objects outside of the immediate context develop around 18 months of age (Westby, 2012). This development coincides with implicit social understanding development, referential talk about objects out of context in language development, and use of words with referential gestures. Embedded requests such as "Would you get me a drink?" emerge around the age of 3 years (Owens, 2012; Read & Cherry, 1978, as cited in McTear & Conti-Ramsden, 1992). Children become more implicit in their speech acts by 5 or 6 years of age and give hints related indirectly to their goal ("She's not playing with me. She's watching my brother").

As children mature, they begin to provide reasons for requests that may involve the other person's desires or rights. ("Dad, it's my turn to ride the bike. He has to share"). By age 8 years, they also begin to understand how requests may emotionally affect the other person and communicate the cost–benefit relationship of the request and compliance or offer options with their requests ("If you help me pick up the toys, I'll let you ride my bike"; McTear & Conti-Ramsden, 1992; Owens, 2012).

Some research on other speech acts such as commissives, expressives, and explanations has been summarized by McTear and Conti-Ramsden (1992). Commissives or promises are expressed as early as age 5 years ("I promise to be good"), but it is not until 9 years of age that children seem to understand the difference between promises and predictions ("You're going to get in trouble"). Expressives, or routine communication such as "I'm sorry," "Please," and "Thank you" are often taught as early as 2 years old, but children do not appear to comprehend the role of these acts until they are older (McTear & Contin-Ramsden, 1992). Although commissives and expressives are acquired at older ages, 3- to 4-year-old children were found to provide explanations when seeking help from the listener and when the listener's actions were unwanted ("Mommy, please use the pink ribbon because it matches my dress") and indirect requests by age 5 (Owens, 2012).

Other research has provided evidence that young children use repair and revision strategies in cases of communication breakdown. Children as young as 2 years of age demonstrated appropriate responses to different clarification requests (McTear & Contin-Ramsden, 1992). Older children with more advanced linguistic abilities (Brown's Stages II and III) developed a variety of repair and revision strategies (McTear & Contin-Ramsden, 1992). Owens (2001) reported that the predominant repair strategy for children younger than 9 years of age is repetition ("I said I want the blue one!"), but 9-year-olds are able to perceive communication breakdowns and provide definitions of terms, increased context, as well as talk about how to repair the breakdown in communication ("I don't want to talk to my mom on the phone because I'll start crying because I miss her").

In addition, children demonstrate knowledge of speech and language characteristics associated by a person's role in life as young as 4 years of age. Children will imitate vocal pitch, loudness, and politeness registers as well as linguistic utterances associated with dramatic roles during symbolic play scenes (Owens, 2012). Initially, toddlers and preschoolers will use *motherese* when pretending to be a mother or simplified one-to two-word utterances when pretending to be a baby or a toddler. As children mature, they begin to take on communication styles for other characters such as pretending to be a doctor, a teacher, a police officer, or a firefighter.

Politeness Rules

How to display appropriate politeness is influenced and judged by one's cultural group, which is also influenced by socioeconomic factors. Politeness rules are also affected by context, age, and conversational partners. Initially, as infants and toddlers, children are developing close relationships with their caregivers. While toddlers play alongside other children, they are not developing close personal friendships with other children. It is not until later preschool ages, that children have developed the linguistic maturity, self-regulation, and the ability to think about someone else's point of view to begin to form friendships with peers (Goldstein & Morgan, 2002).

Linguistic interactions and participant behaviors are largely affected by the context of the interaction (Abbeduto & Short-Meyerson, 2002). Utterances are expected to be appropriate toward the goal or intent and contingent to the interaction. Participants are also expected to appropriately and accurately interpret responses and information relative to the goal and/or intention. Abbeduto and Short-Meyerson (2002) summarize research that provides evidence of young children adjusting the length and complexity of their utterances for younger children, providing more detail to someone who may not have knowledge of the event, and increasing their use of polite forms when talking with adults or less familiar participants. They conclude that these adjustments are made based on children's past experiences with the participants, as well as their beliefs about the age-related differences in linguistic ability and "authority" (Abbeduto and Short-Meyerson, 2002, p. 37).

Indirect requests, inferences, and use of ambiguous language develop during the school-age years ("I can't see the book"; "That dog isn't very friendly"; "It's raining cats and dogs"). Owens (2012) summarizes pragmatic development during the school-age years. He reports that children recognize nonliteral meanings in indirect requests and consider others' intentions by age 8. Between 16 and 18 years of age, children use sarcasm, double meanings (*politics = many bloodsucking insects*), and metaphors ("My heart is broken"), and discriminate between others' and their own perspectives. Thus, pragmatic development continues to develop and refine across childhood into adulthood. All pragmatic behaviors, intentionality, speech acts, repair strategies, and politeness rules, are expected, self-monitored, regulated, and expressed dynamically during conversational exchanges.

Conversational Exchanges

Grice (1975) proposed four maxims that are needed for cooperative conversation. These maxims are related to qualitative judgments of quantity, quality, relation, and manner.

- Contributions should be informative as needed for the exchange.
- Contributions should be true based on adequate evidence.
- Contributions should be relevant.
- Contributions should be clear, brief, and orderly.

Grice also described how these maxims could be used to mean or implicate unspoken messages by using conventional and conversational implicature (McTear & Conti-Ramsden, 1992). Conventional implicatures are meanings related to an utterance that are unspoken because of the nature of cooperative maxims. For example, if a speaker states that he or she was studying abroad for the summer semester, according to the maxim of quantity and relevance, the speaker provided a limited amount of relevant information. The conventional implicature could be that the person was also in a different country to study abroad. Conversational implicature, on the other hand, is when an indirect statement is communicated to infer or implicate another meaning. For example, if Speaker A asks Speaker B, "Will you be able to come to my wedding?" Speaker B could use conversational implicature to avoid hurting Speaker A's feelings by saying, "I'm sorry. I was planning on studying abroad for the summer." This response meets the definition of conversational implicature in the following ways:

1. It infers that the wedding date and her duration of studying abroad are at the same time.
2. Speaker B could cancel the statement by adding more information ("I think I may return from studying abroad in time for your wedding").
3. The statement is attached to the semantic content but not the linguistic form.
4. The statement is calculable and cooperative.
5. It is nonconventional in that the meaning is beyond what is spoken ("I am not sure whether I can attend").
6. It is indeterminate in meaning if the same statement was spoken in a different context and time (such as spoken to share information about what one did over the summer).

The cooperative maxims and use of implicature in conversation can result in an infinite number of combinations and inferences. Based on one's history and experience, individual variability in comprehension and use of these strategies can be dynamic and uniquely individual. The study of conversational discourse also includes such strategies as taking turns, and topic initiation, maintenance and closure. Verbal responding increases between 2 and 3 years of age, a 3-year-old can take two to three turns during a conversation as compared to about 50% of 5-year-olds who can talk about a topic through approximately 10 to 12 turns (Owens, 2012). Similarly, initiating, maintaining, and discontinuing topics develop as children gain linguistic competence. Toddlers have a limited ability to maintain a topic beyond a question and response format such as "What do you want to do, go outside or read a book?" However, 3- to 4-year-olds can maintain the topic about 75% of the time (Owens, 2012). Yet, by age 3.5 years, most of the children's utterances are on an initiated topic. They also monitor and change informational exchanges based on what they determine their listener knows or does not know. Mental state vocabulary increases between 4 and 7 years of age (Moore, Harris, & Patriquin, 1993). School-age children are able to initiate, maintain, take numerous turns, and stop or switch topics in conversation (Owens, 2012).

FACTORS AFFECTING SOCIAL COMMUNICATION COMPETENCE

Several factors can influence social communication styles and abilities. As mentioned previously, socioeconomic status (SES) and culture are some of the factors that are discussed in this chapter. In addition, communication disabilities such as language impairment, autism, attention-deficit disorders, and social-emotional disorders or trauma can greatly influence one's social communication. The impact of these types of disorders on social communication are discussed in Section II of this volume.

Socioeconomic Status

It has been well documented that children living in poverty are at increased risk of poorer language outcomes in vocabulary and complex syntax exposure and development (Dollaghan et al., 1999; Hart & Risley, 1995; Hoff, 2003; Huttenlocher, Vasilyeva, Cymerman, & Levine, 2002) and tend to receive lower scores on standardized measures (Hart & Risley 1995; Heath, 1983; Qi, Kaiser, Milan, & Hancock, 2006; Qi, Kaiser, Milan, McLean, & Hancock, 2003). These children also have fewer models of mainstream pragmatics and social communication styles and may learn neighborhood discourse styles and behaviors that may not be understood or accepted in mainstream environments. In mainstream environments, these pragmatic communication styles may be misinterpreted resulting in misunderstanding, possible conflict, and negative social outcomes, such as suspension or being expelled from school (Delpit, 1995; Harry, 1992; Kalyanpur & Harry, 1999; Terrell & Terrell, 1996). Poorer linguistic outcomes and limited exposure to different styles of social communication may negatively affect social communication development and ability as well as academic achievement. More preschool students were referred for special education services based on a particular subset of behaviors, violent physical reactions, impulsive behaviors, and noncompliance (Nungesser & Watkins, 2005). Preschool teachers reported that they perceived the home environment as the key contributing factor for these behaviors, and few believed communication played a role in social competence. In fact, the Child Mental Health Foundation and Agencies Network Project (2000) projected that children with limited social skills may be placed in lower academic tracks, which decreases the number of positive social interactions these children may have with peers. Researchers have found that children living in impoverished neighborhoods have been over-identified for special education services (Donovan & Cross, 2002; Hosp & Reschly, 2004). In these studies, demographic and economic factors predicted placement of children into multiple categories of disability (mental retardation, emotional disturbance, or learning disability). Demographic variables included rate of ethnic groups, English proficiency, and number of families with a person with a disability. Economic variables included housing value, family income, adult education level, and number of children at risk. When academic achievement was paired with economic and demographic factors, it also predicted the outcome of a disability category (Hosp & Reschley, 2004). In other words, when children live in environments where they receive less exposure to vocabulary and complex syntax at home and have little opportunity to receive this kind of linguistic exposure or discourse model in their neighborhoods, they have lower academic achievement and are at increased risk of performing similarly as children with disabilities.

Hierarchy of Dependence

Culture is passed from one generation to the next through parenting practices that teach social and communication behaviors to the children (Vygotsky, 1934/1986; Wertsch, 1985). Cultural values are also communicated through the media, policies, laws, and the philosophies or pedagogy of institutions, such as schools (Vygotsky, 1934/1986; Wertsch,

1985). Cultural variations in communicative interactions appear to vary across continua of dependence and power/distance in interpersonal relationships (Hwa-Froelich & Vigil, 2004).

All cultures tend to value behaviors that are (a) more independent with other cultural members, (b) a mix of independent and interdependent behaviors, or (c) more interdependent with other cultural members (Greenfield & Cocking, 1994; Hofstede, 1984, 2001; Hofstede, Pederson, & Hofstede, 2002). Triandis (1995) termed these behaviors as either individualistic or collective. Independent or individualistic values support the idea that it is best to be separate and different from others, whereas dependent or collective values support the view that it is better to be dependent upon and similar to others. These cultural frameworks affect parental goals and interaction behaviors when interacting with their children. Children from diverse backgrounds may react to or interpret mainstream social communication in different ways (Delpit, 1995).

The values of independence/interdependence influence parental views of intentionality, language content, and use (Lustig & Koester, 2009). More independent cultures, such as the US culture, view infants as intentional at birth (Heath, 1983). In contrast, more interdependent cultures, such as some Asian cultures, do not believe infants are intentional until they can express real words. As a consequence, early vocalizations and cries were not attended to consistently (Heath, 1983; Westby, 2012). Linguistic content also varies among independent and dependent cultures. For example, independent individuals tend to communicate using more *I* and *you* pronouns with an emphasis on individuality, independence, personal privacy, and needs (Kim & Choi, 1994; Lustig & Koester, 2009; Lynch & Hanson, 2011). In contrast, the Latino culture is more interdependent, and social competence is viewed as a priority. Thus, Latino children may express polite social words prior to words expressed for requesting or labeling (Sternberg, 2007; Westby, 2012).

Linguistic use can vary along this continuum from messages communicating an individual's intention to messages seeking confirmation, agreement, or invitation to participate. Because infants are viewed as intentional in independent cultures, adults often label objects that infants look at or hand the object to the infant to explore. Infants from a more independent framework may develop requesting and labeling early (Westby, 2012). Parents from dependent cultures may focus on other communicative functions than labeling and requesting. In contrast, interdependent cultures may stress increased politeness toward and inclusion of others. For example, Farver and Shinn (1997) found that Korean children used more tag questions ("The children will stay in the castle, OK?") than did US preschool children when playing with the same stimuli. They hypothesized that the Korean children were demonstrating more interdependent communication strategies showing more concern and attention to their peers' feelings and need to be included.

Interpersonal Relationships

Cultures also exhibit differences along the continuum of power and distance in social roles which influence communicative interactions (Green, 2002; Lynch & Hansen, 2011; Ochs & Schieffelin, 1986; Rogoff, 2003). In cultures that view relationships along a continuum of increased power and distance, persons are expected to know their place and role in different situations. In other words, persons viewed as having more power expect and are treated by persons who have less power with more formal communication and specific behavioral rules for interactions such as addressing elders with differing degrees of formal address or special treatment (Delgado-Gaitan, 1994; Greenfield, 1994; Ho, 1994; Nsamenang & Lamb, 1994; Scollon & Scollon, 1995; Suina & Smolkin, 1994; Tapia Uribe, Levine, & Levine, 1994). To show more or less deference to someone viewed as having more or less power, persons modify their nonverbal and verbal communication (Hofstede, 2001; Triandis, 1995). For example, to show more deference to an elder, some cultures use an indirect eye gaze and address elders by *Mr.* or *Mrs. Smith* and use first names for younger cultural members. In Chinese, *jiějie* is a special name reserved for the oldest sister, whereas *meimei* is the name used for all younger sisters, showing more respect for older than younger children. Another example is shown by Vietnamese parents who socialize their children to "talk sweet" as a way of showing respect to their elders and teachers (Hwa-Froelich & Vigil, 2004; Hwa-Froelich & Westby, 2003). In addition, gender roles may significantly differ from the mainstream and gender communication styles may reflect these role differences (Hwa-Froelich, 2004).

In cultures of less power/distance, individuals are viewed as having equal power relationships. Communicative interactions display equal power through direct, honest sharing of opinions, polite, indirect directions, and more verbal than gestural or tactile communication. Directions are often framed as questions or suggestions to allow for individual and independent choice rather than complete compliance (Hwa-Froelich & Vigil, 2004). For example, in Western cultures it is acceptable to address others by their first names regardless of age or power differential. Special address is reserved for honorary members such as the prime minister or the president or in special contexts such as judicial proceedings.

In conclusion, factors of SES and culture must be considered in providing assessment and intervention services across the life span. SES was a factor in the case example of Shelly. Her parents lacked the education and knowledge they needed to interact and care for Shelly which placed her at risk of failure to thrive. The early childhood special educator and speech-language pathologist (SLP) helped Shelly's parents reorganize their belongings and increase lighting in the living room to allow Shelly to safely explore her environment. They helped the parents learn how to share storybooks with Shelly by labeling pictures or talking about what they saw in the pictures and asking questions to link the pictures to experiences they had shared with Shelly. They helped the parents recognize and facilitate collaborative talk about the pictures, taking conversational turns, and staying on the same topic for three to four turns. To improve Shelly's prosody and inflection, the early childhood teacher and SLP modeled exaggerated inflection and slower prosodic patterns during conversational speech. Over time, Shelly began to imitate these prosodic patterns until her conversational speech began to sound more natural and less monotonous. With the help of early intervention services, Shelly was able to learn and develop functional communication and her parents learned how to contingently respond to Shelly's communication and provide age-appropriate language stimulation and learning experiences. Cultural and social variations may affect performance on assessments that could be misinterpreted especially in the area of social communication. It is important that practitioners be aware of families' cultural expectations to appropriately address the communication goals and needs of individual clients and prepare them for the multiple communicative contexts in which they interact.

DISCUSSION QUESTIONS

1. What is the difference between primary and secondary intersubjectivity?
2. How does intersubjectivity support and facilitate social understanding development?
3. What kind of social interactions facilitate nonverbal communication development?
4. Describe the three stages of early pragmatic language development.
5. What do children have to know to develop speech acts?
6. How do politeness rules affect social communication?
7. What are the maxims for cooperative conversational language?
8. Describe how poverty may influence one's social communication.

9. Describe how cultural differences in dependence and independence may affect social communication.
10. Describe how cultural differences in interpersonal relationships may influence social communication.

INSTRUCTIONAL RESOURCES

Joint attention across developmental disabilities. Retrieved from www.youtube.com/watch?v=tif4U3OjT2M
Life's First Feelings video. Retrieved from http://vimeo.com/44930499
Primary intersubjectivity Still face experiment. Retrieved from www.youtube.com/watch?v=apzXGEbZht0

REFERENCES

Abbeduto, L., & Short-Meyerson, K. (2002). Linguistic influences on social interaction. In H. Goldstein, L. A. Kaczmarek, & K. M. English (Eds.), *Promoting social communication* (pp. 27–54). Baltimore, MD: Brookes.

Anderson, P. (1998). *Nonverbal communication: Forms and functions* (2nd ed.), Long Grove, IL: Waveland Press.

Austin, J. (1962). *How to do things with words.* London, UK: Oxford University Press.

Baldwin, D. A., & Moses, L. J. (1994). Early understanding of referential intent and attentional focus: Evidence from language and emotion. In C. Lewis & P. Mitchell (Eds.), *Children's early understanding of mind. Origins and development* (pp. 133–156). Hillsdale, NJ: Erlbaum.

Banajee, M., DiCarlo, C., & Stricklin, S. (2003). Core vocabulary determination for toddlers. *Augmentative and Alternative Communication, 19,* 67–73. doi:10.1080/0743461031000112034

Baron-Cohen, S. (1997). *Mindblindness. An essay on autism and theory of mind.* Cambridge, MA: MIT Press.

Bates, E. (1976). *Language in context.* New York, NY: Academic Press.

Bauman-Waengler, J. (2009). *Introduction to phonetics and phonology.* Boston, MA: Pearson.

Beck, C. T. (1996). Postpartum depressed mothers' experiences interacting with their children. *Nursing Research, 45*(2), 98–104. Retrieved from http://journals.lww.com/nursingresearchonline/pages/default.aspx

Beer, J. S., & Ochsner, K. N. (2006). Social cognition: A multi-level analysis. *Brain Research, 1079,* 98–105. doi:10.1016/j.brainres.2006.01.002

Brown, R. (1973). *A first language: The early stages.* London, UK: George Allen & Unwin.

Bruner, J. (1983). *Child's talk.* New York, NY: W.W. Norton.

Bruner, J. S. (1999). The intentionality of referring. In P. Zelazo & J.W. Astington (Eds.), *Developing theories of intention: Social understanding and self-control* (pp. 329–339). Mahwah, NJ: Erlbaum.

Butterworth, G. (1994). Theory of mind and the facts of embodiment. In C. Lewis & P. Mitchell (Eds.), *Children's early understanding of mind. Origins and development* (pp. 115–132). Hillsdale, NJ: Erlbaum.

Campanella, S., & Belin, P. (2007). Integrating face and voice in person perception. *Trends in Cognitive Sciences, 11*(12), 535–543. doi:10:1016/j.tics.2007.10.001

Camras, L. A., & Allison, K. (1985). Children's understanding of emotional facial expressions and verbal labels. *Journal of Nonverbal Behavior, 9,* 84–94. doi:10.1007/BF00987140

Capone, N., & McGregor, K. (2004). Gesture development: A review for clinical and research practices. *Journal of Speech, Language, and Hearing Research, 47,* 173–187. doi:10.1044/1092–4388(2004/015)

Carpendale, J., & Lewis, C. (2006). *How children develop social understanding.* Malden, MA: Blackwell Publishing.

Caron, R., Caron, A., & Myers, R. (1982). Abstraction of invariant facial expression in infancy. *Child Development, 53,* 1008–1015. doi:10.2307/1129141

Chapman, R. (1978). Comprehension strategies in children. In J. F. Kavanaugh & W. Strange (Eds.), *Speech and language in the laboratory, school, and clinic* (pp. 308–327). Cambridge, MA: MIT Press.

Chiat, S., & Roy, P. (2008). Early phonological and sociocognitive skills as predictors of later language and social communication outcomes. *Journal of Child Psychology and Psychiatry, 49,* 635–645. doi:10.1111/J.1469–7610.2008.01881.x

Child Mental Health Foundation and Agencies Network Project. (2000). *A good beginning: Sending America's children to school with the social and emotional competence they need to succeed.* Bethesda, MD: National Institute of Mental Health.

Clarke-Stewart, A. (1973). Interactions between mothers and their young children: Characteristics and consequences. *Monographs of the Society of Research in Child Development, 38*(6, Serial No. 7), 1–109. Retrieved from www.jstor.org/pss/1165928

Coh, J. F., Matias, R., Tronick, E. Z., Connell, D., & Lyons-Ruth, K. (1986). Face-to-face interactions of depressed mothers and their infants. In E. Z. Tronick & T. Field (Eds.), *Maternal depression and infant disturbance* (New Directions for Child Development, Vol. 34, pp. 31–45). San Francisco, CA: Jossey-Bass.

Crago, M. B., & Eriks-Brophy, A. (1994). A culture, conversation, and interaction. In J. F. Duchan, L. Hewitt, & R. M. Sonnenmeier (Eds.), *Pragmatics from theory to practice* (pp. 43–58). Englewood Cliff, NJ: Prentice Hall.

Crais, E. R., Watson, L. R., & Baranek, G. T. (2009). Use of gesture development in profiling children's prelinguistic skills. *American Journal of Speech-Language Pathology*, *18*, 95–108. doi:10.1044/1058-0360(200 8/07–0041)

Delgado-Gaitan, C. (1994). Socializing young children in Mexican-American families: An intergenerational perspective. In P. M. Greenfield & R. R. Cocking (Eds.), *Cross-cultural roots of minority development* (pp. 55–86). Hillsdale, NJ: Erlbaum.

Delpit, L. (1995). *Other people's children.* New York, NY: The New Press.

Dollaghan, C. A., Campbell, T. F., Paradise, J. L., Feldman, H. M., Janosky, J. E., Pitcairin, D., & Kurs-Lasky, M. N. (1999). Maternal education and measures of early speech and language. *Journal of Speech, Language, and Hearing Research*, *42*, 1432–1443.

Donovan, S., & Cross, C. T. (Eds.). (2002). *Minority students in special and gifted education.* Washington, DC: National Academy Press.

Dunn, J., Brown, J., Slomkousky, C., Tesla, C., & Youngblade, L. (1991). Young children's understanding of other people's feelings and beliefs: Individual differences and their antecedents. *Child Development*, *62*, 1352–1366. doi:10.2307/1130811

Edmonston, N., & Thane, N. (1992). Children's use of comprehension strategies in response to relational words: Implications for assessment. *American Journal of Speech-Language Pathology*, *1*, 30–35.

Farver, J. M., & Shinn, Y. L. (1997). Social pretend play in Korean- and Anglo-American preschoolers. *Child Development*, *68*(3), 544–556. doi:10.2307/1131677

Ferguson, C. A., Menn, L., & Stoel-Gammon, C. (Eds.). (1992). *Phonological development: Models, research, implications.* Timonium, MD: York Press.

Goldstein, H., Kaczmarek, L. A., & English, K. M. (Eds.). (2002). *Promoting social communication.* Baltimore, MD: Brookes.

Goldstein, H., & Morgan, L. (2002). Social interaction and models of friendship development. In H. Goldstein, L. A. Kaczmarek, & K. M. English (Eds.), *Promoting social communication* (pp. 5–25). Baltimore, MD: Brookes.

Gordon-Brannan, M. (1994). Assessing intelligibility: Children's expressive phonologies. *Topics in Language Disorders*, *14*, 17–25. Retrieved from http://journals.lww.com/topicsinlanguagedisorders/pages/default.aspx

Green, L. J. (2002). *African American English.* New York, NY: Cambridge University Press.

Greenfield, P. M. (1994). Independence and interdependence as developmental scripts: Implications for theory, research and practice. In P. M. Greenfield & R. R. Cocking (Eds.), *Cross-cultural roots of minority child development* (pp. 1–37). Hillsdale, NJ: Erlbaum.

Greenfield, P. M., & Cocking, R. R. (Eds.). (1994). *Cross-cultural roots of minority child development.* Hillsdale, NJ: Erlbaum.

Greenwood, C. R., Walker, D., & Utley, C. (2002). Relationships between social-communicative skills and life achievements. In H. Goldstein, L. A. Kaczmarek, & K. M. English (Eds.), *Promoting social communication* (pp. 345–370). Baltimore, MD: Brookes.

Grice, H. P. (1975). Logic and conversation. In P. Cole, and J. L. Morgan, (Eds.), *Speech acts* (pp. 41–58). New York, NY: Academic Press.

Halliday, M. (1975). *Learning how to mean: Explorations in the development of language*. New York, NY: Arnold.

Harry, B. (1992). *Cultural diversity and the special education system: Communication and empowerment*. New York, NY: Teachers College Press.

Hart, B., & Risley, T. R. (1995). *Meaningful differences in the everyday experiences of young American children*. Baltimore, MD: Brookes.

Heath, S. B. (1983). *Ways with words: Language, life, and work in communities and classrooms*. Cambridge, UK: Cambridge University Press.

Ho, D. Y. F. (1994). Cognitive socialization in Confucian heritage children. In P. M. Greenfield & R. R. Cocking (Eds.), *Cross-cultural roots of minority child development* (pp. 285–314). Hillsdale, NJ: Erlbaum.

Hoff, E. (2003). The specificity of environmental influence: Socioeconomic status affects early vocabulary development via maternal speech. *Child Development, 74*, 1368–1378. doi:10.1111/1467–8624.00612

Hofstede, G. (1984). *Culture's consequences, international differences in work-related values*. Newbury Park, CA: Sage.

Hofstede, G. (2001). *Culture's consequences: Comparing values, behaviors, and organizations across nations* (2nd ed.). Thousand Oaks, CA: Sage.

Hofstede, G. J., Pedersen, P. B., & Hofstede, G. (2002). *Exploring culture: Exercises, stories, and synthetic cultures*. Yarmouth, ME: Intercultural Press.

Hosp, J. L., & Reschly, D. J. (2004). Disproportionate representation of minority students in special education: Academic, demographic, and economic predictors. *Exceptional Children, 70*(2), 185–199.

Huttenlocher, J., Vasilyeva, M., Cymerman, E., & Levine, S. (2002). Language input and child syntax. *Cognitive Psychology, 45*, 337–374. doi:10.1016/S0010–0285(02)00500–5

Hwa-Froelich, D. A. (2004). Play assessment for children from culturally and linguistically diverse backgrounds. *Perspectives on Language, Learning and Education and on Communication Disorders and Sciences in Culturally and Linguistically Diverse Populations, 11*(2), 6–10. doi:10.1044/cds11.2.5

Hwa-Froelich, D. A. (2012a). Social communication development. In D. A. Hwa-Froelich *Supporting development in internationally adopted children* (pp. 177–203). Baltimore, MD: Brookes.

Hwa-Froelich, D. A. (2012b). Theoretical foundations for the development of internationally adopted children. In D. A. Hwa-Froelich (Ed.), *Supporting development in internationally adopted children* (pp. 1–19). Baltimore, MD: Brookes.

Hwa-Froelich, D. A., & Vigil, D. C. (2004). Three aspects of cultural influence on communication: A literature review. *Communication Disorders Quarterly, 25*(3), 110–118. doi:10.1177/15257401040250030201

Hwa-Froelich, D. A., & Westby, C. E. (2003). Frameworks of education: Perspectives of Southeast Asian parents and Head Start staff. *Language, Speech and Hearing in Schools, 34*, 299–319. doi:10.1044/0161–1461(2003/025)

James, D. G. H. (2001). The use of phonological processes in Australian children aged 2 to 7:11 years. *Advances in Speech-Language Pathology, 3*, 109–128. Retrieved from http://informahealthcare.com/doi/pdf/10.3109/14417040109003718

James, D., van Doorn, J., & McLeod, S. (2002). Segment production in mono-, di- and polysyllabic words in children aged 3–7 years. In F. Windsor, L. Kelly, & N. Hewlett (Eds.), *Themes in clinical phonetics and linguistics* (pp. 287–298), Hillsdale, NJ: Erlbaum.

Kaczmarek, L. A. (2002). Assessment of social-communicative competence. In H. Goldstein, L. A. Kaczmarek, & K. M. English (Eds.), *Promoting social communication children with developmental disabilities from birth to adolescence* (pp. 55–115). Baltimore, MD: Brookes.

Kalyanpur, M., & Harry, B. (1999). *Culture in special education*. Baltimore, MD: Brookes.

Kim, U., & Choi, S. (1994). Individualism, collectivism, and child development: A Korean perspective. In P. M. Greenfield & R. R. Cocking (Eds.), *Cross-cultural roots of minority child development* (pp. 227–257). Hillsdale, NJ: Erlbaum.

Koneya, M., & Barbour, A. (1976). *Louder than words: Nonverbal communication*. Columbus, OH: Merrill Publishing.

Legerstee, M. (2005). *Infants' sense of people: Precursors to a theory of mind*. Cambridge, UK: Cambridge University Press.

Lewis, M. D. (1997). Personality self-organization: Cascading constraints on cognition-emotion interaction. In. A. Fogel., M. C. D. P. Lyra, & J. Valsiner (Eds.), *Dynamics and indeterminism in developmental and social processes* (pp. 193–216). Mahwah, NJ: Erlbaum.

Lustig, M. W., & Koester, J. (2009). *Intercultural competence: Interpersonal communication across cultures* (6th ed.). Boston, MA: Allyn & Bacon.

Lynch, E. W., & Hanson, M. J. (2011). *Developing cross-cultural competence: A guide for working with young children and their families* (3rd ed.). Baltimore, MD: Brookes.

McClure, E. B. (2000). A meta-analytic review of sex differences in facial expression processing and their development in infants, children, and adolescents. *Psychological Bulletin, 126*, 38–59. doi:10.1037//0033–2909 .126.3.424

McTear, M. F., & Conti-Ramsden, G. (1992). *Pragmatic disability in children*. San Diego, CA: Singular.

Moore, C., Harris, L., & Patriquin, M. (1993). Lexical and prosodic cues in the comprehension of relative certainty. *Journal of Child Language, 20*, 153–167.

National Institute of Child Health and Human Development Early Child Care Research Network. (2000). The relation of child care to cognitive and language development. *Child Development, 71*(4), 960–980. doi:10.1111/1467–8624.00202

Nelson, K. (1973). *Structure and strategy in learning to talk* (Monographs of the Society for Research in Child Development, 38, Serial No. 149). Hoboken, NJ: Wiley.

Ninio, A., & Snow, C. E. (1996). *Pragmatic development.* Boulder, CO: Westview Press.

Nowicki, S., Jr., & Duke, M. P. (1994). Individual differences in the nonverbal communication of affect: The diagnostic analysis of nonverbal accuracy scale. *Journal of Nonverbal Behavior, 18*, 9–35. doi:10.1007/BF02169077

Nsamenang, A. B., & Lamb, M. E. (1994). Socialization of Nso children in the Bamenda grassfields of northwest Cameroon. In P. M. Greenfield & R. R. Cocking (Eds.), *Cross-cultural roots of minority child development* (pp. 133–146). Hillsdale, NJ: Erlbaum.

Nungesser, N. R., & Watkins, R. V. (2005). Preschool teachers' perceptions and reactions to challenging classroom behavior: Implications for speech-language pathologists. *Language, Speech, and Hearing Services in Schools, 36*, 139–151. doi:10.1044/0161–1461(2005/013)

Ochs, E., & Schieffelin, B. (1986). *Language socialization across cultures.* Cambridge, UK: Cambridge University Press.

Owens, R. E., Jr. (2001). *Language development* (5th ed.). Boston, MA: Allyn and Bacon.

Owens, R. E., Jr. (2012). *Language development* (8th ed.). Boston, MA: Allyn and Bacon.

Qi, C. H., Kaiser, A. P., Milan, S., & Hancock, T. (2006). Language performance of low-income, African American and European American preschool children on the Peabody Picture Vocabulary Test-III. *Language, Speech, Hearing Services in Schools, 37*, 1–12.

Qi, C. H., Kaiser, A. P., Milan, S., McLean, Z., & Hancock, T. (2003). The performance of low-income African American children on the Preschool Language Scales-3. *Journal of Speech, Language, and Hearing Research, 43*, 576–590. doi:10.1044/1092–4388(2003/046)

Rogoff, B. (2003). *The cultural nature of human development.* New York, NY: Oxford University Press.

Rothman, A. D., & Nowicki, S., Jr. (2004). A measure of the ability to identify emotion in children's tone of voice. *Journal of Nonverbal Behavior, 28*(2), 67–92. doi:10.1023/B:JONB.0000023653.13943.31

Scollon, R., & Scollon, S. W. (1995). *Intercultural communication.* Malden, MA: Blackwell Press.

Searle, J. (1969). *Speech acts: An essay in the philosophy of language*. Cambridge, UK: Cambridge University.

Siegel, D. J. (1999). *The developing mind: How relationships and the brain interact to shape who we are*. New York, NY: Guilford Press.

Solantus-Simlua, T., Punamaki, R., & Beardslee, W. R. (2002). Children's responses to low parental mood. *Journal of the American Academy of Child and Adolescent Psychiatry, 41*, 287–295. doi:10.1097/00004583-200203000-00008

Sorce, J. F., Emde, R. N., Campos, J., & Klinnert, M. D. (1985). Maternal emotional signaling: Its effect on the visual cliff behavior of 1-year-olds. *Developmental Psychology, 21*, 195–200. doi:10.1037//0012-1649.21.1.195

Sroufe, L. A. (1997). Psychopathology as an outcome of development. *Development and Psychopathology, 5*, 251–268. doi:10.1017/S0954579497002046

Stafford, L., & Bayer, C. L. (1993). *Interaction between parents and children*. Newbury Park, CA: Sage.

Sternberg, R. J. (2007). Who are the bright children? The cultural context of being and acting intelligent. *Educational Researcher, 36*(3), 148–155. doi:10.3102/0013189X07299881

Suina, J. H., & Smolkin, L. B. (1994). From natal culture to school culture to dominant society culture: Supporting transitions for Pueblo Indian students. In P. M. Greenfield & R. R. Cocking (Eds.), *Cross-cultural roots of minority child development* (pp. 115–132). Hillsdale, NJ: Erlbaum.

Tapia Uribe, F. M., Levine, R. A., & Levine, S. E. (1994). Maternal behavior in a Mexican community: The changing environments of children. In P. M. Greenfield & R. R. Cocking (Eds.), *Cross-cultural roots of minority child development* (pp. 41–54). Hillsdale, NJ: Erlbaum.

Terrell, S. L. & Terrell, F. (1996). The importance of psychological and sociocultural factors in providing clinical services to African American children. In A. G. Kamhi, K. E. Pollock, & J. L. Harris (Eds.). *Communication development and disorders in African American children* (pp. 55–72). Baltimore, MD: Brookes.

Trevarthen, C. (1979). Communication and cooperation in early infancy. A description of primary intersubjectivity. In M. Bullowa (Ed.), *Before speech: The beginning of human communication* (pp. 321–347). Cambridge, UK: Cambridge University Press.

Trevarthen, C. (1992). An infant's motives for speaking and thinking in the culture. In A. H. Wold (Ed.), *The dialogical alternative: Towards a theory of language and mind* (pp. 99–137). Oslo, Norway: Scandinavian University Press.

Triandis, H. C. (1995). *Individualism and collectivism*. Boulder, CO: Westview Press.

Vygotsky, L. (1986). *Thought and language* (A. Kozulin, Trans.). London, UK: MIT Press. (Original work published in 1934)

Walden, T. A., & Ogan, T. A. (1988). The development of social referencing. *Child Development, 59,* 1230–1240. doi:10.2307/1130486

Wertsch, J. V. (1985). *Vygotsky and the social formation of mind.* Cambridge, MA: Harvard University Press.

Westby, C. E. (2012). Social-emotional bases of communication development. In B. B. Shulman & N. C. Capone (Eds.), *Language development: Foundations, processes, and clinical applications* (pp. 133–176). Boston, MA: Jones & Bartlett.

Wetherby, A. M. (1991). Profiling pragmatic abilities in the emerging language of young children. In T. Gallagher (Ed.), *Pragmatics of language: Clinical practice issues* (pp. 249–281). San Diego, CA: Singular.

Wetherby, A. M., & Prizant, B. M. (2002). *Communication and symbolic behavior scales: Developmental profile.* Baltimore, MD: Brookes.

Winsler, A., Carlton, M. P., & Barry, M. J. (2000). Age-related changes in preschool children's systematic use of private speech in a natural setting. *Journal of Child Language, 27,* 665–687.

Section II
EVIDENCE-BASED PRACTICE FOR
SOCIAL COMMUNICATION DISORDERS

6

ASSESSMENT AND INTERVENTION FOR CHILDREN WITH PRAGMATIC LANGUAGE IMPAIRMENT

Catherine Adams

A pragmatic impairment is a mismatch between language and context.
—Volden and Lord (1991)

LEARNING OBJECTIVES

Readers will

1. Become aware of incidence/prevalence statistics and the nature of pragmatic language impairment.
2. Gain knowledge about the relationship between pragmatic language impairment, social communication disorder, high-functioning autism, Asperger Syndrome, and Specific Language Impairment.
3. Be familiar with appropriate formal and informal assessment procedures, particularly for pragmatics and high-level language skills in pragmatic language impairment.
4. Gain information about evidence-based assessment and intervention practices for children with pragmatic language impairment.

CASE STUDY

Lucas was aged 7 years, 11 months when he was assessed for participation in a speech-language intervention research project. Lucas had a history of language delay, unintelligibility, and comprehension difficulties in the early years. Motor milestones and birth history was normal. There was no history of speech and language difficulties in the extended family. Lucas had passed all his hearing tests during the preschool period, and there was no concern about his current hearing status. At age 3 years he showed little inclination for imaginative or cooperative play with other children. He attended a nursery school since the age of 3.5 years, where there was some concern over his lack of engagement with staff and children and his limited expressive language. Lucas is an only child; he lives with his parents and has an extended family living nearby.

Lucas was referred for an initial speech-language assessment at the age of 4 years 8 months. At that stage he could produce simple sentences but his comprehension was significantly delayed. His receptive and expressive vocabularies were limited for his age, and he was considered to have a language disorder. He received a period of speech-language intervention in the community pediatric clinic that focused on listening and attention skills. As Lucas was about to enter mainstream education at age 5 years, a case conference was held to discuss management. The staff felt that Lucas would not require attendance in a special education unit for children with language impairment, but that he could continue to receive speech-language therapy and additional support via a learning assistant in the classroom. Lucas continues to receive this support to the present time.

At age 7, Lucas is intelligible and fluent, and to the lay observer, he appears to have normal expressive language skills. However, his literacy skills are developing slowly, and he is falling behind his peer group. Lucas's teacher has reported that he had literacy difficulties.

His parents' main concerns are that he is making very slow progress at school, and he gets confused when speaking to the extent that they do not know what he is talking about. They report that it is difficult to sustain a conversation with Lucas. They are aware it is not easy for peers to engage with him and he appears increasingly socially isolated. Lucas is very talkative and tends to dominate the topics of conversation, preferring to talk about familiar TV programs and computer games. He has only one friend with whom he spends some time but mostly he prefers to play on his computer at home.

The history and current reports of communication for Lucas suggest that he has significant language and pragmatic difficulties that require a full investigation. These difficulties are compounded by some social interaction difficulties. Lucas's lack of progress in language and literacy and his growing social difficulties indicate that he requires action to prevent further problems in the school year and into adolescence. His parents and education staff require specialist advice about the nature of the underlying impairment and guidelines on how to support language and pragmatic development.

Preliminary information about Lucas suggested that he has a Pragmatic Language Impairment (PLI). This condition has recently also been referred to as Social Communication Disorder (SCD). For the purposes of clarity, the condition will be referred to as PLI, but the two terms can be used interchangeably. The emergence of these categorical and descriptive labels as well as issues of diagnosis are addressed in this chapter.

CHARACTERISTICS OF PRAGMATIC LANGUAGE IMPAIRMENT AND ITS RELATION TO OTHER CONDITIONS

Definitions and Labels

PLI is a type of developmental language impairment in which there is disproportionate difficulty with pragmatics and social communication compared to the structural aspects of language such as grammar and vocabulary. Children with PLI show a range of pragmatic impairment and language impairment features and may have a history of autistic traits. As children who have PLI move into the later stages of language development (at around age 4 years), the marked difficulty with pragmatics and social communication becomes more apparent. Typically these difficulties interfere significantly with social functioning and acceptability. In addition, they may retain long-term developmental difficulties with language structure and discourse.

The term *Pragmatic Language Impairment* was first introduced by Bishop (2000), who instigated the classic definition of a mismatch between pragmatics and structural language abilities. Prior to 2000, this condition was labeled semantic-pragmatic language disorder (Rapin & Allen, 1987). PLI has always been a controversial term; it is not included in the current *Diagnostic and Statistical Manual of Mental Disorders* (5th ed.; *DSM-5*; American Psychiatric Association [APA], 2013), and many autism researchers have firmly placed these children in the broader autism phenotype, suggesting that the term *PLI* is redundant. There is, however, evidence that children identified as having PLI do not meet diagnostic criteria for autism (Bishop & Norbury, 2002; Leyfer, Tager-Flusberg, Dowd, Tomblin, & Folstein, 2008), and this led to the retention by some of the term *PLI*. An ongoing debate exists regarding the relationship between autism and Specific Language Impairment

(SLI), specifically as to whether PLI represents an *intermediate condition* (Bishop & Norbury, 2002), or represents a complex *comorbid condition* in which autism and SLI coexist (Tager-Flusberg, Paul, & Lord, 2005). Matters are complicated by the fact that symptomatology is overlapping. The pragmatic deficits observed in PLI may be indistinguishable from those of high-functioning autism (HFA). Common features of language impairment, such as grammatical impairments and limitations in vocabulary have been found in SLI and HFA, even when well-defined criteria for diagnostic group inclusion are met (Kjelgaard & Tager-Flusberg, 2001; Leyfer et al., 2008).

The term *PLI* is likely to be replaced by Social Communication Disorder. The development of revised guidelines in the *DSM-5* (APA, 2013) has created a new category of Social Communication Disorder (SCD) in the Neurodevelopmental Disorders/Language Impairment pathway. In this formal diagnostic terminology, SCD is distinguished from Autism Spectrum Disorder (ASD) and SLI.

DIAGNOSTIC CRITERIA FOR SCD IN *DSM-5*

In *DSM-5*, the following are given as diagnostic criteria for SCD:

- Persistent pragmatic difficulties which affect social function.
- Persistent language difficulties which may affect comprehension and expression.
- Absence of ASD (absence of restricted, repetitive patterns of behaviour).
- Evidence from early childhood.

The adoption of a categorical diagnostic label (SCD) to replace PLI may be welcomed in terms of referral for services. The label has an advantage in that it implies, correctly, that the communication impairment has social consequences. Research has shown, however, that there is a closer relationship with ASD than *DSM-5* suggests and that there may be relatively mild, but significant social issues which impact the child who has SCD (Gibson, Adams, Lockton, & Green, 2013; Whitehouse, Watt, Line, & Bishop, 2009) which could be overlooked in a non-autism diagnosis.

CURRENT INCIDENCE/PREVALENCE ESTIMATES

Although there is anecdotal information that speech-language pathologists are being asked to provide services for more children who have pragmatic language impairments, precise incidence and prevalence estimates are not available. There are two reasons for this: (a) PLI is not widely recognized as a diagnostic category, and (b) recognition of the condition is likely to be delayed until the child's language profile can show clear signs of pragmatic impairment, and this may not be until after 4 years of age.

There are some relevant statistics, however, which shed some light on the possible prevalence of PLI. Because PLI is a condition that is related to both HFA and SLI, it is likely that the current populations of children identified with these conditions contain a, relatively small, proportion of children who have PLI. The incidence of SLI has been shown to be around 7% (Tomblin et al., 1997), and about 60% of children identified with SLI will go on to have language difficulties well into their elementary school years (Stothard, Snowling, Bishop, Chipchase, & Kaplan, 1998). In a study of provision of special education in the UK for children with persistent SLI, Botting and Conti-Ramsden (1999) found that of this group, nearly a quarter could be described as having PLI. Autism has a slightly lower prevalence than SLI (Yeargin-Allsopp et al., 2003). It could be proposed that PLI might be most likely associated with the autism spectrum condition, Pervasive Developmental Disorder (PDD), because this represents a less severe form of autistic spectrum disorder. The incidence of PDD has been estimated to be as high as 60/10,000 (0.6%) (Fombonne, 2003). PLI is therefore a significant but rarer type of language disorder than is SLI.

General population studies provide another route to estimation of the prevalence of pragmatic language difficulties, but at present there is only one study which has a sufficiently well-constructed observational measure and a contemporary approach to the diagnosis of PLI. This is the work of Ketelaars, Cuperus, van Daal, Jansonius, and Verhoeven (2010) in which parents from a community sample of 1,396 preschool children (mean age 56 months) completed the Children's Communication Checklist-2 (Bishop, 2003), an assessment of communication from which a pragmatic composite score is computed (see the Assessment section). Ketelaars et al., using a specific recommended cut off for PLI, were able to identify 7.5% of the population as having significant pragmatic difficulties in comparison to their overall communication scores. Several of these children went on to have clinical diagnoses of autism and language deficits. Using the same measures, Ketelaars et al. found that 32.7% of children in an SLI group had identifiable pragmatic impairments. However, it is not known if these would meet criteria for PLI or were secondary to a broader communication disorder (see the Definitions and Labels section).

It is difficult to draw any precise conclusions about the prevalence or incidence of PLI. Studies have drawn on different populations and with different methods and measures. Definitions of PLI are not sufficiently well developed and validated to allow precise identification of the condition, and it is likely that all of the studies so far are describing children with a range of diagnosed conditions who also have pragmatic difficulties. Definitive information will have to wait for better delineations of the nature of pragmatic difficulties.

THE NATURE OF PRAGMATIC LANGUAGE IMPAIRMENT

The nature of the communication disorder in children with PLI has three main components: pragmatic deficits, structural language deficits and social interaction deficits. Although children will show some deficits in all three components, they may vary independently in severity so that individual communication profiles may diverge within the group. Children with PLI rarely demonstrate all of the behaviors listed in the following, and heterogeneity should be anticipated.

Pragmatic Deficits

Pragmatics is a domain of linguistics that defines how language form is adapted and used to convey meaning in social situations. Pragmatic behaviors are typically exhibited in social situations and in discourse at above-sentence level, for example in conversations, in casual verbal exchanges between interlocutors and in accounts of events or narratives. Children who have PLI may present difficulty with all these verbal exchanges, and the normal smooth flow of conversation/interactions is disrupted.

The main pragmatic characteristics of children with PLI are set out below and based on accounts from Bishop and Adams (1989) and Adams (2001, 2013):

- Turn-taking difficulties: The child is unable to judge when turn-taking signals are being provided by the interlocutor and/or is unable to provide those signals, and consequently, there is over-talking (verbal overlaps and clashes) in the interaction.
- Lack of responsivity to interlocutor: The child does not respond to a verbal invitation or direct question, and the typical sequence of exchange of speech acts is disrupted.
- Poor coherence/cohesion of events in discourse: The child provides accounts of events or descriptions that are difficult to

understand as ideas are illogically sequenced or not adequately related to each other.

- Tendency to dominate discourse or conversation: The child talks more often than would be expected in a social situation. This is more than chattiness; there is a compulsion to talk.
- Misjudging required information: The child provides too much information for the interlocutor (related to conversational dominance), and the important information is lost in the detail. He or she will appear pedantic to the observer. The child may also provide too little information, so that the interlocutor is not sure what is being talked about.
- Topic management problems: The child does not follow the expected conventions which govern the way in which topic (what is being talked about) is handled in conversation/discourse. Children with PLI may show sudden topic shifts or drift into an unrelated topic.
- Initiations of exchanges: The child with PLI may initiate conversational exchanges more frequently than expected by making many unsolicited statements or by asking many questions. However, some children with PLI can do just the opposite—they appear to be relatively passive and make very few initiations.
- Paralinguistic behaviors such as abnormalities of intonation similar to those seen in HFA (Peppé, McCann, Gibbon, O'Hare, & Rutherford, 2006), and stereotyped language/learned phrases (Bishop & Adams, 1989) may also be present and have significant impact on overall pragmatic profiles.

Structural Language Deficits

Children who have PLI and who have passed the preschool years demonstrate a range of difficulties in acquiring language forms. Again this is highly variable, with some children having significant and severe language impairment and others presenting as relatively verbally fluent and able. The range of language impairment characteristics in PLI is as follows:

- Difficulties with sentence grammar and lexical semantics: Children with PLI frequently show persistent minor errors of syntax (Bishop & Adams, 1989). However, structural language impairments are variable throughout this group (Adams et al., 2012) and that where they do occur they tend to be less marked than those found in typical SLI (Freed, Adams, & Lockton, 2011). Word finding and semantic difficulties (Adams, 2001), particularly with abstract words (Botting & Adams, 2005) have also been reported (Ketelaars, Hermans, Cuperus, Jansonius, & Verhoeven, 2011).

- Discourse comprehension problems: For a child with these issues, he or she is unable to follow the complex language forms appearing in real time. From a pragmatic perspective, the child who does not understand often dissembles or makes up an unrelated response (McTear, 1985), which can appear pragmatically odd.
- Difficulty interpreting non-literal language: In a highly idiomatic language such as English, the child with PLI may have difficulty in understanding language forms such as idioms, metaphors, jokes and sarcasm. Children with SLI also have problems with these forms (Vance & Wells, 1994) and there is no evidence that children with PLI are disproportionately poor at interpreting this sort of language processing.
- Difficulty in making inferences: The child with PLI typically shows limited ability to make appropriate inferences, particularly in naturalistic discourse, and may therefore misinterpret meanings. There is mixed evidence of disproportionate impairment of inferential comprehension in children with PLI (Adams, Clarke, & Haynes, 2009; Norbury & Bishop, 2002).
- Misinterpretation of meanings in context: Children with PLI or SLI have difficulty in disambiguating homonyms and may not be able to identify the correct meaning of the word. Accounts of homonym misinterpretation (Bishop, 2000), as for inference comprehension, in PLI are largely anecdotal and there is no evidence of a specific deficit in PLI compared to SLI (Norbury, 2005).
- Narrative disorganization: The child shows disorganized narratives (stories, accounts of recent events) resulting in unintelligible discourse and listener confusion (Adams, 2001).

Social Interaction Deficits

Bishop (2000) refers to the social interaction deficits in children with PLI as being mild in nature and insufficient to indicate autism spectrum disorder and this is reflected in clinical descriptive accounts in the literature (Adams, 2001). Group studies of children with PLI have indicated poor peer social interaction ratings (Botting & Conti-Ramsden, 1999) and limitations of social cognition compared to children with SLI (Shields, Varley, Broks, & Simpson, 1996). Empirical observational research by Gibson et al. (2013) has shown that a well-defined group of children with PLI displayed some difficulties with social interaction (as observed on the school playground) but that these were less severe than children with HFA. Broader social communication features in children with PLI such as limited use of gesture to supplement communication and gaze aversion suggestive of ASD traits have been reported (Bishop, Chan, Adams, Hartley, & Weir, 2000). Children with PLI therefore are typically at risk of mild social interaction and social relationship difficulties. It is likely that this will be reflected in limited friendships and consequently restricted opportunities to develop social interaction skills in the typical contexts of childhood.

Associated Developmental Difficulties in PLI

Behavioral difficulty is a common correlate of language impairment. Research has shown that in children with SLI, pragmatic abilities are associated with behavioral and emotional difficulties in development (St. Clair, Pickles, Durkin, & Conti-Ramsden, 2011). There is increasing evidence of a link between social communication difficulties in early life and later behavioral difficulties (Donno, Parker, Gilmour, & Skuse, 2010; St. Pourcain et al., 2011; see Chapter 11). Ketelaars, Cuperus, Jansonius, and Verhoeven (2010) found that behavioral problems are closely associated with pragmatic competence in a community sample. The same research showed that children with PLI frequently show externalizing behavioral problems, particularly hyperactivity and limited prosocial behaviors. A qualitative study Baxendale, Lockton, Gaile, and Adams (2013) provided accounts of family difficulties and problems in friendships for children with PLI. This is an area where more research is required since the implications for social integration and well-being as well as intervention are significant.

Children with PLI are likely to show additional learning needs often associated with children with SLI, including difficulties with reading comprehension and accuracy (Freed et al., 2011). Long-term outcomes for individuals who have PLI reveal a specific difficulty in forming adult relationships in later life (similar to that in ASD) and some persistent difficulties with social use of language. However, adults with a PLI history have relatively normal literacy and structural language skills, fewer autism symptoms than comparable ASD individuals, and better work skills outcomes than adults with a history of SLI (Whitehouse et al., 2009).

REFERRAL PRACTICES AND ASSESSMENT METHODS

Although there are no retrospective studies of early language history, clinical accounts suggest that children with PLI show late emergence of language, including receptive language delay (sometimes severe) and an early history of mild autistic features (such as echolalia) with impaired social relationships (Adams, 2001). Since the full profile of PLI tends to emerge as grammatical and vocabulary development progresses, recognition of the condition may not happen until after age 4.

Referral should be made to a speech-language pathologist for expert assessment of communication skills. Referral to a child medical practitioner (pediatrician) for an overall developmental assessment and/or child psychiatrist for assessment of autism characteristics and diagnosis/exclusion of autism spectrum disorder should also be made. Because children with PLI often have additional learning needs with literacy, careful monitoring of reading, writing, spelling, and numeracy must be ensured within the education system.

Principles of Assessment

Assessment of the communication of the child with PLI is an expert and specialist undertaking. Speech-language practitioners' evaluation of the communication features of pragmatic language impairment should be based on six key principles:

- Assessment should be comprehensive enough to adequately evaluate language skills, pragmatic ability, and social interaction during communication.
- Evaluation must be individualized, because PLI is variable in presentation; this will allow scrutiny of characteristics of the individual which may be targeted in intervention.
- Evaluation should be carried out as part of multidisciplinary teamwork to ensure that appropriate ASD diagnostic practice and expert language assessment information are available for overall identification of strengths and needs.
- A mixture of contexts should be used during assessment. The context of assessment is crucial; children with PLI tend to do better with structured contexts so a mixture of formal, informal and naturalistic contexts is essential. Expert assessment should be extended to non-clinical contexts (home, classroom, and playground) to obtain a representative profile of social interactions.
- Carers' and teachers' accounts of communication and social functioning should be actively elicited. The people who live and work with the child on an everyday basis will be the source of key information that will not be accessible in clinical evaluation. Evaluation should include interviews with carers and teachers

to gain additional information about the impact of communication deficit on daily life and peer relationships.

Language Assessment

The speech-language practitioner should use standardized tests to identify the language competency of children with PLI. Although many tests are available, an indicative list of tests suitable for this purpose is:

- Clinical Evaluation of Language Fundamentals (CELF-4; Semel, Wiig, & Secord, 2006a): includes subtests of Concepts and Following Directions, Formulated sentences, Understanding paragraphs, and Word classes.
- Test of Word Finding (German, 2000) and Test of Word Knowledge (Wiig & Secord, 1992): subtests include definitions, multiple-meaning words (homonyms), figurative language and receptive and expressive vocabulary.
- Test of Language Competence (Wiig & Secord, 1989): subtests include Making Inferences, Re-creating Speech Acts and Figurative Language.
- Expressive Receptive Recall of Narrative Instrument (ERRNI; Bishop, 2004): a test that requires the child to tell a story from a set of pictures, to recall the story content without the pictures and to answer questions designed to tap into overall inferential comprehension.
- Assessment of Comprehension and Expression (ACE; Adams, Cooke, Crutchley, Hesketh, & Reeves, 2001): contains subtests of Narrative, Non-Literal Comprehension and Inferential Comprehension.

The speech-language practitioner may supplement formal testing of language with informal procedures such as observation of narrative constriction and understanding of inference in stories. Many tasks fall within this category, and these are likely to vary according to local practice and experience. Two tasks which have been used in research with children who have PLI are (a) the Strong Narrative Assessment Procedure (SNAP; Strong, 1998): this elicits narratives using picture materials and provides a method of analysis of narratives; and (b) the Happé Strange Stories (Happé, 1994): a series of short stories which aim to tap into comprehension of and explanations for use of non-literal forms of language including jokes and sarcasm. O'Hare, Bremner, Happé and Pettigrew (2009) published norms and means for 5- to 12-year-olds for short version of the Happé Strange Stories task. However, Young, Diehl,

Morris, Hyman, and Bennetto (2005) found that SNAP did not identify any unique characteristics of narrative in children with PLI.

Pragmatics Assessment

Preschool assessments may include parent/carer report of communication skills or direct observation. In Wetherby and Prizant's (2002) Communication and Symbolic Behavior Scales–Developmental Profile (CSBS-DP), observation of pragmatics were carried out from recordings using a simple checklist of communicative behaviors, including use of voice to communicate, affective signaling and communicative gestures. The Clinical Evaluation of Language Fundamentals–Preschool, second edition (Semel, Wiig, & Secord, 2006b), contains a Pragmatics Profile section which enables the practitioner to describe language use; however, this is not standardized. The Language Use Inventory (LUI; O'Neill, 2007) is a checklist, completed by parents/carers, recording the child's uses of language and gesture to communicate intention. It also includes items related to understanding of others' knowledge. The LUI is not standardized but has good internal consistency and discriminant validity and therefore stands out in the preschool field as a well-developed and evaluated scale. Other informal methods such as the Peanut Butter Protocol (Carpenter & Strong, 1988; Creaghead, 1984) provide a means of eliciting communicative intent. In this task the child is tempted to use a sequence of communicative intents by the provision of given situation prompts, such as a jar of cookies that is difficult to open. Similar elicitation and suggestions for informal tasks are provided by Roth and Spekman (1984). A more comprehensive review of pragmatic assessment for early language learners is provided by Paul and Norbury (2012).

Preschool assessment methods are unlikely to evaluate the more complex pragmatic features of PLI reported above. Adams and Lloyd (2005), for example, used a modified version of the Peanut Butter Protocol with a group of elementary school-age children with PLI but found that they could complete this task easily; that is they were able to demonstrate the full range of communicative intents elicited via this procedure and did not differ from typically developing children.

Pragmatic assessments for school-age children are available in the form of pragmatic behavior checklists, teacher and parent/carer report forms and standardized tests. The earliest observational checklist was the Pragmatic Protocol (Prutting & Kirchner, 1987) which is suitable for children 4 years and older who have substantive expressive language skills. The protocol allows the practitioner to profile aspects of language and communication (including pragmatics) as appropriately or inappropriately used. Examples of communicative acts included in the protocol are Utterance acts (e.g., intelligibility and prosody), Propositional acts (e.g., specificity and accuracy of lexical selection), illocutionary and perlocutionary acts (e.g., speech act pair analysis, topic introduction and maintenance) and turn taking. The Pragmatic Protocol has considerable merit as a checklist but it has not been validated and it contains ratings of non-pragmatic variables such as prosody. The CELF-4 (Semel et al., 2006a) also contains a Pragmatic Profile appropriate for older children. This is a criterion-referenced assessment consisting of a checklist of pragmatic features to be completed by the speech-language practitioner, the teacher or a parent/carer. Scores are allocated on frequency of occurrence of listed pragmatic behaviors, and totaled scores provide an indication of performance compared to children who have typical language development. This is one of the few assessments to offer some norm-comparative information. Other pragmatic checklists are available that can function as observational guides, but these have not been validated and their reliability is currently unknown.

In language testing, context and mode of delivery are typically strictly controlled. The nature of pragmatics as a set of rich descriptions of the use of language in naturalistic contexts does not lend itself well to this controlled paradigm. Consequently, formal tests of pragmatics are rare. Some aspects of pragmatics and supporting language skills are addressed in the Test of Pragmatic Language–2 (Phelps-Teraski & Phelps-Gunn, 2007). This assessment contains a comprehensive set of picture stimuli accompanied by short texts/stories to which the child is asked to respond. Items are designed to tap into various aspects of pragmatic and emotional/social understanding. This test has the advantage of having a set of standardized norms from 6 years 0 months to 18 years 11 months. Its potential to identify pragmatic language impairment is compromised by its heavy reliance on complex language input, and it has been shown to be less reliable than other standardized instruments (e.g., CCC-2; see the following discussion) at identifying pragmatic language impairment (Volden & Philips, 2010). The Social Language Development Test: Elementary (Bowers, Huisingh, & LoGiudice, 2008) has similar elements to the Test of Pragmatic Language, but uses a method in which children's responses to portrayed peer interactions are elicited. Aspects of pragmatics which are included are multiple interpretations of social episodes, negotiation with peers and inference of emotions in context. The Social Language Development Test is aimed at 6- to 11-year-olds and has satisfactory test–retest reliability and good internal consistency.

There have been a number of attempts to develop a clinically relevant and manageable observation scale for pragmatics or social communication in childhood. The most recent of these is the Social Communication Coding System (Olswang, Coggins, & Svensson, 2007) that codes social communication behaviors (such as passivity, prosocial behavior) in a classroom setting. Whereas this is not a pure pragmatics assessment, it enables the practitioner to take into account the broader social interaction abilities of children with PLI. The scale has also been subjected to satisfactory validity and reliability testing (Olswang, Svensson, Coggins, Beilinson, & Donaldson, 2006) and has good concurrent validity with parent/teacher report (Olswang, Svensson, & Astley, 2010).

Evaluation and Differential Diagnosis of PLI

The current best practice in identifying the presence of PLI can be obtained using the Children's Communication Checklist–2 (CCC-2; Bishop, 2003). On the CCC-2, a parent, a carer or a familiar adult rates the frequency of occurrence of a range of structural language, pragmatic and autistic-like communication behaviors in the child. Two summary scores are then derived: a General Communication Composite that indicates the presence of communication impairment and a Social Interaction Deviance Composite that can indicate the presence of a disproportionate pragmatic impairment. The CCC-2 is well validated although there are some accepted limitations on its diagnostic accuracy (Norbury, Nash, Baird, & Bishop, 2004) and some risk of inconsistent parent reports (Geurts & Embrechts, 2008). In further research, Geurts and Embrechts (2010) studied the convergent validity of the CCC-2 and the Nijmegen Pragmatics Test, a direct observational measure in children with language impairment and typical development. Some convergence of scores/observations between the two tests was found, but there is still a need for caution in using a single measure to identify the presence of PLI.

Diagnostic criteria that distinguish children with PLI from other conditions are as follows (note that these require further validation research). PLI is differentiated from SLI by consideration of disproportionality of the impairment of pragmatics compared to the impairment in structural aspects of language such as grammar, vocabulary, and phonology. The Social Interaction Deviance Composite (SIDC) score of the CCC-2 can indicate the likely presence of PLI, but should not be used in isolation, as there is no precise cut-off between SLI and PLI. Children with severe receptive language impairments, for example, can present odd pragmatic behaviors (likely to be reported as frequent behaviors by parents on CCC-2) that are compensatory strategies to remain engaged in interaction. It is necessary therefore, to inspect carefully high-rated items on CCC-2's Pragmatic Composite scale. The best diagnostic practice is to combine use of the CCC-2 SIDC with high-level language assessment findings and specialist speech-language practitioner opinion.

Intellectual impairment is distinguished from PLI using a non-verbal IQ cut-off. Individuals who have a PLI have non-verbal IQ scores greater than 70; individuals with an intellectual impairment have non-verbal IQ scores that are less than 70. This is identical to the IQ cut-off used for SLI diagnosis. Narrower definitions of SLI use a nonverbal score cut-off that is greater than 85. In clinical practice, children with PLI with a non-verbal IQ in the range of 70 to 85 are likely to present with a similar profile of language impairment as children with PLI who have non-verbal IQ greater than 85.

It has been proposed that SCD/PLI can be differentiated in diagnosis from ASD, because SCD/PLI do not demonstrate the repetitive behaviors and restricted interests dimension of ASD. However, this evaluation is usually outside the scope of practice of the speech-language practitioner. Diagnosis of autism spectrum disorder should be carried out by a qualified practitioner (pediatrician/psychiatrist). Information about language impairment status would not invalidate a diagnosis of ASD – the two co-occur frequently. However, the absence of an ASD diagnosis in the presence of a significant impairment in pragmatics would be indicative of SCD according to the *DSM-5*.

CASE HISTORY: ASSESSMENT

Lucas was referred to the intervention research project by his local speech-language pathologist. She described him as having trouble understanding and interpreting social contexts and non-verbal communication and as having a significant pragmatic difficulty and some difficulty with non-literal language. A summary of formal assessment findings is shown in Table 6.1.

Lucas's conversational skills were then assessed using an experimental checklist of pragmatic features (Targeted Observation of Pragmatics in Children's Conversation [TOPICC]; Adams, Lockton, Gaile, & Freed, 2011). On this assessment he was observed to have difficulty with management of topic, responsiveness to the interlocutor and with making accurate judgements of listener knowledge (for the purpose of outcome interpretation, his score on TOPICC was overall severity score = 17. Lower scores indicate improvement). Lucas's parents completed the

Table 6.1 Assessment Summary for Lucas at the Pre-Intervention Stage

Test	Findings
CELF-4 (UK version)	Core language standard score = 66 Expressive language standard score = 69 Receptive language standard score = 61
Expressive Receptive Recall of Narrative Instrument (Bishop, 2004)	Story comprehension = 2nd centile Initial story telling = 1st centile
British Picture Vocabulary Test (Dunn, Dunn, & Whetton, 1997)	Receptive vocabulary = 22nd centile
Children's Test of Non-Word Repetition (Gathercole & Baddeley, 1996)	Below the 10th centile
Children's Communication Checklist-2 (parent report; Bishop, 2003)	General Communication composite = 28 (indicates communication impairment) Social Interaction Deviance Composite = 5 (indicative of disproportionate pragmatic impairment)

Social Communication Questionnaire (Rutter, Bailey, & Lord, 2003). The total score on this assessment indicated that Lucas may fall into the Pervasive Developmental Disorder category, but this would need to be confirmed with more detailed investigation of social functioning. In addition, opinions and observations regarding Lucas's current social communication, social interaction ability, peer relations, and language ability were solicited from his parents and his class teacher.

EVIDENCE-BASED INTERVENTION PRACTICES FOR SOCIAL COMMUNICATION PROBLEMS ACROSS THE LIFE SPAN

The standard Cochrane systematic review of language and communication disorders treatments (Law, Garrett, & Nye, 2003, 2010) contains no eligible studies of pragmatic interventions. Gerber, Brice, Capone, Fujiki and Timler (2012), in a further systematic review, examined the quantity and levels of available evidence for the effects of conversational and/or pragmatics treatments for children with pragmatic language difficulties. The review found insufficient quantity or type of evidence available to carry out a meta-analysis. Most studies found were small-scale or exploratory and the stated contents of intervention or goals varied across studies, making even narrative comparison difficult.

The only randomized controlled trial for older children with PLI is that of Adams et al. (2012) which was published after Gerber et al.'s review. There are no published clinical guidelines based on empirical research. At a lower level of evidence, single case studies and case series have universally indicated that children with PLI can make progress in social communication and language skills, given the right support (Adams, Lloyd, Aldred, & Baxendale, 2006; Merrison & Merrison, 2005; Timler, Olswang, & Coggins, 2005a).

Choice of social communication intervention will depend on the age and communication status of the child. Consideration is first given to intervention models in the preschool period.

Preschool Intervention Approaches

Preschool speech-language treatments are likely to be aimed at encouraging use of language and establishing skills that underpin social interaction and language comprehension. This would typically take the form of advice and training of parents and carers. The intervention model of choice is likely to be the *developmental–social model*, in which facilitation of social interaction via verbal and non-verbal means is encouraged through a child-centred approach. This model has many variants and has been widely reported; for example versions of the developmental-social model are the Hanen method (Manolson, 1992), responsive interaction (Kaiser, Hancock, & Hester, 1998), and the child-oriented approach advocated by Fey (1986). The central tenet of the developmental–social model and all its variants is the facilitation of social interaction and appropriate communicative intents. A review of relevant methods and their effectiveness can be found in Roberts and Kaiser (2011). Specific examples of early developmental–social interventions are reported in robust clinical trials.

Because PLI is not typically diagnosed in the early preschool years, evidence of intervention effects are best extrapolated from trials of toddlers with ASD. Two robust clinical trials of developmental–social interventions for toddlers with autism have demonstrated evidence of positive treatment effects on parental communication synchrony (Green et al., 2010) and joint engagement (Kasari, Gulsrud, Wong, Kwon, & Locke, 2010). Further consideration of these interventions is provided in Fannin and Watson's chapter in this volume.

Elementary School-Age Interventions

The two principle models supporting direct individual intervention during the school years are those of Brinton and Fujiki (1995) and Adams (2005, 2008). Brinton and Fujiki's social communication intervention focuses on the facilitation of conversational interaction with children with a range of language impairments, including SLI. Pragmatic competence is viewed as part of an integrated model in which language expression and comprehension skills contribute to social communication and to social interaction which, in turn, contribute to peer interactions, friendships, and social well-being (Brinton, Fujiki, & Robinson, 2005). The overall aims in this model are primarily ones of social integration and self-esteem, mediated through specific language-based pragmatic targets, such as taking turns in a conversation (Fujiki, 2009). Brinton, Robinson, and Fujiki (2004) described an intensive conversational program, entitled *The Conversation Game*, for children who have language impairments. Further information on these approaches can be found in Chapter 8 in this volume.

Adams's Social Communication Intervention Programme (SCIP) is based on a model of social communication in which competencies in social interaction/understanding and language ability interact during early development. From this process emerges pragmatic competence. That is pragmatics is viewed as an emergent phenomenon in a dynamic system (Karmiloff-Smith, 1998) rather than an isolated linguistic skill. The SCIP model of intervention therefore contains therapy goals in three main components:

- language processing (receptive and expressive high-level language);
- pragmatics and metapragmatics;
- language-mediated social understanding and social interpretation.

The SCIP therapy resource (Adams & Gaile, 2014) is organized into these key components of intervention, each containing a large number of therapy goals and activities (e.g., basic narrative skills, topic management, interpreting social context cues). SCIP Intervention was developed for children aged between 6 and 11 years of age. It can be adapted to provide appropriate materials for a wide range of children's social communication and language needs and for children who have high-functioning ASD or for older children with language impairments.

SCIP Intervention adheres to the same principles of integration of language and social communication goals as Brinton's and Fujiki's. It provides a phased method of intervention. In Phase 1 children are prepared for social communication practice via work on underpinning communication skills, such as comprehension monitoring and metapragmatic knowledge. In Phase 2, individual social communication, pragmatic, and language needs are mapped to individual needs and the child participates in therapeutic activities with the practitioner and co-workers/parents. In the final stage of SCIP Intervention, each child participates with carers, buddies and teaching staff in a set of personalized therapy activities that extend work done in Phase 2 beyond the treatment context. Both Adams's (2008) and Fujiki and Brinton's (1995) models underline the importance of the level of language input, the use of 'meta' language in therapy and the essential use of functional contexts to support social learning. SCIP Intervention uses a series of intervention principles, which underpin all management decisions (shown in Table 6.2).

The effectiveness of SCIP intervention was examined in a randomized controlled trial (Adams et al., 2012). Eighty-six children with PLI (aged between 6 and 11 years) were allocated randomly to SCIP versus Treatment as Usual groups. Children in the intervention group received 20 individual therapy sessions in school from a specialist research speech and language therapist or a closely supervised therapy assistant. Evidence in favour of the intervention was found in measures of parent-/carer-rated pragmatic competence, blind-rated change in conversational skills, parent/carer opinion of post-treatment change in social communication and language skills and teacher opinions of post-treatment change in classroom learning skills.

Table 6.2 Principles of Intervention in SCIP Intervention

Principle	Description
Adaptation	Develop, adopt, and practice communication strategies which are less disruptive to social interaction
Language support	Strengthen some aspects of language processing by structured practice and building confidence and fluency in language tasks
Environment modification	Modify the language environment to support interpretation of language in social interactions
Metapragmatic learning	Facilitate pragmatic conventions using metacognitive methods appropriate for school-age children
Generalization to socially meaningful contexts	Incorporate individual social needs/situations into language and pragmatic therapy

Evidence from other researchers exists primarily at the level of single case-studies. Timler, Olswang, and Coggins (2005a) evaluated a social communication intervention in which a child was supported to appraise social communication situations from various perspectives, including those of peers. Stages of the intervention are presented but this approach has not been trialled to date with a clinical population.

Social Skills Training (SST) refers to a set of approaches that aim to teach specific social behaviors as a means of enhancing interaction. Social skills training programs typically consist of a series of programed activities that are often carried out in a group context (Segrin & Givertz, 2003) and are founded on learning and behavioristic treatment principles. SSTs have the advantage of being relatively simple to implement and not requiring specialist knowledge. The disadvantage of SST in relation to PLI is that there is no specific support for language processing in the form of language scaffolding. Although there is some evidence of social skills gains in some populations because of SST (Matson, Matson, & Rivet, 2007; Reichow & Volkmar, 2010) evidence of generalization of learned skills is weak. The meta-analysis by Koenig, De Los Reyes, Cicchetti, Scahill, and Klin (2009) of SST evidence concluded that methodological limitations and problems of generalization existed in most SST effectiveness studies.

Classroom, Group, and Peer Interventions

Evidence of intervention effects for classroom treatments exist at the level of the single case study only. Timler, Olswang and Coggins (2005b) devised a social communication intervention which incorporated classroom peers into social communication therapy for a child with social communication difficulties. Peers were found to facilitate communication targets and support generalization. Timler and Vogler-Elias (2007) presented a single case study of a child with social communication needs in which a range of people in the child's school, including the clinician, the teacher and peers, mediated the communication training. This study also provides practical guidelines on classroom-based intervention. Expert opinion (Adams & Gaile, 2014) recommends the use of buddies or peers in SCIP intervention, both for reasons of generalization and to provide age- and culture-appropriate models of talk.

Parent Programs

There are no programs of intervention for older children with PLI that are specifically written for parents. Both Fujiki (2009) and Adams and Gaile (2014) stress the important role of the parent or carer in both planning and carrying out social communication intervention. The parent or carer's role in mediating everyday social communication situations which are problematic, place him or her in an ideal position to monitor the implementation of strategies learned in therapy and to reflect on progress made. Baxendale et al. (2013) found that parents/carers involved in the SCIP trial valued being provided with information about ongoing therapy and used this information to adopt communication strategies at home.

Overall, evidence relating to intervention for children who have PLI is indicative of positive effects. Case series and prospective case studies of conversational treatments have suggested potential efficacy of speech-language treatments. A single robust trial of a specialist pragmatic/language intervention has suggested positive outcomes for social communication. There remain many questions still remaining regarding individuals' response to intervention and issues of intensity and who can best deliver therapy.

CASE STUDY: TREATMENT AND OUTCOMES

At the end of assessment, Lucas entered the treatment arm of the Social Communication Intervention Project (Adams et al., 2012). During the intervention process, Lucas took part in 20 face-to face individual intervention sessions with the speech-language practitioner. Lucas's parents attended some treatment sessions, and his support assistant attended more than half of the sessions. A buddy from Lucas's class joined in later sessions in order to provide relevant social context and models in the intervention. Intervention components in Lucas's Phase 2 SCIP Intervention (Individualized phase) are shown in Table 6.3.

Table 6.3 Content of the Individualized Phase of SCIP Intervention for Lucas

Components of SCIP Intervention		
Language Processing	Pragmatics	Social Understanding/ Social Interpretation
Vocabulary and Word Knowledge	Conversation and metapragmatic skills (including requests for clarification)	Understanding social context cues in interactions
Improving Narrative Construction	Understanding information requirements	Understanding emotion cues in interactions
Enhanced Comprehension Monitoring	Understanding and managing topic in conversation	Understanding thoughts and intentions of others

Lucas was reassessed 6 months after the end of intervention, using raters blind to intervention versus control group status when possible. His parents and teacher reported that, whereas he still had significant communication problems, they had seen great improvement in listening, narrative, confidence in communication skills, and in conversation abilities: "We can actually have a conversation with him at the end of the school day now." Lucas's teacher reported noticing a significant change in his participation in classroom discussions and in attention paid to group instructions. Conversational ability was reassessed by an independent researcher blind to the fact that Lucas had received intervention. TOPICC overall score had decreased from 17 to 12 with significant improvements observed in responsiveness and decreased conversational dominance. Narrative ability (ERRNI) had improved slightly, but his Clinical Evaluation of Language Fundamentals–Revised (CELF-R; Semel, Wiig, & Secord, 1989) scores remained static. Lucas remained a child with a severe, persistent communication problem, but there had been significant gains according to those who know him best.

DISCUSSION QUESTIONS

1. What might be the relationship between pragmatic language impairment and high-functioning autism?
2. Does the category of Social Communication Disorder in *DSM-5* clarify the diagnostic issues described in this chapter?
3. What principle features do pragmatic language impairment and specific language impairment have in common, and why might this discussion be crucial to intervention planning?
4. What are the broader social consequences of pragmatic language impairment for the child and his family?
5. Describe a package of assessment for a 10-year-old child suspected of having pragmatic language impairment.
6. Describe an intervention program for the same child, showing how the current evidence base supports the choices made.
7. How could practitioners balance the need for individualized treatment for children who have pragmatic language impairment when resources are finite?
8. Describe some ways in which communication intervention can be personalized for the child with pragmatic language impairment.
9. Which measures of conversation, pragmatics, and language could be employed as appropriate outcome measures at the single case level?

CLINICAL RESOURCES

Description of Conditions

Social Language Use and Pragmatics (ASHA): www.asha.org/public/speech/development/pragmatics.htm
What Is Pragmatic Language Impairment?: www.slideshare.net/RALLICampaign/what-is-pli
www.asha.org/slp/PragLangDis/

Examples of Therapy Resources

Black Sheep Press: Talkabout Friends, Talkabout School, Practical Pragmatics: www.blacksheeppress.com
Fun Decks: Emotions, Multiple Meanings: www.superduperinc.com
Introducing Inference (M. Toomey): www.taskmasteronline.co.uk
Schubi Picture Sequences: Tell It, Sentimage, Combimage: www.winslow-cat.com
Talkabout Activities: Developing Social Communication Skills (A. Kelly): www.speech-therapy.org
Think It Say It pictures: www.proedinc.com

REFERENCES

Adams, C. (2001). Clinical diagnostic studies of children with semantic-pragmatic language disorder. *International Journal of Language and Communication Disorders, 36,* 289–306.

Adams, C. (2005). Social Communication Intervention: Rationale and description. *Seminars in Speech and Language, 26,* 181–189.

Adams, C. (2008). Intervention for children with pragmatic language impairments: Frameworks, evidence and diversity. In C. F. Norbury, J. B. Tomblin, & D. V. M. Bishop (Eds.), *Understanding developmental language disorders: From theory to practice* (pp. 189–204). London, UK: Psychology Press.

Adams, C. (2013). Pragmatic language impairment. In F. R. Volkmar (Ed.), *Handbook of autism* (p. 3429). New York, NY: Springer. Retrieved from www.springer.com

Adams, C., Clarke, E., & Haynes, R. (2009). Inference and sentence comprehension in children with specific or pragmatic language impairments. *International Journal of Language and Communication Disorders, 44,* 30–318.

Adams, C., Cooke, R., Crutchley, A., Hesketh, A., & Reeves, D. (2001). *Assessment of Comprehension and Expression (6–11).* Windsor, UK: NFER-Nelson.

Adams, C., & Gaile, J. (2014). *Managing children's pragmatic and social communication needs in the early school years.* Cheshire, UK: Napier Hill Press.

Adams, C., & Lloyd, J. (2005). Elicited and spontaneous communicative functions and stability of conversational measures with children who have pragmatic language impairments. *International Journal of Language & Communication Disorders, 40*, 333–347.

Adams, C., Lloyd, J., Aldred, C., & Baxendale, J. (2006). Exploring the effects of communication intervention for developmental pragmatic language impairments: A signal-generation study. *International Journal of Language and Communication Disorders, 41*, 41–66.

Adams, C., Lockton, E., Gaile, J., & Freed, J. (2011, Spring). TOPICCAL applications: Assessment of children's conversation skills. *Speech and Language Therapy in Practice,* pp. 7–9.

Adams, C., Lockton, E., Gaile, J., Freed, J., Earl, G., McBean, K., . . . Law, J. (2012). The Social Communication Intervention Project: A randomised controlled trial of the effectiveness of speech and language therapy for school-age children who have pragmatic and social communication problems with or without autism spectrum disorder. *International Journal of Language and Communication Disorders, 47*(3), 233–244.

American Psychiatric Association. (2013). *Diagnostic and statistical manual of mental disorders: DSM-5* (5th ed.). Washington, DC: Author.

Baxendale, J., Lockton, E., Gaile, J., & Adams. C. (2013). Parent and teacher perceptions of participation and outcomes in an intensive communication intervention for children with pragmatic language impairment. *International Journal of Language and Communication Disorders, 48*, 41–53.

Bishop, D. V. M. (2000). Pragmatic language impairment: A correlate of SLI, a distinct subgroup, or part of the autistic continuum? In D. V. M. Bishop & L. B. Leonard (Eds.), *Speech and language impairments in children: Causes, characteristics, intervention and outcome* (pp. 99–113). Hove, UK: Psychology Press.

Bishop, D. V. M. (2003). *The Children's Communication Checklist–2.* London, UK: Harcourt Assessment.

Bishop, D. V. M. (2004). *Expression, reception and recall of narrative instrument.* London, UK: Harcourt Assessment.

Bishop, D.V.M., & Adams, C. (1989). Conversational characteristics of children with semantic-pragmatic disorder. II: What features lead to a judgement of inappropriacy? *British Journal of Disorders of Communication, 24*, 241–263.

Bishop, D. V. M., Chan, J., Adams, C., Hartley, J., & Weir, F. (2000). Conversational responsiveness in specific language impairment: Evidence of disproportionate pragmatic difficulties in a subset of children. *Development and Psychopathology, 12*, 177–199.

Bishop, D. V. M., & Norbury, C. F. (2002). Exploring the borderlands of autistic disorder and specific language impairment: A study using standardised diagnostic assessments. *Journal of Child Psychology and Psychiatry, 43*, 917–929.

Botting, N., & Adams, C. (2005). Semantic and inferencing abilities in children with communication disorders. *International Journal of Language & Communication Disorders, 40,* 49–66.

Botting, N., & Conti-Ramsden, G. (1999). Pragmatic language impairment without autism: The children in question. *Autism, 3,* 371–396.

Bowers, L., Huisingh, R., & LoGiudice, C. L. (2008). *Social Language Development Test: Elementary.* East Moline, IL: Linguisystems.

Brinton, B., & Fujiki, M. (1995). Conversational intervention for children with specific language impairment. In M. Fey, J. Windsor, & S. F. Warren (Eds.), *Language intervention: Preschool through the intermediate years* (pp. 183–211). Baltimore, MD: Brookes.

Brinton, B., Fujiki, M., & Robinson, L. (2005). Life on a tricycle: A case study of language impairment from 4 to 19. *Topics in Language Disorders, 25,* 338–352.

Brinton, B., Robinson, L., & Fujiki, M. (2004). Description of a program for social language intervention: "If you can have a conversation, you can have a relationship." *Language, Speech, and Hearing Services in Schools, 35,* 283–290.

Carpenter, A. E., & Strong, J. C. (1988). Pragmatic development in normal children: Assessment of a testing protocol. *NSSLHA Journal, 16,* 40–49.

Creaghead, N. (1984). Strategies for evaluating and targeting pragmatic behaviors in young children. *Seminars in Speech and Language, 5,* 241–252.

Donno, R., Parker, G., Gilmour, J., & Skuse, D. J. (2010). Social communication deficits in disruptive primary-school children. *British Journal of Psychiatry, 196,* 282–289.

Dunn, L. M., Dunn, L. M., & Whetton, C. W. (1997). *The British Picture Vocabulary Scale-2* (2nd ed.). Windsor, UK: NFER-Nelson.

Fey, M. (1986). *Language intervention with young children.* Boston, MA: Allyn & Bacon.

Fombonne, E. (2003). Epidemiological surveys of autism and other pervasive developmental disorders: An update. *Journal of Autism and Developmental Disorders, 33,* 365–382.

Freed, J., Adams, C., & Lockton, E. (2011). Literacy skills in primary school-aged children with pragmatic language impairment: A comparison with children with specific language impairment. *International Journal of Language & Communication Disorders, 46,* 334–347.

Fujiki, M. (2009). Pragmatics and social communication in child language disorders. In R. Schwartz (Ed.), *Handbook of child language disorders* (pp. 406–423). New York, NY: Psychology Press.

Gathercole, S. E., & Baddeley, A. D. (1996). *The Children's Test of Nonword Repetition.* New York, NY: Psychological Corporation.

Gerber, S., Brice, A., Capone, N., Fujiki, M., & Timler, G. (2012). Language use in social interactions of school-age children with language impairments: An evidence-based systematic review of treatment. *Language, Speech and Hearing Services in the Schools, 43,* 235–249.

German, D. (2000). *Test of Word Finding* (2nd ed.). San Antonio, TX: Psychological Corporation.

Green, J., Charman, T., McConachie, H., Aldred, C., Slonims, V., Howlin, P., & Pickles, A. (2010). Parent-mediated communication-focused treatment in children with autism (PACT): A randomised controlled trial. *The Lancet, 375*, 2152–2160.

Geurts, H. M., & Embrechts, M. (2008). Language profiles in ASD, SLI, and ADHD. *Journal of Autism and Developmental Disorders, 38*, 1931–1943.

Geurts, H. M., & Embrechts, M. (2010). Pragmatics in pre-schoolers with language impairment. *International Journal of Language and Communication Disorders, 45*, 436–447.

Gibson, J, Adams, C., Lockton, E., & Green, J. (2013). Social communication disorder outside autism? A diagnostic classification approach to delineating pragmatic language impairment, high functioning autism and specific language impairment. *Journal of Child Psychology and Psychiatry, 54*, 1186–1197.

Happé, F. (1994). An advanced test of theory of mind: Understanding of story characters' thoughts and feelings by able autistic, mentally handicapped, and normal children and adults. *Journal of Autism and Developmental Disorders, 24*, 129–153.

Kaiser, A. P., Hancock, T. B., & Hester, P. P. (1998). Parents as co-interventionists: Research on applications of naturalistic language teaching procedures. *Infants & Young Children, 10*, 46–55.

Karmiloff-Smith, A. (1998). Development itself is the key to understanding developmental disorders. *Trends in Cognitive Sciences, 2*, 389–398.

Kasari, C., Gulsrud, A. C., Wong, C., Kwon, S., & Locke, J. (2010). Randomized controlled caregiver mediated joint engagement intervention for toddlers with autism. *Journal of Autism and Developmental Disorders, 40*, 1045–1056.

Ketelaars, M. P., Cuperus, J., van Dall, J., Jansonius, K., & Verhoeven, L. (2010). Pragmatic language impairment and associated behavioural problems. *International Journal of Language & Communication Disorders, 45*, 204–214.

Ketelaars, M. P., Hermans, S. I. A., Cuperus, J., Jansonius, K., & Verhoeven, L. (2011). Semantic abilities in children with pragmatic language impairment: The case of picture naming skills. *Journal of Speech, Language and Hearing Research, 54*, 87–98.

Kjelgaard, M. M., & Tager-Flusberg, H. (2001). An investigation of language impairment in autism: Implications for genetic subgroups. *Language and Cognitive Processes, 16*, 287–308.

Koenig, K., De Los Reyes, A., Cicchetti, D., Scahill, L., & Klin, A. (2009). Group intervention to promote social skills in school-age children with pervasive developmental disorders: Reconsidering efficacy. *Journal of Autism and Developmental Disorders, 39*, 1163–1172.

Law, J., Garrett, Z., & Nye, C. (2003). Speech and language therapy interventions for children with primary speech and language delay or disorder. *The Cochrane Library*, 2003(3): Article No. CD004110. (Updated 2010).

Law, J., Garrett, Z. & Nye, C. (2010). Speech and language therapy interventions for children with primary speech and language delay or disorder. *Cochrane Database of Systematic Review, 2010*(5), CD004110.

Leyfer, O. T., Tager-Flusberg, H., Dowd, M., Tomblin, B., & Folstein, S. E. (2008). Overlap between autism and specific language impairment: Comparison of Autism Diagnostic Interview and Autism Diagnostic Observation Schedule Scores. *Autism Research, 1*, 284–296.

Manolson, A. (1992). *It takes two to talk: A parent's guide to helping children communicate*. Toronto, ON: The Hanen Centre.

Matson, J. L., Matson, M. L., & Rivet, T. T. (2007). Social skills treatments for children with autism spectrum disorders. *Behaviour Modification, 31*, 682–707.

McTear, M. F. (1985). Pragmatic disorders: A question of direction. *International Journal of Language & Communication Disorders, 20*, 119–127.

Merrison, S., & Merrison, A. J. (2005). Repair in speech and language therapy interaction: Investigating pragmatic language impairment of children. *Child Language Teaching and Therapy, 21*, 191–211.

Norbury, C. F. (2005). Barking up the wrong tree? Lexical ambiguity resolution in children with language impairments and autistic spectrum disorders. *Journal of Experimental Child Psychology, 90*, 142–171.

Norbury, C. F., & Bishop, D. V. (2002). Inferential processing and story recall in children with communication problems: A comparison of specific language impairment, pragmatic language impairment and high functioning autism. *International Journal of Language & Communication Disorders, 37*, 227–251.

Norbury, C. F., Nash, M., Baird, G., & Bishop, D. V. M. (2004). Using a parental checklist to identify diagnostic groups in children with communication impairment: A validation of the Children's Communication Checklist-2. *International Journal of Language & Communication Disorders, 39*, 345–364.

O'Hare, A. E., Bremmer, L., Happé, F., & Pettigrew, L. M. (2009). A clinical assessment tool for advanced theory of mind performance in 5 to 12 year olds. *Journal of Autism and Developmental Disorders, 39*, 916–928.

Olswang, L. B., Coggins, T. E., & Svensson, L. (2007). Assessing social communication in the classroom: Observing manner and duration of performance. *Topics in Language Disorders, 27*, 111–127.

Olswang, L. B., Svensson, L., & Astley, S. (2010). Observation of classroom social communication: Do children with fetal alcohol spectrum disorders spend their time differently than their typically developing peers? *Journal of Speech, Language and Hearing Research, 53*, 1687–1703.

Olswang, L. B., Svensson, L., Coggins, T. E., Beilinson, J. S., & Donaldson, A. L. (2006). Reliability issues and solutions for coding social communication performance in classroom settings. *Journal of Speech, Language and Hearing Research, 49*, 1058–1071.

O'Neill, D. K. (2007). The language use inventory for young children: A parent-report measure of pragmatic language development for 18- to 47-month-old children. *Journal of Speech, Language and Hearing Research, 50*, 214–228.

Paul, R., & Norbury, C. F. (2012). *Language disorders from infancy through adolescence* (4th ed.). St. Louis, MO: Mosby.

Peppé, S., McCann, J., Gibbon, F., O'Hare, A., & Rutherford, M. (2006). Assessing prosodic and pragmatic ability in children with high-functioning autism. *Journal of Pragmatics, 38*, 1776–1791.

Phelps-Teraski, T., & Phelps-Gunn, D. (2007). The *Test for Pragmatic Language–2*. Austin, TX: Pro-Ed.

Prutting, C. A., & Kirchner, D. M. (1987). A clinical appraisal of the pragmatic aspects of language. *Journal of Speech and Hearing Disorders, 52*, 105–119.

Rapin, I., & Allen, D. A. (1987). Developmental dysphasia and autism in preschool children: Characteristics and subtypes. In *Proceedings of the First International Symposium on Specific Speech and Language Disorders in Children* (pp. 20–35). London, UK: AFASIC.

Reichow, B., & Volkmar, F. R. (2010). Social skills interventions for individuals with autism: Evaluation for evidence-based practices within a best evidence synthesis framework. *Journal of Autism and Developmental Disorders, 40*, 149–166.

Roberts, M. Y., & Kaiser, A. P. (2011). The effectiveness of parent-implemented language interventions: A meta-analysis. *American Journal of Speech-Language Pathology, 20*, 180.

Roth, F. P., & Spekman, N. J. (1984). Assessing the Pragmatic Abilities of Children: Part 2. Guidelines, Considerations, and Specific Evaluation Procedures. *Journal of Speech and Hearing Disorders, 49*, 12–17.

Rutter, M., Bailey, A., & Lord, C., (2003). *The Social Communication Questionnaire*. Los Angeles, CA: Western Psychological Services.

Segrin, C., & Givertz, M. (2003). Methods of social skills training and development. In J. O. Greene & B. R. Burleson (Eds.), *Handbook of communication and social interaction skills* (pp. 135–176). Mahwah, NJ: Erlbaum.

Semel, E., Wiig, E. H., & Secord, W. (1989). Clinical Evaluation of Language Fundamentals—Revised Edition. San Antonio, TX: Psychological Corporation.

Semel, E., Wiig, E. H., & Secord, W. (2006a). *Clinical Evaluation of Language Fundamentals—Fourth Edition UK*. Oxford, UK: Pearson Assessment.

Semel, E., Wiig, E., & Secord, W. (2006b). *Clinical Evaluation of Language Fundamentals—Preschool 2 (UK version)*. Oxford, UK: Pearson Assessment.

Shields, J., Varley, R., Broks, P., & Simpson, A. (1996). Social cognition in developmental language disorders and high level autism. *Developmental Medicine & Child Neurology, 38*, 487–495.

St. Clair, M.C., Pickles, A., Durkin, K., & Conti-Ramsden, G. (2011). A longitudinal study of behavioral, emotional and social difficulties in individuals with a history of specific language impairment (SLI). *Journal of Communication Disorders, 44*, 186–199.

Strong, C. J. (1998). *Strong Narrative Assessment Procedure*. Austin, TX: ProEd.

Stothard, S. E., Snowling, M. J., Bishop, D. V. M., Chipchase, B. B., & Kaplan, C. A. (1998). Language-impaired preschoolers: A follow-up into adolescence. *Journal of Speech, Language and Hearing Research, 41*, 407–418.

St. Pourcain, B., Mandy, W., Heron, J., Golding, J., Smith, G., & Skuse, D. (2011). Links between co-occurring social-communication and hyperactive-inattentive trait trajectories. *Journal of the American Academy of Child and Adolescent Psychiatry, 50*, 892–902.

Tager-Flusberg H., Paul, R., & Lord, C. E. (2005). Language and communication in autism. In F. Volkmar, R. Paul, A. Klin, & D. J. Cohen (Eds.). *Handbook of autism and pervasive developmental disorder* (3rd ed., Vol. 1, pp. 335–364). New York, NY: Wiley.

Timler, G., Olswang, L. B., & Coggins, T. E. (2005a). "Do I know what I need to do?" A social communication intervention for children with complex clinical profiles. *Language, Speech, and Hearing Services in Schools, 36*, 73–85.

Timler, G. R., Olswang, L. B., & Coggins, T. E. (2005b). Social communication interventions for preschoolers: Targeting peer interactions during peer group entry and cooperative play. *Seminars in Speech and Language, 26*, 170–180.

Timler, G. R., & Volger-Elias, D. (2007). Strategies for promoting generalisation of social communication skills in pre-schoolers and school-aged children. *Topics in Language Disorders, 27*, 167–181.

Tomblin, J. B., Records, N. L., Buckwalter, P., Zhang, X., Smith, E., & O'Brien, M. (1997). Prevalence of specific language impairment in kindergarten children. *Journal of Speech, Language, and Hearing Research, 40*, 1245–1260.

Vance, M., & Wells, B. (1994). The wrong end of the stick: Language-impaired children's understanding of non-literal language. *Child Language Teaching and Therapy, 10*, 23–46.

Volden, J., & Lord, C. (1991). Neologisms and idiosyncratic language in autistic speakers. *Journal of Autism and Developmental Disorders, 21*, 109–130.

Volden, J., & Phillips, L. (2010). Measuring pragmatic language in speakers with autism spectrum disorders: Comparing the Children's Communication Checklist–2 and the Test of Pragmatic Language. *American Journal of Speech-Language Pathology, 19*, 204–212.

Wetherby, A. M., & Prizant, B. M. (2002). *Communication and symbolic behavior scales: Developmental profile*. Baltimore, MD: Brookes.

Whitehouse, A. J. O., Watt, H. J., Line, E. A., & Bishop, D. V. M. (2009). Adult psychosocial outcomes of children with specific language impairment, pragmatic language impairment and autism. *International Journal of Language and Communication Disorders, 44,* 511–528.

Wiig, E., & Secord, W. (1989). *Test of Language Competence—Expanded Edition.* San Antonio, TX: Psychological Corporation.

Wiig, E. H., & Secord, W. (1992). *Test of Word Knowledge: TOWK: Examiner's manual.* San Antonio, TX: Psychological Corporation.

Yeargin-Allsop, M., Rice, C., Karapurkar, T., Doernberg, N., Boyle, C., & Murphy, C. (2003). Prevalence of autism in a US metropolitan area. *Journal of the American Medical Association, 289,* 49–55.

Young, E. C., Diehl, J. J., Morris, D., Hyman, S. L., & Bennetto, L. (2005). The use of two language tests to identify pragmatic language problems in children with autism spectrum disorders. *Language, Speech, and Hearing Services in Schools, 36,* 62–72.

7

SOCIAL COMMUNICATION ASSESSMENT AND INTERVENTION FOR CHILDREN ON THE AUTISM SPECTRUM

Danai K. Fannin and Linda R. Watson

People are always looking for the single magic bullet that will totally change everything. There is no single magic bullet.

—Temple Grandin, PhD

LEARNING OBJECTIVES

Readers will be able to

1. Specify the current incidence and prevalence of Autism Spectrum Disorders (ASD).
2. Describe the most recent adjustments in ASD diagnosis using the new *DSM-5* criteria and their ramifications on Asperger's Disorder (ASP) diagnosis.
3. Differentiate between ASP and ASD.
4. Describe referral guidelines and recommended medical and educational assessment practices.
5. Define the level of evidence for current treatment approaches for ASD across the lifespan and various environments (e.g., home, classroom).

Hanaa is a 6-year, 3-month-old girl who presented with a medical diagnosis of severe autism. She lives with her parents, Mr. and Mrs. A, two older sisters (10 years old and 8 years old, respectively), and one younger sister (aged 4 years), with both Arabic and English spoken in the home. Mr. A works while Mrs. A stays at home. At her first birthday, Hanaa was able to say "mama" and "baba" but stopped saying words at 18 months of age. Mr. and Mrs. A became concerned about Hanaa's communication difficulties at the age of 2 years, 6 months. At age 4 year, Hanaa's pediatrician referred her to a university speech-language pathology clinic for an evaluation. She had been receiving language treatment at school with the goals of expanding functional communication, reciprocal interaction, commenting, advocating for self-help, and repairing communication breakdowns. At the time of referral, Mr. and Mrs. A believed she understood commands but had difficulty vocalizing her wants and needs. Instead, she became quiet or angry when she was not understood. Hanaa expressed her needs by leading people to what she wanted, pointing to objects, or bringing objects to others. Of the few words she had, some were in English (e.g., one, two, three) and some were in Arabic (e.g., sayyāra [car]); Mr. and Mrs. A reported that she rarely interacted with her family socially.

Hanaa also had sleep disturbances and feeding delays, prompting Mr. and Mrs. A to feed her and give her an over-the-counter supplement to help her sleep. She could drink from a cup but had strong food preferences. In fact, Hanaa was hospitalized for 12 days after she went 3 days without eating or drinking. Additionally, Hanaa had been taken to the emergency room on a number of occasions for ear infections and accompanying fevers.

The evaluating Speech-Language Pathologist (SLP) observed play sessions between Mrs. A and Hanaa, and Mrs. A seemed comfortable playing with her daughter. However, Hanaa was difficult to engage in play routines because of her sensory-seeking behaviors (e.g., running around the room and climbing on cabinets). While the SLP attempted to play with Hanaa, she exhibited self-stimulating behaviors such as mouthing objects and spinning in circles when looking into the mirror. She did not produce intelligible vocalizations, respond to vocalizations, respond to her name, or seek eye contact. Hanaa sometimes extended her arm to show an object, sometimes gave an object, and often raised her arms to request being picked up. Hanaa consistently displayed play skills corresponding to the Functional Play level (Indiscriminate Actions to Combinations) and inconsistent, emerging Pre-Symbolic Play behaviors with maximum prompting from an adult (Bakeman & Adamson, 1984). Hanaa demonstrated proto-imperative communication functions by lifting her hand in a palm-up position (request) and pushing an adult's hand away (protest). Hanaa did not consistently demonstrate proto-declarative (i.e., showing something to get attention) functions, and she did not point to share interesting objects or events. When considering joint engagement, Hanaa was at the Object-Engaged level of joint engagement states (Bakeman & Adamson, 1984), when she primarily focused on objects during parallel play.

After a 12-week program designed to increase Hanaa's joint attention/joint engagement, Mrs. A reported improvement in Hanaa's social interaction with her sisters and acquisition of some additional words. At age 6, however, Hanaa returned to the clinic, and the SLP providing treatment reported limited communication skills and persistent sensory-seeking behaviors.

This case exemplifies different issues in assessment and intervention planning for people with Autism Spectrum Disorder (ASD), including persisting core deficits after treatment, cultural differences in family language use, and sensory integration impairments that affect behavior and feeding. Hanaa demonstrates developmental delays in language, play skills, social skills, and joint attention, as well as repetitive behaviors. Because of the difficulty in treating functionally nonverbal people with severe autism, these individuals frequently are excluded from treatment studies. Furthermore, those from culturally and linguistically diverse (CLD) backgrounds are even more absent from ASD research (Pierce et al., 2014). Both of these factors (i.e. nonverbal, bilingual environment) might contribute to why treatment for Hanaa has not yet been as effective as desired. A combination of treatment strategies at an increased dose, reduction of sensory seeking behaviors, and the addition of Augmentative and Alternative Communication (AAC) methods might be the answer for some nonverbal children such as Hanaa who do not initially respond to treatment.

Research concerning evidence-based practice for ASD is still needed, and indeed, such research is ongoing. The following chapter describes the current state of evidence for diagnostic assessment and communication/social interaction treatment of ASD across settings and the lifespan. Because reviews of evidence were conducted before the advent of the new *DSM-5* diagnosis of ASD, other terms (e.g., Autistic Disorder [AD]), Pervasive Developmental Disorder Not Otherwise Specified (PDD-NOS), high-functioning autism, autism) utilized in individual studies and resources will be used throughout the chapter. Because of the multiple names used for Asperger's Disorder (e.g., Asperger Disorder, Asperger Syndrome, Asperger's Syndrome, Asperger's syndrome) the term Asperger's Disorder (ASP) will be used.

Multiple systematic evidence reviews have been conducted related to different aspects of detection, diagnosis, and treatment of individuals with ASD. We make use of those sources throughout this chapter, while offering two general cautions to readers. First, different evidence reviews use different criteria for the types of studies that will be included in a review; for example, in the evidence synthesis of ASD interventions issued by the Agency for Healthcare Research Quality (Warren et al., 2011), studies of behavioral treatment with fewer than 10 participants and those that did not aggregate results across participants were excluded, leading to the exclusion of a large body of research on interventions for individuals with ASD that has used single case designs, whereas the National Autism Center (NAC; 2009) included single-case design studies in its evidence synthesis. Second, evidence syntheses, which are tremendously useful to practitioners, are inevitably "out-of-date" by the time they are published, because these projects require searching a body of literature using a cutoff date, followed by the complex process of analyzing, synthesizing, and disseminating that evidence. In the meantime, new studies are being published that can strengthen, clarify, or, in some cases, contradict the evidence previously available.

DEFINITIONS, INCIDENCE, AND PREVALENCE

ASD is a developmental disability distinguished by early emerging core deficits in social interaction and communication that affects development into adulthood (Howlin, 1997). The following core deficits differentiate children with ASD from typically developing children and other developmental delays with similar characteristics: (a) joint attention (i.e., actively sharing and following the attention of others by coordinating attention to people, events, or objects), (b) social communication (i.e., various nonverbal and verbal skills necessary for reciprocal social interaction and development of peer relationships), and (c) repetitive behaviors (i.e., stereotyped motor mannerisms, narrow interests, fixation on parts of objects, and/or rigidity of routines): (Mundy, Sigman, Ungerer, & Sherman, 1986; Volkmar, Lord, Bailey, Schultz, & Klin, 2004; Wetherby, Watt, Morgan, & Shumway, 2007).

The pathophysiology of this neurological disorder has not yet been fully determined; it is likely multifactorial and variable from one individual with ASD to the next (Parellada et al., 2014). For this reason, behavioral and educational interventions have been most frequently used to target the core symptoms of ASD, rather than administration of biomedical treatments (NAC, 2009). Research now indicates that the prevalence of autism and related disorders in the United States may be as high as 1 in 68 children (Autism and Developmental Disabilities Monitoring Network, 2014), and up to 1 in 50 school-age children (Blumberg et al., 2013), exceeding the prevalence of other severe childhood developmental disorders. Approximately 500,000 children and adolescents are estimated to meet criteria for ASD, making it a significant public health concern (Mandell, Cao, Ittenbach, & Pinto-Martin, 2006).

Fewer prevalence studies have been conducted internationally and numbers are presented with the caveat that there were methodological problems (e.g., low sample size) with the gathering of data. Studies conducted in the countries of Oman, Israel, France, Indonesia, Iceland, China, and Portugal report low prevalence of 1.4 per 10,000 children, 10 per 10,000, 5.35 per 10,000, 11.7 per 10,000, 13.32 per 10,000, 16.1 per 10,000, and 16.7 per 10,000, respectively (Hughes, 2011). Other countries, including Canada, Australia, Sweden, Denmark, and Brazil report higher prevalence of 64.9 per 10,000, 39.2 to 51 per 10,000, 72.6 per 10,000, 68.5 per 10,000, and 27.2 per 10,000 respectively. When the United States prevalence is translated to 10,000 children, the number is approximately 113 per 10,000, which is more consistent with countries like the United Kingdom (94 per 10,000), and Japan (181.1 per 10,000). Most of these international studies are recent but some date as far back as 1992. Thus, based on current prevalence in the United States and the more recent international studies, the numbers in those earlier studies have likely risen.

Although there are no known differences in ASD incidence by race, socioeconomic status (SES), nationality, or ethnicity, Dyches, Wilder, Sudweeks, Obiakor, and Algozzine (2004) suggest that cultural factors may influence: (a) how and when symptoms of ASD are defined and viewed, (b) to what extent stigma of disability status exists across cultures, and (c) if there are differences in how families accept ASD diagnoses. Clinician bias may also play a role in how certain cultures diagnose and treat ASD. People from various backgrounds may face unique obstacles when managing disability but there is a lack of research on how culture may affect treatment outcomes. Thus, until more research on assessment and intervention for those from CLD backgrounds is conducted, clinicians must bear in mind that populations that have provided evidence for best practices in ASD have primarily employed samples of middle-SES people of European descent (Dyches et al., 2004). Because of the increased number of people identified with ASD, the urgency to meet the needs of all families with ASD has been heightened.

CHARACTERISTICS OF ASD AS DEFINED BY THE *DSM-5*

The *Diagnostic and Statistical Manual of Mental Disorders (DSM)* is a diagnostic guide for mental illnesses used by social workers, researchers, physicians, psychologists, and those in forensic fields (Kupfer,

Regier, & Kuhl, 2008). In the previous version of the *DSM* (4th ed., text rev.; *DSM-IV-TR*; American Psychiatric Association [APA], 2000), the umbrella category of "Pervasive Developmental Disorders" included several distinct diagnoses. Individuals with the most symptoms and most classic symptoms were classified as having Autistic Disorder (AD). Those with intelligence and adaptive functioning within normal limits and no history of extreme language delay were likely to meet the criteria for ASP. The rare group of children who developed relatively typically for the first 2 to 5 years followed by progressive developmental deterioration and the development of social, affective, and repetitive behaviors were diagnosed with Childhood Disintegrative Disorder. The diagnosis of Rett's Disorder was also based on a pattern of very early normal psychomotor development followed by the loss of motor skills, deceleration of head growth, severe impairments in receptive and expressive language, and a loss of social engagement early in development (often a transient symptom). Finally, individuals who did not meet the criteria for one of the aforementioned diagnoses and showed deficits in social reciprocity similar to those seen in AD were diagnosed with PDD-NOS. Using this system, diagnosticians have been reliably distinguishing people on the autism spectrum from those who are typically developing or those with other disorders. Differentiation among the various pervasive developmental disorders has not been as consistent and valid across settings and diagnosticians, however (Borden, 2011). For this and other reasons, a revision of diagnostic criteria was needed to more rigorously confine diagnosticians to the features of "autism spectrum disorder" and characterize other factors such as intelligence, language level, or severity as continuously variable, rather than categorical features (APA, 2013).

In May 2013, the fifth edition of *DSM* (APA, 2013) was published with anticipated and controversial changes to the autism diagnosis. The *DSM-5* manual incorporates the previous diagnoses of AD, ASP, and other Pervasive Developmental Disorders into the single diagnosis of ASD (Borden, 2011). Diagnosis is based on symptoms in two broad domains: social-communication and restrictive/repetitive behaviors. A diagnosis of ASD under *DSM-5* entails specifying the severity of symptoms in each of these domains, as well as an indication of whether there is accompanying intellectual impairment, language impairment, and/or known genetic or medical factors or environmental conditions. The public, composed of parents, individuals on the autism spectrum, and health care workers have raised concerns about the new definition of ASD, especially regarding the elimination of ASP and PDD-NOS as distinct diagnoses (Ghazi-uddin, 2010; Kite, Gullifor, & Tyson, 2013; Leventhal-Belfer, 2012).

Concerns have included the possibility that an ASD diagnosis would be stigmatizing for those with milder symptoms and parents would therefore be less likely to pursue an evaluation for mildly affected children (Kite et al., 2013) or, conversely, that the *DSM-5* criteria are too strict and would exclude people with milder, high-functioning autism, especially females (Frazier et al., 2012). Research, however, indicated that the *DSM-5* was valid in Phase I field trials with 97% specificity, but 81% sensitivity that prompted a suggested relaxed algorithm in Phase II field trials to catch 12% of people with ASD who may potentially be missed (Frazier et al., 2012). Further, supporters of the revision found that the poor prognoses for functional outcomes in adults with AD and PDD-NOS appear to be similar for degree of disability and marital status (Mordre et al., 2012). This finding reinforces the importance of individuals with milder symptoms continuing to meet the criteria for ASD, thereby allowing access to services.

ASPERGER'S DISORDER

ASP is a developmental disorder that has an impact on one's social skills and ability to communicate effectively, despite cognitive and language skills being within the normal range. Persisting interests in specific subjects and social awkwardness are two characteristics typical of ASP. In the *DSM-IV-TR* (APA, 2000), the primary feature distinguishing ASP's from AD was the absence of childhood language delays, resulting in ASP being differentiated from AD solely based on early language development (Bennett et al., 2008; Cuccaro et al., 2007). Indeed, several research reviews have concluded that individuals with ASP show quantitative but not qualitative differences from those with high-functioning autism (i.e., AD with IQs within the normal range), and therefore, ASP should be considered a variant of autism rather than a distinct disorder (Frith, 2004; Sanders, 2009). Furthermore, in light of the controversies over no longer distinguishing ASP's from AD in the *DSM-5*, it is important to recognize that the criteria for ASP in the *Diagnostic and Statistical Manual of Mental Disorders* (4th ed.; *DSM-IV*; American Psychiatric Association, 1994) and *Diagnostic and Statistical Manual of Mental Disorders* (4th ed., text rev.; DSM-IV-TR; American Psychiatric Association, 2000) were also widely criticized (Klin, McPartland & Volkmar, 2005).

Historically, *DSM* criteria have been very influential, but other diagnostic classification systems also are used, with widespread global reliance on the World Health Organization's (WHO's) *International Classification of Diseases-10* (*ICD-10*), currently in its 10th edition. The *ICD-10* (WHO, 1996) diagnostic criteria for Pervasive Developmental Disorders were closely aligned with those in the *DSM-IV-TR*. Work on the *ICD-11* is currently underway, but the extent to which it will be aligned with the *DSM-5* is not yet clear.

REFERRAL GUIDELINES

The first professionals with opportunities to notice signs of communication disorders are often family practitioners or pediatricians. The American Academy of Pediatrics (AAP) recommends screening for all at the ages of 9 months, 18 months, and 24 to 30 months, using a standardized tool and surveillance for ASD at every well-child visit (Centers for Disease Control and Prevention [CDC], 2013; Johnson, Myers, & the Council on Children with Disabilities, 2007). Surveillance includes listening carefully to parents, maintaining a developmental history, making informed observations, identifying risk and protective factors, and documenting the process and findings. The American Academy of Neurology and the Child Neurology Society practice parameter on autism identifies several symptoms that should trigger an immediate referral (Filipek et al., 2000):

- By 12 months of age, the child is not babbling, pointing, or using other gestures.
- By 16 months the child has no single words.
- By 24 months the child has no two-word phrases.
- The child loses language skills at any age.

If any of the following risk factors are present during the birth to three-year age range, an ASD screener should be administered (see Table 7.1). If multiple of the following risk factors are present, however, the child can be referred directly for a comprehensive assessment (i.e., an ASD screening is not necessary; Johnson et al., 2007):

- There is an older sibling diagnosed with ASD.
- An adult knowledgeable about child development has a concern that the child may have ASD.
- The child seems as if he or she cannot hear, despite a normal hearing evaluation.
- The child lacks joint attention gestures.
- The child shows idiosyncratic repetitive behaviors (e.g., fixation on certain objects, hand flapping, self-injury, perseveration on certain topics).
- The child has inappropriate or delayed play behaviors.
- The child uses delayed or immediate echolalic verbalizations and/or has delayed receptive language.

Signs of ASD are often observable by 12 months of age and knowledgeable and experienced clinicians can reliably diagnose ASD in many children as early 24 months (American Speech-Language-Hearing Association [ASHA], 2006). Despite the fact that ASD-sensitive screeners for children as young as 9 months exist, many children are not identified until years later (Mandell et al., 2010). In fact, the median age for initial ASD diagnosis in the United States is around 53 months, and even for children who meet the *DSM-IV-TR* criteria for AD, the median age is a relatively old 48 months (Autism and Developmental Disabilities Monitoring Network, 2014). Thus, continued vigilance for symptoms that would indicate screening or assessment is important.

Children with ASD who remain unidentified at school age are often those with good language and cognitive skills. The following behaviors in the primary grades should trigger screening or referral to a psychologist, SLP, or primary-care provider (Reilly, Campbell, & Keran, 2009):

- Abnormal intonation and/or rhythm of connected speech.
- Voice volume too soft or loud.
- Difficulty with back-and-forth conversation, despite age-appropriate language structure.
- Discrepancy between academic ability and "social intelligence," particularly during unstructured social interactions.
- Little interest in other children.
- Difficulty joining play appropriately (e.g., hitting, interrupting without asking to play).
- Difficulty developing and maintaining relationships, especially with same-age peers.
- Lack of awareness of personal space, and/or marked intolerance for intrusions of others into his or her personal space.
- Failure to understand sarcasm or metaphor.
- Unusually intense and focused preoccupation with an interest; may involve collecting, listing, or numbering.
- Persistent difficulties in coping with change.

SCREENING

While there has been considerable research on ASD screening tools, the most recent systematic review rated the quality of evidence as low for most available tools (National Institute for Clinical Excellence [NICE], 2011). Meisels (1989) recommends that both sensitivity and specificity of developmental screening tools for young children be at least 80%, whereas Barnes (1982) considers sensitivity in the 70% to 80% range to be adequate for developmental screening. Table 7.1 lists ASD screening tools reviewed by several sources for quality of evidence, along with information on specificity and sensitivity. The NICE evidence ratings should be considered conservative, because they only apply to studies published between 1990 and 2010 and thus do not reflect more recent studies.

RECOMMENDED MEDICAL AND EDUCATIONAL ASSESSMENT

Table 7.1 Evidence-Based ASD Screeners

Screeners	Type of Evidence	Ages
Modified Checklist for Autism in Toddlers (M-CHAT; Robins, Fein, Barton, & Green, 2001)[a]	Very Low Quality[b] 74% Sensitivity[b] 42% Specificity[b]	16–30 months
Communication and Symbolic Behavior Scales–Developmental Profile (CSBS-DP) Infant-Toddler Checklist (ITC; Wetherby & Prizant, 2002)	No studies met criteria for evidence review[b] 88.9% Sensitivity/Specificity[c]	6–24 months
Screening Tool for Autism in Two-Year-Olds (STAT; Stone, Coonrod, & Ousley; 2000; Stone, Coonrod, Turner, & Pozdol, 2004; Stone & Ousley, 1997)	No studies met criteria for evidence review[b] 92% Sensitivity[c] 85% Specificity[c]	24–36 months
Social Communication Questionnaire (SCQ; Rutter, Bailey, & Lord, 2003).	Very Low Quality[b] 71% Sensitivity[b] 62% Specificity[b]	4–40 years*
Checklist for Autism in Toddlers (CHAT; Baird et al., 2000; Baron-Cohen, Allen, & Gillberg, 1992; Baron-Cohen, et al., 1996).	No studies met criteria for evidence review[a,b] Strong Evidence[d] 38% Sensitivity[c] 98% Specificity[c]	18–24 months

Note. Research designs designated as "Very Low Quality" evidence were uncontrolled observational studies.

[a] A new version of this tool, the Modified Checklist for Autism in Toddlers, Revised with Follow-up (M-CHAT-R/F; Robins, Fein, & Barton, 2009) is now available and recommended by the authors.

[b] Rated by the National Institute for Health and Clinical Excellence (NICE, 2011).

[c] Rated by the American Speech-Language-Hearing Association (ASHA, 2006). "Strong Evidence" defined as two or more studies that had adequate evidence of efficacy, at least moderate applicability to the topic, and evidence that consistently and strongly supported the recommendation.

[d] Rated by the New York State Department of Health, Early Intervention Program (NYSDH, 1999).

*Can be used for children as young as 24 months but evidence exists for 4+ years old (one study included children with intellectual disability).

RECOMMENDED ASSESSMENT PRACTICES

If a screener and/or clinical observation indicate risk for ASD, a full evaluation should be conducted. The evaluation protocol should not rely on standardized ASD tools exclusively. Rather, it should include measures of the function of behaviors, cognition, adaptive behavior, play, motor skills, language, and concomitant mental conditions (Boyd, Conroy, Asmus, McKenney, & Mancil, 2008; Taylor-Goh, 2005). All of these areas of assessment are needed to (a) differentiate ASD from other disorders with similar symptoms (e.g., Specific Language Impairment, Social [Pragmatic] Communication Disorder), (b) determine ASD severity, and (c) specify accompanying impairments (e.g., intellectual impairment, language impairment, medical or genetic condition, behavioral disorder, catatonia, mental disorder). However, there is no evidence that these additional assessments produce a more accurate ASD diagnosis. Instead, information derived from a comprehensive assessment protocol provides a more detailed explanation of the client's behaviors, aiding development of a more needs-based management plan (NICE, 2011).

The collaborative work of a multidisciplinary team can make the diagnostic process more complete and efficient from the perspective of the family. The composition of multidisciplinary autism teams in health care settings varies but may include a psychologist, a psychiatrist or developmental pediatrician, an SLP, an Occupational Therapist (OT), a Developmental Therapist (DT), a Physical Therapist (PT), and a neurologist. Depending on the findings and the expertise represented on the team, an individual may be referred for further evaluation, such as genetic testing and DNA analysis to check for conditions such as Fragile X. Multidisciplinary autism teams are not universally available; thus, individuals may be diagnosed with ASD by one professional, often a psychiatrist or clinical psychologist. Nonmedical diagnoses of ASD can be made in schools and other clinical settings. In schools, diagnostic teams may include a school administrator, an SLP, an OT, a PT, a school psychologist, and a DT when available. An educational diagnosis can serve the purpose of qualifying the child for services in schools even if the child does not have a medical diagnosis (ASHA, 2006). In early childhood and school settings, an arena type assessment where all evaluators simultaneously observe the child communicating, playing, problem solving, and participating in other tasks may be conducted but many early intervention programs or educational settings do not allow for schedules to be coordinated among all evaluators. Thus, the child may be assessed at different times by individual professionals who then convene at an Individual Family Service Plan (IFSP)/Individual Education Program (IEP) meeting to determine eligibility and plan services.

In a systematic review spanning 2000 to 2012, Falkmer, Anderson, Falkmer, and Horlin (2013), determined that the gold standard of ASD evaluation consists of a multidisciplinary team combining the Autism Diagnostic Observation Schedule (ADOS; Lord et al., 2000) and Autism Diagnostic Interview–Revised (ADI-R; Le Couteur, Lord, & Rutter, 2003; which has the best accuracy levels at 80.8%), other assessments, and clinical judgment. The creators of the *ADOS* and *ADI-R* stress that these should not be the only tools used to make diagnostic decisions but, instead, should be used as part of a comprehensive assessment protocol. By combining information from assessment tools, parent/teacher report, observation, and clinical judgment, professionals can diagnose autism based on *ICD-10* and *DSM-5* criteria (Scottish Intercollegiate Guidelines Network [SIGN], 2007). Standardized evaluation tools are still being validated and developed, and not all tools in regular use have been deemed evidence based. Using the Appraisal for Guidelines in Research Evaluation II (AGREE II) Framework (Brouwers et al., 2010) that was adopted by most North American and European countries in 1990, the National Center for Evidence-Based Practice in Communication Disorders (N-CEP) scored various ASD assessment guidelines for their scientific rigor, categorizing them as Highly Recommended, Recommended with Provisos, and Not Recommended (ASHA, 2009). Table 7.2 presents specific assessment tools for adults and children with ASD that were found in Highly Recommended guidelines and, therefore, have the most rigorous evidence. The NICE (2011) guidelines highlight assessment tools with evidence of sensitivity and specificity at a minimum of 80%, with the lower 95% confidence interval estimate above 70%. These tools also align with the *ICD-10* and *DSM-5*, from which the medical diagnosis and diagnostic codes are derived.

EVIDENCE-BASED INTERVENTION FOR AUTISM SPECTRUM DISORDERS ACROSS THE LIFE SPAN

Despite the fact that one must meet specific criteria to be diagnosed with ASD, considerable heterogeneity of behaviors, background factors, and presentation of symptoms exists within the population. Intervention studies have rarely compared two well-specified treatments or

Table 7.2 Highly Recommended Guidelines for ASD Assessment Tools

Diagnostic Tools	Type of Evidence	Ages Studied
Autism Diagnostic Interview-Revised (ADI-R; Le Couteur, Lord, & Rutter, 2003)	Very Low Quality[a] Low Quality[a] Gold standard[b] Limited Evidence[c]	Adults with and without learning disability Children with intellectual disability 12+ months
Autism Behavior Checklist (ABC; when used with other diagnostic tools; Krug, Arick, & Almond, 1980)	Very Low Quality[a] Strong Evidence[c]	School age Not recommended under 3 years[c]
Ritvo Autism Asperger Diagnostic Scale–Revised (RAADS-R; Ritvo et al., 2011).	Very Low Quality[a]	Adults with no learning disability
Adult Asperger Assessment (AAA) (includes Autism-Spectrum Quotient [ASQ] and Empathy Quotient [EQ]; Baron-Cohen, Wheelwright, Robinson, & Woodbury-Smith, 2005)	Very Low Quality[a]	Adults with no learning disability
Autism Diagnostic Observation Schedule (ADOS-G; Lord et al., 2000)	Very Low Quality[a]	Adults with learning disability
Autism Diagnostic Observation Schedule (ADOS-2; Lord, Rutter, DiLavore, Risi, & Gotham, 2012)	Low Quality[a] Very Low Quality[a] Good accuracy and correspondence with DSM/gold standard[b]	Preschool Children with intellectual disability
Childhood Autism Rating Scale (CARS; Schopler, Reichler, & Rochen Renner, 1999)	Strong Evidence[c] Good for autism but not other ASDs[b]	Early childhood, preschool

(*Continued*)

Table 7.2 (*Continued*)

Diagnostic Tools	Type of Evidence	Ages Studied
Parent Interview for Autism (PIA; Stone & Hogan, 1993).	No study met inclusion criteria for review[c] Strong Evidence[c]	2–4 years
Diagnostic and Statistical Manual (4th ed, text rev; DSM-IV-TR; APA, 2000); *Diagnostic and Statistical Manual* (5th ed.; DSM-5; APA, 2013). *International Classification of Diseases (ICD-10).* (WHO, 1996)	Very Low Quality[a] Low Quality[a] Gold standard[b] Limited Evidence[c]	Diagnosed under 24 months and up to 36 months (99% of children <24 months retained autism diagnosis a year later, 100% with another ASD retained diagnosis a year later, but 41% thought not to have ASD did indeed have it a year later) (95% of children <24 mo. retained autism diagnosis a year later, 84% with another ASD retained diagnosis a year later, and 0% thought not to have ASD did indeed have it a year later)

Note. Research designs Note. Research designs designated as "Very Low Quality" evidence were uncontrolled observational studies. "Low Quality" evidence were controlled observational studies.
[a] Rated by the National Institute for Health and Clinical Excellence (NICE, 2011).
[b] Rated by the American Speech-Language-Hearing Association (ASHA, 2006). "Strong Evidence" defined as two or more studies that had adequate evidence of efficacy, at least moderate applicability to the topic, and evidence that consistently and strongly supported the recommendation.
[c] Rated by the New York State Department of Health, Early Intervention Program (NYSDH, 1999).

investigated the implications that heterogeneity among individuals with ASD has in response to an intervention; thus, even when a treatment has good evidence for efficacy, we cannot assume it will work well for all with ASD. Unfortunately, many clinicians, researchers, and caregivers have claimed that their treatment of choice has been proven successful (Prelock & McCauley, 2012), ignoring the complexities of evaluating the evidence for interventions tested with this population.

The complexities of evaluating evidence extend to systematic reviews of ASD treatments. First, organizations that sponsor reviews have had various foci, leading to inconsistencies in interventions selected across reviews. For example, the National Autism Center (with many members who are behavior analysts who research autism treatments specifically) included studies of ASD treatment only. Therefore, several studies from certain areas (e.g., occupational therapy and physical therapy) were excluded from the NAC (2009) review because these studies of sensory processing or motor skill treatments tend to include other disabilities beyond ASD. Additionally, the Agency for Healthcare Research and Quality (AHRQ; Warren et al., 2011) report excludes some research on Applied Behavioral Analysis (ABA) treatments because these treatments did not meet their quality/strength of research criteria, while other reviews included ABA studies (Missouri Autism Guidelines Initiative, 2012). As another example, the National Professional Development Center's (NPDC) report (Odom, Collet-Klingenberg, Rogers, & Hatton, 2010) only contains Focused Behavioral Interventions, thereby excluding Comprehensive Behavioral Treatments. Second, time spans of the reviews vary from 1957 to 2007 (NAC, 2009) to more recent research from 2000 to 2010 (Warren et al., 2010). Thus, the number and era of studies reviewed are not identical. Third, the reviews varied in their classification of evidence-based practice where some only reported studies meeting their *evidence of effectiveness* criteria, while others placed the studies in continuous categories such as *established, emerging,* or *unestablished*. Last, some reviews grouped treatments into "packages" (e.g., Behavioral Packages, Antecedent Packages) while others identified treatments individually. These varying intervention classification methods appeared to indicate differences in findings at first glance, but when comparing across reviews while taking the semantically different classifications into account, determinations of which treatments were evidence based were not found to be considerably different (Missouri Autism Guidelines Initiative, 2012).

There is continuing consensus that guidelines for best ASD intervention practices should include (a) early intervention; (b) systematic, developmentally appropriate activities and learning opportunities; (c) intensive instruction with active engagement; (d) peer and family involvement for generalization and educational achievement; (e) individualized services and supports via an IEP; (f) a systematic process for measuring outcomes; and (g) structured environments for learning (Iovannone, Dunlap, Huber, & Kincaid, 2003; National Research Council [NRC], 2001). Development of treatment for ASD is steadily advancing and, although all treatments discussed in this chapter may not have *established* effectiveness, several have shown promising results for positive outcomes. For the purposes of this chapter, interventions that meet the higher levels of evidence, *established* or *emerging*, according to the National Autism Center's (2009) *National Standards Report*, will be described:

- *Established*: Adequate evidence exists to confidently determine that the treatment results in beneficial effects for those with ASD.
- *Emerging*: One or more studies imply beneficial effects for those with ASD but more high-quality, scientifically rigorous studies are needed to reliably confirm positive outcomes before it is determined that the treatment is effective.

For other systematic reviews of ASD interventions, readers may refer to the Clinical Resources section at the end of this chapter. Because of the plethora of treatments that have been studied with this population, this section is divided into comprehensive treatment programs, structural or peer-based programs, and focused intervention programs. The purpose will be to summarize the evidence base for these programs, while a more detailed description of the interventions themselves can be found in individual articles referenced in the chapter, or Prelock and McCauley's (2012) textbook on ASD treatment.

Comprehensive Treatment Programs

Comprehensive programs address goals across different domains of development and functioning, and usually can be applied across several settings (e.g., school, home, individual settings); most have accompanying manuals, trainings, and/or certifications. The next segment of the chapter provides descriptions of behavioral, naturalistic, and structural and peer-based programs within comprehensive programs.

Behavioral Packages

Interventions using **ABA** principles are characterized by a common chain of events: (a) the occurrence of a stimulus for a desired behavior, (b) the client demonstrating a response, and (c) the interventionist giving a verbal or tangible reinforcer if the response is correct or withholding the reinforcer and assisting the client if the response is incorrect. One of the most extensively studied treatments for ASD, Behavioral Packages are at the *established* level of evidence for improvement of academic, interpersonal, communication, learning readiness, personal responsibility, self-regulation, and play for people from birth to 21 years old (Birnbrauer & Leach, 1993; Lovaas, 1987; Matson, Matson, & Rivet, 2007; NAC, 2009; Reichow & Volkmar, 2010; Stahmer & Schreibman, 1992). They also have been found effective in reducing problem behaviors, Restricted, Repetitive, Nonfunctional Patterns of Behavior and improving Sensory or Emotional Regulation (Iwata, Dorsey, Slifer, Bauman, & Richman, 1982; NAC, 2009).

Although behavioral interventions have the most evidence of effectiveness, a number of concerns have been raised. The studies have primarily included verbal participants with a verbal treatment delivery, so the treatments have not been proven to be as effective with those who are nonverbal (Walton & Ingersoll, 2013). Many intervention programs using ABA principles have relied largely on the use of adult-directed, highly structured discrete trial training strategies, and those interventions have often failed to demonstrate generalization of skills across settings (Wetherby & Woods, 2006, 2008). Much of the research has used single-case design methods, which have strong internal validity but unknown external validity (i.e., generalizability to individuals with different characteristics from those studied). Finally, evidence that Behavioral Packages are effective in addressing social pragmatic deficits is lacking. Although ASP is no longer considered separate from ASD, finding evidence-based treatment for those with Asperger phenotypes is of utmost importance, especially for interventionists who use only behavioral intervention, as they would be implementing a treatment that lacks evidence for those with primarily social pragmatic deficits (Wilczynski, Rue, Hunter, & Christian, 2012). Due to these drawbacks, researchers have tested more naturalistic applications of ABA principles, such as Pivotal Response Training (L. Koegel, Camarata, Valdez-Menchaca, & Koegel, 1998; see below), and clinicians have customized treatments to individual clients by modifying their behavioral methods to include elements from developmental approaches that have more evidence of generalizability (Wilczynski, 2012).

Challenging behavior (e.g., tantrums, hitting, shouting) is common not only for people with ASD but anyone who has difficulty communicating. Until one is taught to make requests and regulate others' behavior, challenging behavior will likely replace functional communication. Thus, **Functional Communication Training** (FCT) is an intervention based on ABA principles that is designed to teach caregivers to determine the purpose of the challenging behavior, choose a more appropriate way to communicate this purpose, and teach the individual how to replace the challenging behavior with the appropriate communication strategy by gradually reducing reinforcements or prompts (Durand, 1990, 2012). When a challenging behavior is dangerous to the person with ASD or others, however, ensuring elimination of dangerous challenging behavior may be prioritized over teaching appropriate replacement behaviors for effective communication (Durand, 2012).

In 2009, Petscher, Rey, and Bailey conducted a meta-analysis of at least 80 FCT studies targeting reduction of a variety of challenging behaviors. Results indicated positive effects and few adverse effects for these participants of various ages and impairments. For ASD specifically, however, Wong et al. (2014) analyzed 12 single-case FCT studies for social, behavior, communication, play, adaptive skills, and school-readiness outcomes for participants between 3 to 18 years old. Some of those studies showed that Response Milieu (provision of opportunities for the client to make choices) and practicing desired functional communication in settings outside the therapy room facilitated generalization of communication skills and augmented the effects of FCT (Carlson, Luiselli, Slyman, & Markowski, 2008; Durand, 1990, 2012; Dyer, Dunlap, & Winterling, 1990; Stokes, Fowler, & Baer, 1978; Watanabe & Sturmey, 2003). Moreover, the NAC (2009) categorizes FCT as a Behavioral Package, which is at the *established* level of evidence for people with ASD and PDD-NOS, birth to 21 years old.

Early Intensive Behavioral Intervention (EIBI; aka the UCLA Treatment) is a Comprehensive Behavioral Treatment for Young Children (birth to 9 years old), characterized by 20 to 40 hours of weekly intensive Discrete Trial Training (DTT; Lovaas, 1977) in the home. Based on ABA principles, DTT is included among the aforementioned definition of behavioral interventions, with trials consisting of a stimulus, response, a consequence or reinforcer, and a brief break (Wilczynski et al., 2012). The NAC's (2009) examination of 22 studies found treatments like EIBI to be effective for increasing communication, higher cognitive functions, interpersonal, motor, personal responsibility, placement, and play while being effective in reducing problem behaviors. Comprehensive Behavioral Treatment for Young Children, which includes EIBI, is at the *established* level of evidence for children with AD and PDD-NOS.

Specifically, EIBI has produced positive outcomes for expressive language, receptive language, socialization, and daily communication skills (Reichow, Barton, Boyd, & Hume, 2012). The quality of this evidence has been limited in widespread generalization of results because of the lack of randomized controlled trials (RCTs) and dosage guidelines. For instance, positive results have been reported for EIBI administered at as little as 12 hours a week, 25 hours per week, or 40 hours per week (Eldevik, Eikeseth, Jahr, & Smith, 2006; Luiselli, Cannon, Ellis, & Sisson, 2000; Meyer, Taylor, Levin, & Fisher, 2001). Hence, questions about EIBI dosage remain.

When considering DTT singularly, the NAC (2009) declared it *established* for those 3 to 21 years old when targeting communication, adaptive, and social skills. An RCT showed significantly improved language development, IQ scores, academic skills, and visual-spatial skills when compared to a 5 hours per week, parent-training group (based on Lovaas et al.'s, 1981, parent program; Smith, Groen, & Wynn, 2000). These twenty-eight 18- to 42-month-old children with autism and PDD-NOS all entered the study with IQs between 35 and 75, but the experimental group participants were more often mainstreamed than the comparison group was (Wilczynski, 2012). Moreover, Sallows and Graupner (2005) showed in their RCT ($N = 23$, mean age = 33 months), that children who had higher pretreatment IQs had the most improvement in IQ scores. Thus, characteristics such as IQ and mainstreaming exposure may influence DTT outcomes, necessitating control of these variables in future research.

In summary, evidence for behavioral interventions is extensive and a variety of positive outcomes can be attained. Yet, the literature still lacks methodologically sound RCTs with larger sample sizes. Furthermore, research on mediating factors (e.g., pretreatment IQ, verbal ability, communication level), maintenance and generalization of acquired skills, and evidence to support the use of EIBI and DTT for social pragmatic skills is imperative.

Naturalistic Teaching Strategies

Naturalistic Teaching Strategies (aka Naturalistic Interventions) encompass treatments that promote functional skills within typical, developmentally appropriate routines, activities, or settings that are natural reinforcers of the targeted skills (Wong et al., 2014). These social-pragmatic approaches are more child directed, facilitating generalization to multiple natural settings (L. Koegel, Koegel, Harrower, & Carter, 1999), but most also identify their foundations in the learning principles of ABA. A review of 10 single-case design studies of children with ASD, birth to 11 years old found Naturalistic Interventions to be effective when addressing behavior, joint attention, play, communication, social, and academic skills (Wong et al., 2014). Based on 32 studies that used high quality quasi-experimental group designs, high quality single subject designs, and RCTs, with outcomes of communication, interpersonal skills, learning readiness, and play, Naturalistic Teaching Strategies are at an *established* level of evidence for children with AD or PDD-NOS, birth to 9 years old (NAC, 2009). The following treatments have been classified as Naturalistic Teaching Strategies.

Training and Education of Autistic and Related Communication Handicapped Children (TEACCH) is an intervention characterized by a structured teaching environment rich with visual cues (NAC, 2009). It also incorporates parent involvement with therapists and educators, as well as broad-spectrum cognitive-behavioral strategies (Lazarus, 1958) that consider the domains of physical sensation, visual cues, interpersonal relationships, and biological factors (Schopler, 1997). This multimodal approach to cognitive-behavior therapy is designed to increase effectiveness of treatment and generalization of desired behaviors (Lazarus, 1958).

The structured teaching methodology capitalizes on students' strengths, and goals based on these strengths are developed for the IEP. A variety of procedures that depend on predictable schedules, specific physical organization of a setting, and individualized teaching methods are combined in the classroom. By customizing these classroom and instructional features to the cognitive styles of individuals with ASD, structured teaching aims to make learning, thinking, and understanding easier for them (Mesibov, Shea, & Schopler, 2004; Walton & Ingersoll, 2013).

Structure may be provided at a very basic level, e.g., by creating an "object schedule" for a nonverbal child with ASD using objects associated with each main activity in his classroom day, or at a more sophisticated level by helping a high-functioning adolescent better adapt to the school environment by using a smartphone calendar and other apps that provide predictability and organizational supports. Despite the individualized nature of TEACCH educational plans, research indicates that TEACCH can positively affect social contact, communication, imitation skills, higher cognitive functions, motor skills, learning readiness, personal responsibility, and general socialization scores for children up to 2.5 years after treatment (NAC, 2009; Panerai, Ferrante, & Zingale, 2002; Walton & Ingersoll, 2013).

A recently published study compared preschool classrooms using the TEACCH approach with ones using a comprehensive peer-mediated program called LEAP (Learning Experiences and Alternative Program for Preschoolers and their Parents) as well as with non-model specific preschool classrooms (Boyd et al., 2014). This study found that children with ASD made progress across an academic year in all three types of classrooms, but that their progress was the same no matter which type of classroom they were in. In order to be included in the study, all classrooms had to be rated as "high quality" based on observations of trained observers using a standardized rating scale. The researchers suggest that it may have been the many common elements across these high quality classrooms that were important in promoting student progress rather than the elements that differentiated among the three types of classrooms.

The TEACCH program is considered to be at the *emerging* level of evidence in the NAC (2009) review because of studies with small sample sizes and a lack of the most rigorous research design (RCT). In an updated meta-analysis of research on TEACCH (Virues-Ortega, Julio, & Pastor-Barriuso, 2013), the authors identified 13 studies for inclusion, and found moderate to large gains in social behavior and maladaptive behavior, but small to negligible effects on cognition, verbal, motor, or perceptual skills. Studies using TEACCH programs varied widely in terms of the age of the individuals included, whether the program was applied in home, school, or community settings and the duration and intensity of the intervention. The relatively small number of studies and their variability prompted the authors to conclude that the results of their meta-analysis should be considered preliminary.

Pivotal Response Treatment (PRT) focuses on pivotal areas of development including motivation, social initiations, responsivity to multiple cues, and self-management (L. Koegel et al., 1998). Pivotal Response Treatment has been used successfully with children, adolescents, and young adults and by concentrating on pivotal areas, change may occur in behaviors not directly targeted such as increased imitative utterances, learning rate, speech intelligibility, and eye gaze alternation (Bruinsma & McNerney, 2012; R. Koegel & Koegel, 1990; R. Koegel, Vernon, & Koegel, 2009).

Quasi-experimental, highly controlled studies have found PRT to be more effective with those who (a) can tolerate the close proximity of others, (b) demonstrate few nonverbal repetitive behaviors, (c) have a high level of verbal repetitive behaviors, and/or (d) are interested in toys (Bruinsma & McNerney, 2012; Scherer & Schreibman, 2005). Hence, as with DTT, mediating factors play a role in treatment response. Although PRT is a naturalistic treatment delivery that motivates the child to learn because they have choices in the play, it is derived from ABA strategies, resulting in its simultaneous categorization as Antecedent Package, Behavioral Package, and Self-Management treatment types. At its core, however, PRT is a play-based treatment that has been scientifically validated, resulting in an *established* level of evidence for those with ASD, 3 to 9 years old (NAC, 2009).

Interventions like **Enhanced Milieu Teaching** (EMT) are based on the therapist- or caregiver–child dyad playing in a naturalistic context (Kaiser, Hancock, & Trent, 2007). EMT is designed for children who have minimal language (i.e., 10 words or Mean Length of Utterance under 3.0) but can imitate words. For detailed information on EMT, see Hancock and Kaiser (2012).

Enhanced Milieu Teaching has resulted in increased targeted language, and improved quality of caregiver conversational turns with children with or at risk for ASD as young as 18 months. Studies at the highest quality (RCT) showed positive results after 24 sessions, that persisted 6 months later (Hancock & Kaiser, 2002). In summary, EMT is among the Naturalistic Teaching Strategies that are at the *established* level of evidence for the outcomes of communication skills, play, interpersonal skills, and learning readiness for those birth to 9 years old with AD and PDD-NOS (NAC, 2009).

The **Early Start Denver Model** (ESDM; Rogers & Dawson, 2010) is a comprehensive early intervention approach based on both ABA and developmental principles. In the initially reported study of ESDM, professionals engaged in one-to-one interactions with toddlers with ASD for 15 hours a week for 2 years, supplemented by parent delivery of ESDM for an additional 5 (or more) hours per week. ESDM yielded large effects in improved cognitive developmental outcomes (Dawson et al., 2009) after 2 years. This intervention shares many characteristics of other interventions using naturalistic teaching strategies, but the randomized controlled trial reporting these results was published after the NAC (2009) synthesis. Another instantiation of the ESDM that has been tested is to provide parent coaching in the ESDM intervention 1 hour per week for 12 weeks, without any additional professional interaction with toddlers with ASD. In an randomized controlled trial, the parent-implemented ESDM did not yield significant changes in either parent or child outcomes after 12 weeks (Rogers et al., 2012), suggesting that the more intense professional involvement and longer length of intervention in the earlier ESDM study contributed to the positive effects.

The **Early Social Interaction Project** (ESI) was also designed for children who are at risk for or have ASD, have minimal language, and are under 3 years old. Early Social Interaction activities are embedded into daily routines and, in the context of child-directed play, adults encourage communication using behavioral strategies such as communicative temptations and reinforcement (Dunst, Hamby, Trivette, Raab, & Bruder, 2000; Woods, Wetherby, Kashinath, & Holland, 2012). See Woods et al., (2012) for further description of ESI.

Significant advancement in social communication skills, as well as collateral improvement in initiation and response to joint attention was found after ESI (Wetherby & Woods, 2006). The evidence for Naturalistic Teaching Strategies that include ESI is *established* with some studies providing evidence of its effectiveness when implemented by parents (NAC, 2009; Woods et al., 2012).

At the end of infancy and into toddlerhood, typically developing children demonstrate specific communication skills and detailed information on this cognitive development is included in Chapter 4 of this text (Bates, Benigni, Bretherton, Camaioni, & Volterra, 1979). **Joint attention** (JA) skills are among these typical communication skills and they occur within the context of a joint engaged state where the adult and child are focused on the same activity, object, or event during routines (Bakeman & Adamson, 1984). Joint attention is integral to language development because children need to have the same joint attentional focus as a communicative partner in order to acquire new words (Tomasello & Farrar, 1986). JA skills consist of protodeclaratives or gestures used to share (e.g., pointing, showing, giving, eye contact) and absence of these skills is a risk indicator for ASD, as well as a core deficit that differentiates ASD from other developmental delays and disorders (Mundy et al., 1986). For more information on JA intervention, see Kasari, Fannin, and Stickles-Goods (2012).

Hwang and Hughes (2000) conducted a meta-analysis of 16 social interactive interventions for 64 children with autism (84% boys, 2 to 12 years old, approximately 48% verbal, 21% echolalic, 31% nonverbal) with only one study (Tiegerman & Primavera, 1984) including participants with profound social communicative delays. This meta-analysis revealed improvements in eye contact, JA gestures, social and affective behaviors, and nonverbal and verbal expressive language. However, few of these gains were generalized and maintained across settings and time. Among treatments designed to improve functional communication by promoting early social communicative skills, however, JA treatment has a growing body of evidence that has revealed better generalization via RCTs.

For example, a JA RCT focused on making preschoolers with autism (3 to 4 years old, average Developmental Quotient of 58) initiators of communication instead of the customary responders, and the experimental JA group initiated joint engagement significantly more often than both the ABA-only control group and a second, Symbolic Play (SP) treatment group (Kasari, Freeman, & Paparella, 2006). Furthermore, JA treatment also improved joint engagement with maintenance of expressive language improvements in the JA and SP groups 6 to 12 months after treatment, in contexts outside the treatment room. Based on six studies of children birth to 5 years old with AD and PDD-NOS, the NAC (2009) determined that JA interventions are at the *established* level of evidence for the outcomes of interpersonal skills and communication.

Developmental, Relationship-Based Intervention involves an adult interacting with the child (18 months to 9 years old) by responding to and imitating the child's communicative attempts (Walton & Ingersoll, 2013). The "relationship" component of developmental, relationship-based intervention stands for the healthy relationship desired between the child and caregiver while the 'developmental' component signifies treating the child at the appropriate developmental level. In a comparative study of preschoolers with ASD and preschoolers with other behavioral and developmental disorders ($N = 72$), both groups improved in language and cognitive areas as a result of a developmental relationship-based intervention model (Rogers & Dillala, 1991). Significant increases in the rate of language acquisition and decreases in autistic symptoms for children diagnosed with PDD were also found in Rogers and Lewis's (1989) study.

A very salient, socially valid outcome measure is a change from an ASD diagnosis to no ASD diagnosis. For instance, Relationship Development Intervention (RDI), a caregiver-based treatment, was administered between 2000 and 2005 to 16 children who met ADOS/ADI-R criteria for autism, and 100% no longer met criteria after treatment (Gutstein, Burgess, & Montfort, 2007).

The **Developmental, Individual-difference, Relationship-based** (DIR) program is another particular intervention that capitalizes on the individual way in which each child processes information (Gerber, 2012). Greenspan and Wieder (1997), the authors of DIR, reviewed records of 200 toddlers and preschoolers who had received a minimum of 2 years of DIR, finding that 8 years posttreatment, 58% of the participants had "good to outstanding" abilities to affectively relate to others, engage, and participate in spontaneous verbal communication turns (Gerber, 2012). These children also scored in the non-autistic range on the Childhood Autism Rating Scale (CARS; Schopler et al., 1999). Another longitudinal study of 10- to15-year-old boys with ASD ($N = 16$) who had received DIR revealed significant improvement in empathy, creativity, and reflection, along with improved academic skills and healthy peer relationships for 58% of the sample (Wieder & Greenspan, 2005).

Floortime is a specific treatment model within DIR, and 45.5% of participants in a study were rated as good to very good in functional development after receiving approximately a year of treatment (Solomon, Necheles, Ferch, & Bruckman, 2007). Gains in JA, joint engagement duration, communication initiation, expressive language, vocabulary, turn-taking routines, and communication frequency occurred when parents were more responsive as a result of the DIR/ Floortime™ training (Mahoney & Perales, 2003, 2005; McConachie, Randle, Hammal, & Le Couteur, 2005). Developmental Relationship-Based Intervention is an *emerging* group of treatments for children from birth to 5 years old with AD and PDD-NOS, resulting in increased skills in communication, higher cognitive functions, interpersonal skills, self-regulation, and motor skills, as well as a decrease in general symptoms of ASD and Sensory or Emotional Regulation (NAC, 2009).

LEAP and Other Peer-Mediated Approaches

School settings provide a natural opportunity to implement **peer-mediated interventions**. Several studies have shown typically developing peers to be realistic models of appropriate social interaction for children, adolescents, and adults with ASD, resulting in increased academic participation, frequency and quality of responding to others, reciprocity, understanding others' social communication, interacting with others, inclusion in classroom settings, and friendship formation across settings (Carter, Sisco, & Chung, 2012; Garrison-Harrell, Kamps, & Kravitz, 1997; Walton & Ingersoll, 2013). For example, Learning Experiences: An Alternative Program for Preschoolers (LEAP) is a naturalistic, classroom-based, behavioral program where typically developing peers model desired social behaviors in order to encourage social development in the children with ASD. According to Odom, Boyd, Hall, and Hume's (2010) systematic review of comprehensive treatment models (CTM), there is strong evidence for LEAP where, although large RCTs are limited, LEAP is well documented, has been replicated, has evidence of efficacy, and was the only CTM to receive the highest rating for fidelity of implementation.

Based on 33 studies, peer-mediated interventions are at the *established* level of evidence for the outcomes of play skills, interpersonal skills, and communication skills for children with Autistic Disorder and PDD-NOS, ages 3 to 14 years old (NAC, 2009). Furthermore, 15 single-case studies showed effectiveness for people with ASD, ages 3 to 18 years old, when targeting joint attention, school-readiness, academic skills, and the aforementioned outcomes evaluated in the NAC report (Wong et al., 2014).

Clinicians must bear in mind certain factors, however, when considering peer-mediated intervention. For instance, although peer-mediated intervention has been implemented with children as young as 3 years old, particular social targets may be more appropriate within certain age ranges. Peer-initiation training, where peers initiate interactions using techniques such as offering to share, requesting assistance, and gaining the child's attention, is most appropriate for those aged 3 through 8 years old when the goal is to help children with ASD gain social and communication skills (Neitzel, 2008); however, training peers to form a social "network" that supports children with ASD in their classrooms is best for children aged 9 to 18 years old (Rotheram-Fuller, Kasari, Chamberlain, & Locke, 2010). Thus, despite the *established* status of peer-mediated treatment, more research is needed to determine specifics such as whether individual peer interactions are more effective than group peer interactions (Cushing, Kennedy, Shukla, Davis, & Meyer, 1997; Walton & Ingersoll, 2013).

Focused Intervention Strategies

Augmentative and Alternative Communication

Focused intervention strategies are typically individualized treatments that include Augmentative and Alternative Communication (AAC), Picture Exchange Communication System (PECS), social stories, and video modeling. AAC can be used in both group and individual settings, with graphic systems like PECS, sign language, and speech-generating devices (SGD) being common types. These communication modalities replace or support verbal language, augmenting the communication of people with ASD (ASHA, 2004; Tincani, 2004). A meta-analysis of 24 case studies examined the impact of three AAC interventions (i.e., PECS, SGD, and non-PECS picture exchange systems) and the overall effect AAC had on behavior outcomes (Ganz et al., 2012). This evidence confirmed that AAC had large positive effects, with the outcome of communication being most affected among the targeted skills. All picture based systems produced effects; however, PECS, as well as SGDs exhibited the largest effect sizes (Ganz et al., 2012).

Researchers have offered evidence refuting the frequent assumption that AAC use will hamper verbal production (Millar, 2009). Millar, Light, and Schlosser's (2006) meta-analysis reviewed literature published more than 28 years that explored the effect of AAC on verbal language for those 2 to 60 years old with intellectual disability or ASD. There was no evidence that AAC inhibits verbal productions. Of the 23 studies, 6 had experimental controls, with 2 of those controlled studies having participants with ASD. Charlop-Christy, Carpenter, Le, LeBanc, and Kellet (2002) reported an increase in communicative functions for three children 3 to 12 years old, and Kouri's (1988) study resulted in significant gains for production of words with a 3-year-old with ASD. The participants may have demonstrated ceiling effects that could have resulted in underestimation of gains attributed to AAC, so more methodologically rigorous research is needed (Millar et al., 2006).

These meta-analyses establish a broad view of the positive effect of AAC on people with disabilities, but because there are several different types of AAC and ASD profiles, examination of specific AAC treatments for ASD is warranted, namely, (a) PECS, (b) speech-generating devices, and (c) video modeling. Beyond the various phenotypes of people with ASD, cultural differences must also be considered; for example, Huer's (2003) research described how there are cultural differences in how people perceive several AAC symbol sets. This research provides additional evidence that individual differences can influence effective use of AAC. Evidence at the *emerging* level exists for AAC for toddlers through adults. Specific modes of AAC that have *emerging* evidence include PECS for children under 9 years of age, SGDs for children 6 to 14 years, and sign language for children ages 3 to 9 years (NAC, 2009).

The **Picture Exchange Communication System** is an aided, low-tech graphic communication approach based on pictures or icons (Bondy & Frost, 1994). It employs an applied behavior modification method of prompting, modeling, and shaping along with a reward system to teach functional nonverbal and verbal communication (Charlop-Christy et al., 2002; Frost & Bondy, 2002). Making the most of the tendency for people with ASD to be visual learners, clients are taught to solve communicative problems by initiating communication or making observations through exchange of pictures for verbal words (Schopler, Mesibov, & Hearsey, 1995). In addition, PECS appears to decrease challenging behaviors that may occur due to the inability to express one's self (Frea, Arnold, & Vittimberga, 2001; Charlop-Christy et al., 2002).

Forty-one PECS studies were analyzed in two meta-analyses of AAC (Schlosser & Wendt, 2008; Sulzer-Azaroff, Hoffman, Horton, Bondy, & Frost, 2009). Although only Schlosser and Wendt (2008), assessed the quality of the studies (one group design and six single subject designs), results of both meta-analyses were consistent with the NAC's (2009) determination that evidence for PECS' effectiveness is limited by negative to small gains in speech skills, small to moderate gains in communication, and low quality in generalization and maintenance (Flippin, Rezka & Watson, 2010). In their RCT of PECS with 4- to 10-year-olds ($N = 84$, 15 schools), Howlin, Gordon, Pasco, Wade, and Charman (2007), showed that spontaneous requests increased significantly but spontaneous language for social purposes did not. Moreover, better outcomes were associated with baseline characteristics such as a lower severity rating on the *ADOS*. In essence, if the child had a few words when PECS training commenced, he or she would benefit more than one who was completely nonverbal. Additionally, the Flippin et al. (2010) meta-analysis revealed that Phase IV (i.e., teaching "I want . . ." sentences), may be the section that has the most impact on speech outcomes. Thus, when designing a treatment plan for ASD, a social communication disorder at its core, clinicians must remember that evidence is tentative for whether PECS is as useful for social communication as it is for initiating requests, and certain phases of the intervention may affect the outcomes differently. In their analysis of two group and four single case design studies, Wong et al., (2014) deemed PECS effective for 3- to 14-year-old children with ASD for social, joint attention, and communication skills. According to the NAC (2009) analysis, evidence for PECS is *emerging* because results are mixed in terms of overall effectiveness.

Speech-generating devices (SGD) are portable, computerized or battery-operated devices that substitute for or supplement verbal expression by producing digitized or synthetic speech when graphic symbols or buttons are triggered (Wegner, 2012). Not only are SGDs effective in enhancing expressive communication; they also have helped reduce challenging behaviors in those with ASD (Millar, 2009). Additionally, SGDs can be used to augment communication input (i.e., receptive language) (Drager, 2009). For example, methods such as Natural Aided Language, Aided Language Stimulation, and the System for Augmenting Language mandate that the communication partner also use the SGD to enhance communicative input to the person with ASD, resulting in increased spoken words and SGD generated utterances from the person with ASD (Cafiero, 2005; Goossens, Crain, & Elder, 1992; Romski & Sevcik, 2003).

Because SGDs are newer than manual sign or graphic systems, there is less research on SGDs for people with ASD. There are multiple choices in the type of device used, software, symbol selection method, and display (Mirenda & Erickson, 2000). Thus, in addition to investigation of whether SGDs enhance human verbal modes of treatment delivery, studies on the most beneficial display types for development of social and functional communication is ongoing (Wegner, 2012). The National Standards Project (NAC, 2009) considers the evidence base for SGDs to be *emerging*, as more research is needed on the best ways to teach use of SGDs, and the best way to design devices that will have the greatest impact on social communication, functional communication, and language development (Wegner, 2012).

Video Modeling Interventions

Hermelin and O'Connor (1970) declared that people with autism have an information-processing deficit, characterized by their visuospatial encoding ability being superior to their auditory processing skills (Quill, 1997). For example, children with ASD were most successful on IQ test tasks that involved block design, matching, form discrimination, pattern analysis, and object assembly when the visual stimuli were constantly available (DeMyer, 1975; Harris, Handleman, & Burton, 1990; Lincoln, Courchesne, Kilman, Elmasian, & Allen, 1988; Siegel, Minshew, & Goldstein, 1996). Thus, treatment that utilizes video is especially appropriate for people with ASD who tend to be visual learners and those who do not readily imitate behaviors in person because of distractors in the in vivo context (Bellini & Akullian, 2007; Bryan & Gast, 2000). Hence, some people with ASD can better focus on salient components of behaviors via video models, as the interventionist can reduce distractions in the video context (Charlop-Christy, Le, & Freeman, 2000).

Video modeling consists of the client seeing a video of another person or themselves appropriately performing a targeted behavior (e.g., functional skills, social skills, language) (Bandura, 1969, 1997; Buggey, 2009). Whereas traditional video modeling shows behaviors to be imitated, self observation is a video modeling variant that allows the client to analyze what *not* to do (Buggey, 2012). For instance, the client views video of an unsuccessful social interaction involving themselves, allowing them to identify errors, devise ways to improve, and highlight achievements. For details on video modeling implementation, see Buggey (2012).

One can consider video modeling to be a combination of technology based and modeling interventions and, although there is evidence of its effectiveness with children of various ASD severity levels, more rigorous studies are necessary since most studies used multiple-baseline, single-subject design, rendering the sample sizes small (Buggey, 2012). For instance, results of the limited number of studies targeting school-age children have been mixed due to small samples, and almost half the participants not responding to treatment, owing to unfamiliarity with the toy used during the task or inability to attend to the videos (Nikopoulos & Keenan, 2003, 2004). In addition, studies targeting adults and school-aged children that discern which group of people (by severity and age) with ASD would most benefit from video modeling are lacking (Buggey, 2012; Walton & Ingersoll, 2013). Other studies revealing negative findings included preschool participants and these results can be explained by the notion that very young children may not have yet developed the cognitive abilities to observe, self-reflect, judge, remember, and apply learning to current and new contexts (Buggey, Hoomes, Williams, & Sherberger, 2011; Clark et al., 1993; Lewis & Brooks-Gunn, 1979). Nonetheless, the majority of video modeling research indicates that it has been appropriate for young children and adolescents diagnosed with ASD, PDD-NOS, ASP, and autism (Bellini & Akullian, 2007; Buggey, 2005; Delano, 2007; Dowrick, 1983; Sansosti & Powell-Smith, 2008; Scattone, 2008). Consequently, modeling interventions that include video modeling are at the *established* level of evidence (NAC, 2009).

Story-Based Intervention Package

As ASD is a social communication disorder, use of story-based intervention is especially appropriate for the goal of minimizing impairments in social knowledge. Story-based intervention involves the person with ASD writing a story that describes a particular situation and provides key information needed for proper social responses (Gray & Garand, 1993). The most popular story-based intervention, **Social Stories**, was intended for those with ASD but has been used successfully with clients with other intellectual deficiencies, as long as they possess basic written and receptive language skills and understand vocabulary at their cognitive level (Schneider & Goldstein, 2010). Types of sentences used in Social Stories include Descriptive, Directive, Perspective, Affirmative, Control, and Cooperative. For details on Social Stories sentences, see Hutchins, (2012a), and Gray (2003).

Some efficacy studies show that Social Stories can affect indirect outcomes including (a) better acclimation to new social situations, (b) demonstration of appropriate behavioral routines, (c) increase and maintenance of appropriate social behaviors for up to 10 months, and (d) reduction in challenging behaviors (Del Valle, McEachern, & Chambers, 2001; Gray & Garand, 1993; Hutchins, 2012b; Scattone, Wilczynski, Edwards, & Rabian, 2002; Toplis & Hadwin, 2006). Limitations in this evidence, however, consist of small samples with primarily single-subject designs. Moreover, participants did not maintain social communication gains once prompts and visual cues were removed, and more complicated targets like securing attention required a higher intensity of treatment to ensure mastery (Thiemann & Goldstein, 2001).

Through story-based interventions, however, the person with ASD can increase their understanding of (a) what people are feeling, doing, or thinking; (b) the sequence of events in a social interaction; (c) social cues and what they mean; and (d) the script for what is customarily said in social interactions (Attwood, 2000; Gray, 1998, 2010; Rowe, 1999). Based on 17 single-case studies for children aged 3 to 18 years old, story-based interventions for the outcomes of interpersonal skills and self-regulation are at the *established* level of evidence for children with AD and children with ASP ages 6 to 14 years old (Gray & Garand, 1993; NAC, 2009); but evidence for those with severe ASD is scarce and inconclusive (Quirmbach, Lincoln, Feinberg-Gizzo, Ingersoll, & Andrews, 2009).

Social skills groups are a form of focused intervention where peers (typical or with disabilities) interact in a group setting to teach interpersonal communication, play, or social skills. According to an analysis of seven group-design and eight single-case studies by Wong et al. (2014), social skills groups are effective for treating the outcomes of play, cognitive skills, behavior, social skills, and communication skills for toddlers to young adults with ASD. Reichow, Steiner, and Volkmar (2012) evaluated the effects of social skills group treatment across five studies ($N = 196$; ages 6–21 years), providing evidence that social skills groups can improve quality of life based on outcomes of decreased loneliness, improved friendship quality, and overall social competence. However, no significant differences between the treatment and control groups were found in understanding idioms, emotional recognition, and child/parental depression.

Although social skills groups show promise as an evidence-based form of peer-mediated treatment, these results cannot yet be generalized to a wider population, because of the lack of RCTs for social skills groups and homogeneity of the samples characterized by exclusively mostly 7- to 12-year-old US participants with average or above average intelligence. Furthermore, there is a dearth of evidence to support effectiveness with adults beyond age 22. Hence, social skills groups are at the *emerging* level of evidence (NAC, 2009). Although some research is beginning to provide evidence that social skills groups can facilitate progression of social competence skills, implementation of this type of peer-mediated treatment in every setting, with all types of participants, should be taken with caution owing to the lack of a robust evidence base (Reichow, Steiner, et al., 2012).

The use of evidence-based treatment can be exemplified in the case of Hanaa, who, approximately 5 months after the university evaluation, participated in a 12-week research treatment program targeting joint attention and joint engagement. Mrs. A was included in sessions to facilitate use of play routines, joint-attention, and joint-engaged states at home. After the program, Mrs. A reported that Hanaa interacted and played more appropriately with her sisters but had not yet gained many words.

At age 6, Hanaa continues to need treatment; a new SLP at the university clinic commenced intervention approximately 2 years after the initial evaluation and aforementioned 12-week treatment. Hanaa exhibits many of the same sensory-seeking behaviors as earlier, making it difficult to get her to focus. Mr. A reported that she gained new words in English and Arabic, but Mrs. A reported that Hanaa has no new words, despite continued treatment at her school. The university SLP concurred with Mrs. A that Hanaa remains functionally nonverbal. The original evaluating SLP at the university who administered the 12-week treatment recalled that the room in which she saw Hanaa was large with multiple distractors (e.g., cabinets to climb, a sink, electric paper-towel dispenser, mirror wall), and recommended that treatment be conducted in a smaller, more sterile room. The current university SLP also requested a swing to address Hanaa's hyposensitivity. Hanaa may also benefit from ABA in order to learn some words, get through daily activities at home, and learn how to use an AAC device. Using ABA might be helpful in establishing words initially, but more joint attention/engagement treatment would directly target Hanaa's attention deficit and social communication. Both SLPs recommended that an SGD be introduced, with the goals of facilitating expressive communication and reducing frustration for both Hanaa and the listener. As the evidence for ASD treatment builds and an increasing number of more challenging participants (i.e., nonverbal, bilingual, severe ASD) such as Hanaa are included in high-quality, controlled treatment studies, clinicians will become more efficient and precise in matching the best, evidence-based intervention to the various phenotypes on the autism spectrum.

DISCUSSION QUESTIONS

1. Bearing in mind the stakeholders (e.g., people with ASD and their caregivers, health care providers, clinicians, educators), discuss the pros and cons of the revised definition of ASD in the *DSM-5*.
2. Examine the following three resources cited for ASD prevalence in the US to identify the research designs used:

   - Autism and Developmental Disabilities Monitoring. (2012). *Prevalence of autism spectrum disorders (ASDs) among multiple areas in the United States in 2008* [PDF file]. Available from www.cdc.gov/ncbddd/autism/documents/ addm-2012-community-report.pdf.

- Centers for Disease Control and Prevention. (2012). Prevalence of autism spectrum disorders—Autism and developmental disabilities. *MMWR Surveillance Summary, 61*(3), 1–19.
- Blumberg, S. J., Bramlett, M. D., Kogan, M. D., Schieve, L. A., Jones, J. R., & Lu, M. C. (2013). Changes in prevalence of parent-reported autism spectrum disorders in school-aged US children: 2007 to 2011–12. *National Health Statistics Reports, 64*, 1–12.

Describe any advantages and/or drawbacks of collecting prevalence data in these ways. Discuss how prevalence reports may change based on the *DSM-5* criteria for ASD.

3. Consider what additional or alternative evidence-based approaches might be implemented with Hanaa. She is currently a functionally nonverbal, bilingual, sensory seeking 6-year-old with severe ASD and no intellectual impairment. What additional information is needed to choose the appropriate treatment? What supplemental treatment approach might fit Hanaa's profile? Based on the evidence presented in this chapter, what treatments might *not* fit Hanaa's profile?

CLINICAL RESOURCES

Association of Science in Autism Treatment: www.asatonline.org

- This website includes book reviews, video demonstrations of interventions, research summaries of treatments, and the Clinical Corner, where questions asked by the public are answered by autism experts.

Autism Internet Modules: www.autisminternetmodules.org/

- This website includes evidence-based practice briefs, case studies, and video examples pertaining to 14 evidence-based ASD interventions.

The National Professional Development Center on Autism Spectrum Disorders: Evidence-based Practice Briefs: http://autismpdc.fpg.unc.edu/content/briefs

- This website includes evidence-based practice briefs for ASD.

The National Professional Development Center on Autism Spectrum Disorders (NPDCASD): http://autismpdc.fpg.unc.edu/

- This website compares the 24 NPDCASD evidence-based practices to those in the National Standards Project. It also provides detailed descriptions of the interventions with directions for implementation.

National Autism Center: www.nationalautismcenter.org/

- This website contains articles, information from the National Standards Project, a Frequently Asked Question section, and an Educator's manual. An updated version of the NAC (2009) report is expected to be disseminated late 2014 or in 2015.

Evaluation of Comprehensive Treatment Models for Individuals with Autism Spectrum Disorders: http://dcautismparents.org/yahoo_site_admin/assets/docs/ABA_14.9261728.pdf

- This is a systematic review of 30 Comprehensive Treatment Models from the early 1970s to 2009, for people with ASD birth to 22 years.

Evidence-based Practices in Intervention for Children and Youth with ASD: http://autismpdc.fpg.unc.edu/content/evidence-based-practices

- This is a systematic review sponsored by the NPDC of approximately 360 Focused Intervention studies from 1997 to 2007, for people with ASD from birth to 22 years.

Vanderbilt Evidence-Based Practice Center on behalf of Agency for Healthcare Research and Quality: www.effectivehealthcare.ahrq.gov/ehc/products/106/656/cer26_autism_report_04-14-2011.pdf

- This is a systematic review sponsored by AHRQ of 159 behavioral, medical, educational, Allied Health, and Complementary and Alternative Medicine studies from 2000 to 2010, for children at-risk for ASD birth to 2 years, and children 2 to 12 years old with ASD.

ASD Services, Final Report on Environmental Scan: www.impaqint.com/sites/default/files/project-reports/Autism_Spectrum_Disorders.pdf

- This is a systematic review sponsored by the Centers for Medicare and Medicaid Services of 271 psychosocial and behavioral interventions from 1998 to 2008 for children birth to 16 years, transitioning youth 17 to 21 years, and adults 21+ with ASD.

REFERENCES

American Psychiatric Association. (1994). *Diagnostic and Statistical Manual of Mental Disorders DSM-IV Fourth Edition*. Washington, DC: American Psychiatric Association Inc.

American Psychiatric Association. (2000). *Diagnostic and statistical manual of mental disorders* (4th ed., text rev.). Washington, DC: Author.

American Psychiatric Association. (2013). *Autism spectrum disorder fact sheet.* Retrieved from www.dsm5.org/Documents/Autism%20Spectrum%20 Disorder%20Fact%20Sheet.pdf

American Psychiatric Association. (2013). *Diagnostic and Statistical Manual of Mental Disorders DSM-V Fifth Edition*. Washington, DC: American Psychiatric Association Inc.

American Speech-Language-Hearing Association. (2004). *Roles and responsibilities of speech-language pathologists with respect to augmentative and alternative communication: Technical report*. Retrieved from www.asha. org/policy/TR2004-00262/.

American Speech-Language-Hearing Association. (2006). *Guidelines for speech-language pathologists in diagnosis, assessment, and treatment of autism spectrum disorders across the life span*. Retrieved from www.asha. org/policy.

American Speech-Language Hearing Association. (2009). *Autism spectrum disorders guidelines*. Retrieved from www.asha.org/members/compendiumSearchResults.aspx?type=0&searchtext=Autism%20Spectrum%20 Disorders

Attwood, T. (2000). Strategies for improving the social integration of children with Asperger syndrome. *Autism, 4*, 85–100.

Autism and Developmental Disabilities Monitoring Network. (2014). Prevalence of autism spectrum disorder among children aged 8 years—Autism and Developmental Disabilities Monitoring Network, 11 sites, United States, 2010. *Morbidity and Mortality Weekly Report, 2014, 63* (2), 1–21.

Baird, G., Charman, T., Baron-Cohen, S., Cox, A., Swettenham, J., Wheelwright, S., & Drew, A. (2000). A screening instrument for autism at 18 months of age: A 6-year follow-up study. *Journal of the American Academy of Child and Adolescent Psychiatry, 39*, 694–702.

Bakeman, R., & Adamson, L. B. (1984). Coordinating attention to people and objects in mother–infant and peer–infant interaction. *Child Development, 55*(4), 1278–1789.

Bandura, A. (1969). *Principles of behavior modification*. Oxford, UK: Holt, Rinehart, & Winston.

Bandura, A. (1997). *Self-efficacy: The exercise of control*. New York, NY: Freeman.

Barnes, K. E. (1982). *Preschool screening: The measurement and prediction of children at-risk*. Springfield, IL: Charles C Thomas.

Baron-Cohen, S., Allen, J., & Gillberg, C. (1992). Can autism be detected at 18 months? The needle, the haystack, and the CHAT. *British Journal of Psychiatry, 161*, 839–843.

Baron-Cohen, S., Cox, A., Baird, G., Swettenham, J., Nightingale, N., Morgan, K., . . . Charman, T. (1996). Psychological markers in the detection of autism in infancy in a large population. *British Journal of Psychiatry, 168*, 158–163.

Baron-Cohen, S., Wheelwright, S., Robinson J., & Woodbury-Smith, M. (2005). The Adult Asperger Assessment (AAA): A diagnostic method. *Journal of Autism and Developmental Disorders, 35*, 807–819.

Bates, E., Benigni, L., Bretherton, I., Camaioni, L., & Volterra, V. (1979). *The emergence of symbols: Cognition and communication in infancy.* New York, NY: Academic Press.

Bellini, S., & Akullian, J. (2007). A meta-analysis of video modeling and video self-modeling interventions for children and adolescents with autism spectrum disorders. *Exceptional Children, 73*, 264–287.

Bennett, T. A., Szatmari, P., Bryson, S. E., Volden, J., Zwaigenbaum, L., Vaccarella, L., . . . Boyle, M. H. (2008). Differentiating autism and Asperger syndrome on the basis of language delay or impairment. *Journal of Autism and Developmental Disorders, 38*, 616–625.

Birnbrauer, J. S., & Leach, D. J. (1993). The Murdoch Early Intervention Program after 2 years. *Behaviour Change, 10*, 63–74.

Blumberg, S. J., Bramlett, M. D., Kogan, M. D., Schieve, L. A., Jones, J. R., & Lu, M. C. (2013). Changes in prevalence of parent-reported autism spectrum disorders in school-aged US children: 2007 to 2011–12. *National Health Statistics Reports, 64*, 1–12.

Bondy, A., & Frost, L. (1994). The Picture Exchange Communication System. *Focus on Autistic Behavior, 9*, 1–19.

Borden, M. C. (2011). *Treating individuals who have autism: DSM-V, ABA, and beyond.* Retrieved from www.childadolescentbehavior.com/Article-Detail/treating-individuals-autism.aspx

Boyd, B. A., Conroy, M. A., Asmus, J. M., McKenney, E. L. W., & Mancil, G. R. (2008). Descriptive analysis of classroom setting events on the social behaviors of children with autism spectrum disorder. *Education and Training in Developmental Disabilities, 43*(2), 186–197.

Boyd, B. A., Hume, K., McBee, M. T., Alessandri, M., Gutierrez, A., Johnson, L., . . . Odom, S. L. (2014). Comparative efficacy of LEAP, TEACCH and non-model-specific special education programs for preschoolers with autism spectrum disorders. *Journal of Autism and Developmental Disorders, 44*, 366–380.

Brouwers, M., Kho, M.E., Browman, G.P., Cluzeau, F., feder, G., Fervers, B., . . . Makarski, J. on behalf of the AGREE Next Steps Consortium. (2010). AGREE II: Advancing guideline development, reporting and evaluation in healthcare. *Canadian Medical Association Journal. 182*, E839-842. doi: 10.1503/cmaj.090449

Bruinsma, Y., & McNerney, E. K. (2012). Pivotal response treatment. In P. A. Prelock, & R. J. McCauley (Eds.), *Treatment of autism spectrum disorders: Evidence-based intervention strategies for communication and social interactions* (pp. 281–312). Baltimore, MD: Brookes.

Bryan, L. C., & Gast, D. L. (2000). Teaching on-task and on-schedule behaviors to high-functioning children with autism via picture activity schedules. *Journal of Autism and Developmental Disorders, 30*(6), 553–567.

Buggey, T. (2009). *Seeing is believing: Video self-modeling for people with autism and other developmental disabilities*. Bethesda, MD: Woodbine House.

Buggey, T. (2005). Video modeling applications with students with autism spectrum disorder in a small private school setting. *Focus on Autism and Other Developmental Disabilities, 20*, 52–63.

Buggey, T. (2012). Effectiveness of video self-modeling to promote social initiations by 3-year-olds with autism spectrum disorders. *Focus on Autism and Other Developmental Disabilities, 27*(2), 102–110.

Buggey, T., Hoomes, G., Williams, S., & Sherberger, B. (2011). Facilitating social initiations with preschoolers with autism using self-modeling. *Focus on Autism, 26*, 25–36.

Cafiero, J. M. (2005). *Meaningful exchanges for people with autism: An introduction to augmentative and alternative communication*. Bethesda, MD: Woodbine House.

Carlson, J. I., Luiselli, J. K., Slyman, A., & Markowski, A. (2008). Choice-making as intervention for public disrobing in children with developmental disabilities. *Journal of Positive Behavior Interventions, 10*(2), 86–90.

Carter, E. W., Sisco, L. G., & Chung, Y. (2012). Peer-mediated support strategies. In P. A. Prelock & R. J. McCauley (Eds.), *Treatment of autism spectrum disorders: Evidence-based intervention strategies for communication and social interactions* (pp. 221–254). Baltimore, MD: Brookes.

Centers for Disease Control and Prevention. (2013). *Autism spectrum disorders: Screening and diagnosis for healthcare providers*. Retrieved from www.cdc.gov/ncbddd/autism/hcp-screening.html#recommendations.

Charlop-Christy, M. H., Carpenter, M., Le, L., LeBlanc, L. A., & Kellet, K. (2002). Using the Picture Exchange Communication System (PECS) with children with autism: Assessment of PECS acquisition, speech, social-communicative behavior, and problem behavior. *Journal of Applied Behavior Analysis, 35*(3), 213–231.

Charlop-Christy, M. H., Le, L., & Freeman, K. A. (2000). A comparison of video modeling with in vivo modeling for teaching children with autism. *Journal of Autism and Developmental Disorders, 30*(6), 537–552.

Clark, E., Beck. D., Sloane, H., Goldsmith, D., Jenson, W., Bowen, J., & Kehle, T. (1993). Self-modeling with preschoolers: Is it different? *School Psychology International, 14*, 83–89.

Cuccaro, M. L., Nations, L., Brinkley, J., Abramson, R. K., Wright, H. H., Hall, A., . . . Pericak-Vance, M. A. (2007). A comparison of repetitive behaviors in Aspergers disorder and high functioning autism. *Child Psychiatry and Human Development, 37*, 347–360.

Cushing, L., Kennedy, C., Shukla, S., Davis, J., & Meyer, K. (1997). Disentangling the effects of curricular revision and social grouping within cooperative learning arrangements. *Focus on Autism and Other Developmental Disabilities, 12*, 231–240.

Dawson, G., Rogers, S., Munson, J., Smith, M., Winter, J., Greenson, J., . . . Varley, J. (2009). Randomized, controlled trial of an intervention for toddlers with autism: The Early Start Denver Model. *Pediatrics, 125*, e17–e23.

Delano, M. E. (2007). Video modeling interventions for individuals with autism. *Remedial and Special Education, 28*, 33–42.

Del Valle, P. R., McEachern, A. G., & Chambers, H. D. (2001). Using social stories with autistic children. *Journal of Poetry Therapy, 14*(4), 187–197.

DeMyer, M. K. (1975). The nature of neuropsychological disability in autistic children. *Journal of Autism and Childhood Schizophrenia, 5*, 109–128.

Dowrick, P. W. (1983). Self-modeling. In P. W. Dowrick & J. Biggs (Eds.), *Using video: Psychological and social applications* (pp. 105–124). New York, NY: Wiley.

Drager, K. D. (2009). Aided modeling interventions for children with autism spectrum disorders who require AAC. *SIG 12 Perspectives on Augmentative and Alternative Communication, 18*(4), 114–120.

Dunst, C. J., Hamby, D., Trivette, C. M., Raab, M., & Bruder, M. B. (2000). Everyday family and community life and children's naturally occurring learning opportunities. *Journal of Early Intervention, 23*(3), 151–164.

Durand, V. M. (1990). *Severe behavior problems: A functional communication training approach.* New York, NY: Guilford Press.

Durand, V. M. (2012). Functional communication training: Treating challenging behavior. In P. A. Prelock & R. J. McCauley (Eds.), *Treatment of autism spectrum disorders: Evidence-based intervention strategies for communication & social interaction* (pp. 107–138). Baltimore, MD: Brookes.

Dyches, T. T., Wilder, K., Sudweeks, R. R., Obiakor, R. E., & Algozzine, B. (2004). Multicultural issues in autism. *Journal of Autism and Developmental Disorders, 34*, 211–222.

Dyer, K., Dunlap, G., & Winterling, V. (1990). Effects of choice making on the serious problem behaviors of students with severe handicaps. *Journal of Applied Behavior Analysis, 23*(4), 515–524.

Eldevik, S., Eikeseth, S., Jahr, E., & Smith, T. (2006). Effects of low-intensity behavioral treatment for children with autism and mental retardation. *Journal of Autism and Developmental Disorders, 36*(2), 211–224.

Falkmer, T., Anderson, K., Falkmer, M., & Horlin, C. (2013). Diagnostic procedures in autism spectrum disorders: A systematic literature review. *European Child and Adolescent Psychiatry, 22*(6), 329–340.

Filipek, P. A., Accardo, P. J., Ashwal, S., Baranek, G., Cook, E. H., Dawson, G., & Volkmar, F. R. (2000). Practice parameter: Screening and diagnosis of autism: Report of the Quality Standards Subcommittee of the American Academy of Neurology and the Child Neurology Society. *Neurology, 55,* 468–479.

Flippin, M., Reszka, S., & Watson, L. (2010). Effectiveness of the Picture Exchange Communication System (PECS) on communication and speech for children with autism spectrum disorders: A meta-analysis. *American Journal of Speech-Language Pathology, 19*(2), 178–195.

Frazier, T. W., Youngstrom, E. A., Speer, L., Embacher, R., Law, P., Constantino, J., . . . Eng, C. (2012). Validation of proposed DSM-5 criteria for autism spectrum disorder. *Child and Adolescent Psychiatry, 51*(1), 28–40.

Frea, W. D., Arnold, C. L., & Vittimberga, G. L. (2001). A demonstration of the effects of augmentative communication on the extreme aggressive behavior of a child with autism within an integrated preschool setting. *Journal of Positive Behavior Interventions, 3,* 194–198.

Frith, U. (2004). Emanuel Miller lecture: Confusions and controversies about Asperger syndrome. *Journal of Child Psychology and Psychiatry, 45*(4), 672–686.

Frost, L., & Bondy, A. (2002). *The Picture Exchange Communication System training manual* (2nd ed.). Newark, DE: Pyramid Education Products.

Ganz, J. B., Earles-Vollrath, T. L., Heath, A. K., Parker, R. I., Rispoli, M. J., & Duran, J. B. (2012). A meta-analysis of single case research studies on aided augmentative and alternative communication systems with individuals with autism spectrum disorders. *Journal of Autism and Developmental Disorders, 42*(1), 60–74.

Garrison-Harrell, L. G., Kamps, D., & Kravitz, T. (1997). The effects of peer networks on social-communicative behaviors for students with autism. *Focus on Autism and Other Developmental Disabilities, 12*(4), 241–256.

Gerber, S. (2012). An introduction to the Developmental, Individual-Difference, Relationship-based (DIR) model and its application to children with autism spectrum disorder. In P. A. Prelock & R. J. McCauley (Eds.), *Treatment of autism spectrum disorders: Evidence-based intervention strategies for communication & social interaction* (pp. 79–106). Baltimore, MD: Brookes.

Ghaziuddin, M. (2010). Should the DSM-5 drop Asperger's syndrome? *Journal of Autism & Developmental Disorders, 40,* 1146–1148.

Goossens, C., Crain, S., & Elder, P. (1992). *Engineering the preschool environment for interactive, symbolic communication.* Birmingham, AL: Southeast Augmentative Communication Conference Publications.

Gray, C. (2003). *Social Stories 10.0.* Arlington, TX: Future Horizons.

Gray, C. (2010). *The new Social Story book.* Arlington, TX: Future Horizons.

Gray, C. A. (1998). Social stories and comic strip conversations with students with Asperger syndrome and high-functioning autism. In E. Schopler &

G. B. Mesibov (Eds.), *Asperger syndrome or high-functioning autism?: Current issues in autism* (pp. 167–198). New York, NY: Plenum Press.

Gray, C. A., & Garand, J. D. (1993). Social stories: Improving responses of students with autism with accurate social information. *Focus on Autistic Behavior, 8*(1), 1–10.

Greenspan, S. I., & Wieder, S. (1997). Developmental patterns and outcomes in infants and children with disorders in relating and communicating: A chart review of 200 cases of children with autistic spectrum diagnoses. *Journal of Developmental and Learning Disorders, 1,* 87–142.

Gutstein, S. E., Burgess, A. F., & Montfort, K. (2007). Evaluation of the relationship development intervention program. *Autism, 11,* 397–411.

Hancock, T. B., & Kaiser, A. P. (2002). The effects of trainer-implemented Enhanced Milieu Teaching on the social communication of children with autism. *Topics in Early Childhood Special Education, 22*(1), 39–54.

Hancock, T. B., & Kaiser, A. P. (2012). Implementing enhanced milieu teaching with children who have *autism* spectrum disorders. In P. A. Prelock, & R. J. Macauley (Eds.), *Treatment of autism spectrum disorders: Evidence-based intervention strategies for communication and social interactions* (pp. 139–162). Baltimore, MD: Brookes.

Harris, S., Handleman, J., & Burton, J. (1990). The Stanford Binet profiles of young children with autism. *Special Services in the School, 6,* 135–143.

Hermelin, B., & O'Connor, N. (1970). *Psychological experiments with autistic children.* Oxford, UK: Pergamon Press.

Howlin, P. (1997). Diagnosis in autism: A survey of over 1200 patients in the UK. *Autism, 1*(2), 135–162.

Howlin, P., Gordon, R. K., Pasco, G., Wade, A., & Charman, T. (2007). The effectiveness of Picture Exchange Communication System (PECS) training for teachers of children with autism: A pragmatic, group randomised controlled trial. *Journal of Child Psychology and Psychiatry, 48*(5), 473–481.

Huer, M. B. (2003). Individuals from diverse cultural and ethnic backgrounds may perceive graphic symbols differently: Response to Nigam, *Augmentative and Alternative Communication, 19*(2), 137–140.

Hughes, V. (2011). *Researchers track down autism rates across the globe.* Retrieved from http://sfari.org/news-and-opinion/news/2011/researchers-track-down-autism-rates-across-the-globe

Hutchins, T. L. (2012a). Social Stories. In P. A. Prelock, & R. J. Macauley (Eds.), *Treatment of autism spectrum disorders: Evidence-based intervention strategies for communication and social interactions* (pp. 139–162). Baltimore, MD: Brookes.

Hutchins, T. L. (2012b). What's the story?: What does the research say about how best to use social stories to help children with ASDs? Retrieved from www.asha.org/Publications/leader/2012/120117/What-s-the-Story/

Hwang, B., & Hughes, C. (2000). The effects of social interactive training on early social communicative skills of children with autism. *Journal of Autism & Developmental Disorders, 30*(4), 331–343.

Iovannone, R., Dunlap, G., Huber, H., & Kincaid, D. (2003). Effective educational practices for students with autism spectrum disorders. *Focus on Autism and Other Developmental Disabilities, 18*(3), 150–165.

Iwata, B. A., Dorsey, M. F., Slifer, K. J., Bauman, K. E., & Richman, G. S. (1982). Toward a functional analysis of self-injury. *Analysis and Intervention in Developmental Disabilities, 2*(1), 3–20.

Johnson, C. P., Meyers, S. M., & the Council on Children with Disabilities. (2007). Identification and evaluation of children with Autism Spectrum Disorders. *Pediatrics, 120*, 1183–1215.

Kaiser, A. P., Hancock, T. B., & Trent, J. A. (2007). Teaching parents communication strategies. *Early Childhood Services: An Interdisciplinary Journal of Effectiveness, 1*(2), 107–136.

Kasari, C., Fannin, D. K. & Stickles Goods, K. (2012). Joint attention intervention for children with autism. In P. A. Prelock, & R. J. Macauley (Eds.), *Treatment of autism spectrum disorders: Evidence-based intervention strategies for communication and social interactions* (pp. 139–162). Baltimore, MD: Brookes.

Kasari, C., Freeman, S., & Paparella, T. (2006). Joint attention and symbolic play in young children with autism: A randomized controlled intervention study. *Journal of Child Psychology and Psychiatry, 47*(6), 611–620.

Kite, D. M., Gullifer, J., & Tyson, G. A. (2013). Views on the diagnostic labels of autism and Asperger's disorder and the proposed changes in the DSM. *Journal of Autism & Developmental Disorders, 43*(7), 1692–1700.

Klin, A., McPartland, J., & Volkmar, F. R. (2005). Asperger syndrome. In F. R. Volkmar, R. Pauk, A. Klin & D. Cohen (Eds.). *Handbook of Autism and Pervasive Developmental Disorders, Third Edition. Volume 1. Diagnosis, development, neurobiology and behavior.* Hoboken, NJ: Wiley.

Koegel, L. K., Camarata, S., Valdez-Menchaca, M., & Koegel, R. L. (1998). Generalization of question asking in children with autism. *American Journal on Mental Retardation, 102*(4), 346–357.

Koegel, L. K., Koegel, R. L. Harrower, J. K., & Carter, C. M. (1999). Pivotal response intervention I: Overview of approach. *Journal of the Association for Persons with Severe Handicaps, 24*, 174–185.

Koegel, R. L., & Koegel, L. K. (1990). Extended reductions in stereotypic behaviors through self-management in multiple community settings. *Journal of Applied Behavior Analysis, 1*, 119–127.

Koegel, R. L., Vernon, T. W., & Koegel, L. K. (2009). Improving social initiations in young children with autism using reinforcers with embedded social interactions. *Journal of Autism and Developmental Disorders, 39*, 1240–1251.

Kouri, T. (1988). Effects of simultaneous communication in a child-directed treatment approach with preschoolers with severe disabilities. *Augmentative and Alternative Communication, 4*(4), 222–232.

Krug, D. A., Arick, J., & Almond, P. (1980). *Autism Screening Instrument for Educational Planning*. Portland, OR: ASIEP Educational Co.

Kupfer, D. J., Regier, D. A., & Kuhl, E. A. (2008). On the road to the DSM-5 and ICD-11. *European Archives of Psychiatry and Clinical Neuroscience, 258*, 2–6.

Lazarus, A. A. (1958). New methods in psychotherapy: A case study. *South African Medical Journal, 32*, 660–664.

Le Couteur, A., Lord, C., & Rutter, M. (2003). *Autism Diagnostic Interview-Revised (ADI-R)*. Los Angeles, CA: Western Psychological Services.

Leventhal-Belfer, L. (2012). Potential ramifications of DSM-5 classification of autistic disorders: Comments from a clinician's perspective. *Journal of Autism and Developmental Disorders, 43*(3), 749–750.

Lewis, M., & Brooks-Gunn, J. (1979). *Social cognition and the acquisition of self*. New York, NY: Plenum Press.

Lincoln, A., Courchesne, E., Kilman, B., Elmasian, R., & Allen, M. (1988). A study of intellectual abilities in high-functioning people with autism. *Journal of Autism and Developmental Disorders, 18*, 505–523.

Lord, C., Risi, S., Lambrecht, L., Cook, E. H. Jr., Leventhal, B. L., DiLavore, P. C., . . . Rutter, M. (2000). The Autism Diagnostic Observation Schedule—Generic: A standard measure of social and communication deficits associated with the spectrum of autism. *Journal of Autism and Developmental Disorders, 30*, 205–223.

Lord, C., Rutter, M., DiLavore, P. C., Risi, S., & Gotham, K. (2012). *Autism Diagnostic Observation Schedule (ADOS-2)*. Los Angeles, CA: Western Psychological Services.

Lovaas, O. I. (1977). *The autistic child: Language training through behavior modification*. New York, NY: Irvington.

Lovaas, O. I. (1987). Behavioral treatment and normal educational and intellectual functioning in young autistic children. *Journal of Consulting and Clinical Psychology, 55*, 3–9.

Lovaas, O. I., Ackerman, A. B., Alexander, D., Firestone, P., Perkins, J., & Young, D. (1981). *Teaching developmentally disabled children: The me book*. Austin, TX: Pro-Ed.

Luiselli, J. K., Cannon, B. O. M., Ellis, J. T., & Sisson, R. W. (2000). Home-based behavioral intervention for young children with autism/pervasive developmental disorder: A preliminary evaluation of outcome in relation to child age and intensity of service delivery. *Autism, 4*(4), 426–438.

Mahoney, G., & Perales, F. (2003). Using relationship-focused intervention to enhance the social-emotional functioning of young children with Autism Spectrum Disorders. *Topics in Early Childhood Special Education, 23*(2), 77–89.

Mahoney, G., & Perales, F. (2005). Relationship-focused early intervention with children with pervasive developmental disorders and other disabilities: A comparative study. *Journal of Developmental & Behavioral Pediatrics, 26*(2), 77–85.

Mandell, D. S., Cao, J., Ittenbach, R., & Pinto-Martin, J. (2006). Medicaid expenditures for children with autism spectrum disorders: 1994–1999. *Journal of Autism and Developmental Disorders, 36*, 475–485.

Mandell, D. S., Morales, K. H., Xie, M., Lawer, L. J., Stahmer, A. C., & Marcus, S. C. (2010). Age of diagnosis among Medicaid-enrolled children with autism. *Psychiatric Services, 61*, 822–829.

Matson, J. L., Matson, M. L., & Rivet, T. T. (2007). Social-skills treatments for children with autism spectrum disorders: An overview. *Behavior Modification, 31*(5), 682–707.

McConachie, H., Randle, V., Hammal, D., & Le Couteur, A. (2005). A controlled trial of a training course for parents of children with suspected autism spectrum disorder. *Journal of Pediatrics, 147*(3), 335–340.

Meisels, S. J. (1989). Can developmental screening tests identify children who are developmentally at-risk? *Pediatrics, 83*, 578–585.

Mesibov, G., Shea, V., & Schopler, E. (2004). *The TEACCH approach to autism spectrum disorders.* New York, NY: Springer.

Meyer, L. S., Taylor, B. A., Levin, L., & Fisher, J. R. (2001). Alpine learning group. In J. S. Handleman & S. L. Harris (Eds.), *Preschool education programs for children with autism* (2nd ed., pp. 135–155). Austin, TX: Pro-Ed.

Millar, D. (2009). Effects of AAC on the natural speech develop of individuals with autism spectrum disorders. In P. Mirenda & T. Iacono (Eds.), *Autism spectrum disorders and AAC* (pp. 171–194). Baltimore, MD: Brookes.

Millar, D., Light, J., & Schlosser, R. (2006). The impact of augmentative and alternative communication intervention on the speech production of individuals with developmental disabilities: A research review. *Journal of Speech, Language & Hearing Research, 49*(2), 248–264.

Mirenda, P., & Erickson, K. A. (2000). Augmentative communication and literacy. In A. M. Wetherby & B. M. Prizant (Eds.), *Autism spectrum disorders: A transactional developmental perspective* (pp. 333–367). Baltimore, MD: Brookes.

Missouri Autism Guidelines Initiative. (2012). *Autism spectrum disorders: Guide to evidence-based interventions.* Retrieved from http://autism-guidelines.dmh.mo.gov/documents/Interventions.pdf

Mordre, M., Groholt, B., Knudsen, A. K., Mykletun, A., Sponheim, E., & Myhre, A. M. (2012). Is long-term prognosis for Pervasive Developmental Disorder Not Otherwise Specified different from prognosis for autistic disorder?: Findings from a 30-year follow-up study. *Journal of Autism and Developmental Disorders, 42*(6), 920–928.

Mundy, P., Sigman, M., Ungerer, J., & Sherman, T. (1986). Defining the social deficits of autism: The contribution of non-verbal communication measures. *Journal of Child Psychology and Psychiatry, 27*(5), 657–669.

National Autism Center. (2009). *National standards report: The national standards project—addressing the need for evidence-based practice guidelines for autism spectrum disorders*. Retrieved from www.nationalautismcenter. org/nsp/reports.php.

National Institute for Health and Clinical Excellence. (2011). *Autism: Recognition, referral, diagnosis and management of adults on the autism spectrum*. London, UK: Author.

National Research Council. (2001). *Educating children with autism*. Washington, DC: The National Academies Press.

Neitzel, J. (2008). *Overview of peer-mediated instruction and intervention for children and youth with autism spectrum disorders*. Chapel Hill, NC: National Professional Development Center on Autism Spectrum Disorders, Frank Porter Graham Child Development Institute, the University of North Carolina.

New York State Department of Health, Early Intervention Program. (1999). *Clinical practice guideline: Report of the recommendations. Autism/Pervasive developmental disorders: Assessment and intervention for young children (Age 0–3 Years)*. Albany, NY: NYS Department of Health.

Nikopoulos, C. K., & Keenan, M. (2003). Promoting social imitation in children with autism using video modeling. *Behavioral Interventions, 18*, 87–108.

Nikopoulos, C. K., & Keenan, M. (2004). Effects of video modeling on social initiations by children with autism. *Journal of Applied Behavior Analysis, 37*, 93–96.

Odom, S. L., Boyd, B. A., Hall, L. J., & Hume, K. (2010). Evaluation of comprehensive treatment models for individuals with autism spectrum disorders. *Journal of Autism and Developmental Disorders, 40*, 425–436. Retrieved from http://dcautismparents.org/yahoo_site_admin/assets/docs/ABA_14.9261728.pdf

Odom, S. L., Collet-Klingenberg, L., Rogers, S., & Hatton, D. (2010). Evidence-based practices for children and youth with autism spectrum disorders. *Preventing School Failure, 54*, 275–282.

Panerai, S., Ferrante, L., & Zingale, M. (2002). Benefits of the Treatment and Education of Autistic and Communication Handicapped Children (TEACCH) program as compared with a non-specific approach. *Journal of Intellectual Disability Research, 46*, 318–327.

Parellada, M., Penzol, M. J., Pina, L., Moreno, C., Gonzalez-Vioque, E., Zalsman, G., & Arango, C. (2014). The neurobiology of autism spectrum disorders. *European Psychiatry, 29*(1), 11–19.

Petscher, E. S., Rey, C., & Bailey, J. S. (2009). A review of empirical support for differential reinforcement of alternative behavior. *Research in Developmental Disabilities, 30*(3), 409–425.

Pierce, N. P., O'Reilly, M. F., Sorrells, A. M., Fragale, C. L., White, P. J., Aguilar, J. M., & Cole, H. A. (2014). Ethnicity reporting practices for empirical research in three autism-related journals. *Journal of Autism and*

Developmental Disorders. Advance online publication. doi:10.1007/s10803-014-2041-x

Prelock, P. A, & McCauley, R. J. (2012). *Treatment of autism spectrum disorders: Evidence-based intervention strategies for communication and social interaction.* Baltimore, MD: Paul H. Brookes.

Quill, K. A. (1997). Instructional considerations for young children with autism: The rationale for visually cued instruction. *Journal of Autism and Developmental Disorders, 27*(6), 697–714.

Quirmbach, L. M., Lincoln, A. J., Feinberg-Gizzo, M. J., Ingersoll, B. R., & Andrews, S. M. (2009). Social stories: Mechanisms of effectiveness in increasing game play skills in children diagnosed with autism spectrum disorders using a pretest posttest repeated measures randomized control group design. *Journal of Autism and Developmental Disorders, 39*(2), 299–321.

Reichow, B., Barton, E. E., Boyd, B. A., & Hume, K. (2012). Early intensive behavioral intervention (EIBI) for young children with autism spectrum disorders (ASD). *Cochrane Database of Systematic Review, 10,* 1–60.

Reichow, B., Steiner, A.M., & Volkmar, F. (2012). Social skills groups for people aged 6 to 21 with autism spectrum disorders (ASD). *Cochrane Database of Systematic Review, 7,* 1–48.

Reichow, B., & Volkmar, F.R. (2010). Social skills interventions for individuals with autism: Evaluation for evidence-based practices within a best evidence synthesis framework. *Journal of Autism and Developmental Disorders, 40*(2), 149–166.

Reilly, C., Campbell, A., & Keran, P. (2009). Screening for Asperger syndrome in school-age children: Issues and instruments. *Educational Psychology in Practice, 25,* 37–52.

Ritvo, R. A., Ritvo, E. R., Guthrie, D., Ritvo, M. J., Hufnagel, D. H., McMahon, W., . . . Eloff, J. (2011). The Ritvo Autism Asperger Diagnostic Scale—Revised (RAADS-R): A scale used to assist the diagnosis of autism spectrum disorders in adults: An international validation study. *Journal of Autism and Developmental Disorders, 41,* 1076–1089.

Robins, D., Fein, D., & Barton, M. (2009). The Modified Checklist for Autism in Toddlers, Revised with Follow-up (M-CHAT-R/F). Retrieved from at www.mchatscreen.com

Robins, D., Fein, D., Barton, M., & Green, J. (2001). The Modified Checklist for Autism in Toddlers (M-CHAT): An initial investigation in the early detection of autism and pervasive developmental disorders. *Journal of Autism and Developmental Disorders, 31*(2), 131–144.

Rogers, S. J., & Dawson, G. (2010). *Early Start Denver Model for young children with autism.* New York, NY: Guilford Press.

Rogers, S. J., & Dillala, D. L. (1991). A comparative study of the effects of a developmentally based instructional model on young children with autism and young children with other disorders of behavior and development. *Topics in Early Childhood Special Education, 11*, 29–47.

Rogers, S. J., Estes, A., Lord, C., Vismara, L., Winter, J., Fitzpatrick, A., . . . Dawson, G. (2012). Effects of a brief Early Start Denver Model (ESDM)-based parent intervention on toddlers at risk for autism spectrum disorders: A randomized controlled trial. *Journal of the American Academy of Child and Adolescent Psychiatry, 51*, 1052–1065.

Rogers, S. J., & Lewis, H. (1989). An effective day treatment model for young children with Pervasive Developmental Disorders. *Journal of the American Academy of Child and Adolescent Psychiatry, 28*(2), 207–214.

Romski, M. A., & Sevcik, R. A. (2003). Augmented input: Enhancing communication development. In J. Light, D. Beukelman, & J. Reichle (Eds.), *Communicative competence for individuals who use AAC* (pp. 147–162). Baltimore, MD: Brookes.

Rotheram-Fuller, E., Kasari, C., Chamberlain, B., & Locke, J. (2010). Social involvement of children with autism spectrum disorders in elementary school classrooms. *The Journal of Child Psychology and Psychiatry and Allied Disciplines, 51*, 1227–1234.

Rowe, C. (1999). The Stanley Segal Award: Do social stories benefit children with autism in mainstream primary schools? *British Journal of Special Education, 26*(1), 12–14.

Rutter M., Bailey, A., & Lord, C. (2003). *Social Communication Questionnaire* (SCQ). Los Angeles, CA: Western Psychological Services.

Sallows, G. O., & Graupner, T. D. (2005). Intensive behavioral treatment for children with autism: Four-year outcome and predictors. *American Journal on Mental Retardation, 110*(6), 417–438.

Sanders, J. L. (2009). Qualitative or quantitative differences between Asperger's Disorder and autism? Historical considerations. *Journal of Autism and Developmental Disorders, 39*, 1560–1567.

Sansosti, F. J., & Powell-Smith, K. A. (2008). Using computer-presented social stories and video models to increase the social communication skills of children with high-functioning autism spectrum disorders. *Journal of Positive Behaviour Interventions, 10*, 162–178.

Scattone, D. (2008). Enhancing the conversation skills of a boy with Asperger's disorder through social stories and video modeling. *Autism Developmental Disorder, 38*, 395–400.

Scattone, D., Wilczynski, S. M., Edwards, R. P., & Rabian, B. (2002). Decreasing disruptive behaviors of children with autism using social stories. *Journal of Autism and Developmental Disorders, 32*(6), 535–543.

Scherer, M. R., & Schreibman, L. (2005). Individual behavioral profiles and predictors of treatment effectiveness for children with autism. *Journal of Consulting and Clinical Psychology, 73*(3), 525–538.

Schlosser, R. W., & Wendt, O. (2008). Effects of augmentative and alternative communication intervention on speech production in children with autism: A systematic review. American *Journal of Speech-Language Pathology, 17,* 212–230.

Schneider, N., & Goldstein, H. (2010). Using social stories and visual schedules to improve socially appropriate behaviors in children with autism. *Journal of Positive Behavior Interventions, 12*(3), 149–160.

Schopler, E. (1997). Implementation of TEACCH philosophy. *Handbook of Autism and Pervasive Developmental Disorders, 2,* 767–795.

Schopler, E., Mesibov, G.B., & Hearsey, K. (1995). Structured teaching in the TEACCH system. In E. Schopler & G.B. Mesibov (Eds.), *Learning and cognition in autism* (pp. 243–268). New York, NY: Plenum.

Schopler, E., Reichler, R.J., Rochen Renner, B. (1999). *Childhood Autism Rating Scale (CARS).* Chapel Hill: University of North Carolina Project TEACCH.

Scottish Intercollegiate Guidelines Network. (2007). *Assessment, diagnosis and clinical interventions for children and young people with autism spectrum disorders: A national clinical guideline* (SIGN Publication No. 98). Edinburgh: Scottish Intercollegiate Guidelines Network (SIGN); NHS Quality Improvement Scotland.

Siegel, J., Minshew, N., & Goldstein, G. (1996). Wechsler IQ profiles in diagnosis of high-functioning autism. *Journal of Autism and Developmental Disorders, 26,* 389–406.

Smith, T., Groen, A. D., & Wynn, J. W. (2000). Randomized trial of intensive early intervention for children with pervasive developmental disorder. *American Journal on Mental Retardation, 105*(4), 269–285.

Solomon, R., Necheles, J., Ferch, C., & Bruckman, D. (2007). Pilot study of a parent training program for young children with autism: The PLAY Project Home Consultation program. *Autism, 11*(3), 205–224.

Stahmer, A.C., & Schreibman, L. (1992). Teaching children with autism appropriate play in unsupervised environments using a self-management treatment package. *Journal of Applied Behavior Analysis, 25*(2), 447–459.

Stokes, T., Fowler, S., & Baer, D. (1978). Training preschool children to recruit natural communities of reinforcement. *Journal of Applied Behavior Analysis, 11*(2), 285–303.

Stone, W. L., Coonrod, E., & Ousley, O. (2000). Brief report: Screening Tool for Autism in Two-year-olds (STAT): Development and preliminary data. *Journal of Autism and Developmental Disorders, 30,* 607–612.

Stone, W. L., Coonrod, E. E., Turner, L. M., & Pozdol, S. L. (2004). Psychometric properties of the STAT for early autism screening. *Journal of Autism and Developmental Disorders, 34,* 691–701.

Stone, W. L., & Hogan, K. L. (1993). A structured parent interview for identifying children with autism. *Journal of Autism and Developmental Disorders, 23*(4), 639–652.

Stone, W. L., & Ousley, O. (1997). *STAT manual: Screening Tool for Autism in Two-year-olds.* Unpublished manuscript, Vanderbilt University, Nashville, TN.

Sulzer-Azaroff, B., Hoffman, A. O., Horton, C. B., Bondy, A., & Frost, L. (2009). The Picture Exchange Communication System (PECS): What do the data say? *Focus on Autism and Other Developmental Disabilities, 24*(2), 89–103.

Taylor-Goh, S. (Ed.). (2005). *Royal college of speech and language therapists clinical guidelines.* Bicester, UK: Speechmark Publishing Ltd.

Thiemann, K. S., & Goldstein, H. (2001). Social stories, written text cues, and video feedback: Effects on social communication of children with autism. *Journal of Applied Behavior Analysis, 34*(4), 425–446.

Tiegerman, E., & Primavera, L. (1984). Imitating the autistic child: Facilitating communicative gaze. *Journal of Autism and Developmental Disorders, 14,* 27–38.

Tincani, M. (2004). Comparing the picture exchange communication system and sign language training for children with autism. *Focus on Autism and Other Developmental Disabilities, 19*(3), 152–163.

Tomasello, M., & Farrar, M. J. (1986). Joint attention and early language. *Child development, 57*(6), 1454–1463.

Toplis, R., & Hadwin, J. A. (2006). Using social stories to change problematic lunchtime behaviour in school. *Educational Psychology in Practice, 22*(1), 53–67.

Virues-Ortega, J., Julio, F. M., & Pastor-Barriuso, R. (2013). The TEACCH program for children and adults with autism: a meta-analysis of intervention studies. *Clinical Psychology Review, 33*(8), 940–953.

Volkmar, F. R., Lord, C., Bailey, A., Schultz, R. T., & Klin, A. (2004). Autism and pervasive development disorders. *Journal of Child Psychology and Psychiatry, 45*(1), 135–170.

Walton, K. M., & Ingersoll, B. R. (2013). Improving social skills in adolescents and adults with autism and severe to profound intellectual disability: A review of the literature. *Journal of Autism and Developmental Disorders, 43*(3), 594–615.

Warren, Z., Veenstra-VanderWeele, J., Stone, W., Bruzek., J., Hahmias, L., Foss-Feig, J. H., . . . McPheeters, M. (2011). *Therapies for children with autism spectrum disorders* (Comparative Effectiveness Review Number 26. AHRQ Publication No. 11-EHC029-EF). Rockville, MD: Agency for Healthcare Research and Quality. Retrieved from www.effectivehealthcare.ahrq.gov/ehc/products/106/656/cer26_autism_report_04–14–2011.pdf

Watanabe, M., & Sturmey, P. (2003). The effect of choice-making opportunities during activity schedules on task engagement of adults with autism. *Journal of Autism and Developmental Disorders, 33*(5), 535–538.

Wegner, J. R. (2012). Augmentative and alternative communication strategies: Manual signs, picture communication, and speech-generating devices. In P. A. Prelock & R. J. Macauley (Eds.), *Treatment of autism spectrum disorders: Evidence based intervention strategies for communication and social interactions* (pp. 27–48). Baltimore, MD: Brookes.

Wetherby, A. M., & Prizant, B. M. (2002). *Communication and Symbolic Behavior Scales—Developmental Profile: Infant Toddler Checklist* (1st normed ed.). Baltimore, MD: Brookes.

Wetherby, A., Watt, N., Morgan, L., & Shumway, S. (2007). Social communication profiles of children with autism spectrum disorders in the second year of life. *Journal of Autism and Developmental Disorders, 37,* 960–975.

Wetherby, A., & Woods, J. (2006). Effectiveness of early intervention for children with autism spectrum disorders beginning in the second year of life. *Topics in Early Childhood Special Education, 26*(2), 67–82.

Wetherby, A. M., & Woods, J. (2008). Developmental approaches to treatment. In K. Chawarska, A. Klin, & F. Volkmar (Eds.), *Autism spectrum disorders in infants and toddlers: Diagnosis, assessment, and treatment* (pp. 170–206). New York, NY: Guilford Press.

Wieder, S., & Greenspan, S. I. (2005). Developmental pathways to mental health: The DIR model for comprehensive approaches to assessment and intervention. In K. M. Finello (Ed.), *The handbook of training and practice in infant and preschool mental health* (pp. 377–401). San Francisco, CA: Jossey-Bass.

Wilczynski, S. M. (2012). Risk and strategic decision-making in developing evidence-based practice guidelines. *Education and Treatment of Children, 35*(2), 291–311.

Wilczynski, S. M., Rue, H. C., Hunter, M., & Christian, L. (2012). Elementary behavioral intervention strategies: Discrete trial training, differential reinforcement and shaping. In P. A. Prelock & R. J. McCauley (Eds.), *Treatment of autism spectrum disorders: Evidence-based intervention strategies for communication & social interaction* (pp. 49–78). Baltimore, MD: Brookes.

Wong, C., Odom, S. L., Hume, K. Cox, A. W., Fettig, A., Kucharczyk, S., . . . Schultz, T. R. (2014). *Evidence-based practices for children, youth, and young adults with autism spectrum disorder.* Chapel Hill: The University of North Carolina, Frank Porter Graham Child Development Institute, Autism Evidence-Based Practice Review Group.

Woods, J., Wetherby, A, Kashinath, S., & Holland, R. (2012). Early social interaction project. In P. A. Prelock & R. J. McCauley (Eds.), *Treatment of autism spectrum disorders: Evidence-based intervention strategies for communication & social interaction* (pp. 189–220). Baltimore, MD: Brookes.

World Health Organization. (1996). *The Tenth Revision of the International Classification of Diseases and Related Health Problems (ICD-10).* Geneva, Switzerland: Author.

8

SOCIAL COMMUNICATION ASSESSMENT AND INTERVENTION FOR CHILDREN WITH LANGUAGE IMPAIRMENT

Martin Fujiki and Bonnie Brinton

The social stuff is everything.
—Mother of a child with Language Impairment

LEARNING OBJECTIVES

Readers will

1. Be able to recognize the nature of social communication disorders in children with language impairment (LI).
2. Be able to define social communication and describe the integration of social interaction, pragmatics, social cognition, and language processing.
3. Be able to describe the difficulties children with LI have performing various social communication tasks and the problematic social and emotional outcomes experienced by these children.
4. Gain knowledge about methods of assessing social communication problems and a comprehensive strategy for performing the assessment.
5. Gain knowledge regarding the efficacy of interventions designed to improve social communication in children with LI.

CASE STUDY

As a toddler, Jennie was slow to acquire both receptive and expressive language. She continued to have difficulty communicating, and at 4:2 (years: months) she qualified for placement in a special education preschool program based on delays in language and pre-academic skills. Jennie's parents and teachers expressed additional concerns. Jennie struggled to attend to pre-academic tasks, she sometimes seemed anxious, and she was occasionally aggressive with peers. At 6:0, Jennie was enrolled in a regular kindergarten classroom. Academic tasks were very challenging for her; she had difficulty understanding lesson content presented in class, and she struggled to express her ideas.

Jennie's performance on the Clinical Evaluation of Language Fundamentals-5 (Semel, Wiig, & Secord, 2013), produced a core language standard score of 78, consistent with her diagnosis of LI. She received speech and language intervention on a pullout basis. In addition to her deficits in language, Jennie had difficulty with multiple aspects of social and emotional learning. Jennxie was unable to label basic emotions beyond *happy*, *sad*, and *mad*, and she struggled to understand emotion cues and to draw social inferences. Jennie was reticent at school and seemed reserved and somewhat fearful interacting with other children. For example, she often stared at other children without interacting with them, and she sometimes stood or sat in the midst of her peers, doing nothing when there were numerous activities going on around her. She frequently chose to play alone with toys, sometimes building something or looking at a book by herself. At times, however, she talked, sang, or engaged in pretend play around her classmates without interacting with them. This behavior tended to draw negative attention from her peers. Jennie's teacher reported that her sociable behavior was limited. Her teacher had never observed her helping, sharing, or sympathizing with other children. In summary, Jennie was at risk for academic and social problems. She existed on the academic and social outskirts of her classroom. She presented with LI in a traditional sense in that her receptive and expressive language abilities were limited for her age. She also had difficulties with social communication that undermined her relationships with her peers as well as her participation and inclusion within her classroom community. It seemed clear that Jennie needed intervention designed to facilitate her language and academic development as well to support her social and emotional learning.

INTRODUCTION

Early definitions of LI[1] generally highlighted the syntactic and semantic limitations that children with this diagnosis experience. As Jennie's case illustrates, however, children with LI can also experience deficits in social interaction. Recent revisions and rethinking of diagnostic categories suggest that within the broad category of LI, there are children who have problems with various aspects of language use that do not stem wholly from structural limitations. At the same time, however, these children do not meet the diagnostic criteria for autism spectrum disorder (ASD) (Bishop & Norbury, 2002). Bishop and Norbury (2002) labeled these children as having pragmatic language impairment (PLI). Children with PLI may be relatively verbal but have difficulty using language appropriately to participate in conversation, to understand what is implied rather than actually stated in words, and to adjust language to specific contexts. Other children identified with LI present with a more traditional collection of symptoms, with marked deficits in the production and comprehension of syntax, morphology, and semantics. This refinement of the general category of LI is reflected in the organization of the 2013 revision of the *Diagnostic and Statistical Manual of Mental Disorders* (5th ed., *DSM-5*; American Psychiatric Association, DSM-5 Task Force, 2013), which separates language disorder from social (pragmatic) communication disorder. These categories of impairment parallel Bishop and Norbury's separation of PLI from structural LI. Even with this separation, however, it is important to recognize that each of these subtypes of impairment is closely associated with the other. Many children who have trouble using language in interaction also show the structural problems that characterize traditional LI. Likewise, many children identified with traditional LI also have interactional concerns. For purposes of this discussion, we consider difficulties employing language in social situations as social communication disorders.

The actual percentage of children with LI who have social interactional problems is difficult to determine. It is of note, however, that such difficulties have been reported in these children for some time (Bishop, Chan, Adams, Hartley, & Weir, 2000; Brinton, Fujiki, & Powell, 1997). Additionally, studies that have profiled the types of linguistic difficulties experienced by children with specific language impairment (SLI) consistently identify a subgroup of children with pragmatic problems (e.g., Bishop & Rosebloom, 1987; Conti-Ramsden, Crutchley, & Botting, 1997). For example, Botting and Conti-Ramsden (1999) considered results from 2 years of evaluation of a large longitudinal sample of children placed in specialized language units for children with SLI in England. These researchers reported that 23% (53 of 234) of the children had notable pragmatic problems.

Although the prevalence of pragmatic problems in these children is important, it is perhaps just as critical to consider that many children with LI have difficulty with a range of social communication tasks. Even children with LI who have not been identified with specific pragmatic issues often experience difficulty with tasks such as entering ongoing interactions, negotiating for resources with peers, and resolving conflicts. As a group, these children also experience a variety of troubling social and emotional outcomes (e.g., fewer friendships, poor peer acceptance, higher levels of emotional difficulties).

In this chapter, we discuss the social communication problems of children with a primary diagnosis of LI. In the literature that we consider, almost all of the children have been identified with LI based on their performance on standardized measures of language. Much of what we write, however, will also be applicable to children who currently could be diagnosed with a social communication disorder (or PLI) using the new *DSM-5* standards. We begin by defining social communication, drawing heavily on the work of Catherine Adams (2005, 2008). We particularly like Adams's idea that successful social communication requires the integration of both pragmatic and structural language behaviors, as well as additional behaviors that reach into the realms of social and emotional learning. We believe that treating children with LI requires a comprehensive approach that not only addresses their structural challenges but also considers the abilities and dispositions essential to their use of language in social interactions. At the same time, children whose difficulties fall primarily within the realm of social communication certainly require approaches that address their interactional challenges.

After discussing social communication, we focus on our target population, children with LI. We consider the social communication difficulties that these children experience with an emphasis on social and emotional learning. After describing potential problems, we present ideas on assessment and intervention. We focus heavily on evidence-based practice, reviewing work that has investigated the efficacy of interventions with these children.

SOCIAL COMMUNICATION: WHAT ARE WE TALKING ABOUT?

Social communication can be defined as the ability to use "language in interpersonally appropriate ways to influence people and interpret events" (Olswang, Coggins, & Timler, 2001, p. 53). The simplicity of this definition is deceptive, however. Social communication is an encompassing notion that can be difficult to pin down. Defining social communication is complicated by the tendency to equate social communication with pragmatics. As Adams (2005) points out, however, although often considered as synonymous with pragmatics, the term *social communication* is more far-reaching. Successful communication in social contexts is a complex phenomenon that includes four areas: social interaction, language processing, pragmatics, and social cognition (as discussed in Chapters 2, 4, and 5). To review briefly each of these areas, social interaction acknowledges the fundamental role of early interactions between children and their caretakers in multiple aspects of development. These interactions begin within the subjective sharing of experience with others, or intersubjectivity. Intersubjectivity is critical to the development of intention, which in turn is fundamental to the acquisition of language (Westby, 2014). Although interactional difficulties seem most pertinent for children in the earliest stages of development, they also merit consideration in older children who have more general developmental problems. In addition, weaknesses in the development of basic social interactional skills may contribute to limitations in the other three aspects of social communication as children mature.

The inclusion of language processing in this framework acknowledges the importance of the structural and lexical components of language. By definition, children with LI have deficits in these aspects of language, and these problems may seriously limit the ability to produce and understand language. Within a social communication approach, limitations in the syntactic and semantic aspects of language do not form the sole focus of intervention, however. These problems are considered, monitored, and, as necessary, addressed in holistic, authentic contexts.

Pragmatic behaviors play a key role in a social communication framework. Conveying communicative intent, managing conversations, and understanding social conventions for politeness are examples of behaviors that fall within the realm of pragmatics. Although it is possible to produce a long list of such behaviors, it can be difficult to draw the line between pragmatics and other areas of development. For example, to engage in conversation, an individual must know how to introduce, maintain, and change topics in conversation. To do this effectively, one must also be able to read the social and emotional cues that a conversational partner conveys. These abilities may extend beyond the traditional boundaries of pragmatics into Adam's fourth area of social cognition.

The umbrella term *social cognition* includes a wide of range of behaviors. In a social communication framework, there is particular emphasis on aspects of social and emotional learning that are critical to successful communication. These abilities include understanding one's own emotions, understanding the emotions of others, and considering the perspectives of others. A number of these abilities involve Theory of Mind (ToM) and are critical to social interaction (for a review see Chapters 2 and 4).

Although social communication problems are often closely associated with autism spectrum disorders (ASD), these difficulties have been observed in children with a range of diagnoses, including not only LI, but also intellectual disability, hearing impairment, and learning disability (e.g., Brown, Odom, & McConnell, 2008). As noted previously, although social communication and structural language problems often co-occur within the broader category of LI, it is also possible for social communication problems to occur without being linked to structural impairments.

THE SOCIAL COMMUNICATION SKILLS OF CHILDREN WITH LI

Jennie presented with LI that was manifested in her language comprehension and production as well as in other aspects of social communication. Research suggests that like Jennie, many children with LI have difficulty with a range of important social communication abilities. We review a sampling of this research in the following sections.

Important Social Tasks and LI

Entering the Interaction

Joining an on-going interaction can be difficult for anyone, and studies have shown that it is particularly challenging for children with LI (Brinton, Fujiki, Spencer, & Robinson, 1997; Craig & Washington, 1993; Liiva & Cleave, 2005). To illustrate, Craig and Washington (1993) introduced two previously unacquainted children. Once these children were engaged in cooperative play, a target child was introduced to them. Children with LI and typically developing peers served as target children. All of the typical target children successfully entered the on-going play. Three of the five target children with LI did not enter the interaction during a 20-minute period (similar results were reported by Brinton, Fujiki, Spencer, et al., 1997, and Liiva & Cleave, 2005).

Integrating One's Self Into Group Interaction

In each of the three studies cited earlier, some children with LI were able to enter the on-going interaction, although most did not do it quickly.

It might be hypothesized that if a child with LI had the skills to enter the interaction, he or she would also have the skills to become an active participant. Brinton, Fujiki, Spencer, et al. (1997) and Liiva and Cleave (2005) both considered this possibility by examining children who were able to join the group. In both studies, after children with LI joined the other children, they were often marginalized in the subsequent group interaction. The triad frequently became a dyad, with the two typical children interacting with each other to the exclusion of the child with LI. These findings parallel observations made by other researchers who have observed group interactions involving children with LI (Grove, Conti-Ramsden, & Donlan, 1993; Guralnick, Connor, Hammond, Gottman, & Kinnish, 1996).

Negotiating for Resources

Children must often negotiate with their peers for resources. This skill is particularly important in the school context where materials, food, and even friends must sometimes be shared. As might be expected, children with LI have difficulty with negotiation tasks (Brinton, Fujiki, & McKee, 1998; Grove et al., 1993). For example, Brinton and colleagues observed triadic interactions, in which a child with LI interacted with two peers to select a treat to be shared by all three children. Children with LI used less sophisticated negotiating strategies (e.g., ordering a peer to perform an action, or disagreeing with a peer's statement without offering a reason for disagreeing) than did typical peers, and they frequently were excluded from the final decision. Although limitations in syntax, vocabulary, and aspects of verbal ability may have played a role, these difficulties could not completely explain the differences observed.

Resolving Disputes

Childhood is filled with conflicts with peers, and children need to learn how to resolve these disputes in positive ways that preserve relationships. To study conflict resolution, researchers have frequently presented children with hypothetical scenarios and asked what strategies they would use to resolve a potential disagreement (e.g., another child will not share materials needed to complete a school assignment; e.g., Erdley & Asher, 1999). Several researchers have used this methodology with children with LI (e.g., Marton, Abramoff, & Rosenzweig, 2005; Timler, 2008). In these studies, children with LI often produced less effective strategies to resolve conflicts. For example, Timler (2008) found that children with LI did not differ from typical peers in the number of strategies produced, but they produced fewer prosocial strategies. Thus, children with LI were less likely than typical children to make a polite request or to suggest a strategy that would meet the needs of both children, such as "Let's flip a coin" (Timler, 2008, p. 750).

Horowitz, Jamsson, Ljungberg, and Hedenbro (2005) used a more direct (and more laborious) methodology to examine conflict resolution. These researchers observed naturally occurring conflicts in preschool age boys. Typical boys interacted with other typical boys, and boys with LI interacted with other boys with LI. The typical boys resolved a significantly greater number of conflicts than did the boys with LI. As might be expected, boys with poor language skills were less able to resolve conflicts verbally, and they did not compensate using nonverbal means. Interestingly, boys with LI were involved in more conflicts that the researchers labeled as "aberrant" (p. 440). That is, a child's behavior intensified to the point of driving the other child away (e.g., friendly wrestling became too rough and the other child withdrew from the play).

Learning in Cooperative Group Activities

Cooperative learning tasks in which several children work together on a project are widely used in school settings. Although cooperative learning models can be highly beneficial, children with LI may not do well in these groups without extra support. For example, Brinton, Fujiki, and Higbee (1998) examined the verbal and nonverbal behaviors produced by children with LI and their typically developing peers in cooperative work settings. Typical children matched for age and language level were also examined. The triads of typical children generally worked collaboratively, resulting in a balanced interaction among the children. The triads with a child with LI (and two typical peers) frequently turned into dyads, with the exclusion of the child with LI. Interestingly, children with LI did not compensate for their language limitations by using nonverbal behaviors. Rather, they contributed fewer nonverbal cooperative behaviors than did the typical children. Brinton, Fujiki, Montague, and Hanton (2000) also observed children with LI interacting in a cooperative work project with two typically developing peers. For children with LI, successful interaction was more influenced by the sociable behaviors of the child (e.g., helping or comforting others, controlling one's temper, sharing materials) than by the child's language level.

In summary, it is likely that the inability to take part successfully in peer interactions could contribute in social and emotional difficulties. This turns out to be the case, as illustrated by the sampling of research reviewed in the next section.

Problematic Social and Emotional Outcomes

There is considerable evidence that children with LI often experience problematic social outcomes. Children with LI as young as 2 years of age scored lower on measures of socialization when compared with typically developing peers (e.g., Paul, Looney, & Dahm, 1991). Preschool children with poor speech and language skills were perceived by peers as less desirable playmates in sociodramatic play than were children with typical language skills (Gertner, Rice, & Hadley, 1994).

Elementary school-age children with LI consistently demonstrate higher rates of social difficulty than do their typical peers. These children have fewer friends and are less well accepted by peers (Fujiki, Brinton, Hart, & Fitzgerald, 1999). Additionally, teachers rate children with LI as having poorer social skills, more problem behaviors, and higher rates of reticent withdrawal than typical children had (Fujiki, Brinton, Morgan, & Hart, 1999; Fujiki, Brinton, & Todd, 1996). Conti-Ramsden and Botting (2004) found high rates of social difficulty in a longitudinal sample of children with LI. These children also reported experiencing higher rates of victimization (bullying) than did typical peers. Lindsay, Dockrell, and Mackie (2008) also found high rates of bullying based on self-ratings, but levels were not significantly different than those experienced by typical children (54% in the group with LI compared to 46% in the typical children).

Adolescents with LI continue to experience a variety of social difficulties. Tomblin (2008) examined data from a large longitudinal sample (children studied from ages 7 to 16 years). At age 16, these individuals had fewer social contacts. Individuals with LI had a higher rate of emotional difficulties (e.g., depression), but these problems were linked to IQ level. The adolescents with LI also had a higher rate of rule breaking than did their typical peers, but this did not extend to more serious criminal behavior. It was of note that the 16-year-olds with LI rated themselves as lower on global self-esteem, but their ratings of satisfaction with life did not differ from those of their typical peers. As Tomblin pointed out, these positive ratings may have been tied to the fact that quality of life at age 16 is heavily influenced by the parents (living arrangement, income, etc.).

Conti-Ramsden and her colleagues at the University of Manchester also followed a large group of children with LI. From ages 7 to 16 years, individuals with LI experienced increasing difficulty interacting with peers (St. Clair, Pickles, Durkin, & Conti-Ramsden, 2011). When sampled at 16 years of age, these adolescents reported fewer friends (Durkin & Conti-Ramsden, 2007) and fewer close relationships (Wadman, Durkin, & Conti-Ramsden, 2011) than did typical peers.

Beitchman and colleagues followed a large group of Canadian children with speech and language problems from age 5 to adulthood (Brownlie et al., 2004). Although levels of socio-emotional difficulty were consistently higher in this group than for typical individuals, these rates decreased somewhat between ages 19 and 25 (Vida et al., 2009). At age 25, these young adults with LI had poorer outcomes in several aspects of life, including educational and occupational status. Their perceptions of quality of life did not differ from typical individuals, but these positive perceptions were closely linked to levels of social support provided by family, friends, and other social contacts. Additionally, the number of individuals who were married or had a partner did not significantly differ between groups (Johnson, Beitchman, & Brownlie, 2010). This finding contrasted with other studies reporting poorer outcomes regarding romantic relationships for adults with LI (e.g., Clegg, Hollis, Mawhood, & Rutter, 2005).

FACTORS INFLUENCING SOCIAL OUTCOMES FOR CHILDREN WITH LI

There is little doubt that LI has an impact on social relationships. There are indications, however, that additional factors also play a role in the social outcomes experienced by children with LI. For one thing, if language deficits alone accounted for poor social outcomes, we would expect almost all children with LI to experience such difficulties. In fact, some do well socially. Durkin and Conti-Ramsden (2007) found that 92% of typical 14-year-olds reported a normal range of social relationships, compared to 54% of individuals with LI. Although these differences are striking, still a sizable group of persons with LI reported a typical social experience.

If LI alone dictated social outcomes, it might also be expected that children with the most severe language problems would also have the most serious social difficulties. Hart, Fujiki, Brinton, and Hart (2004) considered this question by looking at the relationship between language and two general domains of social behavior—sociability and withdrawal. These researchers found that severity of LI was linked to problematic sociable behavior. Children with less impaired language generally demonstrated higher levels of both prosocial and likeable behaviors than did children with more impaired language. In contrast, there was little connection between various subtypes of withdrawn behavior (e.g., reticent withdrawal, solitary passive withdrawal) and language level. This finding suggests that social behaviors that require children to extend themselves (offering comfort, sharing, etc.) are more influenced by language skills than behaviors that do not.

It is likely that a number of variables influence social outcomes in children with LI. Some of these factors are probably internal (e.g., nature and severity of the language difficulties, temperament) and others external (e.g., availability and nature of educational programs, social support from family and friends). One developmental domain that has received relatively little attention in the study of LI is emotional intelligence. Given the strong connection between social and emotional competence (Thompson, 2011), however, a case can be made that emotional development merits consideration. Further, there are indications that aspects of emotional intelligence, particularly those related to ToM, may play a key role in the social interactions of children with LI.

Emotional Intelligence and Children With LI

A number of studies have suggested that there is a connection between aspects of emotional intelligence and the social competence of children with LI. For example, Fujiki, Spackman, Brinton, and Hall (2004) used a regression analysis to show that emotion regulation and language predicted 43% of the variability in social reticence scores in elementary school-age children with LI. Other work has indicated that some children with language problems experience difficulty with additional aspects of emotional intelligence, particularly the ability to recognize and understand the emotions of other people. These difficulties involve basic recognition of emotion expressed on faces as well as in voices (Boucher, Lewis, & Collis, 2000; Courtright & Courtright, 1983; Fujiki, Spackman, Brinton, & Illig, 2008; Spackman, Fujiki, Brinton, Nelson, & Allen, 2006). Illustrative of this work, Fujiki et al. (2008) presented a seven-sentence passage to elementary school-age children and their typically developing peers. The passages were constructed to minimize the syntactic and semantic demands of the task. The same passage was again read by actors using prosody to express happiness fear, anger, and sadness. The children with LI had significantly more difficulty than did typically developing peers identifying the emotion being expressed.

Children with LI also have difficulty with more complex emotion understanding tasks, such as inferring emotional reactions of others (Ford & Milosky, 2003; Spackman, Fujiki, & Brinton, 2006) and understanding when to hide an emotional reaction for social purposes (Brinton, Spackman, Fujiki, & Ricks, 2007). For example, Ford and Milosky (2003) asked kindergarteners with LI and typical peers to infer the emotion that a character named Twinky would experience, given a basic scenario (e.g., "Twinky wanted a teddy bear for his/her birthday. S/he opened a present with a big fluffy teddy bear. Twinky was _____"; p. 24). The emotions of happy, sad, mad, and surprised were tested. Children with LI had significantly more difficulty making emotional inferences. In fact, the children with LI were not only less accurate at inferring what emotions Twinky would experience; they also made more valence errors, confusing positive and negative emotions. Spackman, Fujiki, and Brinton (2006) replicated these results with older elementary children with LI. Although these children did not make many valence errors, they still performed significantly more poorly than did their typical peers.

Summary

Children with LI have difficulty with a range of social tasks, including entering ongoing interactions, negotiating with peers, and resolving disputes. It follows that they would also experience a number of poor social outcomes, including poor peer acceptance and higher rates of social and emotional problems. In considering why these children experience social difficulties, one might consider linguistic deficits as an obvious explanation. There are indications, however, that LI alone does not explain all of the variance seen in these children. Aspects of social cognition such as emotion understanding also play an important role.

ASSESSMENT OF SOCIAL COMMUNICATION

Assessment of social communication can be conceptualized as a questioning process. That is, we formulate several questions, and proceed to address those questions by employing various diagnostic procedures. Traditionally, we have formulated our questions focusing primarily on the individual suspected of having a problem. In a social communication approach, it is important to extend those questions to include the persons who have a stake in that individual's welfare. In the following section, we discuss the influence of stakeholders and the important contexts in which the child interacts with others. We then review questions we might pose in evaluating the various aspects of social communication.

Stakeholders

- Who are the stakeholders concerned in the child's development?
- What are the priorities of these stakeholders?
- What are the family and cultural considerations that have an impact on the child's communication?

- Who are the persons within the child's social circles?
- What are the important contexts in which the child interacts with persons in the social circles?
- How well does the child interact within these contexts?

Stakeholders are the prominent people in the child's life. Stakeholders include the child's family members, teachers, special service providers, and others who have an interest in the child's welfare. For most children, parents (or caretakers), followed by other family members, will be most important. In recent years there has been a great deal of attention focused on the importance of considering a family's cultural perspective in both assessment and intervention. This focus is critically important in assessing social communication. Interactional behaviors are heavily influenced by cultural norms and expectations. For example, parents' beliefs about communicating with their children (how much a parent talks to the child, when and where they talk, what they talk about, etc.) are often dictated by cultural standards (Goldstein & Horton-Ikard, 2010). In order to understand the interactional behaviors that are observed, it is necessary to understand what is considered appropriate within a particular culture.

A second reason for considering the cultural perspective of the family is that the cultural biases and stereotypes clinicians bring to the assessment process can influence clinical outcomes. This concern is not limited to speech-language pathology services. For example, there is considerable evidence that quality of medical treatment can be negatively influenced by the cultural biases of service providers (Smedley, Stith, & Nelson, 2003). It is important to consider how one's own cultural views line up with those of the family. This is fundamental when working with persons from different racial, linguistic, and ethnic backgrounds. It may also be an issue in cases where cultural differences are more subtle, however.

Important Communicative Partners and Communication Contexts

Understanding the perspectives of stakeholders can help in identifying important communicative partners and contexts. It is important to consider both the interactional partners with whom the child talks as well as the contexts in which those interactions occur. One way to gather this information is through interviewing caretakers and other important stakeholders. If appropriate, the clinician will also want to interview the child directly. A successful interview will require developing both trust and rapport with the individual and family. Ethnographic interviewing is a strategy that may be helpful in accomplishing both of these goals (Westby, Burda, & Mehta, 2003). This procedure involves a series of open-ended questions asked within a two-way interaction.

Blackstone and Hunt Berg's (2003) social network analysis is a useful way of organizing information regarding important communicative partners and contexts. The child's potential conversational partners are organized into social circles. The innermost circle consists of family members. Moving outward, subsequent circles include close friends, acquaintances, and finally those who are paid to interact with the individual (teachers, SLPs, etc.). This system was developed for persons with complex communication needs (including users of augmentative and alternative communication [AAC]), but it can provide useful information for individuals with a range of communication abilities. The examiner can supplement the social network analysis with information such as whom the child talks to the most, the contexts in which the child interacts, and the topics the child enjoys talking about. It may be the case that a child has many conversational partners, but most of them are paid or in some way obligated to interact (e.g., the classroom teacher, soccer coach, Sunday school teacher).

Assessing Components of Social Communication

Assessment of the child's general development provides an important backdrop for the evaluation. Our specific focus, however, is on the major aspects of social communication. As noted, the first component, social interaction, is particularly relevant for children in the earliest stages of language acquisition. For older children, the primary focus will usually be on language processing, pragmatics, and social cognition (Adams, Lockton, Gaile, Gillian, & Freed, 2012). A comprehensive review of methods and procedures that assess these abilities is beyond the scope of this chapter. Although we mention some specific procedures, we focus on the general questions to address in assessment. We suggest examples in the following section, but both the questions posed and the procedures employed to address these questions should be geared to the needs of individual children.

Language Processing

- Does the child have the expressive and receptive vocabulary to express personal experience, convey information, understand and tell stories, and participate in academic learning tasks and units?
- Does the child understand and produce the sentence structure needed to share experience and describe cause-and-effect relationships?

- Does the child have the expressive and receptive vocabulary to label, describe, express, and understand emotion?

Assessment of language processing largely involves considering the structural and semantic aspects of language production and comprehension. Deficits in these aspects of language are common in children with LI and may play a role in the limitations of children with related diagnoses such as PLI. Speech language pathologists and others who work with children with LI are highly familiar with both standardized tests and informal assessment tools that can be used to assess these problems. From a social communication perspective, however, it is important to go beyond documenting deficits in expressive and/or receptive language abilities. Rather, emphasis is placed on determining how children's strengths and limitations in language processing contribute to their interactions with others in a variety of educational and social contexts. Accordingly, we want to know how the child's language processing abilities support sharing personal experiences and comprehension of story structures and literature. In addition, it is also important to assess how the child's language processing facilitates participation in classroom learning activities. We pay particular attention to the vocabulary and structures that allow children to understand and convey emotion. This involves emotion words (especially those that go beyond the basic emotions, "happy, mad, sad") as well as complex sentence structures used to link emotions with the sources that elicit them (e.g., *If Tommy sees the dragon, then he will be scared*).

Pragmatics

- Can the child express a variety of communicative intents?
- Does the child take turns in conversation appropriately?
- Does the child manipulate topic in conversation appropriately?
- Is the child responsive to questions and requests for repair?
- Can the child request repair when needed?
- Does the child recognize and adjust conversational contributions according to accepted standards of politeness?

The assessment of pragmatics can include a range of behaviors, beginning in the early stages of language development with a focus on communicating intention. Most children with LI can express a variety of intents, but they may do so with limited words and structures. When addressing questions about pragmatics, it is important to focus on conversational behaviors that represent moments of cooperation between speaker and listener. For example, does the child exchange turns appropriately? Can the child initiate and maintain topics, and is the child responsive to topics introduced by other speakers? Does the child respond to requests for conversational repair (e.g., "What?" "A blue one?"), and can the child request repair when needed? (Requesting repair depends on comprehension monitoring which may be problematic for children with LI.)

Although there are standardized assessments that consider pragmatic behaviors, there are notable limitations to examining pragmatics in highly standardized contexts. A good place to start the assessment of pragmatic behaviors is by observing the child in social conversations. These direct observations may be supplemented by the impressions of individuals who know the child well (e.g., teacher, parent). Measures that use a rating scale or report form format such as the Children's Communication Checklist, second edition (Bishop, 2003) or the Language Use Inventory (O'Neill, 2007), can provide a useful way of organizing the impressions of stakeholders. These types of instruments have several advantages. Rating scales take advantage of the observations of people who have known the child over extended periods. They are relatively efficient to use and can provide information about important but infrequently occurring behaviors. On the negative side, these scales sample impressions of behaviors, not actual behaviors. Additionally, they can be influenced by the biases of the rater (e.g., too lenient or too stringent). Rating scales may also be subject to variability related to specific settings, times, and other factors that might skew the impressions of the rater (Merrell, 2003). The fact remains, however, that when used with care and recognition of potential limitations, these types of measures can provide highly useful information.

As helpful as rating scales are, it is important to analyze how a child actually performs in conversation. Various methods of conversational analysis have the potential to provide a description of a child's interactional behavior (e.g., Brinton & Fujiki, 1989). These procedures can be very time consuming, however. Some researchers have developed methodologies for online analyses of interactional behaviors (e.g., Olswang, Coggins, & Svensson, 2007), making these detailed analyses more feasible in clinical situations.

In addition to the analysis of natural conversation, the clinician may also want to examine specific abilities using tasks designed to elicit these behaviors. There are numerous examples of these tasks in the literature. For example, we used a topic task to probe the abilities of children with LI to maintain a topic introduced by a conversational partner (Brinton, Fujiki, & Powell, 1997). In this task, the examiner introduced some topics in association with an object (e.g., "My brother wants me to wear these. I don't know about that," spoken while placing an odd pair of sunglasses on the table). Other topics were introduced verbally only (e.g., "I walked to school this morning. I saw a dog. It almost bit me"; examples from Brinton, Fujiki, & Powell, 1997, p. 5). All of the children were able to maintain some topics, but children with LI produced far more utterances that did not maintain the topic than did typical peers. As another example, we performed a number of studies in which we inserted stacked sequences of requests for repair (e.g., "Huh? What? What?) to probe children's ability to adjust their input to accommodate listeners (Brinton, Fujiki, & Sonnenberg, 1988). Children with LI tend to be limited in the sophistication of their responses (e.g., repeating their original repair rather than adjusting it in response to the listener's difficulty, or responding off topic as the sequence progressed). Tasks such as these may be inserted into natural interactions to probe specific aspects of conversational behavior.

Social Cognition

- Does the child regulate emotion appropriately?
- Does the child recognize facial expressions of emotion?
- Can the child label/express experienced emotion appropriately?
- Can the child infer what others might be thinking in a specific scenario?
- Can the child infer what others might be feeling in a specific scenario?
- Does the child understand that others may experience emotions different from his or her own in a given situation?
- Can the child infer the social motivations of characters in stories?
- Can the child anticipate the emotions his or her actions might elicit?

As noted, social cognition is an umbrella term that encompasses a wide range of abilities and behaviors. We focus on several aspects of social and emotional learning that are (a) important to social interaction and academic success and (b) have been shown to be at risk for children with LI. For example, it is helpful to consider how well children with LI regulate emotion. Two aspects of emotion regulation, calming down and gearing up, affect a child's motivation and availability to learn. We are concerned with how well children calm themselves when they are experiencing intense emotion, and we are just as concerned with how children are able to gear themselves up to enter interactions or accomplish difficult tasks. Observation and caregiver and teacher report can be useful in determining how well children regulate emotion in various contexts.

It can be helpful to probe several types of emotion knowledge that play important roles in social communication. Although children begin to learn to interpret facial expressions of emotion in infancy, this remains a difficult task for some children with LI. Various tasks (some standardized) can be employed to determine how well children interpret emotion in still pictures (e.g., Ekman, 2014) and videos (e.g., Brinton, Robinson, & Fujiki, 2004). It is also helpful to probe how children express emotion. Specifically, do they have the vocabulary to label emotion and do they understand the emotion display rules of their community? It is also helpful to explore ToM tasks. Current conceptualizations of ToM consider both a more traditionally recognized "cognitive" ToM (e.g., used to complete a false belief task) and an "emotional" ToM (see Westby, Chapter 2 of this volume). This affective ToM has to do with understanding the emotional perspectives of others and recognizing that those perspectives may differ from one's own, even in identical situations. It can be useful to examine how well children infer the emotion a person might experience in a basic scenario (e.g., see task used by Ford & Milosky, 2003). This task provides information about how well children link sources (e.g., events, scenarios) with the emotions they are likely to elicit in individuals with various backgrounds and dispositions. The ability to make these kinds of social inferences will underpin children's comprehension of stories and literature.

Some children with LI have difficulties interacting because they cannot predict the emotions that their own actions might elicit in others. This difficulty may well be tied to problems recognizing the emotion cues that others convey. It may be possible to help children with LI reflect on the emotional reactions of those with whom they interact.

Summary

In this section we posed several questions that, when geared to the needs of an individual child such as Jennie, may guide assessment. It is important to begin with the stakeholders and the culture within which the child communicates. In Jennie's case, it was important to obtain information from her mother and her teacher regarding her general developmental history and her current social communication needs at home and in the classroom. We were then prepared to employ formal testing, teacher/parent report measures, observation, and specific tasks to probe the four components of Jennie's social communication. Standardized testing measures documented impairment in both expressive and receptive language processing. Teacher interviews highlighted Jennie's difficulty with academic work, particularly story comprehension and literacy tasks. Teacher report measures also suggested difficulties with both social cognition and pragmatics manifest in reticent behavior, limited prosocial skills, and a lack of responsiveness to peers. A series of probes of social and emotional learning, particularly emotion understanding, revealed that Jennie did not easily recognize facial expression of emotion. She often did not label emotions accurately, and she had difficulty predicting what emotion an event might elicit. Jennie presented with language impairment in the traditional sense, but she also demonstrated associated difficulties with social cognition and pragmatics. By synthesizing and integrating information obtained from multiple sources, we were able to get a sense of Jennie's functioning in the contexts that were important in her social world.

SOCIAL COMMUNICATION INTERVENTION

In the following section, we begin by considering work to improve the social and emotional learning of typically developing children. We then review research focusing on interventions to improve social communication skills in children with LI.

Social and Emotional Learning Programs for Typically Developing Children

Social communication depends heavily on social and emotional learning. Social and emotional learning refers to the processes by which children learn to "understand and manage emotions, set and achieve positive goals, feel and show empathy for others, establish and maintain positive relationships, and make responsible decisions" (Collaborative for Academics, Social, and Emotional Learning [CASEL] Guide, 2012, p. 4). In recent years, there has been a good deal of work devoted to designing and implementing educational programs to facilitate social and emotional learning in school settings. To date, there is strong evidence that when these programs are implemented in a comprehensive, rigorous manner, they are highly successful. For example, Durlak, Weissberg, Dymnicki, Taylor, and Schellinger (2011) reported a meta-analysis of 213 studies involving 270,034 students. Results indicated that children and adolescents who participated in educational programs targeting social and emotional learning had significantly better outcomes than controls on assessments of emotional problems, behavioral disorders, social skills, and emotional competence. Significant differences were not limited to social and emotional domains, however, but were also observed in measures of academic performance including grades and achievement test scores.

Social Communication Interventions for Children With Language Deficits

The evidence for social communication intervention programs for children with disabilities is mixed. In addition, there are relatively few studies investigating interventions designed to facilitate social and emotional competence specifically in children with LI (Gerber, Brice, Capone, Fujiki, & Timler, 2012). There have been a number of investigations, however, examining aspects of social functioning in a similar (overlapping) population. For example, studies have examined social skill training interventions for children with learning disabilities (LD). Kavale and Mostert (2004) conducted a meta-analysis of 53 studies examining social skill interventions for children with LD and found modest effects. Kavale and Mostert suggest that a number of factors may be responsible for this outcome, including the use of intervention packages that lack a fundamental rationale for how procedures are combined and applied, the lack of sufficient intensity of training, and the difficulty in conceptualizing and then measuring variables of interest. In the following section, we review a few of the studies reporting successful outcomes for children with LI. Although our discussion is not comprehensive, the studies discussed are representative of this work.

Randomized Controlled Trial for Social Communication Skills

Adams and colleagues (Adams, Lockton, Freed, et al., 2012; Adams, Lockton, Gaile, et al., 2012) have conducted the only randomized control trial (to date) to facilitate social communication skills in children with LI (specifically focusing on PLI). Adams and her colleagues administered a comprehensive intervention program to a group of 57 children with pragmatic problems. Outcomes were then compared with a group of 28 children who received treatment as usual. The intervention addressed multiple areas of social communication, including ToM, social inferencing, and conversational ability. Specific intervention targets were geared to the problems experienced by individual children, however. Children in the treatment group did not produce greater gains than the control group in structural language and narrative language abilities as measured by the Clinical Evaluation of Language Fundamentals–4 (Semel, Wiig, & Secord, 2006). Positive improvement was noted in blind ratings of quality of conversation, however. Additionally, parent and teacher ratings of pragmatic ability also improved in comparison to controls (see Adams, Chapter 6 in this volume). The intervention represented a well-thought-out, comprehensive treatment package that was adjusted to meet the needs of specific students. The individualized nature of this program was relatively unique and likely contributed to positive outcomes.

Single-Subject Research Involving Children With LI

Although the Adams randomized control trial is arguably the most notable group intervention study available, there is much to learn from research using other methods, particularly well-designed single-subject research. Because there is notable heterogeneity among children with LI, single-subject design studies evaluating specific interventions can show how individuals with unique strengths and limitations respond to treatment.

Single-subject designs have been used to target a variety of social communication behaviors in children with LI (e.g., Craig-Unkefer & Kaiser, 2002; Goldstein, Wickstrom, Hoyson, Jamieson, & Odom, 1988; Stanton-Chapman, Denning, & Roorbach Jamison, 2012; Stanton-Chapman, Kaiser, Vijay, & Chapman, 2008). It should be noted that some of these studies included children presenting with a variety of deficits, most frequently involving a combination of language and behavioral problems (although children with diagnoses of intellectual disability or ASD were excluded). The researchers in many of these studies used a similar intervention format. The children received instruction and then were provided with an opportunity to practice skills. The practice (often integrated into a procedure such as script training or sociodramatic play) was followed by an opportunity to review performance. For example, Stanton-Chapman and colleagues have conducted a number of studies employing such procedures. In one of the more recent studies, Stanton-Chapman et al. (2012) followed eight preschoolers at risk for social, behavior, and language problems. The children were seen for intervention in dyads. Treatment began with a 10-minute segment in which the children were instructed as to the possible roles they would assume during a sociodramatic play scenario (e.g., grocery store, doctor's office). The clinician then read a story focusing on the scenario. During the story, instruction was provided targeting specific social communication strategies (initiating, responding, using the person's name, and turn taking). These strategies were introduced one at a time over the course of the first 12 sessions. After listening to the story, children selected their roles and received additional instruction as to how the targeted strategy might be used. Instruction time was also devoted to teaching the vocabulary needed to execute the play scenario.

The actual play session made up the second component of the intervention (also 10 minutes long). The clinician helped the children to select appropriate costumes and the other items needed to act out the roles. The children then acted out the play scenario. The clinician was not directly involved in the play, but provided prompts for the children to use the targeted strategies as well as appropriate vocabulary words. Prompts were delivered according to predetermined rates and conditions (e.g., if a child did not engage in a targeted behavior after the first minute, the clinician provided a prompt). The play session was then followed by a 5-minute review session. The clinician first reviewed the role played by the children. Next, targeted vocabulary items were presented followed by specific social communication strategies. The intervention produced increases over baseline levels of production of both positive verbal initiations and appropriate responding to the bids of peers.

Additional Studies of Social Communication Abilities

Case Study Designs

Additional studies describing social communication interventions for children with LI are available. Many, but not all of these investigations use case study or multiple case study designs and are exploratory in nature. Interventions have focused on behaviors such as increasing conversational responsiveness (Brinton et al., 2004), facilitating the production of positive comments (Fujiki, Brinton, McCleave, Anderson, & Chamberlain, 2013), and enhancing pragmatic and social cognitive behaviors (Adams, Lloyd Aldred, & Baxendale, 2006). These studies have employed a variety of methods, including the instruction–practice–review procedures described previously. Although the outcomes of these case studies have been promising, they also highlight the persistence of social communication problems in individual children as well as the challenge of monitoring change in authentic interactional contexts.

Group Designs

A number of authors have studied interventions designed for larger groups of children with LI. For example, Schuele, Rice, and Wilcox (1995) conducted an intervention within a classroom context. Specifically, Schuele and colleagues examined the impact of redirecting child initiations from adults to peers. This strategy, implemented by the classroom teacher, produced an increase in peer initiations in the four children studied.

Richardson and Klecan-Aker (2000) performed a treatment study focusing on aspects of social communication in a group of children with language learning impairment. The children, who were placed in two self-contained classrooms, were formally diagnosed with LD, but language deficits were documented through a standardized, global language test. Intervention focused on facilitating conversational skills and object description as well as receptive identification and expressive labeling of facial expressions of emotion. Improvements were noted in initiating and maintaining conversational topic, object description, and identification of emotions.

Summary

There is an impressive body of evidence demonstrating that carefully designed programs to facilitate social and emotional learning in typical children result in significant gains in social, behavioral, and academic performance. In comparison, research examining the efficacy of intervention targeting social communication in children with LI is sparse. The relatively small number of treatment studies reflects the complexity of designing and implementing studies that assess and measure children's knowledge, performance, and growth within and across varied domains of development. Both treatment and assessment demand consideration of multiple behaviors within authentic communicative contexts. Nevertheless, recent studies provide evidence that social communication interventions can be effective at facilitating growth, at least to the point where stakeholders observe a positive difference. Additional efficacy research is needed to identify the most critical social communication abilities to target, to refine our treatment approaches, and to determine the most effective intensity and duration of treatment.

CASE STUDY OUTCOMES

Like most children with LI, Jennie presented with complex educational needs. On one hand, she demonstrated the kinds of structural language deficits that have traditionally been associated with LI. Facilitating Jennie's language structure and expanding her vocabulary seemed essential to her academic progress. That was only part of the picture, however. Jennie's difficulty with pragmatics and social cognition limited her ability to comprehend academic content, to understand stories and events, to participate in learning contexts, and to form positive relationships with her peers.

Jennie's abilities and challenges could best be addressed within a social communication approach. Such an approach allowed a broad perspective on Jennie's development and the integration of language processing, pragmatic, and social cognition goals in intervention. An intervention program was designed to facilitate simultaneously the production of complex sentences, the acquisition of new vocabulary (including emotion words), the comprehension of story structures, the interpretation of emotion cues, and the association of events and situations with the emotions they might elicit. Treatment sessions were built around a trio of components. The first involved storybooks with clear event structures and prominent emotional content. The clinician shared a book with Jennie, emphasizing (a) the facial expressions of emotions pictured, (b) the sources of emotions, (c) the emotion labels, (d) the sentence structures used to link scenarios with the emotions they elicited, and (e) the outcomes of prosocial behaviors of characters. Jennie then participated in an enactment using toys and prompts. She was encouraged to use appropriate sentence structures to express and explain the emotions and motivations of characters and to model emotion cues including facial expressions.

The second component consisted of a brief segment of direct instruction on various aspects of emotion understanding such as learning emotion words, interpreting emotion cues, or modeling facial expressions of emotion. The third component involved a journaling activity. Jennie dictated sentences to the clinician relating the main idea of the story, what she had liked about the session, and what she found challenging. The clinician modeled appropriate sentence structures and words, read Jennie's dictation back to her, and assisted Jennie in "revising" her dictation as needed. Jennie was encouraged to draw a picture, write a letter or word, or put a sticker in her journal. Jennie found these activities challenging, but she gradually learned to focus on the emotional content of the stories, the perspectives of the characters in the stories, a variety of emotion words, and more appropriate language structures. Within a few months, her repertoire of emotion words began to expand, as did her ability to recognize and correctly label emotion. These gains supported her comprehension of stories. It was clear, however, that Jennie would continue to need intervention emphasizing the integration of language and social and emotional learning.

DISCUSSION QUESTIONS

1. How has the conceptualization of language impairment (LI) evolved over time?
2. What is social communication and how is it different from pragmatics?
3. How does "cognitive" theory of mind differ from "affective" theory of mind?
4. What are some common social tasks that are difficult for children with LI?

5. What are some of the social and emotional problems that children with LI may experience?
6. What are some reasons to believe that limited language is not the only factor that leads to social and emotional problems in children with LI?
7. Describe some aspects of emotional competence that are difficult for children with LI.
8. Why is it important to consider "stakeholders" as well as the child when assessing the social communication skills of a child?
9. What type of questions should be asked about social cognition when performing a social communication assessment?
10. Are social and emotional learning programs for typical children effective? What can these programs tell us about similar programs for children with LI?
11. What do single subject research studies add to our understanding of the efficacy of social communication interventions?

CLINICAL RESOURCES

American Psychiatric Association. Definition of social communication disorder: www.dsm5.org/Documents/Social%2520Communication%2520Disorder%2520Fact%2520Sheet.pdf

American Speech-Language-Hearing Association, Social Communication Disorders in School-Age Children. Clinical topics: www.asha.org/Practice-Portal/Clinical-Topics/Social-Communication-Disorders-in-School-Age-Children/

American Speech-Language-Hearing Association, Social Communication Benchmarks: www.asha.org/uploadedFiles/ASHA/Practice_Portal/Clinical_Topics/Social_Communication_Disorders_in_School-Age_Children/Social-Communication-Benchmarks.pdf

American Speech-Language-Hearing Association, Social Communication Components of Social Communication: www.asha.org/uploaded Files/ASHA/Practice_Portal/Clinical_Topics/Social_Communication_Disorders_in_School-Age_Children/Components-of-Social-Communication.pdf

NOTE

[1] In this chapter we refer to developmental language difficulties in the face of relatively typical nonverbal cognitive abilities using the term "language impairment" rather than specific language impairment in recognition of the fact that the impairment is not as specific as once believed. We

occasionally use the term *SLI* when authors have used it to describe the children they have studied, however.

REFERENCES

Adams, C. (2005). Social communication intervention for school-age children: Rationale and description. *Seminars in Speech and Language, 26,* 181–188.

Adams, C. (2008). Intervention for children with pragmatic language impairments. In C. F. Norbury, J. B. Tomblin, & D. V. M. Bishop (Eds.), *Understanding developmental language disorders* (pp. 189–204). New York, NY: Psychology Press.

Adams, C., Lloyd, J., Aldred, C., & Baxendale, J. (2006). Exploring the effects of communication intervention for developmental pragmatic language impairments: A signal-generation study. *International Journal of Language & Communication Disorders, 41,* 41–65.

Adams, C., Lockton, E., Freed, J., Gaile, J., Earl, G., McBean, K., . . . Law, J. (2012). The Social Communication Intervention Project: A randomized controlled trial of the effectiveness of speech and language therapy for school-age children who have pragmatic and social communication problems with or without autism spectrum disorders. *International Journal of Language & Communication Disorders, 47,* 233–244. doi:10:111/J.1460–6984.2011.00146.x

Adams, C., Lockton, E., Gaile, J., Gillian, E., & Freed, J. (2012). Implementation of a manualized communication intervention for school-aged children with pragmatic and social communication needs in a randomized controlled trial: The Social Communication Intervention Project. *International Journal of Language & Communication Disorders, 47,* 245–256. doi:10.1111/j.1460–6984.2012.00147.x

American Psychiatric Association, DSM-5 Task Force. (2013). *Diagnostic and statistical manual of mental disorders* (5th ed.). Arlington, VA: Author.

Bishop, D. V. M. (2003). *The Children's Communication Checklist* (2nd ed.). London, UK: Harcourt Assessment.

Bishop, D. V. M., Chan, J., Adams, C., Hartley, J., & Weir, F. (2000). Conversational responsiveness in specific language impairment: Evidence of disproportionate pragmatic difficulties in a subset of children. *Development and Psychopathology, 12,* 177–199.

Bishop, D. V. M., & Norbury, C. F. (2002). Exploring the borderlands of autistic disorder and specific language impairment: A study using standardized diagnostic instruments. *Journal of Child Psychology and Psychiatry and Allied Disciplines, 43,* 917–929.

Bishop, D. V. M., & Rosenbloom, L. (1987). Classification of childhood language disorders. In W. Yule & M. Rutter (Eds.), *Language development and disorders* (pp. 16–41). London, UK: Mac Keith Press.

Blackstone, S. W., & Hunt Berg, M. (2003). *Social networks: A communication inventory for individuals with complex communication needs and their communication partners.* [Inventory booklet]. Monterey, CA: Augmentative Communication, Inc.

Boucher, J., Lewis, V., & Collis, G. M. (2000). Voice processing abilities in children with autism, children with specific language impairments, and young typically developing children. *Journal of Child Psychology & Psychiatry, 41,* 847–857.

Botting, N., & Conti-Ramsden, G. (1999). Pragmatic impairment without autism. *Autism, 3,* 371–396. doi:10.1177/1362361399003004005

Brinton, B., & Fujiki, M. (1989). *Conversational management with language-impaired children.* Rockville, MD: Aspen.

Brinton, B., Fujiki, M., & Higbee, L. (1998). Participation in cooperative learning activities by children with specific language impairment. *Journal of Speech, Language, and Hearing Research, 41,* 1193–1206.

Brinton, B., Fujiki, M., & McKee, L. (1998). The negotiation skills of children with specific language impairment. *Journal of Speech, Language, and Hearing Research, 41,* 927–940.

Brinton, B., Fujiki, M., Montague, E. C., & Hanton, J. L. (2000). Children with language impairment in cooperative work groups: A pilot study. *Language, Speech, and Hearing Services in Schools, 31,* 252–264.

Brinton, B., Fujiki, M., & Powell, J. M. (1997). The ability of children with language impairment to manipulate topic in a structured task. *Language, Speech and Hearing Services in Schools, 28,* 3–11.

Brinton, B., Fujiki, M., Spencer, J. C., & Robinson, L. A. (1997). The ability of children with specific language impairment to access and participate in an ongoing interaction. *Journal of Speech, Language, and Hearing Research, 40,* 1011–1025.

Brinton, B., Fujiki, M., & Sonnenberg, E. A. (1988). Responses to requests for clarification by linguistically normal and language-impaired children in conversation. *Journal of Speech and Hearing Disorders, 53,* 383–391.

Brinton, B., Robinson, L. A., & Fujiki, M. (2004). Description of a program for social language intervention: "If you can have a conversation, you can have a relationship." *Language, Speech and Hearing Services in Schools, 35,* 283–290. doi:10.1044/0161-1461(2004/026)

Brinton, B., Spackman, M. P., Fujiki, M., & Ricks, J. (2007). What should Chris say? The ability of children with specific language impairment to recognize the need to dissemble emotions in social situations. *Journal of Speech, Language, and Hearing Research, 50,* 798–811.

Brown, W. H., Odom, S. L., & McConnell, S. R. (2008). *Social competence of young children: Risk, disability, and intervention.* Baltimore, MD: Brookes.

Brownlie, E. B., Beitchman, J. H., Escobar, M., Young, A., Atkinson, L., Johnson, C. J., . . . Douglas, L. (2004). Early language impairment and young adult delinquent and aggressive behavior. *Journal of Abnormal Child Psychology*, *32*, 453–467.

Clegg, J., Hollis, C., Mawhood, L., & Rutter, M. (2005). Developmental language disorders—a follow-up in later adult life. Cognitive, language and psychosocial outcomes. *Journal of Child Psychology and Psychiatry*, *46*, 128–149.

Collaborative for Academic, Social, and Emotional Learning. (2012). CASEL Guide: Effective social and emotional learning programs: Preschool and elementary school edition. Chicago, IL: Author. Retrieved from http://casel.squarespace.com/guide

Conti-Ramsden, G., & Botting, N. (2004). Social difficulties and victimization in children with SLI at 11 years of age. *Journal of Speech, Language, and Hearing Research*, *47*, 145–161. doi:10.1044/1092–4388(2004/013)

Conti-Ramsden, G., Crutchley, A., & Botting, N. (1997). The extent to which psychometric tests differentiate subgroups of children with SLI. *Journal of Speech, Language, and Hearing Research*, *40*, 765–777.

Courtright, J., & Courtright, I. (1983). The perception of nonverbal vocal cues of emotional meaning by language disordered and normal children. *Journal of Speech and Hearing Research*, *26*, 412–417.

Craig, H. K., & Washington, J. A. (1993). The access behaviors of children with specific language impairment. *Journal of Speech and Hearing Research*, *36*, 322–336.

Craig-Unkefer, L. A., & Kaiser, A. P. (2002). Improving the social communication skills of at-risk preschool children in a play context. *Topics in Early Childhood Special Education*, *22*, 3–13.

Durkin, K., & Conti-Ramsdsen, G. (2007). Language, social behavior, and the quality of friendships in adolescents with and without a history of specific language impairment. *Child Development*, *78*, 1441–1457.

Durlark, J. A., Weissberg, R. P., Dymnicki, A. B., Taylor, R. D., & Schellinger, K. B. (2011). The impact of enhancing students' social and emotional learning: A meta-analysis of school-based universal interventions. *Child Development*, *82*, 405–432.

Ekman, P. (2014). Paul Ekman group. Retrieved February 26, 2014, from www.paulekman.com/products/

Erdley, C. A., & Asher, S. (1999). A social goals perspective on children's social competence. *Journal of Emotional and Behavioral Disorders*, *7*, 156–167.

Ford, J. A., & Milosky, L. M. (2003). Inferring emotional reactions in social situations: Differences in children with language impairment. *Journal of Speech, Language, Hearing Research*, *46*, 21–30.

Fujiki, M., Brinton, B., Hart, C. H., & Fitzgerald, A. (1999). Peer acceptance and friendship in children with specific language impairment. *Topics in Language Disorders*, *19*(2), 34–48.

Fujiki, M., Brinton, B., McCleave, C. P., Anderson, V. W., & Chamberlain, J. P. (2013). A social communication intervention to increase the production of validating comments. *Language, Speech and Hearing Services in Schools, 44*, 3–19. doi:10.1044/0161–1461(2012/11–103)

Fujiki, M., Brinton, B., Morgan, M., & Hart, C. H. (1999). Withdrawn and sociable behavior of children with specific language impairment. *Language, Speech, and Hearing Services in Schools, 30*, 183–195.

Fujiki, M., Brinton, B., & Todd, C. (1996). Social skills of children with specific language impairment. *Language, Speech, and Hearing Services in Schools, 27*, 195–202.

Fujiki, M., Spackman, M. P., Brinton, B., & Hall, A. (2004). The relationship of language and emotion regulation skills to reticence in children with specific language impairment. *Journal of Speech, Language, and Hearing Research, 47*, 647–662.

Fujiki, M., Spackman, M. P., Brinton, B., & Illig, T. (2008). The ability of children with language impairment to understand emotion conveyed by prosody in a narrative passage. *International Journal of Language and Communication Disorders, 43*, 330–345. doi:10.1080/13682820701507377

Gerber, S., Brice, A., Capone, N. C., Fujiki, M., & Timler, G. R. (2012). Language use in social interactions of school-age children with language impairments: An evidence-based systematic review of treatment. *Language, Speech, and Hearing Services in Schools, 43*, 235–249. doi:10.1044/0161–1461(2011/10–0047)

Gertner, B. L., Rice, M. L., & Hadley, P. A. (1994). Influence of communicative competence on peer preferences in a preschool classroom. *Journal of Speech and Hearing Research, 37*, 913–923.

Goldstein, B. A., & Horton-Ikard, R. (2010). Diversity considerations in speech and language disorders. In J. S. Damico, N. Muller & M. J. Ball (Eds.), *The handbook of language and speech disorders* (pp. 38–556). Malden, MA: Wiley-Blackwell.

Goldstein, H., Wickstrom, S., Hoyson, H., Jamieson, B., & Odom, S. L. (1988). Effects of sociodramatic script training on social and communicative interaction. *Education and Treatment of Children, 11*, 97–117.

Grove, J., Conti-Ramsden, G., & Donlan, C. (1993). Conversational interaction and decision-making in children with specific language impairment. *European Journal of Disorders of Communication, 28*, 141–152.

Guralnick, M. J., Connor, R. T., Hammond, M. A., Gottman, J. M., & Kinnish, K. (1996). The peer relations of preschool children with communication disorders. *Child Development, 67*, 471–489.

Hart, K., Fujiki, M., Brinton, B., & Hart, C. H. (2004). The relationship between social behavior and severity of language impairment. *Journal of Speech, Language, and Hearing Research, 47*, 647–662. doi:10.1044/1092–4388(2004/050)

Horowitz, L., Jansson, L., Ljungberg, T., & Hedenbro, M. (2005). Behavioural patterns of conflict resolution strategies in preschool boys with language impairment in comparison with boys with typical language development. *International Journal of Language & Communication Disorders, 40,* 431–454.

Johnson, C. J., Beitchman, J. H., & Brownlie, E. B. (2010). Twenty-year follow-up of children with and without speech-language impairments: Family, educational, occupational, and quality of life outcomes. *American Journal of Speech-Language Pathology, 19*(1), 51–65. doi:10.1044/1058–0360(200 9/08–0083)

Kavale, K. A., & Mostert, M. P. (2004). Social skills interventions for individuals with learning disabilities. *Learning Disability Quarterly, 27,* 31–43.

Liiva, C. A., & Cleave, P. L. (2005). Roles of initiation and responsiveness in access and participation for children with specific language impairment. *Journal of Speech, Language, and Hearing Research, 48,* 868–883.

Lindsay, G., Dockrell, J., & Mackie, C. (2008). Vulnerability to bullying in children with a history of specific speech and language difficulties. *European Journal of Special Needs Education, 23,* 1–16. doi:10.1080/08856250701791203

Marton, K., Abramoff, B., & Rosenzweig, S. (2005). Social cognition and language in children with specific language impairment. *Journal of Communication Disorders, 38,* 143–162. doi:10.1016/j.jcomdis.2004.06.003

Merrell, K. W. (2003). *Behavioral, social, and emotional assessment of children and adolescents* (2nd ed.). Mahwah, NJ: Erlbaum.

Olswang, L. B., Coggins, T. E., & Svensson, L. (2007). Assessing social communication in the classroom. *Topics in Language Disorders, 27*(2), 111–127.

Olswang, L. B., Coggins, T. E., & Timler, G. R. (2001). Outcome measures for school-age children with social communication problems. *Topics in Language Disorders, 21*(4), 40–73.

O'Neill, D. K. (2007). The language use inventory for young children: A parent-report measure of pragmatic language development for 18- to 47-month-old children. *Journal of Speech, Language, and Hearing Research, 50,* 214–228. doi:10.1044/1092–4388(2007/017)

Paul, R., Looney, S. S., & Dahm, P. S. (1991). Communication and socialization skills at ages 2 and 3 in "late-talking" young children. *Journal of Speech and Hearing Research, 34,* 858–865.

Richardson, K., & Klecan-Aker, J. S. (2000). Teaching pragmatics to language-learning disabled children: A treatment outcome study. *Child Language Teaching and Therapy, 16,* 23–42. doi:10.1177/02656590000 1600103

Schuele, C. M., Rice, M. L., & Wilcox, K. A. (1995). Redirects: A strategy to increase peer initiations. *Journal of Speech and Hearing Research, 38,* 1319–1333.

Semel, E., Wiig, E. H., & Secord, W. (2006). *Clinical evaluation of language fundamentals* (4th ed. UK). Hove, UK: Harcourt Assessment.

Semel, E., Wiig, E., & Secord, W. (2013). *Clinical evaluation of language fundamentals* (5th ed). San Antonio, TX: Pearson.

Smedley, B., Stith, A. Y., & Nelson, A. R. (2003). *Unequal treatment: Confronting racial and ethnic disparities in health care.* Washington, DC: National Academy Press.

Spackman, M. P., Fujiki, M., & Brinton, B. (2006). Understanding emotions in context: The effects of language impairment on children's ability to infer emotional reactions. *International Journal of Language & Communication Disorders, 41,* 173–188.

Spackman, M. P., Fujiki, M., Brinton, B., Nelson, D., & Allen, J. (2006). The ability of children with language impairment to recognize emotion conveyed by facial expression and music. *Communication Disorders Quarterly, 26,* 131–143.

St. Clair, M. C., Pickles, A., Durkin, K., & Conti-Ramsden, G. (2011). A longitudinal study of behavioral, emotional and social difficulties in individuals with a history of specific language impairment (SLI). *Journal of Communication Disorders, 44,* 186–199. doi:10.1016/j.jcomdis.2010.09.004

Stanton-Chapman, T. L., Denning, C. B., & Jamison Roorbach, K. (2012). Communication skill building in young children with and without disabilities in a preschool classroom. *Journal of Special Education, 46,* 78–93. doi:10.1177/0022466910378044

Stanton-Chapman, T. L., Kaiser, A. P., Vijay, P., & Chapman, C. (2008). A multicomponent intervention to increase peer-directed communication in head start children. *Journal of Early Intervention, 30,* 188–212. doi:10.1177/1053815108318746

Thompson, R. (2011). The emotionate child. In D. Cicchetti & G. I. Goisman (Eds.), *Minnesota Symposia on Child Psychology: The origins and organization of adaptation and maladaptation* (pp. 13–53). Hoboken, NJ: Wiley. Retrieved from http://onlinelibrary.wiley.com.erl.lib.byu.edu/book/10.1002/9781118036600

Timler, G. R. (2008). Social knowledge in children with language impairments: Examination of strategies, predicted consequences, and goals in peer conflict situations. *Clinical Linguistics & Phonetics, 22*(9), 741–763.

Tomblin, J. B. (2008). Validating diagnostic standards for specific language impairment using adolescent outcomes. In C. F. Norbury, J. B. Tomblin, & D. V. M. Bishop (Eds.), *Understanding developmental language disorders* (pp. 93–114). New York, NY: Psychology Press.

Vida, R., Brownlie, E. B., Beitchman, J., Adlaf, E., Atkinson, L., Escobar, M., . . . Bender, D. (2009). Emerging adult outcomes of adolescent psychiatric and substance use disorders. *Addictive Behaviors, 34,* 800–805. doi:10.1016/j.addbeh.2009.03.035

Wadman, R., Durkin, K., & Conti-Ramdsen, G. (2011). Close relationships in adolescents with and without a history of specific language impairment. *Language, Speech and Hearing Services in Schools, 42,* 40–51.

Westby, C. (2014). Social-emotional bases of pragmatic and communication development. In N. Capone Singleton & B. B. Shulman (Eds.), *Language development: Foundations, processes, and clinical applications* (2nd ed., pp. 119–146). Burlington, MA: Jones & Bartlett Learning.

Westby, C., Burda, A., & Mehta, Z. (2003). Asking the right questions in the right ways. *ASHA Leader.* Retrieved from ASHA.org website: www.asha. org/Publications/leader/2003/030429/f030429b/

9

SOCIAL COMMUNICATION ASSESSMENT AND INTERVENTION FOR CHILDREN WITH ATTENTION PROBLEMS

Geralyn R. Timler and Katherine E. White

The language and communication difficulties in children with ADHD may remain undetected unless language functioning is made a formal part of the diagnostic assessment for ADHD.
—Tannock and Schachar (1996, pp. 147–148)

As most therapies are verbally based, including the cognitive behavioral and social skills training techniques often applied to children with ADHD, it is notable that language competence is rarely evaluated systematically before such therapies are undertaken.
—Cohen et al. (2000, p. 360)

LEARNING OBJECTIVES

Readers will be able to

1. State the incidence/prevalence rates for Attention-Deficit/ Hyperactivity Disorder (ADHD) and Fetal Alcohol Spectrum Disorder (FASD).
2. Describe the behavioral phenotype that leads to diagnoses of ADHD and FASD.
3. Summarize language and social communication profiles of children with ADHD and children with FASD.

4. Describe evidence-based assessment and intervention practices for children with ADHD and FASD.

Gregory (Greg) is a 7-year-old who has a diagnosis of Attention-Deficit/Hyperactivity Disorder (ADHD), articulation disorder, and language disorder. Greg and two younger brothers, ages 5 and 2, live with both parents. When Greg was 18 months old, his parents reported that he seemed "more active" and was much less likely to respond to "no" than were his siblings. In addition, Greg was "not able to get the sounds of words out." When Greg was 3, their pediatrician thought that some of Greg's behavioral problems might be related to his communication difficulties and recommended Greg be evaluated by a speech-language pathologist (SLP). Greg was diagnosed with a speech sound disorder and subsequently received speech therapy services at a local special education preschool program. Although Greg's communication skills began to improve, his parents had increasing concerns about his behavior. Greg was easily distracted by sounds in the neighborhood even when he was watching television. He continued to be "on the go" both at home and in his group therapy sessions. Just after his fourth birthday, Greg's parents had him evaluated by a neurologist. The neurologist and an interdisciplinary team of a pediatrician and clinical psychologist confirmed Greg's speech disorder and suggested that Greg might have ADHD and be at high risk for dyslexia. Because of his ADHD diagnosis, Greg was eligible for special education services under the category of "Other Health Impairment." His speech services intensified in kindergarten and primarily focused on increasing speech intelligibility. In addition to school-based services, Greg's parents have sought out further support from a university clinic and an intensive summer program aimed at supporting literacy skills. At the end of first grade, his parents identified that he is "especially good at math" but that reading is difficult for him. Although Greg likes school, his parents have some emerging concerns about his peer relationships. They report that Greg has few friends. At home, he frequently interrupts his brothers or ignores their questions to him.

Greg's attentional and behavioral difficulties and communicative development are typical of some children with ADHD. Approximately half of all school-age children and adolescents with ADHD have a co-occurring communication disorder (Mueller & Tomblin, 2012). Language impairment is one of the most common co-occurring diagnoses in children with ADHD. Fortunately, Greg's attentional problems and communicative disorders were diagnosed relatively early—during the preschool years. Even though children with ADHD are at higher risk for communicative difficulties than are children without ADHD, these difficulties are likely to remain unidentified unless a systematic screening protocol is implemented at the time the child's behavioral difficulties are evaluated. Suggestions for such a protocol are provided in a later section of this chapter.

Children with ADHD are not the only population of children with attentional problems who are served by SLPs. Children prenatally exposed to alcohol who receive one of several diagnoses under the umbrella term of Fetal Alcohol Spectrum Disorder (FASD) often have co-occurring attention deficits and social communication problems. Descriptions of the diagnostic characteristics, incidence, and speech and language profiles of children with ADHD and FASD are presented in subsequent sections. The Assessment and Intervention sections include overlapping recommendations and guidelines for addressing the social communication concerns of children with ADHD and FASD.

ADHD: DEFINITIONS, INCIDENCE, AND PREVALENCE

Definitions

Attention-deficit/hyperactivity disorder (ADHD) is a neurodevelopmental disorder that is diagnosed based on the presence of developmentally inappropriate levels of hyperactivity/impulsivity or inattention (American Psychiatric Association [APA], 2013). Hyperactivity refers to excessive motor activity including excessive fidgeting, tapping, or talking. Impulsivity is characterized by acting without thinking about the possible harm of an action or acting quickly to get an immediate reward even when the reward might be greater if the individual delays the action. Finally, inattention includes behaviors such as wandering off task because of difficulties sustaining focus and persistence; these behaviors are *not due* to comprehension difficulties or purposeful noncompliance. Children and adults may receive one of three specified diagnoses of ADHD including predominantly inattentive presentation (i.e., six or more symptoms of inattention for at least 6 months and fewer than six symptoms of hyperactivity or inactivity for at least 6 months), predominantly hyperactive/impulsive presentation (i.e., six or more symptoms of hyperactivity or inactivity) or combined presentation. The severity of the impact of inattentiveness and/or hyperactivity/impulsivity can be rated as mild, moderate, or severe depending on the level of impact the symptoms have on social and occupational functioning (APA, 2013). The *Diagnostic and Statistical Manual of Mental Disorders* (4th ed., text rev.; *DSM-IV-TR*; 2000) required that the symptoms of ADHD be present in a child by the age of 7 and that the child demonstrate "clinically significant" impairment in at least two settings such as school, work, or home. The recently published *Diagnostic and Statistical Manual of Mental Disorders* (5th ed.; *DSM-5*; APA, 2013) has modified the inclusionary criteria to behaviors that "interfere with or reduce the quality of social, academic, or occupational functioning" prior to the age of 12 years (p. 60).

Importantly, children with ADHD do not usually demonstrate too little attention; rather the difficulty is in *regulating* attention. These difficulties are characterized by problems inhibiting attention to nonrelevant stimuli (e.g., background noises in the classroom such as a noisy ceiling fan) and thus, focusing too intensely on extraneous stimuli while ignoring relevant stimuli such as teacher instruction. In fact, ADHD has been described as a disorder of "too much attention to too many things" with limited focus on any one task (Contractor, Mayhall, Pataki, Johnson, & Windle, 2013, p. 2).

A widely studied model proposed to account for the attention regulation difficulties in children with ADHD is the *executive functions* model (Barkley, 1997). Executive functions (EF) refer to a variety of higher order cognitive processes that support self-regulation when planning, attending, conducting, persevering, evaluating/revising, and completing a goal directed behavior or task. Some of these cognitive processes include inhibition, working memory, planning, cognitive flexibility, and nonverbal fluency (Pennington & Ozonoff, 1996). A number of studies have revealed that children with ADHD have particular difficulties in tasks that require inhibition, such as delaying the start of—or stopping—a response that has been started (Barkley, 1997; Willcutt, Doyle, Nigg, Faraone, & Pennington, 2005); however, problems in spatial working memory, planning, and task vigilance have also been found in some children (Pennington & Ozonoff, 1996; Willcutt et al., 2005).

Because EF deficits are so common in children with ADHD, it has been hypothesized that these deficits underlie the social communication difficulties in children with attention problems (Tannock & Schachar, 1996). This hypothesis is intuitively appealing when one considers the complex demands of social interactions. Social interactions may require one to wait for a turn, ignore teasing, or avoid telling a peer that something said was "stupid" even if you believe it was! Although EF deficits likely contribute to social communication deficits in some children with ADHD, recent evidence has revealed that not all children with ADHD demonstrate executive function deficits during lab-based EF performance tasks (Sonuga-Barke & Halperin, 2012; Willcutt et. al., 2005).

Moreover, at least one study has found no relationship between performance on EF experimental tasks and pragmatic language abilities in children with ADHD (Parigger, 2012); however, some studies do find an association when parent ratings of EF and pragmatic language abilities are examined (e.g., Nilsen, Mangal, & MacDonald, 2013). Current understanding of the relationship between ADHD symptoms and EF disorders is that while EF disorders are strongly associated with ADHD, the evidence does not "support the hypothesis that EF deficits are the single necessary and sufficient cause of ADHD in all individuals" (Willcutt et al., 2005, p. 1342). As such, EF deficits likely contribute to social communication deficits in some but not all children with ADHD.

A second model, the motivation-based dysfunction model, has been developed to account for the impulsivity piece of ADHD (Sonuga-Barke, 2005). One version of this model focuses on the research and clinical evidence that some children with ADHD have difficulty waiting for rewards and prefer receipt of immediate rewards even when slightly longer delays would result in much larger rewards (Lopez-Vergara & Colder, 2013). Another component of this model is that some children with ADHD show a hypersensitivity to punishment such that anxiety in expectation of a punishment (e.g., losing tokens or points) reduces task performance.

The EF and the motivation-based dysfunction models provide unique implications for assessment and treatment of social communication disorders in children with various presentations of ADHD. Assessment and intervention strategies to account for these models are described in the Assessment and Treatment sections.

Incidence and Prevalence

Due to the recent changes in the *DSM-5* (APA, 2013) diagnostic criteria for ADHD, the incidence of ADHD is expected to rise (Lowry, 2013). Current estimates of prevalence in the United States are that 11% of school-age children, ages 4 to 17, have ADHD (Centers for Disease Control and Prevention [CDC], 2013a). Prevalence rates vary across the US with western states reporting that 6% of school-age children are affected while southern and eastern states report rates above 10% (CDC, 2013a). In any case, ADHD is considered the most common neurobehavioral disorder of childhood. Boys are more likely to be diagnosed with ADHD than girls; recent estimates suggest that 13.2% of school-age boys in the US have ADHD (CDC, 2013a), reflecting an approximate 2:1 ratio of boys to girls (APA, 2013). When girls do receive a diagnosis of ADHD, they are more likely than boys to be diagnosed with inattentive presentation (APA, 2013).

International estimates of ADHD are highly variable (for review, see Storebø et al., 2011). For example, reported rates in the United Kingdom are that 3.6% of boys and 0.9% of girls, ages 5 to 15 years have ADHD (Ford, Goodman, & Meltzer, 2003). In one study from Columbia, South America, reported prevalence was much higher: 19.9% for boys and 12.3% for girls (Pineda, Lopera, Palacio, Ramirez, & Henao, 2003). One explanation for varying rates suggests that ADHD is a socially, culturally, and geographically influenced condition (Faraone, Sergeant, Gillberg, & Biederman, 2003; Polanczyk, Silva de Lima, Horta, Biederman, & Rohde, 2007). Inspired by this explanation, Faraone et al. (2003) and Polanczyk et al. (2007) conducted systematic reviews of the prevalence literature and found that overall, there was no significant difference between the prevalence of ADHD in the United States compared to other geographic locations. Although some areas did show relatively lower rates, there were too few studies available for review from these locations to make any concrete conclusions from the data (Faraone et al., 2003; Polanczyk et al., 2007). Polanczyk and colleagues (2007) suggest that "the ADHD/HD worldwide-pooled prevalence is 5.29% (95% CI=5.01–5.56)" (p. 946) and concluded that given these data, an individual's culture or background does not make him or her any more or less likely to be diagnosed with ADHD. Overall, the worldwide variability of the prevalence of ADHD is most likely due to factors such as diagnostic criteria used, extent to which the elements of the criteria were applied, methods used to make a diagnosis, and characteristics of the sample population (Faraone et al., 2003). Yet, differences in culturally appropriate practices and expectations for child behavior cannot be ruled out as contributing to small variations in geographic and ethnic prevalence rates (APA, 2013).

ADHD: LANGUAGE AND SOCIAL (PRAGMATIC) COMMUNICATION DEVELOPMENT

Overview

Children with ADHD represent a highly heterogeneous group. Some children have typical speech and language development while others have deficits in one or more areas of speech, language, and literacy skills (see reviews by Boada, Willicut, & Pennington, 2012; Mueller & Tomblin, 2012; Redmond, 2004; Tannock & Schachar, 1996; Timler 2014). Although one of the most common co-occurring deficits in children with ADHD is language impairment (LI), estimates about the rates of this co-occurrence vary widely; reported co-occurrence rates have ranged from approximately 33% to 90% (Cohen et al., 1998; Gualtieri, Koriath, Van Bourgondien, & Saleeby, 1983; Timler, 2014; Tirosh & Cohen, 1998). Rates vary by referral source and the focus of the communication assessment (Mueller & Tomblin, 2012). Co-occurrence rates are lower if the focus is on syntactic and semantic skills; rates are higher if the focus is on pragmatic language skills because difficulties in social interaction are a core deficit for children with ADHD. In fact, the *DSM-5* lists several behavioral symptoms of ADHD that overlap with social (pragmatic) communication deficits including "excessive talking," "little attention to detail," and "frequent interruptions" (APA, 2013). It is likely that co-occurring LI in many children with ADHD remains unrecognized because LI, in general, is under-identified in school-age children (Tomblin et al., 1997). As such, the speech-language pathologist has an important role to play in the interdisciplinary assessment of children with ADHD, in particular to screen for potential language impairment in children who are referred for concerns with behavior and poor academic performance.

Language Development and Disorders in Children With ADHD

Both delays in the onset of first words and the emergence of sentences have been reported in some toddlers and preschoolers who later receive a diagnosis of ADHD (Bruce, Thernlund & Nettelbladt, 2006; Tannock & Schachar, 1996). Initial referral for young children is likely to focus on expressive language concerns. Yet, when parents are asked to complete formal report measures that include receptive language items (e.g., "Does your child have trouble understanding explanations/instructions?" "Does your child misinterpret what is said?"), they rate these items just as negatively as (or more so than) expressive language items such as "Does your child have difficulty carrying on a conversation?" (Bruce et al., 2006).

Lower parent ratings of communication skills in multiple domains underscore the importance of comprehensive assessment of receptive and expressive language skills in content (e.g., vocabulary, figurative language), form (e.g., syntax), and use (e.g., narration, conversation) of language. Children with ADHD make more inferencing errors in referential comprehension tasks than children without ADHD (McInnes, Humphries, Hogg-Johnson, & Tannock, 2003; Nilsen et al., 2013). Some children have specific deficits in comprehension of figurative language (e.g., "The young girl held the baby like a *fine china plate*"); these deficits appear to contribute to compromised performance in social problem solving tasks, such as formulating less appropriate solutions to hypothetical conflicts with peers (Im-bolter, Cohen, & Farnia, 2013).

In addition to identification of difficulties in receptive language tasks, research efforts have focused on identifying the expressive language profile of school-age children with ADHD. Specifically, one research aim has been to examine whether children with ADHD and co-occurring LI have more impaired linguistic profiles than children who only have LI. Redmond and colleagues (Redmond, Ash, & Hogan, 2013) tested children who had both ADHD and LI and compared their performance on several linguistic measures to children with ADHD only, children with LI only, and typically developing controls. Children with both ADHD and LI had difficulty in repetition tasks and verb tense accuracy; however, they did not have more difficulties than children with LI who did not have attention deficits. In other words, an ADHD diagnosis did not seem to intensify the symptoms of LI in young school-age children who have both conditions. Moreover, the performance of children with ADHD only was similar to age-matched typical peers.

A second focus of research has been to examine whether the syntactic and semantic language profiles of children with ADHD differ from children with LI who do not have attentional issues. In a series of systematic investigations, Redmond and his colleagues have revealed that children with ADHD who were carefully screened to rule out a co-occurring LI at the time of testing, did not demonstrate clinical markers of LI (Redmond, 2004, 2005; Redmond, Thompson, & Goldstein, 2011). Specifically, only children with LI demonstrated lower performance on tasks that required repetition of nonsense words and sentences of varying length and grammatical complexity. Moreover, whereas young school-age children with LI made errors in marking of verb tense such as omitting the past tense –ed, children with ADHD did not make these errors.

Pragmatic language skills of children with ADHD have been examined in narrative and conversational discourse. Narrative samples elicited via standardized tests (e.g., the Test of Narrative Language [TNL]; Gillam & Pearson, 2004) and wordless picture books reveal that some children with ADHD, particularly those who have a co-occurring LI, produce shorter stories, have fewer story grammar elements, and more cohesion errors than typically developing children (Cohen et al., 2000; Luo & Timler, 2008; Parigger, 2012; Vallance, Im, & Cohen, 1999). Cohesion is maintained by linguistic devices that tie meaning across utterances such as pronouns and conjunctions. In the sentences "Sam and John went climbing" and "He fell down," *he* is a cohesion error because we don't know which boy fell down).

The conversation samples of school-age children with ADHD are likely to be characterized by inappropriate pragmatic language behaviors such as interrupting the communication partner, providing nonspecific and insufficient feedback to that partner, and producing more sentence revisions and repetitions, sometimes referred to as mazes or speech disruptions (Cohen et al., 2000; Kim & Kaiser, 2000; Purvis & Tannock, 1997; Redmond, 2004).

In summary, the clinical implications of these findings are that nonword repetition, sentence recall, and tense-marking tasks can provide accurate discrimination of young children with ADHD who do and do not have co-occurring LI in semantic and syntactic domains (Redmond et al., 2013). Children with ADHD usually do not have syntactic deficits unless they have a co-occurring LI. Social (pragmatic) communication difficulties in inferencing tasks, conversation, and narration are core deficits for many children with ADHD even in the absence of LI in syntactic domains.

FASD: DEFINITIONS, INCIDENCE, AND PREVALENCE

Definitions

One of the most serious threats to a developing fetus during pregnancy is exposure to alcohol. The CDC (2011) has stressed that alcohol consumption during pregnancy is not safe at any time or in any amount. In fact, the US Surgeon General advised that complete avoidance of alcohol before or during pregnancy is the only guaranteed way to prevent FASD (National Institutes of Health, 2010).

FASD is an umbrella term that includes a range of diagnoses associated with prenatal alcohol exposure. Fetal Alcohol Syndrome (FAS) is the most severe type of FASD. The Institute of Medicine (Stratton, Howe, & Battaglia, 1996) established four diagnostic criteria for FAS: (a) growth deficiency including growth delays during gestation and the first 12 years of life; (b) the FAS facial phenotype including short palpebral fissures, small midface, flat philtrum, and thin upper lip; (c) evidence of central nervous system dysfunction characterized by a broad range of possible deficits including seizure disorder, intellectual disability, learning disabilities, and ADHD; and (d) gestational alcohol exposure, which may or may not be confirmed. Severity codes for each of these criteria have been developed to create a four-digit diagnostic code that indicates the magnitude of expression of each feature ranked on a 4-point scale with 1 reflecting a complete absence of the FAS feature and 4 reflecting the full manifestation (Astley, 2004). For example, a child with a four-digit code of 3344 would receive a corresponding diagnosis of atypical FAS. The individual digits, respectively, represent moderate growth deficiency, moderate expression of the FAS facial features, clear evidence of organic brain damage, and confirmed risk of significant gestational alcohol intake as provided by the birth mother or an individual who directly observed maternal drinking.

Although FAS has received the most attention in the empirical literature, over time researchers have developed a better understanding of other diagnostic categories within the spectrum. These are known as Alcohol-Related Effects and include Alcohol-Related Neurodevelopmental Disorder (ARND) and Alcohol-Related Birth Defects (ARBD; Stratton et al., 1996). The Substance Abuse and Mental Health Services Agency (SAMHSA; 2004) reports that individuals with one (or both) of these Alcohol-Related Effects exhibit characteristics typical of prenatal exposure to alcohol, but do not present the facial anomalies of FAS. An individual with ARND may experience abnormal central nervous system (CNS) development and/or delays in behavioral and cognitive development struggling specifically with attention deficits, poor visual focus, hyperactivity, delayed speech and language development, and learning disabilities (SAMHSA, 2004; Stratton et al., 1996). In contrast, an individual with ARBD may experience bone, kidney, heart, eye, and/or hearing defects (SAMHSA, 2004).

Of importance to SLPs who serve individuals with prenatal alcohol exposure, is that the specific diagnostic classification (i.e., FAS, ARND, or ARBD) does not predict the severity of the functional deficits that can have an impact on a child's learning and social interactions. These functional deficits include "hyperactive behavior, difficulty paying attention, poor memory, difficulty in school (especially in math), learning disabilities, speech and language delays, intellectual disability or low IQ, [and] poor reasoning and judgment skills" (CDC, 2011, p. 1), in addition to "lack of impulse control, lack of sustained close relationships, [and] inability to recognize social or physical risk" (Woods, Greenspan, & Agharkar, 2011, pp. 17–18). Individuals with FASD show impairments in several areas of executive functioning including cognitive flexibility, response inhibition, planning, reasoning, and working memory (see reviews by Coggins, Timler, & Olswang, 2007; Rasmussen, Wyper, & Talwar, 2009). Some of these symptoms are commonly found in other disorders such as ADHD, which complicates the process of diagnosing an FASD, particularly when alcohol consumption cannot be confirmed.

Incidence and Prevalence

Deficits associated with prenatal alcohol exposure persist throughout life. Prevalence, rather than incidence, is usually used to describe FASD rates among all age groups (May & Gossage, 2001). In the data presented, we use the authors' terminology. More information is available about FAS than other conditions. FAS prevalence rate in the US is "at least 2 to 7 per 1,000" (May et al., 2009, p. 189). The CDC has recently funded several surveillance programs to update prevalence rates for cases of FAS, ARND, and ARBD (CDC, 2010). It is likely that the number of cases of FASDs across the entire spectrum is significantly greater, possibly even three times greater, than what has been reported for FAS alone (CDC, 2012).

Differences in demographics and social circumstances influence prevalence rates, as the occurrence of FASD is not uniformly examined among all socioeconomic (SES) levels and ethnic/racial backgrounds (May & Gossage, 2001). Prevalence rates vary across American Indian, Native Hawaiian, and Alaska Native populations and are reported to be approximately 1.5 to 2.5 per 1,000 live births (SAMHSA, 2007). FAS prevalence rates in Alaska alone are much higher; rates of 5.6 per 1,000 live births for American Indians/Alaska Natives have been reported. The historical factors of violence, oppression, displacement, and loss of self-determination along with poverty and teen pregnancy are thought to contribute to the drinking culture of some Native American populations (SAMHSA, 2007). Another high risk population in the US is children in foster care; these children are "10 to 15 times more likely than the general population to have FASD" (Astley, Stachowiak, Clarren, & Clausen, 2002, p. 712). Although certain populations appear to be at higher risk than others in the US, clinicians must be aware that children from any cultural background are at risk of FASD if they have been prenatally exposed to alcohol. Universal factors that influence the risk of FASD include the mother's socioeconomic status, employment status, education, relationship status, health state, additional drug use, cultural norms, and household environment, among others (May & Gossage, 2011).

International rates of FAS are highly variable and many countries are just beginning surveillance studies. For example, Canadian reports have typically relied on US rates, although studies are now in progress to identify risk within aboriginal communities and other populations (CDC, 2013b; Fogarty International Center, n.d.). Rates in Europe reflect some of the same demographic and social circumstances as the US. It is estimated that approximately half of the Russian children living in orphanages may have prenatal alcohol exposure (Woods et al., 2011). FAS rates in Italy, where drinking is a relatively common cultural practice, have recently been estimated to be 4.0 to 12.0 per 1,000 (May et al., 2011). Population-based studies suggest that South Africa has the highest overall rate of FASD in the world (Woods et al., 2011); rates of 88 to 89 per 1,000 children" have been reported (May & Gossage, 2011,

p. 19). As more research is conducted and awareness about the different types of FASD spreads, it is likely that more children will be identified around the world and FASD rates will continue to rise.

FASD: LANGUAGE AND SOCIAL (PRAGMATIC) COMMUNICATION DEVELOPMENT

A brief overview of communication concerns in children and adolescents with FASD is provided here (for more comprehensive reviews see Coggins et al., 2007; Thorne, Coggins, Carmichael Olson, & Astley, 2007).

Alcohol is a teratogen to the human brain, and as such, children with prenatal alcohol exposure have a range of abilities and disabilities. Children and adolescents with identified IQs below 70 will qualify for special education services under the category of intellectual disability. Children and adolescents with IQs above 70 will also need school supports because by definition, children with FASD have one or more neurological deficits in attention, learning, and speech and language skills.

Individuals with FASD are at increased risk for both conductive and sensorineural hearing loss; a hearing screening should be conducted at the time of initial diagnosis (Cone-Wesson, 2005). Most studies of speech and language skills in children and adolescents with FASD have examined performance on various norm-referenced language tests and obtained a range of findings from clinically significant to within normal limits (Thorne et al., 2007). Criterion-referenced analyses of narrative samples have uniformly revealed difficulties in organization and cohesion (Coggins et al., 2007; Thorne et. al., 2007). Parents report organizational difficulties in conversation skills (Timler, Olswang, & Coggins, 2005), but fine-grained analyses of conversation samples have not yet appeared in the research literature. Children with FASD have difficulty in perspective-taking tasks, particularly Theory of Mind tasks (Timler et al., 2005). Theory of mind represents the ability to infer the mental state of others, that is, to interpret and predict another's knowledge, intentions, beliefs, emotions, and desires, especially when this knowledge may differ from the child's own knowledge" (Timler et al., 2005, p. 74). Parents and teachers of children with FASD almost uniformly report concerns about social skills and problem behaviors (Streissguth et al., 2004; Timler et al., 2005).

A final consideration for clinicians who serve individuals with FASD is that these children and adolescents often live in adverse social environments characterized by poverty, multiple foster placement, neglect (particularly if adult members in the home continue to drink), and abuse. Coggins and colleagues (2007) have used the term *double jeopardy* to describe the compound negative effects of alcohol exposure and poor living conditions on children's language and learning development.

REFERRAL GUIDELINES AND ASSESSMENT PRACTICES FOR CHILDREN WITH ADHD AND FASD

Medical and Psychological Referrals

SLPs who provide early intervention services are likely to see children who have attentional issues but have not been formally evaluated. In these situations, the role of the SLP is to carefully document and describe the behavior concerns as well as determine through family and teacher interviews if others share these concerns. When concerns are documented, the SLP should refer the family to the child's pediatrician for further evaluation and referral to appropriate providers.

Both ADHD and FASD are complex diagnoses that are ideally ascertained by a team of healthcare providers including developmental pediatricians (e.g., to prescribe and monitor medications for attention and other disorders and to identify the facial features of FAS), neurologists (e.g., to rule out associated seizure disorders), psychologists (e.g., to assess executive functioning, intelligence, and learning), and social workers (to identify family needs and community resources). The educational needs of students with ADHD and FASD are addressed by regular and special educators and by school psychologists (who provide testing as well as social skills training). The SLP's roles in medical and educational settings are to provide a comprehensive profile of the child's strengths and challenges in communication skills and to develop and provide treatment for identified communication challenges (Hill, 2000). In addition, the SLP may be asked to monitor potential fluctuations in the student's behavior and attention skills in response to changes in stimulant medication or to provide evidence to support a needed change in medication (e.g., the child appears sleepy possibly indicating that the child is overmedicated or the child becomes more inattentive and anxious so that the prescribed medication no longer provides optimal effects).

Clinical procedures for the diagnosis of ADHD usually require completion of multiple parent and teacher report measures (American

Academy of Pediatrics, Subcommittee on Attention-Deficit/Hyperactivity Disorder, Steering Committee on Quality Improvement and Management, 2011). Two widely used measures include the Child Behavior Checklist (CBCL; Achenbach & Rescorla, 2001) and the Conners 3rd Edition (Conners 3; Conners, 2008). The examiner manuals report accepted levels of reliability and validity. The CBCL has parent and teacher versions available for rating of preschoolers and school-age children; scaled scores are provided for social problems, attention problems, affective problems and other DSM categories. The Conners assessment includes long and short versions for parents, teachers, and self-report (ages 8–48). Scaled scores are available for executive functioning, externalizing, and internalizing behaviors. Both measures ask parents to indicate the severity/frequency with which behavioral difficulties occur (e.g., cannot sit still). Higher values indicate the presence of elevated behavioral difficulties. Although SLPs do not typically ask parents to complete these measures, an item analysis could identify social communication skills that may need further assessment, if the SLP has access to such measures.

In some diagnostic clinics, children are prescribed a *placebo trial* that includes a mix of placebo and stimulant medication for treatment of attention disorders. *Blind* placebo trials are implemented to provide evidence that a medication is providing desired changes rather than *illusory* changes teachers and parents want to see because they believe that the child is medicated. In fact, studies of placebo trials have revealed that approximately 3% to 10% of children show positive changes as measured by parent and teacher ratings of behaviors (Storebø et al., 2011). In placebo trials, the child's caregivers are prescribed multiple bottles of medication that are unmarked so that the person dispensing the prescription does not know whether the pill is medicine or a placebo. Observers at home and school, including parents, teachers, and SLPs, are then able to provide an unbiased assessment of the child's responses to the medication (or no medication). Educators and SLPs may be asked to complete weekly or daily behavior rating scales to provide these unbiased observations.

Speech-Language-Social (Pragmatic) Communication Assessment

Children with ADHD and FASD are at increased risk for speech and language disorders and these disorders can remain unidentified when providers, educators, and families focus on children's behavior problems and consider learning issues as a lack of motivation rather than potential learning and language deficits. As such, the SLP should advocate for communication screening of all children with ADHD and

FASD. Parent report measures, such as the Children's Communication Checklist-2 US Edition (CCC-2; Bishop, 2006), provide a time-efficient screening method for identifying children who require further assessment of comprehension skills. In a recent study of 32 young children with ADHD, ages 5 to 8, the CCC-2 identified 100% of the children ($n = 10$) whose performance on a norm-referenced language test revealed a language impairment (Timler, 2014). More details about the CCC-2 can be found in Chapter 6.

For children who fail a language screening, a comprehensive language assessment is necessary to identify structural language deficits (i.e., deficits in syntax and semantics). Standardized general language tests, nonword repetition, sentence recall, and tense-marking tasks appear to be particularly helpful for identifying syntactic deficits in language production (Redmond et al., 2011, 2013). Language comprehension should be assessed at the sentence and paragraph level to examine recall of factual information and ability to answer questions that require inferencing skills. In addition, comprehension of idioms and figurative language should be tested. As discussed earlier, students with pragmatic language deficits in these areas perform poorly on social problem-solving tasks (e.g., What could you say and do here?); these tasks are often used in social communication interventions to teach students how to approach problematic social situations.

Comprehensive assessment of social (pragmatic) communication deficits requires a variety of assessment tools including norm-referenced tests, rating scales (e.g., the CCC-2 is particularly useful), criterion-referenced procedures and naturalistic observations at home and school. Some of the procedures used for social communication assessment of children with language impairments are also appropriate for children with attentional issues; readers are encouraged to review the assessment sections in Chapters 6 and 8 for descriptions of relevant assessment tools.

Because children with attention problems frequently have difficulty managing longer discourse units, two data-based methods widely used in the ADHD and FASD literature to identify pragmatic language deficits include collection of conversation and narrative samples. Analysis of conversation samples using the Pragmatic Protocol (Prutting & Kirchner, 1987) has revealed inappropriate speech-act pair analysis (i.e., the child's utterance is not responsive to the communication partner's utterance), interruption/overlap with the partner, inappropriate feedback to the partner, poor cohesion, and reduced specificity (Cohen et al., 1998, 2000; Kim & Kaiser, 2000; Vallance et al., 1999). The Pragmatic Protocol or a similar checklist for analysis of conversation samples is likely to not only provide evidence of children's social communication difficulties, but guide intervention planning, particularly if multiple language samples are obtained across interactions with adults and peers. Narrative samples have been collected using a variety of elicitation techniques including the Test of Narrative Language (Gillam & Pearson, 2004), wordless picture books (e.g., Mayer, 1969) and videos. Relevant analysis techniques include cohesion and story grammar analysis (e.g., see Cohen et al., 2000; Luo & Timler, 2008; Thorne et al., 2007). Narrative samples provide a clinically efficient method for viewing children's planning and organization skills as well as perspective taking abilities (e.g., to account for the needs of the listener when telling stories).

Assessment of Executive Functions

Neuropsychologists and clinical psychologists administer norm-referenced tests to assess executive functions in children and adolescents. One test is the Comprehensive Assessment of Neuropsychological Development in Children–2nd Edition (NESPY-2; Korkman, Kemp, & Kirk, 2007) a developmental neuropsychological assessment for children ages 3 to 16 years. The executive functioning/attention domain includes seven subtests which assess various EF processes of inhibition, self-regulation, monitoring, vigilance, selective and sustained attention, maintenance of response set, planning, flexibility in thinking and figural fluency. Other NEPSY-2 domains include language and communication, sensorimotor functions, visuospatial functions, learning and memory, and social perception. This test is not usually administered by SLPs; however, the neuropsychologist's summary of a child's NEPSY-2 performance can provide direction for further communication assessment.

Although the language tests administered by SLPs do not typically provide direct assessment of EF, SLPs can document test behaviors that reveal something about children's EF skills. For example, the SLP can note whether a child self-corrects, asks for repetition of directions, answers too quickly or slowly, is distracted by extraneous sounds, repeats directions, or displays little evidence of planning for extended oral and written tasks (e.g., narratives). In other words, the SLP can note the child's self-regulation behaviors during formal assessment.

Similar to pragmatic language assessment, there is not one single test or subtest that provides a comprehensive picture of executive function skills or specific guidelines for functional treatment plans. The problem is that performance-based tests, which focus on one or more aspects of executive functioning, provide some degree of structure and organization for the student. This structure may mask executive function deficits that are more apparent in the student's everyday natural environment (Wittke, Spaulding, & Schechtman, 2013). As such, a student may score within normal limits on a performance test of EF even though this student demonstrates difficulties in multiple aspects of task completion in school and home settings. Therefore, clinicians are encouraged to use behavioral observations, multi-informant interviews, and ratings scales/questionnaires to identify functional concerns and to develop functional treatment plans.

Dawson and Guare (2010) provide an example of a comprehensive open-ended semistructured interview with questions focusing on time management, working memory, task and material organization, task initiation, follow-through and flexibility, response inhibition, emotional control, sustained attention, goal-directed persistence, and metacognition. Student and teacher versions are available. The student version begins with an explanation of executive function skills: "I'm going to ask you some questions about situations related to your success as a student. All of these are situations in which you have to use planning and organizational skills in order to be successful" (Dawson & Guare, 2010, p. 177). Situations such as "getting started with homework" and "remembering assignments" are presented followed by suggestions for follow-up questions to provide more details about the specific challenges of each situation.

Norm- and criterion-referenced rating scales for parents, teachers, and school-age students (i.e., self-report) are also available. One norm-referenced instrument, the Behavior Rating Inventory of Executive Function (BRIEF: Gioia, Isquith, Guy, & Kenworthy, 2000) consists of 86 items that are rated for students, ages 5 to 18 years; separate parent and teacher versions are available to provide comparison across informants. A preschool version, for ages 3 to 5, (BRIEF-P; Gioia, Espy, & Isquith, 2003) and a student self-report version, for ages 11 to 18 years (BRIEF-SR; Guy, Isquith, & Gioia, 2004) are also available. Acceptable levels of reliability and validity are reported in the examiner manuals for each BRIEF version. Criterion-referenced student self-rating forms provide another method for assessing student awareness of EF skills (Dawson and Guare, 2010). For example, students rate described behaviors on a scale from one (big problem) to five (no problem). Example items include "I act on impulse," "I put off homework or chores until the last minute," and "It's hard for me to put aside fun activities in order to start homework."

EVIDENCE-BASED INTERVENTION PRACTICES

Interventions for children with ADHD and FASD include pharmacological (e.g., stimulant) treatments and comprehensive behavior change programs to address academic, compliance, and social communication skills. Pharmacological treatments have been reported to have a beneficial effect on major symptoms of hyperactivity, impulsivity, and inattention in about 80% of children treated but medication alone is not sufficient to improve social communication skills (see Storebø et al., 2011, for review). Social communication interventions have been developed for implementation in pullout one-to-one or small-group sessions, in the classroom through environmental modifications and strategies provided by the teacher in conjunction with other team members including SLPs and parents, and at home through parent training programs. For children with identified co-occurring deficits in semantic, syntactic, and pragmatic skills, the SLP provides direct intervention. For children with social communication disorders who do not have specific linguistic deficits, the SLP may provide co-treatment with a school psychologist or counselor to implement a social skills or social-cognitive training program. Finally, the SLP may serve as a consultant to parents, classroom teachers, and other providers to suggest linguistic modifications for social skills curricula, particularly when children receiving the curricula have language comprehension difficulties (Hill, 2000; Redmond & Timler, 2007).

Individual/Small-Group Interventions

Individual/small-group interventions aimed specifically at children for ADHD with language and social communication concerns has received little empirical attention in the SLP research literature. As such, the intervention guidelines and strategies described here are primarily from anecdotal evidence and recommendations from clinical experts. Most of this information is borrowed from interventions developed for children with other diagnoses. For example, children with ADHD and FASD may respond to interventions developed for children with pragmatic language impairment (see Chapter 6) and structural language impairment (see Chapter 8) although these recommendations remain to be tested. Some of the visual support strategies for children with autism spectrum disorder described by Fannin and Watson (Chapter 7) are also likely to be relevant. Modifications in these interventions may be needed, however, to address the executive function disorders observed in some children with ADHD and FASD. Watson and Westby (2003) suggest a variety of strategies to support children's self-regulation including use of visual cues and checklists (to supplement verbal input and support working memory), videotaping of children's performance to facilitate learning and evaluation of targeted behaviors, implementation of structured daily routines, and use of systematic behavior modification strategies (i.e., specific corrective feedback and positive reinforcement schedules). In addition, students with attention problems will likely need explicit instruction in how to read the emotions of others and express their own emotions in socially appropriate ways.

Interventions that have been adapted and tested specifically for children with attention problems focus on teaching children how to adjust and monitor their verbal and nonverbal behaviors during social interactions, how to read subtle social cues conveying listener interest, understanding, and emotions, and why reading of these cues is important for the child's success in social interactions (Storebø et al., 2011). Common teaching methods include multisensory input (e.g., videos, peer modeling, picture and word checklists), explicit and concrete step-by-step instruction, adult modeling of social communication targets, role-play of targets with peers, specific and constructive feedback, and procedures to teach children self-monitoring and evaluation. Teacher and parent support and training are other common components of many of these interventions in order to support generalization of children's skills from the small-group setting to home and classroom settings (Bertrand, 2009; Storebø et al., 2011). Table 9.1 provides summaries of four intervention studies; these studies are representative of the types of intervention targets and measures that have been used to facilitate social communication, executive functions, and self-regulation in school-age children with ADHD and FASD (for comprehensive review of intervention programs and strategies see Bertrand, 2009; Storebø et al., 2011; Watson & Westby, 2003; Zwi, Jones, Thorgaard, York, & Dennis, 2011).

For children with motivational issues who struggle with immediate need for reinforcement, the SLP and other team members will need to identify desired *rewards* and optimal schedules of delivery for these rewards. One evidence-based strategy for provision of systematic feedback and rewards for children with ADHD is the Daily Behavior Report Card (DBRC) intervention (Vannest, Davis, Davis, Mason, & Burke, 2010). This intervention usually includes four components: clear description of the desired behavior(s) that is understood by the child, periodic evaluation by the teacher as to the presence or absence of the behavior, daily behavior monitoring and feedback, and parent involvement to provide earned rewards for achievement of the behavior. A recent meta-analysis of single case experimental designs revealed a range of effect sizes for this intervention; however, the largest and strongest effects were demonstrated when parents were involved in the delivery of the reward for appropriate behaviors (Jurbergs, Palcic, & Kelley, 2010; Vannest et al., 2010). Several of the interventions described in Table 9.1 implemented token systems and progress charts, set up so that

TABLE 9.1 Examples of Empirically Tested Interventions for Children with FASD and ADHD

Intervention	Description	Outcomes
Children's Friendship Training (CFT; (O'Connor et al., 2006, 2012)	A parent-assisted intervention implemented in a community clinic for 85 children 6–12 years old with and without FASD. CFT goals focus on peer acceptance and friendship building facilitated through small-group sessions and parent-supervised play dates. Parents received handouts outlining session skills and weekly socialization homework assignments that included social coaching by parents during play with a peer. Specific CFT training modules include the following: • Conversational skills • Peer entry • Expanding and developing friendship networks • Handling teasing • Practicing good sportsmanship and good host behavior during play dates with friend	Compared to the standard of care group, children receiving treatment demonstrated more improvement in measures assessing social knowledge about appropriate behavior and had higher ratings on a self-concept measure including overall reduction in social anxiety; no differences were observed in parent ratings of social skills and problem behaviors (Note: prior investigation of this program implemented in a university setting found differences in parent rating of social skills; O'Connor et al., 2006). Children with FASD responded to the intervention as well as children without FASD who have social problems.
Neurocognitive Habilitation Program Curriculum, with adaptations from the Alert Program' (Bertrand, 2009; Wells, Chasnoff, Schmidt,	An intervention developed for children with FASD, ages 6–12, who are in the child welfare system and have executive function deficits. Intervention aims focus on self-regulation techniques and strategies for improving memory, cause-and-effect reasoning, sequencing, planning, and problem solving. Visual imagery is used to teach children that their brains are like a car engine and they can make their bodies run in high, low, or just-right gears. Caregivers were taught to recognize changes in children's arousal	Compared to a no-treatment control group (n = 38), children receiving treatment (n = 40) demonstrated significant increases in composite scores on a report measure of executive functions and on a narrative measure (i.e., treatment children had fewer unrealistic solutions to story problems).

(*Continued*)

TABLE 9.1 (*Continued*)

Intervention	Description	Outcomes
Telford, & Schwartz, 2012; Williams & Shellenberger, 1996)	levels, to facilitate desired emotional and behavioral responses, and to engage in reciprocal and meaningful activities with their children.	
Contingency Management Training (COMET) and Making Socially Accepting Inclusive Classrooms (MOSAIC; Mikami et al., 2013)	Two classroom-based interventions were compared. Participants included 24 children with ADHD and 113 typically developing peers between the ages of 6.8–9.8 years. The COMET training targeted increases in socially appropriate behaviors of children through use of teacher-provided expectations for desired behaviors, a token system with points earned or lost based on child behavior, and explicit teacher feedback about reasons for the exchange of points. Teachers publicly announced point totals of all children at the end of activities and the school day, with high earners receiving public awards including leadership roles and prizes from a school store. The MOSAIC training used the same token system but teachers provided private (not public) feedback about reasons for point loss and point totals were shared 1:1 with children. Teachers were encouraged to model positive interactions with children with ADHD focusing on praising them for interests and behaviors; teachers used daily awards to publicly discuss children's strengths (unrelated to children's behavior during the day). These strategies were implemented to encourage typical peers to view children with ADHD more positively. MOSAIC-condition teachers also encouraged inclusion of all children and peers lost points when a child was ostracized; teachers created teams of children with and without ADHD for class projects.	Random assignment to COMET or MOSAIC classrooms and repeated measures crossover design (so that some children received both interventions) revealed significantly higher (more positive) results on peer measures in the MOSAIC condition. Specifically, children with ADHD received fewer negative nominations of "I really do not like [him or her]" and more friendship nominations from peers, boys had fewer negative interactions at recess (no differences were noted for girls), and boys and girls received more positive messages from peers in a memory book. No significant differences were detected in the reduction of inappropriate social behaviors by children with ADHD.

Intervention	Description	Outcomes
Play-Based Intervention (Cordier, Munro, Wilkes-Gillan, & Docking, 2013; Wilkes, Cordier, Bundy, Docking, & Munro, 2011)	A play intervention for 14 children with ADHD, ages 5–12, to facilitate improved social play between a child with ADHD and a typically developing playmate. Intervention components include video modeling (to help children understand the purpose and benefit of targeted social behaviors), video feedback (to help children recognize, understand, and regulate their emotions), and therapist and peer modeling of pretend play. Parents were taught strategies to develop children's social skills and were encouraged to set up playdates.	Pre- and posttreatment design revealed significant gains on play assessment; children also demonstrated increases in appropriate pragmatic behaviors with a typically developing peer during naturalistic free play observation sessions; moreover, children with ADHD and LI showed similar improvements, suggesting that this play intervention is appropriate for children with co-occurring disorders.

children had frequent reminders of progress (e.g., receipt of a token and visual feedback of *good work* at least several times in a session). In addition to a focus on positive feedback, it seems important for clinicians to identify whether an individual child finds loss of a reward particularly aversive, so that such a loss increases the child's anxiety and distracts the child even further. In such cases, the clinician needs to structure sessions and breakdown tasks into doable steps so that the child's opportunity for the reward is optimized and the threat of punishment (i.e., removal or loss of points) is minimized or nonexistent.

Classroom-Based Interventions

Children with ADHD are at increased risk for peer victimization (e.g., bullying) and peer rejection, even in circumstances in which they are simultaneously the instigators of such activities (Nijmeijer et al., 2008). Hyperactivity and impulsivity have a particularly negative effect on peer perceptions and the term *reputational bias* has been used to describe the views of peers about children with ADHD; this bias is likely to remain even after students with ADHD improve their social communication skills (Mikami et al., 2013). As such, some children do not have the opportunity to display new acquired social communication skills and to experience the positive natural consequences of appropriate social behaviors (e.g., being allowed to enter a peer group). A protective factor against victimization is to have one or more reciprocal friendships (Nijmeijer et al., 2008; Redmond, 2011). The intransience of reputational bias and the protective value of reciprocal friendships underscore the importance of addressing classroom peers when developing social communication interventions.

Children with attentional issues do better in classrooms with clear and consistent rules and expectations for desired behaviors. Classroom accommodations to support academic success include posted daily work schedules, written notices for homework assignments, quiet work areas, and seating close to teacher and near positive peer models (Dobie et al., 2012). Classroom climate and teacher expectations also play an important role in supporting social communication success. Teacher implemented strategies focus on children with attention problems and importantly, classroom peers as well.

The study by Mikami et al., 2013, summarized in Table 9.1, provides an example of a comprehensive teacher implemented classroom intervention. In the Making Socially Accepting Inclusive Classrooms (MOSAIC) condition, students with and without ADHD received tokens for positive behaviors, lost tokens for negative behaviors, and were given explicit feedback about the token exchange in private conversations with the teacher. Feedback was private to avoid adding to negative reputational bias; note that in the other treatment condition, public feedback was given. In addition to monitoring of student behavior, teachers modeled positive interactions with target students and publicly praised their strengths. Teachers also provided explicit classroom expectations for inclusion of all students so that peers lost points if a target student was ostracized. While no differences were noted in target students' use of undesirable social behaviors across both conditions, peers viewed target students significantly more favorably in the MOSAIC condition. As such, teacher expectation and behavior contributed to changing the views of classroom peers towards target students.

Parent Training

Parent training programs focus on teaching strategies to promote prosocial and compliance behaviors, as well as positive interactions between the parent and the child. Many parent-training programs provide specific instruction in how to set up and monitor playdates so that children have opportunities for positive interactions with typically developing peers. A recent meta-analysis of parent training programs revealed mixed results. Some studies demonstrated positive changes in the reduction of parent stress and child anxiety and withdrawal while others saw little change (Zwi et al., 2011). Parent training was a component of three of the child focused intervention studies presented in Table 9.1 (Cordier et al., 2013; O'Connor et al. 2012; Wells et al., 2012). Parents and caregivers attended trainings while children received direct instruction. Training content included specific instruction for helping children to regulate their emotions and use prosocial skills. The outcomes of these studies suggest that change is more likely when parents are partners in the intervention process. More research is needed regarding how best to deliver parent training (individual or group) and to identify parent and child behavior that are most amenable to change in parent training programs.

Community programs that focus primarily on parent support (without direct intervention for children) have also been examined. One evidence-based parent training program is the Family Check-Up (FCU) intervention, a program composed of periodic assessment and two intervention components: motivational interviewing and teaching of family management practices (Gill, Hyde, Shaw, Dishion, & Wilson, 2008). During motivational interviewing sessions, the therapist shares assessment data, collected from parent rating scales and naturalistic observations, with a goal of facilitating the parent's motivation to change the child's problematic behaviors. Family stressors and environmental risk factors are identified and addressed to facilitate parent motivation (e.g., resources for treating a parent's depression are identified if needed). The family management component focuses on teaching strategies for setting limits, proactive parenting, positive reinforcement, and relationship building. Therapists use role-play and in vivo practice in sessions with the child and the parent; these activities are focused on specific behavioral problems identified during the family and child assessment. For example, one strategy for helping a parent to facilitate prosocial behavior in a young child is the Good Behavior Game (Gill et al., 2008). This game teaches parents to use a timer and instruct their children to play nicely for 10 minutes in order to earn a reward; parents are given instruction in how to identify reasonable and motivating rewards, explain what *playing nicely* means, asking children to repeat this explanation, and using a sticker chart to track the child's positive play. Promising results from randomized control trials have documented the efficacy of the FCU program in families of toddlers who are at increased for conduct disorders (Gill et al., 2008) and in families of adolescents with behavioral disorders (Dishion & Kavanagh, 2003; Stormshak, Fosco, & Dishion, 2010).

CASE STUDY

Returning to the case study, Greg's parents brought him to a University Speech-Language-Hearing clinic. Because Greg's difficulties in speech and language skills (e.g., semantics and syntax) had been identified in an earlier assessment, the current assessment focused on Greg's pragmatic language and social communication skills. Greg's mother completed the CCC-2 (Bishop, 2006) and the BRIEF (Gioia et al., 2000) as did the teacher. The Social Language Development Test–Elementary (SLDT-E: Bowers, Huisingh, & LoGiudice, 2008), a norm referenced measure for 6:0–11:11 year olds, was administered to assess Greg's social knowledge about strategies for interpreting and negotiating social interactions with peers. The TNL was administered, and story grammar analyses were completed in addition to computation of standard scores. Two conversation samples with the clinician and Greg's brother were obtained. The results revealed multiple areas of need related to Greg's social communication skills. The clinician completed item analyses to identify specific areas of need for Greg's intervention plan. The clinician, Greg's teacher and parents developed an intervention plan to improve turn-taking skills and to decrease inappropriate conversation behaviors such as interrupting. All agreed to provide reinforcement in the form of praise and opportunities for special activities at home and school when Greg was observed to implement appropriate strategies for turn taking. The rules for turn taking in conversation were defined and discussed and Greg developed a pictorial checklist of these rules. The clinician modeled *good* and *not so good* turn taking, and Greg was able to classify these models correctly. Next, Greg practiced these skills during small-group cooperative activities in the classroom; Greg was asked to document at least three times when he waited for his turn to talk during each of these activities. He reported the results of his self-monitoring to the teacher, who praised his reporting efforts but did not comment on his reporting accuracy as she was unable to supervise these activities consistently. Greg's mother reviewed the turn-taking rules at the dinner table and Greg and his brothers were asked to identify one good turn for each sibling. Greg's team avoided focusing on inappropriate turns to decrease attention on negative behaviors. Greg's mother reported fewer outbursts from Greg during these dinnertime activities.

CONCLUSION

Children with ADHD and FASD can present complex challenges for clinicians. Some children score within normal limits on norm-referenced social language measures but have significant functional deficits in home and school settings. Best assessment practices for intervention planning include criterion-referenced conversation and narrative analyses; parent, teacher, and self-report measures of pragmatic language and executive functioning; and behavior observations at home and school. Effective interventions to address social communication difficulties in children with attention problems require a team effort by clinicians, mental health providers, teachers, and parents. The *fix* for social communication problems is not an easy one, but it is worth the time and investment.

DISCUSSION QUESTIONS

1. What are some differences in the description of ADHD in the *DSM-IV-TR* and *DSM-5*?
2. What is executive functioning? Describe the executive functioning deficits that are observed in some children with attention problems.
3. What is the motivation-based dysfunction model? How could an SLP account for the implications of this model when providing intervention for children with attention problems?
4. What are the language characteristics of children with ADHD with and without co-occurring language impairment?

5. Describe what is known about the social (pragmatic) communication profiles of children with FASD.

6. What is the role of the SLP in the assessment of children with ADHD and FASD?

7. Describe three evidence-based assessment procedures that could be used to identify structural language deficits in children with ADHD who may or may not have co-occurring LI.

8. Why are conversation and narrative analyses procedures useful for description of social communication profiles in children with attention problems?

9. Describe three strategies to facilitate social communication skills in children with attention problems.

10. What are some approaches for facilitating generalization of social communication skills demonstrated in pullout sessions to home and school settings?

CLINICAL RESOURCES

ADHD

ADD Warehouse: www.addwarehouse.com/

American Academy of Pediatrics: www.aap.org/healthtopics/adhd.cfm

Attitude Magazine: www.additudemag.com/

Children and Adults with Attention Deficit Disorders (CHADD), National Resource Center on ADHD: www.chadd.org

Dawson, P., & Guare, R. (2010). *Executive skills in children and adolescents: A practical guide to assessment and intervention* (Guilford Practical Intervention in Schools Series, 2nd ed.). New York, NY: Guilford Press.

Dobie, C., Donald, W.B., Hanson, M., Heim, C., Huxsahl, J., Karasov, R., . . . Steiner, L. (2012). *Diagnosis and management of attention deficit hyperactivity disorder in primary care for school-age children and adolescents.* Bloomington, MN: Institute for Clinical Systems Improvement. Available from the Institute for Clinical Systems Improvement website: https://www.icsi.org/guidelines__more/catalog_guidelines_ and_more/catalog_guidelines/catalog_behavioral_health_guidelines/ adhd/

K12 Academics: www.k12academics.com/addadhd.htm

National Institutes of Mental Health: www.nimh.nih.gov/health/topics/ attention-deficit-hyperactivity-disorder-adhd/index.shtml

SchoolBehavior.com: www.schoolbehavior.com/disorders/attention-deficit-hyperactivity-disorder

FASD

Centers for Disease Control and Prevention (CDC): Fetal Alcohol Spectrum Disorders (FASDs) website www.cdc.gov/ncbddd/fasd/index.html

Blaschke, K., Maltaverne, M., & Struck, J. (2009). Fetal alcohol spectrum disorders education strategies: Working with students with a fetal alcohol spectrum disorder in the education system. Retrieved from www.usd.edu/medical-school/center-for-disabilities/fetal-alcohol-spectrum-disorders-education-strategies-handbook.cfm

Medline Plus Fetal Alcohol Spectrum Disorders web page with additional resources: www.nlm.nih.gov/medlineplus/fetalalcoholspectrumdisorders.html

National Institutes of Health: National Institute on Alcohol Abuse and Alcoholism (NIAAA) website: www.niaaa.nih.gov

National Organization on Fetal Alcohol Syndrome (NOFAS): www.nofas.org

Recovering Hope (Video) by the Substance Abuse and Mental Health Services Administration: www.youtube.com/watch?v=m7zfJCW9Yco

Substance Abuse and Mental Health Services Administration (SAMHSA): Fetal Alcohol Spectrum Disorders Center for Excellence website: www.fascenter.samhsa.gov

US National Library of Medicine, National Institutes of Health: Fetal Alcohol Spectrum Disorders website: www.nlm.nih.gov/medlineplus/fetalalcoholspectrumdisorders.html

REFERENCES

Achenbach, T. M., & Rescorla, L. A. (2001). *Manual for the ASEBA school-age forms and profiles.* Burlington: University of Vermont, Research Center for Children, Youth, and Families.

American Academy of Pediatrics, Subcommittee on Attention-Deficit/Hyperactivity Disorder, Steering Committee on Quality Improvement and Management. (2011). ADHD: Clinical practice guideline for the diagnosis, evaluation, and treatment of attention-deficit/hyperactivity disorder in children and adolescents. *Pediatrics, 128*(5), 1007–1022. doi:10.1542/peds.2011-2654

American Psychiatric Association. (2000). *Diagnostic and Statistical Manual of Mental Disorders-4th Edition, Text Revision (DSM-IV-TR).* Washington, DC: Author.

American Psychiatric Association. (2013). *Diagnostic and statistical manual of mental disorders* (5th ed.). Washington, DC: Author.

Astley, S. (2004). *Diagnostic guide for fetal alcohol spectrum disorders: The 4-Digit Diagnostic Code–third edition.* Seattle: University of Washington.

Astley, S. J., Stachowiak, J., Clarren, S. K., & Clausen, C. (2002). Application of the fetal alcohol syndrome facial photographic screening tool in a foster care population. *The Journal of Pediatrics, 141*(5), 712–717. doi:10.1067/mpd.2002.129030

Barkley, R. A. (1997). Behavioral inhibition, sustained attention, and executive functions: Constructing a unifying theory of ADHD. *Psychological Bulletin, 121,* 65–94.

Bertrand, J. (2009). Interventions for children with fetal alcohol spectrum disorders (FASDs): Overview of findings for five innovative research projects. *Research in Developmental Disabilities, 30,* 986–1006. doi:10.1016/j.ridd.2009.02.003

Bishop, D. (2006). *Children's Communication Checklist–2* (US ed.). San Antonio, TX: Harcourt Assessment, Inc.

Boada, R., Willicut, E. W., & Pennington, B. P. (2012). Understanding the comorbidity between dyslexia and attention-deficit/hyperactivity disorder. *Topics in Language Disorders, 32*(3), 264–284.

Bowers, L., Huisingh, R., & LoGiudice, C. (2008). *The Social Language Development Test-Elementary.* East Moline, IL: LinguiSystems.

Bruce, B., Thernlund, G., & Nettelbladt, U. (2006). ADHD and language impairment: A study of the parent questionnaire FTF (Five to Fifteen). *European Child and Adolescent Psychiatry, 15,* 52–60.

Centers for Disease Control and Prevention. (2010). Tracking fetal alcohol syndrome. Retrieved from www.cdc.gov/ncbddd/fasd/research-tracking.html

Centers for Disease Control and Prevention. (2011). Facts about FASDs. Retrieved from www.cdc.gov/ncbddd/fasd/facts.html

Centers for Disease Control and Prevention. (2012). Fetal alcohol spectrum disorders (FASDs) data and statistics. Retrieved from www.cdc.gov/ncbddd/fasd/data.html

Centers for Disease Control and Prevention. (2013a). Attention-deficit/hyperactivity disorder (ADHD): Data and statistics. Retrieved from www.cdc.gov/NCBDDD/adhd/data.html

Centers for Disease Control and Prevention. (2013b). Past activities— international research. Retrieved from www.cdc.gov/ncbddd/fasd/pastactivities-international.html

Coggins, T., Timler, G., & Olswang, L. (2007). Impact of prenatal alcohol exposure and maltreatment on the social communicative abilities of school-age children with Fetal Alcohol Spectrum Disorders. *Language, Speech, and Hearing Services in Schools, 38,* 117–127.

Cohen, N., Menna, R., Vallance, D., Barwick, M., Im, N., & Horodezky, N. (1998). Language, social cognitive processing, and behavioral characteristics of psychiatrically disturbed children with previously identified and unsuspected language impairments. *Journal of Child Psychology and Psychiatry, 39,* 853–864. doi:10.1017/S0021963098002789

Cohen, N., Vallance, D., Barwick, M., Im, N., Menna, R., Horodezky, N., & Isaacson, L. (2000). The interface between ADHD and language impairment:

An examination of language, achievement, and cognitive processing. *Journal of Child Psychology and Psychiatry, 41*(3), 353–362.

Cone-Wesson, B. (2005). Prenatal alcohol and cocaine exposure: Influences on cognition, speech, language, and hearing. *Journal of Communication Disorders, 38*, 279–302.

Conners, C. K. (2008). *Conners Comprehensive Behavior Rating Scale Manual* (3rd ed.). San Antonio, TX: Pearson.

Contractor, Z., Mayhall, C., Pataki, C., Johnson, C., & Windle, M. (2013). Pediatric attention deficit hyperactivity disorder. *Medscape Reference* [serial online]. July 29, 2013. Retrieved from http://emedicine.medscape.com/article/912633-overview

Cordier, R., Munro, N., Wilkes-Gillan, S., & Docking, K. (2013). The pragmatic language abilities of children with ADHD following a play-based intervention involving peer-to-peer interactions. *International Journal of Speech-Language Pathology, 15*(4), 416–428. doi:10.3109/17549507.2012.713395

Dawson, P., & Guare, R. (2010). *Executive skills in children and adolescents: A practical guide to assessment and intervention* (Guilford Practical Intervention in Schools Series, 2nd ed.). New York, NY: Guilford Press.

Dishion, T. J., & Kavanagh, K. (2003). *Intervening in adolescent problem behavior: A family-centered approach.* New York, NY: Guilford.

Dobie, C., Donald, W. B., Hanson, M., Heim, C., Huxsahl, J., Karasov, R., . . . Steiner, L. (2012). *Diagnosis and management of attention deficit hyperactivity disorder in primary care for school-age children and adolescents.* Bloomington, MN: Institute for Clinical Systems Improvement.

Faraone, S. V., Sergeant, J., Gillberg, C., & Biederman, J. (2003). The worldwide prevalence of ADHD: Is it an American condition? *World Psychiatry, 2*(2), 104–113. Retrieved from www.ncbi.nlm.nih.gov/pmc/articles/PMC1525089/

Fogarty International Center. (n.d.). Researchers tackle fetal alcohol syndrome in Russia. Retrieved from www.fic.nih.gov/News/Examples/Pages/fas-russia.aspx

Ford, T., Goodman, R., & Meltzer, H. (2003). The British child and adolescent mental health survey 1999: The prevalence of DSM-IV disorders. *Journal of the American Academy of Child and Adolescent Psychiatry, 42* (10), 1203–1211.

Gill, A., Hyde, L. W., Shaw, D. S., Dishion, T. J., & Wilson, M. N. (2008). The family check-up in early childhood: A case study of intervention process and change. *Journal of Clinical Child and Adolescent Psychology, 37*, 893–904. doi:10.1080/1537441080235985

Gillam, R., & Pearson, N. (2004). *Test of Narrative Language (TNL).* Austin, TX: Pro-Ed.

Gioia, G. A., Isquith, P. K., Guy, S., & Kenworthy, L. (2000). *The Behavior Rating Inventory of Executive Function (BRIEF)*. Odessa, FL: Psychological Assessment Resources.

Gioia, G. A., Espy, K. A., & Isquith, P. K. (2003). *The Behavior Rating Inventory of Executive Function-Preschool Version (BRIEF-P)*. Odessa, FL: Psychological Assessment Resources.

Gualtieri, C. T., Koriath, U., Van Bourgondien, M. E., & Saleeby, N. (1983). Language disorders in children referred for psychiatric services. *Journal of the American Academy of Child Psychiatry, 22*, 165–171.

Guy, S., Isquith, P. K., & Gioia, G. (2004). *The Behavior Rating Inventory of Executive Function-Self Report (BRIEF-SR)*. Odessa, FL: Psychological Assessment Resources.

Hill, G. (2000). A role for the speech-language pathologist in multidisciplinary assessment and treatment of attention-deficit/hyperactivity disorder. *Journal of Attention Disorders, 4*(2), 69–79.

Im-bolter, N., Cohen, N., & Farnia, F. (2013). I thought we were good: Social cognition, figurative language, and psychopathology. *Journal of Child Psychology and Psychiatry*, doi:10.1111/jcpp.12067

Jurbergs, N., Palcic, J., & Kelley, M. (2010). Daily behavior report cards with and without home-based consequences: Improving classroom behavior in low income, African American children with ADHD. *Child & Family Behavior Therapy, 32*(3), 177–195. doi:10.1080/07317107.2010.500501

Kim, O., & Kaiser, A. (2000). Language characteristics of children with ADHD. *Communication Disorders Quarterly, 21*, 154–165.

Korkman, M., Kirk, U., & Kemp, S. (2007). *Comprehensive Assessment of Neuropsychological Development in Children, 2nd Edition (NEPSY-2)*. San Antonio, TX: The Psychological Corporation.

Lopez-Vergara, H., & Colder, C. R. (2013). An examination of the specificity of motivation and executive functioning in ADHD symptom-clusters in Adolescence. *Journal of Pediatric Psychology, 38*(10) 1081–1090.

Lowry, F. (2013, November 12). Broader definition of ADHD will 'do more harm than good.' *Medscape Reference*. Retrieved from www.medscape.com/viewarticle/814208

Luo, F., & Timler, G. (2008). Narrative organization skills in children with attention deficit hyperactivity disorder and language impairment: Application of the causal network model. *Clinical Linguistics and Phonetics, 22*, 25–46.

May, P. A., & Gossage, J. P. (2001). Estimating the prevalence of fetal alcohol syndrome: A summary. *Alcohol Research & Health, 25*(3), 159–167. Retrieved from http://pubs.niaaa.nih.gov/publications/arh25-3/159-167.htm

May, P. A., Gossage, J. P., Kalberg, W. O., Robinson, L. K., Buckley, D., Manning, M., & Hoyme, H. E. (2009). Prevalence and epidemiologic characteristics of FASD from various research methods with an emphasis on recent in-school studies. *Developmental Disabilities Research Reviews*, 15, 176–192. doi:10.1002/ddrr.68

May, P. A., Fiorentino, D., Coriale, G., Kalberg, W. O., Hoyme, H. E., Aragon, A. S., Buckley, D. . . . Ceccanti, M. (2011). Prevalence of children with severe fetal alcohol spectrum disorders in communities near Rome, Italy: New estimated rates are higher than previous estimates. *International Journal of Environmental Research and Public Health*, 8, 2331–2351. doi:10.3390/ijerph8062331

May, P. A., & Gossage, J. P. (2011). Maternal risk factors for fetal alcohol spectrum disorders: Not as simple as it might seem. *Alcohol Research & Health*, 34(1), 15–26.

Mayer, M. (1969). *Frog where are you?* New York, NY: Dial Press.

McInnes, A., Humphries, T., Hogg-Johnson, S., & Tannock, R. (2003). Listening comprehension and working memory are impaired in attention-deficit hyperactivity disorder irrespective of language impairment. *Journal of Abnormal Child Psychology*, 31(4), 427–443.

Mikami, A., Griggs, M., Lerner, M., Emeh, C., Reuland, M., Jack, A., & Anthony, M. (2013). A randomized trial of a classroom intervention to increase peers' social inclusion of children with attention-deficit/hyperactivity disorder. *Journal of Consulting and Clinical Psychology*, 81, 101–112. doi:10.1037/a0029654

Mueller, K., & Tomblin, B. (2012). Examining the comorbidity of language impairment and attention-deficit/hyperactivity disorder. *Topics in Language Disorders*, 32, 228–246. doi:10.1097/TLD.0b013e318262010d

National Institutes of Health. (2010). Fetal alcohol spectrum disorders. Retrieved from http://report.nih.gov/nihfactsheets/viewfactsheet. aspx?csid=27

Nijmeijer, J. S., Minderaa, R. B., Buitelaar, J. K., Mulligan, A., Hartman, C. A., & Hoekstra, P. J. (2008). Attention-deficit/hyperactivity disorder and social dysfunctioning. *Clinical Psychology Review*, 28, 692–708.

Nilsen, E., Mangal, L., & MacDonald, K. (2013). Referential communication in children with ADHD: Challenges in the role of a listener. *Journal of Speech, Language, and Hearing Research*, 56, 590–603. doi:10.104 4/1092–4388(2012/12–0013)

O'Connor M., Frankel F., Paley B., Schonfeld A., Carpenter, E., Laugeson, E. & Marquardt, R. (2006). A controlled social skills training for children with fetal alcohol spectrum disorders. *Journal of Consulting and Clinical Psychology*, 74, 639–648.

O'Connor, M., Laugeson, E., Mogil, C., Lowe, E., Welch-Torres, K., Keil, V., & Paley, B. (2012). Translation of an evidence-based social skills intervention for children with prenatal alcohol exposure in a community mental health setting. *Alcoholism: Clinical and Experimental Research*, 36(1), 141–152. doi:10.1111/j.1530–0277.2011.01591.x

Parigger, E. (2012). *Language and executive functioning in children with ADHD.* Amsterdam: University of Amsterdam Press.

Pennington, B. F., & Ozonoff, S. (1996). Executive functions and developmental psychopathology. *Journal of Child Psychology and Psychiatry, 37*, 51–87.

Pineda, D., Lopera, F., Palacio, J., Ramirez, D., & Henao, G. (2003). Prevalence estimations of attention-deficit/hyperactivity disorder: differential diagnoses and comorbidities in a Columbian sample. *International Journal of Neuroscience, 113*(1), 49–71.

Polanczyk, G., Silva de Lima, M., Horta, B. L., Biederman, J., & Rohde, L. A. (2007). The worldwide prevalence of ADHD: A systematic review and metaregression analysis. *American Journal of Psychiatry, 164*(6), 942–948. doi:10.1176/appi.ajp.164.6.942

Prutting, C., & Kirchner, D. (1987). A clinical appraisal of the pragmatic aspects of language. *Journal of Speech and Hearing Disorders, 52*, 118–119.

Purvis, K., & Tannock, R. (1997). Language abilities in children with attention deficit hyperactivity disorder, reading disabilities, and normal controls. *Journal of Abnormal Child Psychology, 25*, 133–144.

Rasmussen, C., Wyper, K., & Talwar, V. (2009). The relation between theory of mind and executive functions in children with fetal alcohol spectrum disorders. *Canadian Journal of Clinical Pharmacology, 16*(2), 370–380.

Redmond, S. (2004). Conversational profiles of children with ADHD, SLI and typical development. *Clinical Linguistics and Phonetics, 18*, 107–125.

Redmond, S. (2005). Differentiating SLI from ADHD using children's sentence recall and production of past tense morphology. *Clinical Linguistics & Phonetics, 19*, 109–127.

Redmond, S. (2011). Peer victimization among students with specific language impairment, attention-deficit/hyperactivity disorder, and typical development. *Language, Speech, and Hearing Services in School, 42*, 520–535. doi:10.1044/0161–1461(2011/10–0078)

Redmond, S. M., Ash, A., & Hogan, T. (2013, June). *Consequences of ADHD comorbidity on the severity of children's LI symptoms.* Poster presented at the Symposium for Research on Child Language Disorders, Madison, WI.

Redmond, S., Thompson, H., & Goldstein, S. (2011). Psycholinguistic profiling differentiates specific language impairment from typical development and from attention deficit/hyperactivity disorder. *Journal of Speech, Language, and Hearing Research, 41*, 688–700.

Redmond, S., & Timler, G. (2007). Addressing the social concomitants of developmental language impairments. In A. Kamhi, J. Masterson, & K. Apel (Eds.), *Clinical Decision Making in Developmental Language Disorders* (pp. 185–202). Baltimore, MD: Brookes.

Sonuga-Barke, E. J. S. (2005). Causal models of attention-deficit/hyperactivity disorder: From common simple deficits to multiple developmental pathways. *Biological Psychiatry, 57*, 1231–1238.

Sonuga-Barke, E. J. S., & Halperin, J. M. (2012). Developmental phenotypes and causal pathways in ADHD: Potential targets for early intervention? *Journal of Psychology and Psychiatry, 51*(4), 368–389.

Storebø, O. J., Skoog, M., Damm, D., Thomsen, P. H., Simonsen, E., & Gluud, C. (2011). Social skills training for Attention Deficit Hyperactivity Disorder (ADHD) in children aged 5 to 18 years. *Cochrane Database of Systematic Reviews* (Issue 12), Art. No. CD008223. Retrieved from www.ncbi.nlm.nih.gov/pubmedhealth/PMH0032941/doi:10.1002/14651858.CD008223.pub2

Stormshak, E., Fosco, G., & Dishion, T. J. (2010). Implementing interventions with families in schools to increase youth school engagement: The family check-up model. *School Mental Health, 2*(2), 82–92. doi:10.1007/s12310-009-9025-6

Stratton, K., Howe, C., & Battaglia, F. (Eds.). (1996). *Fetal alcohol syndrome: Diagnosis, epidemiology, prevention, and treatment.* Washington, DC: National Academy Press.

Streissguth, A., Bookstein, F., Barr, H., Sampson, P., O'Malley, K., & Young, J. (2004). Risk factors for adverse life outcomes in fetal alcohol syndrome and fetal alcohol effects. *Developmental and Behavioral Pediatrics, 25*(4), 228–238. doi:0196–206X/00/2504–0228

Substance Abuse and Mental Health Services Administration. (2004). The language of fetal alcohol spectrum disorders. Retrieved from www.fasdcenter.samhsa.gov/documents/WYNKLanguageFASD2.pdf

Substance Abuse and Mental Health Services Administration. (2007). Fetal alcohol spectrum disorders among Native Americans. Retrieved from www.fasdcenter.samhsa.gov/documents/WYNK_Native_American_Teal.pdf

Tannock, R., & Schachar, R. (1996). Executive dysfunction as an underlying mechanism of behaviour and language problems in attention deficit hyperactivity disorder. In J. H. Beitchman, N. J. Cohen, M. M. Konstantareas, & R. Tannock (Eds.), *Language, learning, and behaviour disorders: Developmental, biological, and clinical perspectives* (pp. 128–155). Cambridge, UK: Cambridge University Press.

Thorne, J. C., Coggins, T. E., Carmichael Olson, H., & Astley, S. J. (2007). Exploring the utility of narrative analysis in diagnostic decision making: Picture-bound reference, elaboration, and fetal alcohol spectrum disorders. *Journal of Speech, Language & Hearing Research, 50*(2), 459–474.

Timler, G. (2014). Use of the Children's Communication Checklist-2 for classification of language impairment risk in young school-age children with attention-deficit/hyperactivity disorder. *American Journal of Speech-Language Pathology, 23*, 73–83. doi:10.1044/1058-0360(2013/12–0164)

Timler, G. R., Olswang, L. B., & Coggins, T. E. (2005). Do I know what I need to do? A social communication intervention for children with complex clinical profiles. *Language, Speech, and Hearing Services in Schools, 36*(1), 73–85.

Tirosh, E., & Cohen, A. (1998). Language deficit with attention-deficit disorder: A prevalent comorbidity. *Journal of Child Neurology, 13*, 493–497.

Tomblin, J. B., Records, N., Buckwalter, P., Zhang, X., Smith, E., & O'Brien, M. (1997). Prevalence of specific language impairment in kindergarten children. *Journal of Speech, Language, and Hearing Research, 40*, 1245–1260.

Vallance, D., Im, N., & Cohen, N. (1999). Discourse deficits associated with psychiatric disorders and with language impairments in children. *Journal of Child Psychology and Psychiatry, 40*(5), 693–704.

Vannest, K., Davis, J., Davis, C., Mason, B., & Burke, M. (2010). Effective intervention for behavior with a daily behavior report card: A meta-analysis. *School Psychology Review, 39*(4), 654–672.

Watson, S., & Westby, C. (2003). Strategies for addressing the executive function impairments of students prenatally exposed to alcohol and other drugs. *Communication Disorders Quarterly, 24*(4), 194–204. doi:10.1177/15257401030240040501

Wells, A., Chasnoff, I., Schmidt, C., Telford, E., & Schwartz, L., (2012). Neurocognitive habilitation therapy for children with fetal alcohol spectrum disorders: An adaptation of the Alert Program©. *American Journal of Occupational Therapy, 66*(1), 24–34. doi:10.5014/ajot.111.002691

Wilkes, S., Cordier, R., Bundy, A., Docking, K., & Munro, N. (2011). A play-based intervention for children with ADHD: A pilot study. *Australian Occupational Therapy Journal, 58*(4), 231–240. doi:10.1111/j.1440-1630.2011.00928.x

Willcutt, E. G., Doyle, A. E., Nigg, J. T., Faraone, S. V., & Pennington, B. F. (2005). Validity of the executive function theory of attention deficit/hyperactivity disorder: A meta-analytic review. *Biological Psychiatry, 57*, 1336–1346.

Williams, M. S., & Shellenberger, S. (1996). *How does your engine run?™ A leader's guide to the alert program™ for self-regulation.* Albuquerque, NM: TherapyWorks, Inc.

Wittke, K., Spaulding T. J., & Schechtman, C. J. (2013). Specific language impairment and executive functioning: parent and teacher ratings of behavior. *American Journal of Speech Language Pathology, 22*(2), 161–172.

Woods, G. W., Greenspan, S., & Agharkar, B. S. (2011). Ethnic and cultural factors in identifying fetal alcohol spectrum disorders. *Journal of Psychiatry & Law, 39*(1), 9–37.

Zwi, M., Jones, H., Thorgaard, C., York, A., & Dennis, J. (2011). Parent training interventions for attention deficit hyperactivity disorder (ADHD) in children aged 5 to 18 years. *Cochrane Database of Systematic Reviews* (Issue 12), Art. No. CD003018. doi:10.1002/14651858.CD003018

10

SOCIAL COMMUNICATION ASSESSMENT AND INTERVENTION FOR CHILDREN EXPOSED TO MALTREATMENT

Deborah A. Hwa-Froelich

I believe the best service to the child is the service closest to the child, and children who are victims of neglect, abuse, or abandonment must not also be victims of bureaucracy. They deserve our devoted attention, not our divided attention.

—Guinn (n.d.).

LEARNING OBJECTIVES

Readers will

1. Become aware of incidence/prevalence statistics and different types of maltreatment.
2. Learn about the language development of children exposed to maltreatment and why they are at increased risk of language impairment and social communication disorder.
3. Be able to describe an evidence-based, transdisciplinary assessment and intervention approach for children exposed to maltreatment who have a social communication disorder.
4. Gain knowledge as to how cultural differences may impact the treatment of children.

CASE STUDY

Harry is a 4-year-old boy adopted from China when he was about 1 year old. Harry received a mixture of institutional care and foster care before he was adopted. His adoptive parents, Mr. and Mrs. Johnson, reported that when he was adopted, he was unable to crawl or walk and had difficulty sitting by himself. The pediatrician reported that Harry was small for his age and malnourished.

When Harry was 15 months old, he was evaluated by an early education program and qualified for physical and speech/language therapies. Harry's motor skills progressed rapidly and within one year's time, he no longer demonstrated motor delays. The speech-language pathologist (SLP) noted rapid progress in receptive language and intelligibility, but his expressive language remained delayed particularly in discourse. Although his parents said Harry played with his brother, the two boys seemed to play beside each other and not converse. Harry became inconsolable when they could not understand what he wanted. Eventually Harry became passive and quiet. When Harry was enrolled in a preschool, he showed regressive behaviors (separation anxiety, reduced eye gaze, solitary play, discomfort with negative emotions displayed by other children, aggressive behaviors) at which time Mr. and Mrs. Johnson sought services from an international adoption clinic. The clinical psychologist observed that the parents seemed tense and uncomfortable with each other when interacting with Harry. Mr. Johnson demonstrated an authoritarian interaction style, and Mrs. Johnson and Harry responded passively by withdrawing. The SLP conducted a play assessment and observed that when playing with dolls pretending to cry, Harry crawled under the table, covered his ears, and closed his eyes.

The psychologist and SLP suspected that Harry demonstrated symptoms of reactive attachment disorder with secondary developmental delays associated with institutional care or neglectful foster care. Harry had learned to cope with negative events by withdrawing or crying, and these coping behaviors were ineffective at home and school. The parents had difficulty reading Harry's cues and interpreting his communication, and the authoritarian parenting style was not a positive match for Harry's emotional needs. Harry needed to develop a secure relationship with both parents as a foundation of security to enable independent emotion regulation at home and preschool as well as communication of wants, needs, and feelings. Mr. and Mrs. Johnson needed to learn how to read Harry's cues to improve their sensitivity, attunement, and attachment with Harry as well as parenting strategies to develop positive ways to interact with Harry. Harry continued to qualify and need early childhood special education, family counseling, and speech-language services to improve his attachment, play development, emotion regulation, expressive language, and socially functional communication.

Harry's case represents the complex needs of children who have experienced maltreatment, for example, neglect and/or abuse. Harry demonstrated developmental delays in relationship development, emotion regulation, expression of emotional themes or emotional communication, general communication, and social and play behaviors. Although Harry was removed from an environment of neglect and possibly abuse, he needed special, individualized support for his unique developmental profile. His parents also needed support to understand Harry's emotional needs and how best to support his development. This case description supports Dynamic Systems Theory in that preadoption and post-adoption environmental factors interfaced with individual variables, which resulted in varied and complex developmental outcomes.

INCIDENCE, PREVALENCE, AND DEFINITIONS

There are many different types of abuse and/or neglect. According to the US Department of Health and Human Services (2012), define physical abuse and neglect as

> *any recent act or failure to act on the part of a parent or caretaker which results in death, serious physical or emotional harm, sexual abuse or exploitation; or an act or failure to act, which presents an imminent risk of serious harm.* (p. vii, italics in original)

Abuse can include physical, sexual, or psychological abuse. Neglect constitutes failure of a caregiver to provide shelter, supervision, medical or mental health treatment, educational and/or emotional needs. Of the different types of maltreatment, neglect was the most commonly reported form of abuse. During 2012, the US Child Protective Services responded to 3,184,000 abuse or neglect reports of abuse or neglect, of which 78.3% were reports of child neglect (Children's Bureau, 2012).

Maltreatment such as abuse and/or neglect is widespread and a world-wide problem. The United Nations 61st General Assembly on the Rights of the Child defined maltreatment as any kind of physical or mental violence, injury or abuse, neglect, exploitation, or sexual abuse (Pinheiro, 2006). Pinheiro (2006) reported that data were collected from 131 governments and convened nine regional consultations across the Caribbean, South Asia, West and Central Africa, Latin and North America, East

Asia and the Pacific, the Middle East, Europe, Central Asia, and North, Eastern, and Southern Africa. He reported that while maltreatment of children varies across cultures and physical environments, most child maltreatment is hidden and unreported. In spite of the hidden nature of maltreatment, World Health Organization (WHO) estimated that:

- 150 million girls and 73 million boys had experienced sexual abuse;
- between 100 and 140 million girls and women had experienced genital mutilation or cutting;
- 80% to 98% of children who received physical punishment experienced it in their homes;
- 20% to 65% of school-age children reported being verbally or physically bullied;
- 133 to 275 million children witness domestic violence in their homes; and
- children with disabilities, ethnic minority children, refugees, and homeless or displaced children are at increased risk (Pinheiro, 2006).

Countries track child abuse and neglect in different ways, resulting in varied incidence and prevalence reports. In spite of this variation, child maltreatment appears to be on the rise. Recent prevalence studies in Western nations show an increase in substantiated and reported cases of abuse and neglect (Australian Institute of Family Studies, 2013; National Society for the Prevention of Childhood Cruelty [NSPCC], 2013; Public Health Agency of Canada, 2008). Although in 2012 the United States reported a decrease in abuse and neglect cases from 2008, the prevalence was still high at 686,000 cases (Children's Bureau, 2012; US Department of Health and Human Services, 2012).

According to the *Diagnostic and Statistical Manual of Mental Disorders* (5th ed.; *DSM-V*; American Psychiatric Association [APA], 2013), the varied types, duration, and frequency of maltreatment can result in a range of disorders. These include (a) Reactive Attachment Disorder, (b) Disinhibited Social Engagement, (c) Acute Stress Disorder, (d) Post-traumatic Stress Disorder, (e) Adjustment Disorders or (f) Trauma- or Stress-Related Disorder not otherwise specified. Reactive attachment disorder is diagnosed when a child demonstrates socially withdrawn/ inhibited behaviors. When children exhibit disorganized attachment or indiscriminate friendly or disinhibited social behaviors, they may have a Reactive Attachment or Disinhibited Social engagement disorder. Acute stress disorder is used to identify individuals demonstrating stress behaviors 2 to 4 weeks following a traumatic event. These behaviors may or may not predict a post-traumatic stress disorder diagnosis. The difference between acute and post-traumatic stress disorders is the duration of symptoms and their connection to disassociation. Post-traumatic stress disorder involves one or a combination of four clusters of behaviors: (a) reexperiencing the event, (b) avoidance of negative thoughts or memories of the event, (c) persistent negative alterations in cognition or mood such as estrangement from others or excessive blame toward others, and (d) heightened arousal and reactivity (for specific detail refer to the *DSM-5*; APA, 2013). An Adjustment disorder is a subtype of stress disorders in which individuals may demonstrate a wide array of stress-related behaviors rather than a specific behavioral pattern described earlier. The category of Trauma- or Stress-Related Disorders not otherwise specified is a diagnosis for persons who exhibit some of these symptoms but not enough or severe enough to qualify under the disorders described earlier (APA, 2013).

LANGUAGE AND SOCIAL COMMUNICATION DEVELOPMENT OF CHILDREN EXPOSED TO MALTREATMENT

Educators and medical professionals are likely to encounter children who have experienced some type of maltreatment (Hwa-Froelich, 2012a). One reason is that children with disabilities are at risk of experiencing maltreatment and may not have the communication abilities to report the abuse. Second, children who have experienced some form of maltreatment are at risk of developmental cognitive, language, and social-emotional delays (Hwa-Froelich, 2012a; Snow, 2009). For example, children exposed to neglect demonstrate more frustration, anger and less flexibility when solving problems, have lower school achievement and IQ scores, are less securely attached, and have negative internal models of themselves and others (Allen & Oliver, 1982; for a review see Hildeyard & Wolfe, 2002; Van der Kolk & Fisler, 1994).

Maltreatment is associated with nonverbal, verbal, and social communication delays (Culp et al., 1991; McFadyen & Kitson, 1996). In a review of the literature, Schore (2001) found that early adverse care often resulted in poorer social information processing of facial expressions, tone of voice, and recognition of emotions and perspectives of others (Camras et al. 1990; Schore, 2001). In addition, children experiencing maltreatment have poorer communication development (Allen & Oliver, 1982) in syntax, expressive vocabulary, and communicative functions than a control group matched by socioeconomic status (SES)

(Coster, Gertsen, Beeghly, & Cicchetti, 1989). These communication delays appear to persist into adolescence. For example, 20 adolescents who had experienced maltreatment during their childhood continued to demonstrate poorer syntax and social communication skills when compared with a control group (McFadyen & Kitson, 1996).

Neglect, as opposed to abuse, appears to have more negative effects on language development (Law & Conway, 1992; Scarborough, Lloyd, & Barth, 2009). Studies including toddlers, preschool-age, and school-age children who were exposed to abuse, neglect, or abuse and neglect compared the children's language performance with a control group matched by SES. Regardless of age, children exposed primarily to neglect performed the lowest on all language measures (Coster et al., 1989; Culp et al., 1991; Fox, Long, & Langlois, 1988). Thus, exposure to neglect places children at increased risk of language delay.

Language and Social Communication Development in Children Remaining with Families

Mothers who mistreat their children may have negative perceptions of their children and interact with them in negative ways (S. R. Wilson, 1999). The communication style of 19 caregivers who were abusive and/ or neglectful toward their children differed from the communication style of 14 caregivers who were not abusive or neglectful (Eigsti & Cicchetti, 2004). The mothers of a maltreated group of children expressed fewer complex utterances, more commands, and did not adjust their language according to their children's age. In contrast, the mothers who did not mistreat their children produced more age-appropriate utterances (more expansions and repetitions with younger children) and more multi-clause utterances and wh-questions. These complex utterances and questions correlated with their children's use of auxiliary verbs and receptive and expressive language scores. They also used fewer commands that were related to their children's higher receptive vocabulary scores. In other words, mothers who neglect and abuse their children communicate fewer complex and age-appropriate utterances adjusted for their child's individual needs. These communication style differences may account for the language delays reported in children exposed to maltreatment and may place these children at risk of poor social communication development.

Social understanding and communication development are dependent on sensitive and attuned caregiver communicative interactions, dialogue about the child's mental states and emotions, as well as conversations about other people's mental states, emotions, and perspectives (Baron-Cohen, 1997). Some research has reported that children exposed to maltreatment demonstrate poorer symbolic play (for a review see Cicchetti & Beeghly, 1987), social or pragmatic language (Manso, Garcia-Baamonde, Alonso, & Barona, 2010) and illogical thinking or thought disorder (Toth, Stronach, Rogosch, Caplan, & Cicchetti, 2011). For example, Beeghly and Cicchetti (1994) reported that 20 toddlers who were exposed to maltreatment expressed fewer internal state words (*want, hurt*) and word types when compared to 20 toddlers in a control group matched by SES. Toddlers who experienced maltreatment and were insecurely attached were at increased risk. In another study controlling SES background and exposure to maltreatment, 203 three- to eight-year-old children from low-SES backgrounds and maltreatment exposure and 315 children not exposed to maltreatment from low- and middle-SES backgrounds were compared on their performance on false belief tasks to measure social understanding (Cicchetti, Rogosch, Maughan, Toth, & Bruce, 2003). Types of abuse included neglect, nonchronic maltreatment, and chronic maltreatment. Children who had experienced nonchronic or chronic maltreatment had lower scores on false belief tasks than the control group and maltreatment predicted social understanding performance. If maltreatment occurred during the toddler years, the children had lower performance on false belief tasks than if maltreatment occurred during infancy. Additionally, the type of maltreatment had differing effects on false belief task performance. Children exposed to physical or emotional abuse performed more poorly on false belief tasks than children who had experienced sexual abuse or neglect (Cicchetti et al., 2003). In other words, early exposure to sexual abuse or neglect had less negative effects on social understanding development than later exposure to physical or emotional abuse.

In summary, for children remaining in the care of their biological caregivers who were the perpetrators of the abuse and/or neglect, the caregivers' communication style, timing, and type of maltreatment affect language and social communication development. Maltreatment, particularly physical or emotional abuse that occurs during the toddler years has negative effects on social understanding development.

Language and Social Communication Development
in Children in Institutional or Foster Care

Children who spend time in institutional care such as group homes or orphanages may not receive consistent, contingent, or sensitive social and communicative experiences to facilitate language or social understanding development. It is well documented that orphanages provide poorer and more neglectful care than foster or adoptive families because of high child-to-caregiver ratios (The Leiden Conference on the

Development and Care of Children Without Permanent Parents, 2012; Tizard, Cooperman, Joseph, & Tizard, 1972; Tizard & Joseph, 1970). Tizard and Joseph (1970) compared 30 children living in institutional settings in the UK with a gender-matched control group of children raised by their biological parents from skilled, semiskilled, and unskilled working-class backgrounds. Children raised by their biological families demonstrated more friendly behaviors, less separation anxiety, higher nonverbal and verbal intelligence scores, and more spontaneous language with more expressive vocabulary and had been exposed to more experiences.

Lack of social interaction and experience associated with institutional rearing may also have negative effects on the development of social understanding. Yagmurlu, Berument, and Celimli (2005) studied 34 children residing in Turkish orphanages in comparison to 76 children living with their biological families from low- or middle-SES backgrounds. Regardless of SES background, the children living with their families had higher false-belief task performance than did children living in orphanages. Thus, residing in institutional environments affects the development of social understanding especially in understanding false beliefs.

If communication delays are the result of exposure to poor quality caregiver–child communicative interactions and the lack of stimulating social experiences, then if children are removed from these situations of maltreatment (e.g., abusive and/or neglectful or institutional environments) and are exposed to improved care, appropriate, and increased social communicative interactions, do they achieve more positive communication development? The goal of social services has been to remove children from abusive and/or neglectful environments and place them into safer environments, such as foster care with the hope that these changes would result in positive developmental outcomes.

In 2003, the US Department of Health and Human Services reported 542,000 children were in foster care (Vig, Chinitz, & Shulman, 2005). The reasons often given for foster care placement included: (a) neglect (30%–59%), (b) parental incapacity (30%–75%), (c) physical abuse (9%–25%), (d) abandonment (9%–23%), and (e) sexual abuse (2%–6%; Vig et al., 2005). These children are at increased risk of being medically fragile, prenatally exposed to drugs, having congenital infections, being born premature, and at risk of having a low birth weight. After birth, they are at risk of shaken baby syndrome, lead exposure, failure to thrive, chronic health problems, attachment problems, regulatory problems, post-traumatic stress disorder, and developmental delays (Vig et al., 2005). In addition, in a qualitative study, focus groups of foster caregivers reported that children exposed to maltreatment had negative self-perceptions, problems understanding and responding to emotions, and either lacked social understanding or could not access social understanding when faced with a stressful situation (Luke & Bannerjee, 2012). In conclusion, children in foster care may have complex medical and developmental profiles requiring specialized care, as well as social-emotional problems.

Consistent foster caregivers and fewer transitions among foster caregivers positively affect development. The development of 3- to 6-year-old children with documented maltreatment of neglect, sexual abuse, physical abuse or emotional abuse, were placed in foster care around 3 years old and after 4 to 5 months of foster care were compared with a group of children living with their biological families matched by education and income (Pears & Fisher, 2005). If they had experienced more transitions in foster care, they had poorer visual-spatial, cognitive, language, and executive functioning. Thus, in spite of removal from adverse care and exposure to 4 to 5 months of safer and more stimulating environments, the lack of consistent caregivers and early exposure to neglect or abuse had persistent negative effects on language and other related skills (visual-spatial skills, language, cognition, and executive function; Pears & Fisher, 2005). Duration of exposure or timing of improved care exposure may affect developmental outcomes.

Timing effects of placement in foster care were studied in 174 children residing in Romanian institutions, children moved from institutions to community foster families, and children born into and raised by their families (Windsor et al., 2011). Five groups of children were randomly selected, placed into community foster care at different ages, or remained in the institution. These groups were compared at 30 and/ or 42 months of age with a group of Romanian children who had never experienced institutional or foster care. If children received foster care prior to 24 months of age (receiving 6–18 months of improved care), they had significantly better language performance at 30 and 42 months of age than did children who received foster care later in life, but they remained delayed compared to children who were never institutionalized.

Some studies found that children exposed to maltreatment tend to have higher rates of special education services and maltreatment type predicted special education treatment (Kurtz, Gaudin, Wodarski, & Howing, 1993; Scarborough & McCrae, 2008). Children exposed to physical abuse were more likely to be diagnosed with social-emotional disturbance, children who were neglected were diagnosed as having cognitive delays, and males and children from culturally or linguistically diverse backgrounds were at increased risk (Scarborough & McCrae, 2008).

International Adoption and Disrupted Language and Social Communication Development

Children who are adopted from different countries may be exposed to large variances in care, language exposure, and social interaction before they are adopted; that is, some experience only institutional care, some experience a mix of relative or foster care and institutional care, and some experience mostly foster care (Hellerstedt et al., 2008). However, their exposure to their birth language may be reduced, inconsistent, or developmentally inappropriate and similar to children living in neglectful environments (The Leiden Conference on the Development and Care of Children without Permanent Parents, 2012; Tizard & Joseph, 1970; Windsor et al., 2011). In fact, longer durations of exposure to this type of care are predictive of poorer developmental outcomes including poorer language development compared to children domestically adopted and children living with their biological families (Cohen, Lojkasek, Zadeh, Pugliese, & Kiefer, 2008; Glennen & Masters, 2002; Roberts et al., 2005; Tan & Yang, 2005).

In the case of international adoption, children are often adopted by families who do not speak their children's birth language. Thus, they experience a disruption in first language acquisition and begin to learn a second first language (for a review see Hwa-Froelich, 2009, 2012b). Does exposure to neglect and disrupted language acquisition adversely influence language development in spite of receiving consistent improved care after adoption into families from a higher SES background?

In general, children adopted from abroad acquire a second first language quickly and perform within normal limits on standardized general language measures (Glennen, 2007; Hwa-Froelich & Matsuo, 2010; Roberts, et al., 2005; Scott, Pollock, Roberts, & Krakow, 2013; Scott, Roberts, & Glennen, 2011; Scott, Roberts, & Krakow, 2008). When compared to children matched by socioecomonic status and age, however, they perform less well, and as they reach school age, the gap widens between children adopted internationally and their peers (Delcenserie & Gensee, 2013; Gauthier & Genesee, 2011; Scott et al., 2011). In a meta-analysis, Scott and colleagues (2011) found that although language outcomes were not different from nonadopted peers at younger ages, children adopted internationally had significantly poorer language performance than their nonadopted peers during school-age. For example, children adopted from China demonstrated poorer language performance when compared to nonadopted peers (Cohen et al., 2008; Gauthier & Genesee, 2011). The reasons for poorer language performance are unknown, and the variables range from duration of institutional care (Cohen et al., 2008; Croft, et al., 2007; Glennen & Masters, 2002; Roberts et al., 2005; Tan & Yang, 2005), disrupted language acquisition (Gindis, 2005), or language learning ability as measured by the age children said their first word in their adopted language (Gauthier & Genesee, 2011). It is also possible that children adopted internationally may demonstrate poorer language performance when compared to an SES-matched peer group but perform within normal limits compared to a population-based sample. Because adoptive families are largely from a higher SES background (Hellerstedt et al., 2008) a comparison peer sample may represent scores one to two standard deviations above the mean on standardized measures. Thus, it may be more appropriate to determine whether weaker performance of a child who is internationally adopted is affecting academic or social participation before referring them for assessment and/or intervention services.

Neurobiological structure and function, processing and interpretation of social communication differences have been reported for children adopted internationally (for a review see Hwa-Froelich, 2012d). Children who experienced Romanian institutional care displayed different electrophysiological patterns in response to pictures of facial expressions and pictures of familiar and unfamiliar persons compared to children who had experienced Romanian foster care and nonadopted children (Moulson, Fox, Zeanah, & Nelson, 2009; Parker, Nelson, & the Bucharest Early Intervention Project Core Group, 2005, 2008).

Children adopted internationally are at risk of social language and social understanding delays. Glennen and Bright (2005) conducted a survey study of 46 children adopted from Eastern Europe who were between 6.6 and 9.1 years of age using two parent-report measures focused on children's communication and social skills:

> The children scored below the test average for subtests measuring social relations (e.g., They may seem distant or may unintentionally hurt peers), use of context (e.g., They tended to misunderstand jokes or were too literal), and nonverbal communication (e.g., They tended to demonstrate poor eye contact or failed to read conversational overtures). (p. 49; Hwa-Froelich, 2012a)

In other words, children adopted from Eastern Europe may have difficulty with social communication and delayed social understanding development. My colleagues and I have also found differences in identifying emotions from facial expressions in 4-year-old children adopted from Asian and Eastern European countries before the age of 2 years compared with a group of nonadopted children matched by age and SES background (Hwa-Froelich, Matsuo, & Becker, in press).

False belief development was measured in 120 six- and seven-year-old children adopted before 3 years old from different countries (Tarullo, Bruce, & Gunnar, 2007). The children were compared across three groups: (a) an institutionalized group who had spent most of their preadoptive lives (10–36 months) in an institution, (b) an age- and gender-matched group who had received mostly foster care (0–2 months institutionalized) prior to adoption, and (c) a US nonadopted group of children. Tarullo and colleagues (2007) controlled for language performance and found that the institutionalized group's false-belief task performance was significantly lower than the other two groups, with the foster care group scoring between the institutionalized and nonadopted groups. These delays in social understanding development may continue into school age. In a longitudinal comparison study of 165 Romanian adoptees and children adopted within the UK (Colvert et al., 2008), social understanding of false belief was measured when the children were approximately 11 years old. The group of Romanian children who were adopted after 6 months of age demonstrated persistent delays in social understanding development. Thus, exposure to institutional care past 6 months of age appears to have long-lasting effects on later social understanding development.

To summarize, children adopted internationally are at risk for neurological structure and function differences that may affect their social communication abilities. As exemplified by Harry, these children may also demonstrate problems interpreting nonverbal communication and social interactions in different social contexts, as well as understanding social and emotional information. The following section describes guidelines for assessment and referral.

MEDICAL AND EDUCATIONAL ASSESSMENT AND REFERRAL GUIDELINES

For us, as professionals working with children, it is important to be observant of possible signs of abuse and neglect and to be persistent reporters of maltreatment. Because of the nature of child abuse and neglect, professionals cannot depend upon caregivers to seek early childhood screenings or assessment. Consequently, many children who demonstrate delayed development from these environments are not identified early and do not receive early intervention services when needed (Dicker & Gordon, 2006). Family system risk factors of abuse and neglect include (a) parents with a history of abuse and neglect, who are socially isolated, and/or who appear to dislike the child or the parenting role and (b) children who were born premature, have physical or mental disabilities, or negative behaviors. Environmental risk factors include poverty; few social support resources and living in a culture that condones physical violence or physical discipline (Scannapieco & Connell-Carrick, 2002). Professionals should enlist the support of their school or medical team which may include a medical doctor, a nurse, a social worker, a school counselor, a psychologist, or a psychiatrist who are mandated reporters of child abuse and/or neglect and are trained in detecting and documenting physical and behavioral signs of abuse or neglect as well as verbal disclosures of maltreatment (Snow, 2009).

A three-tiered approach of prevention, reporting and stopping maltreatment, as well as assessment/intervention services, is recommended (Hyter, Atchison, Henry, Sloane, & Black-Pond, 2001; Scannapieco & Connell-Carrick, 2002; Snow, 2009; Trocmé & Caunce, 1998). Parents and professionals should receive information and training on the types of parent behavior and child experiences that constitute abuse and neglect. Professionals also need a list of procedures and contact information to report maltreatment to Child Protective Services or Social Rehabilitative Services in the United States. Potential signs of abuse or neglect can be found on the Child Welfare Information Gateway under Identification of Child Abuse and Neglect (www.childwelfare.gov/can/identifying/) which lists possible behaviors or signs. Table 10.1 summarizes these signs. Anyone in the US can contact Childhelp anonymously (Childhelp National Child Abuse Hotline 1.800.4.A.CHILD or 1.800.422.4453), which is staffed 24 hours a day, 7 days a week, with professional crisis counselors with accessibility to a database of 55,000 emergency, social service, and support resources (other contacts include the Office for Children, Youth, and Family Support in Australia; Children's Aid Societies in Canada; Gateway Services Teams for Children's Social Work at the Health and Social Care [HSC] Trust, or the NSPCC in the United States). Even if no action is taken on initial reports, it is important to continue to observe and report future incidences to build a case of chronic abuse and/or neglect that may lead to more positive outcomes for the child. Multiple observations by different observers help to provide evidence and support that maltreatment occurred to build a strong case for government intervention or removal of the child from the maltreating environment. Once notification has been completed, assessment and intervention should be completed to insure the child's social-emotional and educational needs are met.

TABLE 10.1 Possible Signs of Child Abuse and Neglect

Child Behaviors	Parent Behaviors	Child/Parent Behaviors
Sudden changes in behavior or performance	Shows little concern for child	Rarely touch or look at each other
Physical or medical problems reported to parents not addressed	Denies presence of or blames child for child's problems in school or at home	View their relationship as negative
Learning or attention problems not caused by physical or psychological problems	Views child as bad, worthless, or burdensome	State they do not like each other
Hypervigilent	Asks others to use harsh physical discipline if child misbehaves	
Lacks adult supervision	Demands physical/academic performance above child's abilities	
Overly compliant, passive, or withdrawn	Depends on the child for care, attention, and satisfaction of emotional needs	
Comes to school or other events early, stays late, does not want to go home		

Note: Adapted from Johnson (2012) and Child Welfare Information Gateway (2007).

Assessment Practice

Children who may have experienced abuse, neglect, and/or trauma need to be assessed by a team of professionals. This team may include pediatricians, school nurses, clinical psychologists, family therapists, social workers, and legal professionals such as police officers or court-appointed officials who receive training and education on working with children exposed to maltreatment or trauma (Horowitz, Owens, & Simms, 2000; Hyter et al., 2001). The purpose of this chapter is to focus on the role of the SLP as a member of this team.

Children exposed to maltreatment and children living in foster care have complex developmental profiles requiring individualized assessments that are ongoing (Vig et al., 2005). Hyter and her colleagues (2001) developed a model of family-centered and transdisciplinary practices for the Child Trauma Assessment Center at Western Michigan

University located in Kalamazoo, MI. This model supports a Dynamic Systems Theoretical approach in that the team recognizes different environmental contexts and other developmental areas may influence children's development. With this understanding, the team frames their services in family-centered practice using an ethnographic interview process and assessing the child in a transdisciplinary manner.

As previously discussed, children exposed to maltreatment are at risk of language and social communication delays as well as delays in executive function and working memory (Delcenserie, Genesee, & Gauthier, 2012; Desmarais, Roeber, Smith, & Pollak, 2012; Eigsti, Weitzman, Schuh, De Marchena, & Casey, 2011; Pears & Fisher, 2005). For this reason, it is recommended that if children have a history of maltreatment and are struggling in school, they receive a thorough speech-language assessment including (a) general language measures, (b) nonverbal and verbal comprehension and expression of social cognition (reading facial expressions and tone of voice, social understanding, and pragmatics), (c) verbal and visual working memory, and (d) executive function. Measures of working memory and executive function are described by Dr. Westby in Chapter 2 and Dr. Timler in Chapter 9. Assessments for children exposed to maltreatment will focus on general language measures that include a subtest of pragmatic or social communication skills or measures that focus on pragmatic language or social understanding.

Because research has documented that exposure to maltreatment may impact multiple developmental areas including language and social communication, a comprehensive assessment is needed that takes into consideration culturally and age-appropriate methods (Horowitz et al., 2000; Hyter et al., 2001). Using an ethnographic interview to gather pertinent and valuable information regarding the child's maltreatment history, cultural and linguistic differences, and the biological, foster, or adoptive parents' observations will assist all professionals in preparation for the assessment (Westby, Burda, & Mehta, 2003). Gathering authentic or portfolio measures of language-based school performance (language, writing, and spelling samples; achievement test scores) and teacher observations and measures may assist SLPs in determining other language areas that may be affected by maltreatment. For children who have experienced maltreatment and speak English as their primary language, mainstream, English-standardized assessments are appropriate. Please refer to Table 10.2 for a list of measures reported in the literature that have been used with children experiencing maltreatment.

TABLE 10.2 Measures of Social Communication in Children Exposed to Maltreatment

General Social Communication Measures	Age Range	Purpose	Research Studies
Communication and Symbolic Behavior Scales–Developmental Profile (CSBS-DP; Wetherby & Prizant, 2002)	1–2 years	Norm-referenced play-based measure of communication, social and symbolic behaviors	Glennen (2007); Hwa-Froelich & Matsuo (2010)
Transdisciplinary Play-Based Assessment, Second Edition (TPBA2; Linder, 2008) or ratings of play behavior	1 month to 6 years	Play-based arena assessment across developmental domains	Daunhauer, Coster, Tickle-Degnen, & Cernak (2010); Hwa-Froelich, (2012c); Kreppner, O'Connor, Dunn, Andersen-Wood, and the English and Romanian Adoptees (ERA) Study Team (1999)
Language Sample	30–33 months	Child and mother conversational analysis of communicative functions, decontextualization, conversational relatedness, and relevance	Coster et al. (1989)
Social Communication Research Tasks			
Stories about emotions, emotional facial expressions	3–7 years	Stories about emotions created by researchers, photos, or drawings of facial expressions	Camras et al. (1990); Camras, Perlman, Wismer Fries, & Pollak (2006); Tarullo et al. (2007)

The Diagnostic Analysis of Nonverbal Accuracy-2, (DANVA2; Nowicki & Duke, 1994)	3–99 years	Error scores are compared to means and standard deviations for each age group.	Colvert et al., 2008; Hwa-Froelich, Matsuo, & Becker (in press)
Theory of Mind tasks	4–6 years	Research tasks: Unexpected contents task (Perner, Frith, Leslie, & Leekman, 1989), Sally-Anne false-belief story (Wimmer & Perner, 1983), explaining action task (Bartsch & Wellman, 1989). Children are expected to 2 questions measuring inter- or intra-ToM for each of the 3 tasks and receive a score of at least 5/6.	Cicchetti et al. (2003); Tarullo et al. (2007); Yagmurlu et al. (2005)
Strange Stories (Happé, 1994)	5–12 years	Research tasks of stories depicting social interactions, jokes, sayings, and false beliefs. Scores are compared to means and standard deviations.	Colvert et al. (2008)
Caregiver–Child Social/Emotional and Relationship Rating Scale	0–8 years	Rating scale for observations of parent–child interaction	McCall, Groark, & Fish (2010)
Parent Report Measures			
Ages and Stages Questionnaire (Squires & Bricker, 2009)	1–66 months	A screening parent-report questionnaire covering gross and fine motor development, problem solving, and social skills.	Walsh & Viana (2012); S. L. Wilson & Weaver (2009)
Children's Communication Checklist-2 (CCC-2; Bishop, 2003)	4:0–16:11 years	Norm-referenced parent report measure of child communication behaviors	Glennen & Bright (2005); Sadiq et al (2012)

Transdisciplinary and ecological assessments are considered best practice when working with young children and their families (Horowitz et al., 2000; Hyter et al., 2001; Paul & Norbury, 2012). For prelinguistic children, parent-report instruments and play-based assessment strategies including parents and siblings are recommended. Observation, mediation and facilitation of play behaviors can help the practitioner assess social-emotional development (expression of emotions, emotion and behavior regulation, sense of self, and social interactions), cognitive development (attention, memory, problem solving, social cognition), communication development (comprehension, expression, pragmatics, articulation), and motor development (Linder, 2008). It also allows family members to participate so interactions among the family members can be observed. The Communication and Symbolic Behavior Scale–Developmental Profile (Wetherby & Prizant, 2002) is a standardized test that measures social, communication and symbolic behaviors of children between the ages of 12 and 24 months. Although play-based assessments continue to be appropriate and recommended for preschool-age children, additional standardized measures are available. After the age of 2, some executive function and selective attention tasks may be administered. Once the child is 4 years old, one can assess nonverbal communication, social understanding, and phonological short-term memory.

For school-age children, formal and informal evidence-based assessments may be used. In all cases, it is recommended to assess receptive and expressive language, pragmatic language, social understanding, short-term and working verbal and visuo-spatial memory, attention (joint and selective), and executive function. Because attention and memory skills may also be influenced by processing speed or auditory processing skills, the SLP should consider assessing these skills. Expressive language delays may not be apparent on general language measures but may affect higher order language skills such as inferential language, narrative language, and reading comprehension, thus these areas may need to be assessed also.

In the case of Harry, a transdisciplinary play-based assessment was performed (Linder, 2008). The SLP and the counselor conducted an ethnographic interview with the parents to gather information about previous assessments and interventions. As a team, they administered a general speech and language assessment and a play-based arena assessment in collaboration with the Occupational and Physical Therapists. The parents were asked to complete the Children's Communication Checklist–2 (Bishop, 2003).

The results of the assessment indicated developmental delays in expressive and pragmatic language, nonverbal communication, and fine motor skills. During the play assessment, Harry demonstrated delays in emotion regulation, attachment, attention, and persistence during problem solving, and reduced complexity in symbolic play. For example, Harry hid when dolls pretended to cry and he did not seek comfort, emotional connection, or joint attention with either parent or siblings. Although Harry qualified for special education services, the early intervention team recommended that Harry receive additional assessment in selective attention, phonological short-term memory, and social understanding or false-belief tasks. The results of these additional assessments indicated that Harry had adequate short-term phonological processing but was not able to express his own mental actions or the thoughts of others, and had difficulty regulating his attention and emotions when experiencing stressful events. Thus, a speech/language intervention using a relationship development framework to improve comprehension and expression of emotions, increasing selective attention, executive function, and expressive and social language were recommended as well as family therapy with a clinical psychologist with experience with families who had adopted children from abroad (S. L. Wilson, 2012).

TREATMENT PRACTICES

Children with a history of maltreatment may have difficulty trusting others and developing close, secure relationships. All professionals, including SLPs, should work closely with families in developing close trusting relationships with these children (Heller, Smyke, & Boris, 2002; Hughes, 2004; Hwa-Froelich, Wilson, Harris, & Ladage, 2012; Vig et al., 2005). It is also essential that judicial and family service systems work to reduce transitions in foster care to enable children to have consistent care to develop trusting relationships (Dicker & Gordon, 2006). A team treatment approach will ensure a consistent and supportive process to meet the child's needs and prevent confusion or conflict among professionals and the caregivers.

Caregiver and Individual Treatment

A positive social communicative environment is dependent upon the development of a trusting relationship with caregivers (for a review see S. L. Wilson, 2012). Young children who have experienced disruption of relationships, such as having multiple and inconsistent caregivers or losing contact with consistent foster caregivers, need special attention devoted to building strong and secure relationships to help them regulate and cope with their internal negative emotions and external stressors.

Children use these strong early relationships to develop a framework for future relationships with others outside of the family, learn to attend to facial expressions, tone of voice, and emotions, regulate their own emotions, and interpret and respond to others' communication and emotions (for a review see Chapters 3, 4, and 5; Barth, Crea, John, Thoburn, & Quinton, 2005; Juffer, Bakermans-Kranenburg, & Van IJzendoorn, 2005; Nickman et al., 2005; Reyes & Lieberman, 2012; Vig et al., 2005).

Most interventions focusing on relationship-based communication have been developed for children with social communication problems such as children with Autism Spectrum Disorder (ASD). These interventions have sufficient evidence of effectiveness and are discussed by Drs. Fannin and Watson in Chapter 7. These include relationship-based models such as, joint attention intervention (Kasari, Fannin, & Goods, 2012), and the Early Social Interaction Project (Woods, Wetherby, Kashinath, & Holland, 2012). Joint attention intervention is a SLP and/ or parent delivered play-based intervention designed to improve overall joint engagement through improvement of initiated joint attention and responses to joint attention (Kasari et al., 2012; Kasari, Gulsrud, Wong, Kwon, & Locke, 2010). The Early Social Interaction Project combines developmentally appropriate practice and family-centered practice, to provide naturalistic instruction to improve children's shared joint attention, intentional, and social communication and to share emotions in naturalistic environments (Woods et al., 2012). Although little research evidence on efficacy is available for the Developmental, Individual Difference, Relationship-Based: Floortime Model (DIR: Floortime; Greenspan & Wieder, 2006), it is based on similar theoretical models as joint attention and the Early Social Interaction Project and has emerging evidence that the treatment approach is effective (Gerber, 2012). This intervention model focuses on "the functional emotional developmental levels (FEDLs)," which are "shared attention and regulation, engagement and relating, two-way intentional communication, complex problem-solving, creative representations and elaboration, and representational differentiation and emotional thinking" (p. 80).

All of these models support facilitation of primary intersubjectivity, joint attention, emotion regulation and inhibition, memory and recall, and social communication, which are skills that would benefit children who have been exposed to maltreatment and/or disrupted relationship development. These models are also based on a developmental hierarchy of relationship development that promote social interaction through play-based activities in which participants learn to communicate and share emotions through positive playful interactions. They include strategies for sharing emotions face-to-face through both nonverbal and verbal communicative interactions that can also be adapted for older children. Once caregivers and children improve their ability to read and interpret each other's communication, facilitation of shared perspectives or joint attention with an inanimate or animate object is possible. Relationship and communication development are refined through stages of coordinated interactions, where children learn how to coordinate their actions and communication with another person. Once nonverbal and verbal communication skills become more coordinated, dynamic and flexible thinking is facilitated when new or unexpected events occur, helping children learn how to reflect on their own and others' actions. Eventually, practitioners can assist children to recall and reflect upon events from multiple perspectives. By helping children achieve and move through stages of relationship development, practitioners and parents facilitate their children's attention, inhibition, memory, and social communication. However, some children may need additional support in any one of these developmental areas.

SLPs should focus on assisting caregivers' abilities to accurately read their children's communication to support the family's positive attunement with one another and primary and secondary intersubjectivity. Primary intersubjectivity can be facilitated by creating and engaging in social face-to-face games, such as peek-a-boo or holding the child at a distance, then moving closer and closer to rub noses or plant kisses. In addition to developing intersubjectivity, treatment could focus on increasing caregivers' explicit, contingent responses to their children's communicative attempts. For example, the caregiver could talk directly to the child and try to interpret the child's vocalizations as intentional comments or requests. Treatment should also include strategies to facilitate caregivers' increased expression of different kinds of words and more complex syntax, to improve the quality of caregiver communicative input. As children move from toddlerhood to preschool age, instruction could include discussions about mental states and emotions leading to taking perspective of one's self and others' mental states to promote social understanding and social communication development (Dunn, Brown, Slomkowski, Tesla, & Youngblade, 1991). SLPs could also provide dynamic practice in associating facial expressions and vocal tones with emotional states by using stories or videos of social interactions and by role-playing common social contexts, such as contexts in which emotions cause people to behavior in certain ways and when events cause people to experience common emotions. For example, a video could be found or created showing a child is hurt and starts to cry and the child's friend tries to console the hurt child.

When working with foster, adoptive, or biological caregivers and their children, practitioners need to understand some of the obstacles that may occur. Juggling all the medical, social, and developmental needs their child may have following exposure to maltreatment, can result in organizational overload for the family (Heller et al., 2002). They may miss appointments or feel stressed and overloaded with the amount of extra care their child needs. They may not have taken "psychological ownership" of their child for a variety of reasons (p. 561). It is important for the child that the parents, regardless of their role, take full parental responsibility for the care of their child. There are several factors involved in developing psychological ownership, such as foster parents creating an emotional distance or not attach to the child so they can avoid feelings of loss if the child is removed or they may feel they lack the power to take responsibility because the biological parents may retain the right to make medical decisions for the child even when the child does not live with them. The foster caregivers may not have the necessary knowledge or understanding of the child's behavioral and developmental needs (Heller et al., 2002). Similar to foster parents, adoptive or biological parents (if the child returns to biological parents who were the source of the maltreatment) may not fully accept the child as a member of their family or may resist forming an attachment for fear that the child may eventually be removed from their care. All families with children exposed to maltreatment need support and assistance in providing adequate medical, social, and developmental care for their children and in developing close, positive relationships.

School-Based Treatment Programs

Only one study using a school mentoring program for children experiencing maltreatment could be found. In this study, 615 children and youths were followed for an average of 21 months (Mallett, 2012). Each child was matched according to individual needs with a certified teacher who served as the child's mentor and met with the child between 1 to 4 hours per week for the duration of the program. After 1 year in the program, the children improved twice as fast as the national norms and after approximately 2 years in the program the children caught up with test norms for intellectual and cognitive abilities, scholastic aptitude, oral language, and overall academic achievement. These rapid gains slowed down by the third year. This study provides preliminary evidence that children who have experienced maltreatment can succeed academically when they receive individualized mentoring. Other studies with children from at-risk backgrounds have also found that children need supportive social relationships to succeed in school (Snow, Porche, Tabors, & Ross-Harris, 2007).

CASE STUDY OUTCOMES

In the case of Harry, the psychologist modeled turn-taking games with Harry and coached the parents as each one learned how to engage Harry in play and take turns during face-to-face games. She modeled exaggerated facial expressions paired with a positive tone of voice to help the parents express exaggerated positive nonverbal behaviors. Harry began to associate and interpret these behaviors with positive interactions. In time, his father learned to change his communicative interactions from giving directions and threats to commenting on Harry's actions, talking about his own actions, and offering choices to help Harry communicate desires, intentions, and goals. As the relationship between Harry and his parents improved, the family began to relax and enjoy each other more during family interactions.

The SLP coached Harry's parents while they played with Harry to help ease them into engaging in child-directed play and language stimulation, modeling how to follow Harry's lead and interests during play as well as how to comment and talk about both Harry's actions and her own. She used storybooks in which the characters were depicted with different facial expressions to teach and demonstrate emotion with exaggerated tone of voice while mirroring the characters' facial expressions. With consultation from the clinical psychologist and SLP, the early childhood educators at Harry's preschool also began to implement relationship-based intervention and facilitated Harry's play development for higher levels of symbolic play around positive emotional themes, and attention and emotion regulation during problem solving or frustrating, challenging events. Gradually, Harry began to have less anxiety when his parents took him to preschool. He began to demonstrate positive emotional themes during his play and had fewer tantrums or physical aggression during stressful events. While his play continued to be less complex than his peers' play behaviors and he avoided others when they displayed negative emotions, his play and emotion regulation skills continued to improve over time.

In summary, as professionals, our assessment and intervention approaches with children exposed to maltreatment should be comprehensive. All professionals should work toward preventing child maltreatment. Once maltreatment has occurred, however, the children and their families should receive a comprehensive, ecological assessment and preventative measures should be implemented to avoid continued exposure to maltreatment. Our interventions should include the participants and contexts in which children live to build safe and secure positive relationships.

DISCUSSION QUESTIONS

1. What are the reasons you think neglect tends to be more debilitating than physical or sexual abuse?
2. What are the developmental outcomes for children who have been exposed to maltreatment?
3. What are the reasons you think that these outcomes are similar for children who are removed from maltreatment and are cared for in foster families or are adopted?
4. Describe the three-tiered approach for preventing child abuse and neglect.
5. Describe the types of assessment that may need to be considered for children exposed to maltreatment.
6. Describe the kinds of interventions that may be needed for children exposed to maltreatment. Consider individual, caregiver, and school programs.

CLINICAL RESOURCES

Centers for Disease Control website: www.cdc.gov/violenceprevention/childmal treatment/

Child Help website: www.childhelp-usa.org/pages/statistics

Children's Bureau website: www.acf.hhs.gov/programs/cb/research-data-technology/statistics-research

Child Trauma Academy: www.childtrauma.org/

Child Trauma Institute: www.childtrauma.com/

Child Welfare Information Gateway: www.childwelfare.gov/can/

National Association of Counsel for Children website: www.naccchildlaw.org/

National Child Traumatic Stress Network: www.nctsn.org/

National Criminal Justice Reference Service: https://www.ncjrs.gov/childabuse/

National Institute of Justice website: www.nij.gov/topics/crime/child-abuse/welcome.htm

Rebuilding Shattered Lives: An Adoption Story: www.youtube.com/watch?v=C8b0rYBT85s

The Future of Children website: http://futureofchildren.org/publications/jour nals/journal_details/index.xml?journalid=71

World Health Organization: www.cdc.gov/violenceprevention/childmaltreat ment/

Zero to Three website: www.zerotothree.org/maltreatment/child-abuse-neglect/child-abuse-and-neglect.html

REFERENCES

Allen, R. E., & Oliver, J. M. (1982). The effects of child maltreatment on language development. *Child Abuse and Neglect, 6,* 299–305.

American Psychiatric Association. (2013). *Diagnostic and statistical manual of mental disorders* (5th ed.). Retrieved from www.dsm5.org/Pages/Default. aspx

Australian Institute of Family Studies. (2013). Child abuse and neglect statistics. Retrieved from www.aifs.gov.au/cfca/pubs/factsheets/a142086/

Baron-Cohen, S. (1997). *Mindblindness. An essay on autism and theory of mind.* Cambridge, MA: MIT Press.

Barth, R. P., Crea, T. M., John, K., Thoburn, J., & Quinton, D. (2005). Beyond attachment theory and therapy: Towards sensitive and evidence-based interventions with foster and adoptive families in distress. *Child and Family Social Work, 10,* 237–268. doi:10.1111/j.1365–2206.2005.00380.x

Bartsch, K., & Wellman, H. M. (1989). Young children's attribution of action to beliefs and desires. *Child Development, 60,* 946–964. Retrieved from www.jstor.org/pss/1131035

Beeghly, M., & Cicchetti, D. (1994). Child maltreatment, attachment, and the self system: Emergence of an internal state lexicon in toddlers at high social risk. *Development and Psychopathology, 6,* 5–30.

Bishop, D. V. M. (2003). *Children's Communication Checklist* (2nd ed.). San Antonio, TX: PsychCorp.

Camras, L. A., Perlman, S. B., Wismer Fries, A. B., & Pollak, S. D. (2006). Post-institutionalized Chinese and Eastern European children: Heterogeneity in the development of emotion understanding. *International Journal of Behavior Development, 30*(3), 193–199.

Camras, L. A., Ribordy, S., Hill, J., Martino, S., Sachs, V., Spaccarelli, S., & Stefani, R. (1990). Maternal facial behavior and the recognition and production of emotional expression by maltreated and nonmaltreated children. *Developmental Psychology, 26*(2), 304–312.

Children's Bureau. (2012). Child maltreatment 2012. Retrieved from www.acf. hhs.gov/programs/cb/resource/child-maltreatment-2012

Child Welfare Information Gateway. (2007). Identification of child abuse and neglect. Retrieved from www.childwelfare.gov/can/identifying/

Cicchetti, D., & Beeghly, M. (1987). Symbolic development in maltreated youngsters: An organizational perspective. In D. Cicchetti & M. Beeghly (Eds.), *Symbolic development in atypical children* (New Directions for Child Development, No. 36, pp. 47–67). San Francisco, CA: Jossey-Bass.

Cicchetti, D., Rogosch, F. A., Maughan, A., Toth, S. L., & Bruce, J. (2003). False belief understanding in maltreated children. *Development and Psychopathology, 15,* 1067–1091. doi:10.1017.S0954579403000440

Cohen, N. J., Lojkasek, M., Zadeh, Z. Y., Pugliese, M., & Kiefer, H. (2008). Children adopted from China: A prospective study of their growth and development. *Journal of Child Psychology and Psychiatry, 49*(4), 458–468. doi:10.1111/j.1469-7610.2007.01853.x

Colvert, E., Rutter, M., Kreppner, J., Beckett, C., Castle, J., Groothues, C., . . . Sonuga-Barke, E. J. S. (2008). Do theory of mind and executive function deficits underlie the adverse outcomes associated with profound early deprivation?: Findings from the English and Romanian adoptees study. *Journal of Abnormal Child Psychology, 36*, 1057–1068. doi:10.1007/s10802-008-9232-x

Coster, W. J., Gersten, M. S., Beeghly, M., & Cicchetti, D. (1989). Communicative functioning in maltreated children. *Developmental Psychology, 25*(6), 1020–1029.

Croft, C., Beckett, C., Rutter, M., Castle, J., Colvert, E., Groothues, C., . . . Sonuga-Barke, E. J. (2007). Early adolescent outcomes for institutionally-deprived and non-deprived adoptees. II: Language as a protective factor and a vulnerable outcome. *Journal of Child Psychology and Psychiatry, 48*, 31–44. Retrieved from http://onlinelibrary.wiley.com/journal/10.1111/%28ISSN%291469-7610

Culp, R. E., Watkins, R. V., Lawrence, H., Letts, D., Kelly, D. J., & Rice, M. L. (1991). Maltreated children's language and speech development: Abused, neglected, and abused and neglected. *First Language, 11*, 377–389.

Daunhauer, L. A., Coster, W. J., Tickle-Degnen, L., & Cernak, S. A. (2010). Play and cognition among young children reared in an institution. *Physical & Occupational Therapy in Pediatrics, 30*(2), 83–97. doi:10.3109/01942630903543682

Delcenserie, A., & Genesee, F. (2013). Language and memory abilities of internationally adopted children from China: Evidence for early age effects. *Journal of Child Language*. Advanced online publication. doi:10.1017/8030500091300041X

Delcenserie, A., Genesee, F., & Gauthier, K. (2012). Language abilities of internationally adopted children from China during the early school years: Evidence for early age effects? *Applied Psycholinguistics*, 1–28. http://dx.doi.org/10.1017/S0142716411000865

Desmarais, C., Roeber, B. J., Smith, M. E., & Pollak, S. D. (2012). Sentence comprehension in postinstitutionalized school-age children. *Journal of Speech, Language, and Hearing Research, 55*, 45–54. doi:10.1044/1092-4388(2011/10-0246).

Dicker, S., & Gordon, E. (2006). Critical connections for children who are abused and neglected: Harnessing the new federal referral provisions for early intervention. *Infants and Young Children, 19*(3), 170–178.

Dunn, J., Brown, J., Slomkowski, C., Tesla, C., & Youngblade, L. (1991). Young children's understanding of other people's feelings and beliefs: Individual differences and their antecedents. *Child Development, 62*, 1352–1366.

Eigsti, I-M., & Cicchett, D. (2004). The impact of child maltreatment on expressive syntax at 60 months. *Developmental Science, 7*(1), 88–102.

Eigisti, E.-M., Weitzman, C., Schuh, J., De Marchena, A., & Casey, B. J. (2011). Language and cognitive outcomes in internationally adopted children. *Development and Psychopathology, 23*, 629–646. doi:10.1017/ S0954579411000204

Fox, L., Long, S., & Langlois, A. (1988). Patterns of language comprehension deficit in abused and neglected children. *Journal of Speech and Hearing Disorders, 53*, 239–244.

Gauthier, K., & Genesee, F. (2011). Language development in internationally adopted children: A special case of early second language learning. *Child Development, 82*(3), 887–901. doi:10.1111/j1467-8624.2011.01578.x

Gerber, S. (2012). An introduction to the Developmental, Individual-Difference, Relationship-based (DIR) model and its application to children with autism spectrum disorder. In P. A. Prelock & R. J. McCauley (Eds.), *Treatment of Autism Spectrum Disorders* (pp. 79–106). Baltimore, MD: Brookes.

Gindis, B. (2005). Cognitive, language, and educational issues of children adopted from overseas orphanages. *Journal of Cognitive Education and Psychology, 4*, 291–315. Retrieved from www.bgcenter.com/adoption-Publication.htm.

Glennen, S. (2007). Predicting language outcomes for internationally adopted children. *Journal of Speech, Language and Hearing Research, 50*, 529–548. doi:10.1044/1092-4388(2007/036)

Glennen, S., & Bright, B. J. (2005). Five years later: Language in school-age internationally adopted children. *Seminars in Speech and Language, 26*(1), 86–101. Retrieved from www.ovid.com/site/catalog/Journal/1176. jsp

Glennen, S., & Masters, G. (2002). Typical and atypical language development in infants and toddlers adopted from Eastern Europe. *American Journal of Speech-Language Pathology, 11*, 417–433. doi:10.1044/ 1058-0360(2002/045)

Greenspan, S. I., & Wider, S. (2006). *Engaging autism: The floortime approach to helping children to relate, communicate, and think*. Philadelphia, PA: Da Capo.

Guinn, K. (n.d.). BrainyQuote.com. Retrieved September 10, 2012, from www. brainyquote.com/quotes/quotes/k/kennyguinn168452.html

Happé, F. (1994). An advanced test of theory of mind: Understanding of story characters' thoughts and feelings by able, autistic, mentally handicapped and normal children and adults. *Journal of Autism and Developmental Disorders, 24*(2), 129–154.

Heller, S. S., Smyke, A. T., & Boris, N. W. (2002). Very young foster children and foster families: Clinical challenges and interventions. *Infant Mental Health Journal, 23*(5), 555–575. doi:10.1002/imhj.10033

Hellerstedt, W.L., Madsen, N.J., Gunnar, M.R., Grotevant, H.D., Lee, R.M., & Johnson, D.E. (2008). The international adoption project: Population-based surveillance of Minnesota parents who adopted children internationally. *Maternal Child Health Journal, 12*(2), 162–171. doi:10.1007/s10995-007-0237-9

Hildeyard, K.L., & Wolfe, D.A. (2002). Child neglect: Developmental issues and outcomes. *Child Abuse & Neglect, 26*, 679–695.

Horowitz, S.M., Owens, P., & Simms, M.D. (2000). Specialized assessments for children in foster care. *Pediatrics, 106*(1), 59–66.

Hughes, D. (2004). An attachment-based treatment of maltreated children and young people. *Attachment & Human Development, 6*(3), 263–278. doi:10.1080/14616730412331281539

Hwa-Froelich, D.A. (2009). Communication development in infants and toddlers adopted from abroad. *Topics in Language Disorders, 29*(1), 27–44. doi:10.1097/01.TLD.0000346060.63964.c2

Hwa-Froelich, D.A. (2012a). Childhood maltreatment and communication development. *Perspectives on School-Age Language, 13*(1), 43–53.

Hwa-Froelich, D.A. (2012b). Prelinguistics, receptive, and expressive language development. In D.A. Hwa-Froelich, *Supporting development in internationally adopted children* (pp. 149–176). Baltimore, MD: Brookes.

Hwa-Froelich, D.A. (2012c). Inhibition, self-regulation, attention, and memory development. In D.A. Hwa-Froelich, *Supporting development in internationally adopted children* (pp. 107–132). Baltimore, MD: Brookes.

Hwa-Froelich, D.A. (2012d). Social communication development. In D.A. Hwa-Froelich, *Supporting development in internationally adopted children* (pp. 177–203). Baltimore, MD: Brookes.

Hwa-Froelich, D.A., & Matsuo, H. (2010). Communication development and differences in children adopted from China and Eastern Europe. *Language, Speech, and Hearing Services in Schools, 41*, 1–18. doi:10.1044/0161-1461(2009/08-0085)

Hwa-Froelich, D.A., Matsuo, H., & Becker, J.C. (in press). Emotion identification from facial expressions in children adopted internationally. *American Journal of Speech-Language Pathology.* doi:10.1044/2014_AJSLP-14-0009

Hwa-Froelich, D.A., Wilson, S.L., Harris, S.E., & Ladage, J.S. (2012). Treatment. In D.A. Hwa-Froelich, *Supporting development in internationally adopted children* (pp. 205–237). Baltimore, MD: Brookes.

Hyter, Y., Atchison, B., Henry, J., Sloane, M., & Black-Pond, C. (2001). A response to traumatized children: Developing a best practices model. *Occupational Therapy in Healthcare, 15*(3–4), 113–140.

Johnson, H. (2012, November 20). Protecting the most vulnerable from abuse. *ASHA Leader, 17*(14), 16–19. Retrieved from www.asha.org/leader.aspx

Juffer, F., Bakermans-Kranenburg, M. J., & Van IJzendoorn, M. H. (2005). The importance of parenting in the development of disorganized attachment: Evidence from a preventive intervention study in adoptive families. *Journal of Child Psychology and Psychiatry, 46,* 263–274. doi:10.1111/ j.1469–7610.2004.00353.x

Kasari, C., Fannin, D. K., & Goods, K. S. (2012). Joint attention for children with autism. In P. A. Prelock & R. J. McCauley (Eds.), *Treatment of autism spectrum disorders* (pp. 139–161). Baltimore, MD: Brookes.

Kasari, C., Gulsrud, A. C., Wong, C., Kwon, S., & Locke, J. (2010). Randomized controlled caregiver mediated joint engagement intervention for toddlers with autism. *Journal of Autism and Developmental Disorders, 40,* 1045–1056. doi:10.1007/s10803–010–0955–5

Kreppner, J. M., O'Connor, T. G., Dunn, J., Anderson-Wood, L., & the English and Romanian Adoption Study Team. (1999). The pretend and social role play of children exposed to early severe deprivation. *British Journal of Developmental Psychology, 17,* 319–332.

Kurtz, P. D., Gaudin, J. M., Wodarski, J. S., & Howing, P. T. (1993). Maltreatment and the school-aged child: School performance consequences. *Child Abuse & Neglect, 17,* 581–589.

Law, J., & Conway, J. (1992). Effect of abuse and neglect on the development of children's speech and language. *Developmental Medicine and Child Neurology, 34*(11), 943–948.

The Leiden Conference on the Development and Care of Children without Permanent Parents. (2012). The development and care of institutionally reared children. *Child Development Perspectives, 6,* 174–180. doi:10.1111/ j.1750–8606.2011.00231.x

Linder, T. (2008). *Transdisciplinary play-based assessment* (2nd ed.). Baltimore, MD: Brookes.

Luke, N., & Bannerjee, R. (2012). Maltreated children's social understanding and empathy: A preliminary exploration of foster carers' perspectives. *Journal of Child Family Studies, 21,* 237–246. doi:10.1007/s10826–011–9468-x

Mallett, C. A. (2012). The school success program: Improving maltreated children's academic and school-related outcomes. *Children & Schools, 34*(1), 13–26.

Manso, J. M. M., García-Baamonde, M. E., Alonso, M. B., & Barona, E. G. (2010). Pragmatic language development and educational style in neglected children. *Children and Youth Services Review, 32,* 1028–1034.

McCall, R. B., Groark, C. J., & Fish, L. (2010). A caregiver-child social/emotional and relationship rating scale (CCSERRS). *Infant Mental Health Journal, 31*(2), 201–219. doi:10.1002/imhj.20252

McFadyen, R. G., & Kitson, W. J. H. (1996). Language comprehension and expression among adolescents who have experienced childhood physical abuse. *Journal of Child Psychology and Psychiatry, 5,* 551–562.

Moulson, M. C., Fox, N. A., Zeanah, C. H., & Nelson, C. A. (2009). Early adverse experiences and the neurobiology of facial emotion processing. *Developmental Psychology, 45*(1), 17–30. doi:10.1037/a001.4035

National Society for the Prevention of Childhood Cruelty. (2013). How safe are our children? Retrieved from www.nspcc.org.uk/Inform/research/findings/howsafe/how-safe-2013_wda95178.html

Nickman, S. L., Rosenfeld, A. A., Fine, P., Macintyre, J. C., Pilowsky, D. J., Howe, R. A. . . . Sveda, S. A. (2005). Children in adoptive families: Overview and update. *Journal of the American Academy of Child Adolescent Psychiatry, 44*(10), 987–995. doi:10.1097/01.chi.0000174463.60987.69

Nowicki, S., Jr., & Duke, M. P. (1994). Individual differences in the nonverbal communication of affect: The diagnostic analysis of nonverbal accuracy. *Journal of Nonverbal Behavior, 18,* 9–35.

Parker, S. W., Nelson, C. A., & the Bucharest Early Intervention Project Core Group. (2005). The impact of early institutional rearing on the ability to discriminate facial expressions of emotion: An event-related potential study. *Child Development, 76*(1), 54–72. Retrieved from www.wiley.com/bw/journal.asp?ref=0009–3920

Parker, S. W., Nelson, C. A., & the Bucharest Early Intervention Project Core Group. (2008). An event-potential study of the impact on institutional rearing on face recognition. *Development and Psychopathology, 17,* 621–639. doi:10.1017/S0954579405050303

Paul, R., & Norbury, C. F. (2012). *Language disorders from infancy through adolescence: Assessment and intervention* (4th ed.). St. Louis, MO: Mosby.

Pears, K., & Fisher, P. A. (2005). Developmental, cognitive, and neuropsychological functioning in preschool-aged foster children: Associations with prior maltreatment and placement history. *Developmental and Behavioral Pediatrics, 26*(2), 112–122.

Perner, J., Frith, U., Leslie, A. M., & Leekam, S. R. (1989). Exploration of the autistic child's theory of mind: Knowledge, belief, and communication. *Child Development, 60*(3), 689–700. doi:10.1111/1467–8624.ep7252771

Pinheiro, P. S. (2006, August). Report of the independent expert for the United Nations study on violence against children. Retrieved from www.unicef.org/violencestudy/reports/SG_violencestudy_en.pdf

Public Health Agency of Canada. (2008). Canadian incidence study of reported child abuse and neglect 2008. Retrieved from www.phac-aspc.gc.ca/cm-vee/csca-ecve/2008/cis-eci-07-eng.php#c3–1

Reyes, V., & Lieberman, A. (2012). Child-parent psychotherapy and traumatic exposure to violence. *Zero to Three.* Retrieved from http://main.zerotothree.org/site/DocServer/Reyes_copy_for_the_Insider.pdf?docID=13741

Roberts, J. A., Pollock, K. E., Krakow, R., Price, J., Fulmer, K. C., & Wang, P. P. (2005). Language development in preschool-age children adopted from China. *Journal of Speech, Language, and Hearing Research, 48*(1), 93–107. doi:10.1044/1092–4388(2005/008)

Sadiq, F. A., Slator, L., Skuse, D., Law, J., Gillberg, C., & Minnis, H. (2012). Social use of language in children with reactive attachment disorder and autism spectrum disorders. *European Child Adolescent Psychiatry, 21,* 267–276. doi:10:1007/s00787–012–0259–8

Scannapieco, M., & Connell-Carrick, K. (2002). Focus on the first years: An eco-developmental assessment of child neglect for children 0 to 3 years of age. *Children and Youth Services Review, 24*(8), 601–621.

Scarborough, A. A., Lloyd, E. C., & Barth, R. P. (2009). Maltreated infants and toddlers: Predictors of developmental delay. *Journal of Developmental and Behavioral Pediatrics, 30*(6), 489–498.

Scarborough, A. A., & McCrae, J. S. (2008). Maltreated infants reported eligibility for Part C and later school-age special education services. *Topics in Early Childhood Special Education, 28*(2), 75–89. doi:10.1077/0271121408320349

Schore, A. N. (2001). The effects of early relational trauma on right brain development, affect regulation, and infant mental health. *Infant Mental Health Journal, 22*(1–2), 201–269.

Scott, K. A., Pollock, K., Roberts, J. A., & Krakow, R. (2013). Phonological processing skills of children adopted internationally. *American Journal of Speech-Language Pathology, 22,* 673–683. doi:10.1044/1058–0360(201 3/12–0133)

Scott, K. A., Roberts, J. A., & Glennen, S. (2011). How well do children who are internationally adopted acquire language? A meta-analysis. *Journal of Speech, Language, and Hearing Research, 54,* 1153–1169. doi:10.104 4/1092–4388(2010/10–0075)

Scott, K. A., Roberts, J., & Krakow, R. A. (2008). Oral and written language development of children adopted from China. *American Journal of Speech Language Pathology, 17,* 150–160. doi:10.1044/1058–0360(2008/015)

Snow, P. C. (2009). Child maltreatment, mental health and oral language competence: Inviting speech-language pathology to the prevention table. *International Journal of Speech-Language Pathology, 11*(2), 95–103. doi:10.1080/17549500802415712

Snow, C. E., Porche, M. V., Tabors, P. O., & Ross-Harris, S. (2007). *Is literacy enough?* Baltimore, MD: Brookes.

Squires, J., & Bricker, D. (2009). *Ages and Stages Questionnaire, 3rd ed.* Baltimore, MD: Brookes.

Tan, T. X., & Yang, Y. (2005). Language development of Chinese adoptees 18–35 months old. *Early Childhood Research Quarterly, 20,* 57–68. doi. org/10.1016/j.ecresq.2005.01.004

Tarullo, A. R., Bruce, J., & Gunnar, M. R. (2007). False belief and emotion understanding in post-institutionalized children. *Social Development, 16*(1), 57–78. doi:10.1111/j.1467-9507.2007.00372.x

Tizard, B., Cooperman, O., Joseph, A., & Tizard, J. (1972). Environmental effects on language development: A study of young children in long-stay residential nurseries. *Child Development, 43,* 337–358.

Tizard, B., & Joseph, A. (1970). Cognitive development of young children in residential care: A study of children aged 24 months. *Journal of Child Psychology and Psychiatry, 11*, 177–186.

Toth, S. L., Stronach, E. P., Rogosch, F. A., Caplan, R., & Cicchetti, D. (2011). Illogical thinking and thought disorder in maltreated children. *Journal of the American Academy of Child and Adolescent Psychiatry, 50*(7), 659–668.

Trocmé, N., & Caunce, C. (1998). The educational needs of abused and neglected children: A review of the literature. *Early Child Development and Care, 106*, 101–135.

US Department of Health and Human Services. (2012). Child maltreatment 2011. Retrieved from www.acf.hhs.gov/sites/default/files/cb/cm11.pdf#page=28

Van der Kolk, B. A., & Fisler, R. E. (1994). Childhood abuse and neglect and loss of self-regulation. *Bulletin of the Meninger Clinic, 58*, 145–168.

Vig, S., Chinitz, S., & Shulman, L. (2005). Young children in foster care: Multiple vulnerabilities and complex service needs. *Infants and Young Children, 18*(2), 147–160.

Walsh, J. A., & Viana, A. G. (2012). Developmental outcomes of internationally adopted children. *Adoption Quarterly, 15*, 241–264. doi:10.1080/109267 55.2012.731029

Westby, C. E., Burda, A. N., & Mehta, Z. (April 29, 2003). Asking the right questions in the right ways: Strategies for ethnographic interviewing. *The ASHA Leader, 8*(8), 4–5, 16–17.

Wetherby, A. M., & Prizant, B. M. (2002). *Communication and Symbolic Behavior Scales–Developmental Profile.* Baltimore, MD: Brookes.

Wilson, S. L. (2012). Social-emotional and relationship development. In D. A. Hwa-Froelich (Ed.), *Supporting development in internationally adopted children* (pp. 59–84). Baltimore, MD: Brookes.

Wilson, S. L., & Weaver, T. L. (2009). Follow-up of developmental attainment and behavioral adjustment of toddlers internationally adopted into the USA. *International Social Work, 52*(5), 679–684. doi:10.1177/0020872809337684

Wilson, S. R. (1999). Child physical abuse: The relevance of language and social interaction research. *Research on Language and Social Interaction, 32*(1&2), 173–184.

Wimmer, H., & Perner, J. (1983) Beliefs about beliefs: Representation and constraining function of wrong beliefs in young children's understanding of deception. *Cognition, 13*, 103–128. doi:10.1016/0010-0277(83)90004-5

Windsor, J., Wing, C. A., Koga, S. F., Fox, N. A., Benigno, J. P., Carroll, P. J., . . . Zeanah, C. H. (2011). Effect of foster care on young children's language learning. *Child Development, 82*(4), 1040–1046. doi:10.1111/j.1467-86242011.01604x

Woods, J. J., Wetherby, A. M., Kashinath, S., & Holland, R. D. (2012). Early social interaction project. In P. A. Prelock & R. J. McCauley (Eds.), *Treatment of autism spectrum disorders* (pp. 189–220). Baltimore, MD: Brookes.

Yagmurlu, B., Berument, S. K., & Celimli, S. (2005). The role of institution and home contexts in theory of mind development. *Applied Developmental Psychology, 26,* 521–537. doi:10.1016j.appdev.2005.06.004

11

SOCIAL COMMUNICATION ASSESSMENT AND INTERVENTION FOR CHILDREN WITH DISRUPTIVE BEHAVIOR PROBLEMS

Carol E. Westby

Ironically, these disorders are defined mainly by the emotions they stir up in adults. Can a youth have a "disruptive behavior disorder" without somebody to disrupt? Does a tree falling in the forest make any sound if no one is there to hear it fall? Kids are called disruptive and disturbed when others in their life space feel disrupted and disturbed. . . . Emotional disturbance is not a solo performance but a dance with multiple partners. No matter who takes the lead, others play supporting roles.

—Brendtro and Shahbazian (2004, pp. 71–72)

LEARNING OBJECTIVES

Readers will

1. Be able to define the criteria for diagnosis of oppositional defiant disorder and conduct disorders.
2. Be able to describe the characteristics of children and adolescents with callous-unemotional, narcissistic, and Machiavellian traits.
3. Be able to describe the patterns of theory of mind strengths and deficits in children and adolescents with different behavioral/ attitudinal patterns.
4. Acquire strategies to assess the language skills of children and adolescents with disruptive behavioral disorders.

5. Become familiar with some of the intervention programs used with children and adolescents with disruptive behavioral disorders.

Alec was not in kindergarten long before it was obvious he was having a difficult time; he was crying, melting down easily over reasonable requests, yelling at and pushing other children, and even talking about dying. He was diagnosed with ADHD and anxiety disorder. Medications were attempted but were not found to be helpful. Alec presented as a child with ADHD and oppositional defiant disorder (ODD). In first grade he had difficulty learning to read. In second grade, he became more resistant to teachers' instructions and his negative moods and aggressive behaviors escalated to the degree that by fourth grade he met the diagnostic criteria for conduct disorders (CDs) with callous-unemotional (CU) traits. For example, he threatened others and picked fights for no apparent reason, was particularly vicious with his sister, and when he was caught stealing or lying, he denied the behavior and blamed others. Alec displayed no concerns for the feelings of others and showed no guilt or remorse when he hurt others or damaged something.

DIAGNOSTIC CRITERIA FOR DISRUPTIVE BEHAVIORAL DISORDERS

This chapter will focus on children who meet the criteria for diagnosis of ODD or CD, two forms of disruptive behavioral disorder (DBD) described in the *Diagnostic Statistical Manual* (5th ed.; *DSM-5*; American Psychiatric Association [APA], 2013). Note: Schools typically use the term emotional and behavioral disorder (EBD) rather than DBD, but EBD is not used in the *DSM-5*. Schools may or may not use the diagnostic criteria associated with ODD and CD when diagnosing students with EBD to qualify them for special education services.

In the *DSM-5*, criteria for ODD are grouped into three types: angry/irritable mood, argumentative/defiant behavior, and vindictiveness, reflecting that the disorder includes both emotional and behavioral symptoms (APA, 2013; Buitelaar et al., 2013). These behavioral and emotional symptoms are frequent and persistent. They may be confined to only one context, although in more severe cases the symptoms are present in multiple settings. Even if individuals show symptoms in only one context, they typically exhibit significant impairments in their social functioning. Many children and teens with ODD also have other behavioral problems, such as attention-deficit/hyperactivity disorder, learning disabilities, mood disorders (such as depression), and anxiety disorders.

ODD symptoms are often part of general problematic interactions with others. Persons with ODD do not regard themselves as oppositional and typically view their anger and argumentative or vindictive behaviors as justified in the face of what they perceive as unreasonable demands.

Diagnosis of CD in the *DSM-5* (APA, 2013) is based on a persistent pattern of behavior in which the basic rights of others or major age-appropriate norms are violated. Symptoms of CD are divided into two related but distinct "aggressive" and "rule-breaking" clusters. In the *DSM-5*, CD is defined based on the presence of 3 of 15 criteria that should have been present in the last 12 months, and of which one must have been present in the past 6 months. These 15 criteria are categorized into four subtypes: (a) aggression to people and animals, (b) destruction of property, (c) deceitfulness or theft, and (d) serious violations of rules. These behaviors are often referred to as antisocial behaviors. Individuals with CD who display aggressive symptoms frequently misperceive the intentions of others as more hostile and threatening than is the case. As a consequence, they maintain that their aggression is reasonable and justified. They also tend to be thrill seeking and reckless and to have a generally negative mood, poor frustration tolerance, irritability, temper outbursts, suspiciousness, and insensitivity to punishment. Aggressive behaviors such a hitting, pushing, slapping, biting, kicking, and spitting are universal among young children, but as children grow older, most learn to inhibit these aggressive behaviors. Children who continue to manifest aggressive and rule-breaking behaviors may receive a diagnosis of CD.

The prevalence of ODD ranges from 1% to 11% with an average prevalence estimate of 3.3%. Prevalence rates for conduct disorders range from 3% to more than 10% with a median of 4%. The prevalence of ODD and CD appears to be fairly consistent across various countries that differ in race and ethnicity. These rates are higher among males than females (ODD, 1.4:1) and rise from childhood to adolescence (APA, 2013). CD is more common in boys (6%–19%) compared with girls (2%–9%), the gap narrows in adolescence. Boys tend to be aggressive whereas girls are more likely to break social rules through offenses such as truancy, lying, and prostitution (Offord, 1987).

ODD indicates risk for early onset of CD (Moffitt et al., 2008). For a significant number of children who develop CD, ODD often emerges first, followed by the onset of the more severe CD symptoms (Frick & Nigg, 2011). In a longitudinal study of children, 71% to 78% of children who developed CD between the ages of 4 and 9 met criteria for ODD earlier in development, whereas the rate was only 30% of those who met criteria for CD after age 10 (Burke, Waldman, & Lahey, 2010). Although there is a strong relationship between ODD and CD, a large percentage of children with ODD do not have CD, nor do they go on to develop CD (Maughan, Rowe, Messer, Goodman, & Meltzer, 2004). Similarly, only a minority of children with CD have a diagnosis of ODD, and the proportion of youths with CD without ODD increases from childhood to adolescence (Burke et al., 2010). Many of the symptoms of ODD and CD overlap. The behaviors of individuals with ODD are typically less severe than those of individuals with CD and do not include aggression toward individuals or animals, destruction of property, or a pattern of theft or deceit. ODD includes problems with emotional dysregulation that are not included in the definition of CD. Thus, students can be diagnosed with both ODD and CD.

The CD diagnosis is subtyped or specified in terms of age of onset of symptoms—childhood onset (prior to age 10) and adolescent onset (after age 10). Children with early onset frequently have had ODD during early childhood, ADHD, and other neurodevelopmental difficulties, for example, deficits in executive functioning, cognitive deficits (low intelligence) and ADHD (with impulsivity and problems in emotional regulation; Frick & Viding 2009; Moffitt, 2006). There are significant differences in life-course trajectories of these two groups. Children in the early-onset group often begin to show mild conduct problems in preschool or early elementary school, and their behavioral problems tend to increase in rate and severity throughout childhood and adolescence. They are more likely to show antisocial and criminal behavior into adulthood and are at greater risk for later mood disorders, anxiety disorders, posttraumatic stress disorder, impulse control disorders, and substance-related disorders as adults. By age 18 the majority meet the criteria for antisocial personality disorder. Although the group represents a small portion (3%–5%) of the total group with CD, they are responsible for about half of the criminal offenses committed by young offenders. Children with early onset CD are also more likely to come from homes with more conflict, live with parents who use less effective parenting, and have behaviors with a genetic basis than are those with adolescence onset. Children with adolescent onset CD are less likely to have temperamental, cognitive problems, and negative family factors, and they tend to have lower genetic risks. Their behaviors are more likely due to negative forms of social learning in their peer groups. If their difficulties persist into adulthood, they are often due to consequences of their adolescent antisocial behavior, for example, a criminal record or dropping out of school.

For the CD diagnosis, the *DSM-5* (APA, 2013) also includes specifiers for callous and unemotional (CU) traits. These CU traits are part of what has been termed the Dark Triad (Paulhus & Williams, 2002), three related, socially undesirable personality traits: psychopathy, which involves callousness, lack of personal affect, and remorselessness; Machiavellianism, characterized by manipulation and exploitation of others, a cynical disregard of morality, and a focus on self-interest; and narcissism, which is a grandiose self-view, a sense of entitlement, egotism, and a desire to establish dominance over others. Emerging research suggests that all three components of the dark triad are distinct constructs that are linked to aggressive behavior in children (Kerig & Stellwagen, 2010) and adults (Baughman, Dearing, Giammarco, & Vernon, 2012). The Dark Triad, particularly Machiavellianism and CU traits, is associated with aggression, emotional instability, and delinquency in adolescents (Muris, Meesters, & Timmermans, 2013). Narcissism is associated with bullying behaviors. There is a strong genetic influence in persons with the Dark Triad of behaviors and persons with combined CD and the CU traits. In contrast, in antisocial youth without CU, the environmental influence is substantial and the genetic influence is small (Viding, Jones, Paul, Moffitt, & Plomin, 2008). Children with a callous and unemotional interpersonal style are at risk for developing the severe and persistent externalizing problems characteristic of childhood-onset CD. Machiavellianism, per se, is not part of the CD criteria, but deceitfulness, as defined in the criteria, is an aspect of Machiavellianism. Whereas CU traits are associated with extreme forms of physical violence (Frick, Cornell, et al., 2003; Frick, Kimonis, Dandreaux, & Farell, 2003), Machiavellianism is more often associated with relational aggression and with covert and sneaky misbehavior (Kerig & Stellwagen, 2010; McIlwain, 2003; Repacholi, Slaughter, Pritchard, & Gibbs, 2003). Relational or covert aggression causes harm by damaging a person's social status or relationships. The covert aggressive behaviors of Machiavellianism are less likely to draw negative attention to the perpetrator than the overt aggression of persons with CU (Kerig & Sink, 2010).

Bullying behavior is one of the criteria for CD. Adolescents high on CD, narcissism, and CU are more likely to engage in bullying (Fanti & Kimonis, 2012; Stellwagen & Kerig, 2013b). Youth and adolescents high on narcissism have strong feelings of entitlement combined with willingness to exploit younger or weaker children for their own personal gain. Bullies use aggression toward peers to achieve their own desired goals. Regardless of levels of CD and CU, those with CU traits are likely to engage in more severe and stable bullying (Fanti & Kimonis, 2012). Although adolescents with CU traits and narcissism are at risk of engaging in bullying, not all individuals who bully are diagnosed with CD.

DBD, SOCIAL-EMOTIONAL COMPETENCE, AND THEORY OF MIND

DBD is frequently associated with abnormalities in social cognition (Frick & Viding, 2009; McMahan & Frick, 2007). Other forms of atypical social cognition, such as impaired emotion recognition (Fairchild, Van Goozen, Calder, Stollery, & Goodyer, 2009) and poor theory of mind (ToM; Donno, Parker, Gilmour, & Skuse, 2010) have also been implicated in the development of childhood-onset CD. Some evidence exists that social cognition moderates the development of childhood conduct problems, by amplifying or attenuating the effects of other risk factors. For example, in early childhood, low maternal emotional support is only predictive of increases in aggression in children who have delayed ToM (Olson, Lopez-Duran, Lunkenheimer, Chang, & Sameroff, 2011). The capacity to understand the subjective states of others (socio-emotional competence) helps regulate antisocial behavior in typical development. Mandy and colleagues (Mandy, Skuse, Steer, St. Bourcain, & Oliver, 2013) proposed that children with ODD who develop childhood onset CD may have an inferior capacity for understanding the subjective states of others compared to children with ODD who do not go on to develop CD. They hypothesize that socio-emotional competence moderates the developmental relationship between ODD and CD symptoms; ODD symptoms pose the greatest risk for subsequent CD symptoms in children with poor socio-emotional competence.

The behaviors associated with some aspects of CD are clearly reflective of deficits in ToM, particularly affective ToM (Baron-Cohen, 2011). ToM involves the ability to recognize one's own thoughts and emotions, the thoughts and emotions of others, and respond appropriately to or empathize with the emotions of others (see Chapter 2 on social neuroscience). Machiavellianism also has been distinguished from CU traits by differences in aspects of ToM. Whereas youth with CU traits demonstrate deficits in both affective empathy ToM (responding with an appropriate emotion to the emotions of others) and affective cognitive ToM (recognition and identification of specific emotions; Blair, Colledge, & Mitchell, 2001; Loney, Frick, Clements, Ellis, & Kerlin, 2003; Woodworth & Waschbusch, 2008), youth high in Machiavellianism are able to read emotions accurately and display a good understanding of other's internal states. They use their cognitive ToM (recognizing mental states and intentions of others) and affective cognitive ToM for manipulation rather than altruism; they lack the affective empathy component of ToM (McIlwain, 2003). Some individuals with CU traits have difficulty with both affective cognitive ToM and affective empathy

ToM (responding with an appropriate emotion to another's emotion) whereas others have cognitive affective ToM but not affective empathy ToM. Youth high on CU are poor at recognizing others' distress cues and fail to experience physiological arousal from these cues. There is some neurological evidence for these affective ToM deficits. Youth with CD in combination with CU traits seem to have deficits in processing signs of fear and distress in others, seem to be less sensitive to punishment and show more fearless or thrill-seeking behavior (Jones, Laurens, Herba, Barker, & Viding, 2009; Marsh, et al., 2008).

Ringleader bullying is associated with average or better ToM abilities (Stellwagen & Kerig, 2013a; Sutton, Smith, & Swettenham, 1999), suggesting that social acumen allows bullies to successfully manipulate victims, recruit followers, and hide their misbehavior. Studies typically show that bullies have at least average cognitive ToM skills and even cognitive affective ToM abilities (Gini, 2006; Monks, Smith, & Swettenham, 2003); they are able to identify thoughts and feelings of others. These competencies may allow them to anticipate others' thoughts and actions and therefore to efficaciously manipulate the group processes underlying the dynamics of bullying. Bullies exhibit deficits in moral motivation and affective empathy. The emotions of others do not trigger an empathic response in them, and even though they know what is morally right or wrong, they did not feel obligated to do the right thing (Gasser & Keller, 2009). Bully-victims (those who are bullied and in response bully others) generally exhibit deficits in all aspects of ToM—cognitive, affective cognitive, and affective empathy. Victims of bullies often have deficits in cognitive and affective cognitive ToM that result in their lack of understanding in how others perceive them and that limit their ability to interpret the behaviors and emotions of others.

DBD AND LANGUAGE DISORDERS

An extensive body of literature has described interrelations among language, learning, and behavioral problems in school-age children. Children who exhibit problem behavior tend to have low language proficiency, and children with low language proficiency tend to exhibit problem behavior (Benner, Nelson, & Epstein, 2002). Although children with a range of maladaptive behavioral profiles are at risk for communication disorders, low language proficiency is often overlooked in children whose challenging behavior is highly salient to adults (e.g., Cohen, Davine, Horodezky, Lipsett, & Isaacson, 1993; Donahue, Cole, & Hartas, 1994). Children's language deficits often are misperceived as low intelligence, inattention, noncompliance, or even as deliberate dishonesty, disrespect, and defiance. For children with DBD, undetected language impairment can have serious consequences. If adults use language that is beyond students' comprehension, they may inadvertently increase problem behaviors (Sutherland & Morgan, 2003). With undiagnosed language impairment, students will be unable to participate effectively in designed interventions. Language deficits limit children's ability to benefit from instruction, talk-based therapies, and complex behavior management plans. All interventions must include consideration of children's linguistic needs.

A meta-analysis of studies of language deficits in children ages 5 to 13 diagnosed with EBD found a prevalence estimate of previously unidentified language deficits of around 81%, indicating that it is likely that four out of five children with EBD had at least mild language impairment that escaped the attention of relevant adults (Hollo, Wehby, & Oliver, 2014). Nearly half the children across the studies, 47%, had moderate to severe deficits. Youth offenders (children and adolescents in the juvenile justice systems) are three times more likely to display language problems than their nonoffending peers (Sanger, Moore-Brown, Magnusson, Svoboda, 2001). Studies of youth offender populations have reported that 65% to 100% of the youth exhibited language impairments on standardized language measures (Bryan, Freer, & Furlong, 2007; Snow & Powell, 2004).

Furthermore, individuals with CD have difficulty with several aspects of narrative discourse. Juvenile offenders asked to tell stories in response to six-frame cartoon stimuli produced as many story grammar elements as nonoffenders, but the plans, direct consequences, and resolutions in their stories were less complete than those of nonoffenders (Snow & Powell, 2005). Wainryb, Komolova, and Florsheim (2010) asked a group of youth offenders to talk about instances in which they had caused harm to another person and nonviolent youth to talk about a time when they did or said something and someone they knew felt hurt by it. The violent youth reported what happened when and who did what in their narratives, but unlike nonviolent youth, they did not organize their stories around goals and the thoughts and feelings of themselves and others. The researchers scored each narrative for references to landscape of action—references to precipitating events, perpetrator's harmful behaviors, victim's responses, and the incident's dénouement and references to landscape of consciousness—references to intentions, emotions, and other mental states (e.g., beliefs, desires). Landscape of consciousness can be thought of as linguistic coding for ToM. Nearly all nonviolent adolescents included references to their own intentions and other mental states in their narratives, and about half included references to their own emotions. By contrast, less than two thirds of the narratives of violent youth included references to their own intentions or their own mental states and about one third included references to their own emotions. The lack of landscape of consciousness references was even more marked when talking about others and not themselves—89% of nonviolent youth but only 10% of violent youth included in their accounts at least one reference to their victim's emotions. Similarly, 54% of nonviolent youth but only 20% of violent youth speculated about their victim's mental states.

Noel (2011) reported similar results with incarcerated youth whom she asked to produce personal narratives in response to prompts such as "Tell me a story about a time someone asked you to do something you knew you weren't supposed to do. Tell me what you were thinking and how you solved the problem." These youth offenders expressed themselves in poorly organized, syntactically simple sentences using few dependent clauses to explicitly signal the temporal and causal relationships within their stories. Of their narratives, 51% did not have a plot, which would involve a character's intention to accomplish a goal. Rather, their stories reflected an action sequence, or they reported others' responses to their identified problems. References to thoughts and emotions, either their own or others', were almost nonexistent. These findings are consistent with research documenting deficits in empathy and social cognition among juvenile delinquents. Responsive empathy has been shown to be a stronger predictor of offender/nonoffender status than self-reported aggression and antisocial attitudes (Robinson, Roberts, Strayer, & Koopman, 2007). This lack of attention to their victims' emotions is particularly troublesome, given the centrality that these attributions have for making moral decisions (Wainryb & Brehl, 2006).

ASSESSMENT FOR CHILDREN AND ADOLESCENTS WITH DBD

Research is showing that there are multiple factors associated with DBD that vary considerably for each person. To provide the most appropriate intervention, children and adolescents should receive comprehensive evaluations that consider individual characteristics and environmental factors for each person (Matthys & Lochman, 2010). (See the factors to consider in Box 11.1.) Ideally, a child or school psychologist with experience with children with DBD should conduct a functional behavior assessment, documenting the disruptive behaviors, when they occur, and how they are responded to. Children and adolescents with ODD or CD are at high risk for having executive function problems that could contribute to the behavioral problems or to ability to participate in interventions, so the psychologist should evaluate the student's executive functions as well as general intelligence.

Box 11.1 Factors to Consider in Assessment

Individual characteristics to be considered:

- Which specific ODD and/or CD criteria are met?
    - Are CU traits present?
    - Are patterns of Machiavellianism or narcissism present?
- Are there possible genetic bases for the DBD?
- Are there comorbid conditions?

    - ADHD
    - Language learning disabilities
    - Reading/math disabilities

- What ToM abilities are present? Absent?

Environmental factors to be considered:

- Contextual family factors

    - Poverty
    - Family structure: single parent, others in the home
    - Parental psychopathology
    - Marital conflict
    - Parent–child attachment

- Parenting practices

    - Nonresponsive parenting
    - Harsh, inconsistent discipline
    - Parental warmth
    - Lack of parental supervision and monitoring

- Peer factors

    - Friendships
    - Peer rejection
    - Moderators of social rejection
    - Child perception of social status
    - Deviant peer groups

- Contextual community and school factors

    - Neighborhood problems
    - School problems

The classroom teacher should document the student's present academic performance, and if the student is not at grade level, the teacher, the school psychologist, or the diagnostician should evaluate the student's reading, math, and working memory abilities. Contextual family factors (e.g., poverty, parent psychopathology) and parenting practices can contribute to children's and adolescents' behavior difficulties and families need to be involved in intervention programs, so a social worker or school counselor should interview family members. If a student exhibits motor planning difficulties or hypersensitivities to environmental stimuli, then an occupational therapist should also be a part of the evaluation team.

Because the majority of children and adolescents with DBD have language/learning and ToM impairments, all students diagnosed with ODD or CD should regularly receive a comprehensive language assessment. Such an assessment should not be limited to evaluation of vocabulary and syntactic skills but should also include evaluation of conversation and narrative discourse skills and the ability to make inferences from oral and written discourse. With awareness of the likelihood of ToM deficits in children and adolescents with DBD, their cognitive and affective ToM skills should also be assessed. Cognitive and affective ToM skills are also essential if social skills and cognitive behavior therapy are to be effective (refer to Chapter 2 for dimensions or types of ToM). There are no standardized tests that assess the range of development of ToM skills, but there are a number of research articles that describe tasks for evaluating first-order ToM (thinking about what someone is thinking or feeling) and second-order ToM (thinking about what someone is thinking or feeling about someone else; e.g., Pons, Harris, de Rosnay, 2004; Wellman & Liu, 2004) and higher order ToM, such as sarcasm, faux pas, and figurative language, in which what is said is different than what is meant (O'Hare, Bremmer, Happé, & Pettigrew, 2009). Because of the high incidence of affective empathy ToM deficits in students with DBD, this area ideally should be assessed. Although some questionnaires and assessments for measuring affective empathy are reported in the literature, they are generally not readily available (the Kids' Empathic Development Scale that assesses empathy of 7- to 10-year-olds in response to scenarios; Reid, Davis, Horlin, Anderson, Baughman, & Campbell, 2013; the Interpersonal Reactivity Index, a self-reported questionnaire for persons 10 years and older that assesses cognitive and affective empathy; Davis, 1980; and the Kiddie Mach; Christie & Geis, 1970, another self-reported questionnaire assesses Machiavellian traits in children 11 years and older). These questionnaires require reasonably good language skills and some degree of intrapersonal ToM (ability to reflect on one's thoughts and emotions), both of which are likely to be problematic in students with DBD.

Because Alec was not making progress in reading at the end of second grade, he was referred for an academic assessment. Testing indicated that Alec had superior visual perceptual skills, average language skills, and low average working memory and processing speed skills. He met criteria for dyslexia. In third grade, he received resource room support for reading and written language. In fourth grade, Alec was placed in a twice-exceptional program for gifted students with learning disabilities. In fifth grade, he was suspended, then transferred to another school with a program for students with EBD, suspended from that program, and then placed in a homebound educational program. Testing at the end of that year revealed markedly lower scores than earlier testing. His overall performance on intellectual testing was in the borderline range. Perceptual skills and comprehension scores were in the borderline range and processing scores were in the extremely low range. Although reading, writing, and math scores indicated significant impairment, his score on the Peabody Picture Vocabulary Test (Dunn & Dunn, 2007) was in the low average range, so Alec was not referred for a language evaluation. In the summer following sixth grade, he attended a language/literacy camp where the Clinical Evaluation of Language Fundamentals, fourth edition (CELF-4; Semel, Wiig, & Secord, 2003) was administered. Alex obtained a score of 68. His narratives were disorganized action or reactive sequences rather than stories with problems and solutions. He made little use of dependent clauses to signal temporal and causal relationships between events.

INTERVENTION FOR CHILDREN AND ADOLESCENTS WITH DBD

DBD are difficult to treat, especially if longstanding and accompanied by CU traits. Many of the interventions that have been used with children and adolescents with DBD have been generic—providing all referred persons with the same curriculum. To be effective, any intervention needs to address the full range of the child's difficulties, at home, school, and the wider community, in a developmentally appropriate way. All the strategies described in this chapter require a certain level of language and ToM skills to participate effectively. Therefore, the most basic treatment for children and adolescents with DBD must recognize and treat language/learning impairments and ToM.

Interventions need to match students' specific strengths and needs. Not attending to these variations can result in interventions that are counterproductive. Persons with CD and combined language or learning impairments are likely to exhibit deficits in social cognitive knowledge, pragmatic skills, and ToM. Students with this pattern of DBD might benefit from interventions that explicitly teach social skills and ToM (Adams et al., 2012). In contrast, some students with CD and Machiavellian or CU traits have good knowledge of expected social conventions and good cognitive ToM skills. Interventions that address these skills for students with Machiavellian traits are at best a waste of time and at worst can provide them with skills that enable them to be more manipulative. With the inclusion of the CU traits to the CD description, there is increased interest in and awareness of the need to address empathy, both cognitive affective ToM, that is, awareness and interpretation of the emotions of others and the ability to regulate one's emotions, and affective empathy, which is the ability to feel and respond to the emotions of others. Some programs or curricula for students with DBD teach aspects of emotional awareness in self and others (Southam-Gerow, 2013), but there has not been any systematic investigation of the effectives of focusing on developing affective ToM in these students.

Designing interventions for children and adolescents with DBD needs to employ a dynamic systems approach, which acknowledges that there are many intrinsic (internal neurologically based) and external (environmental) factors that influence all aspects of development. These factors interact in different ways within each individual. Nelson, Craven, Xuan, and Arkenberg (2004) have used the term "dynamic tricky mix" to refer to this variable mix of environmental and intrinsic factors with different children. Because the individual and environmental factors differ for each child and interact in different ways, no one invention is likely to be equally effective for everyone. Interventions should be informed by increasing the understanding of the psychopathology underlying conduct problems. Therefore, for early-onset ODD or CD, interventions should focus on psycho-education and support for parents and school, to avoid reinforcing undesirable behaviors. Problems with language, literacy and the ability to cope with peers, and the various types of ToM should also be identified and addressed. Treating co-morbid psychiatric conditions such as ADHD or depression is crucial. Interventions for DBD need to address both environmental and individual characteristics that contribute to the DBD (see Figure 11.1). A variety of approaches have been used to treat students with DBD including schoolwide interventions, parent training in behavior management, child-directed interventions focused on social skills or cognitive behavior management, or multisystemic systems that integrate components from all the approaches. Despite the fact that the majority of students with DBD have language

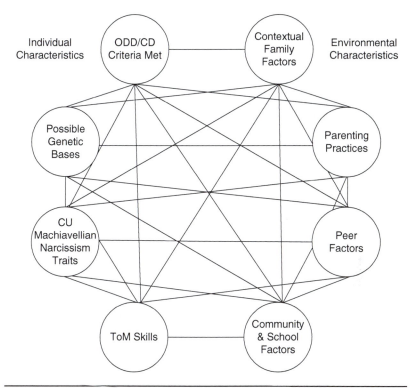

FIGURE 11.1 Dynamic Tricky Mix of Individual and Environmental Treatment Factors

impairments and deficits in ToM, there is not a body of literature on the effects of simultaneously addressing the language and ToM impairments.

Schoolwide Interventions

With increasing awareness of instances of bullying, schools are implementing school or district-wide programs to prevent and reduce violence. Positive behavioral supports (PBS) is among the most well-known of these programs. PBS employs principles of applied behavior analysis and nonpunitive, proactive, systematic techniques. The theory behind PBS is that problem behavior continues to occur because it is consistently followed by the child to get something positive or to escape something negative. PBS strategies fit the needs of children with DBD, particularly those with CU traits, who are known to be unresponsive to interventions that take away privileges for misbehavior. PBS focuses on the contexts and outcomes of the behavior to determine the functions of the behavior, and in so doing, the goal is to make the problem behavior less effective for the child and make desired behaviors more functional. All school staff are trained in PBS so there is consistency in expectations and strategies for managing behavior in all school contexts. Schoolwide PBS programs have three tiers (Tobin & Sugai, 2005). The primary level is intended to be a schoolwide prevention program that involves using effective teaching practices, explicitly teaching behavior that is expected and acceptable in the school environment, using consistent correction practices, and creating reinforcement systems that are used schoolwide (Nelson, Martella, & Marchand-Martella, 2002).

Children and adolescents with DBD require more than tier one interventions. The second intervention tier is for students who do not respond to the primary prevention strategies. Secondary interventions usually include social skills training and academic support typically delivered in small groups. Children with DBD, who exhibit persistent disciplinary problems, will require the third intervention tier. At this level, school staff conduct a functional behavioral assessment of the student, determining antecedent events that precede the inappropriate behavior, describing the behavior, and identifying the consequences of the behavior that might explain what is reinforcing it. This information is then used to design intervention programs to increase prosocial behaviors by giving clearer instructions and positive reinforcement. Antisocial behavior is decreased by a range of behavioral techniques such as extinction, overcorrection, time-out from positive reinforcement, and teaching and reinforcing prosocial behavior that is incompatible with the antisocial behavior. At Tiers 2 and 3, PBS plans are individualized and include procedures for monitoring, evaluating, and reassessing the process.

Meta-analysis of schoolwide and individual PBS programs have demonstrated effectiveness. Schoolwide programs have resulted in significant reductions in student suspensions and disciplinary referrals (Bradshaw, Mitchell, & Leaf, 2010). Meta-analysis of studies of individual students with a variety of different disabilities participating in PBS programs indicated moderate effects in increasing appropriate skills and decreasing problem behavior (Goh & Bambara, 2012). Unfortunately, studies have seldom investigated generalization or long-term effects of individualized PBS.

Parent Management Training

Because conduct problems often arise in disadvantaged families, broader family problems may need to be targeted. This can be challenging because family members may not recognize their role in the child's problems or may not have the motivation to be involved in interventions.

Because some of the behaviors associated with DBD are highly inheritable, particularly CU traits, a number of parents of children with DBD are likely to exhibit behavioral problems themselves, which may compromise their response to training. Children with DBD put stress on their families, even healthy families with involved, caring parents. Hence, parents of any child with significant behavioral problems can potentially benefit from parent management training.

The rationale for parent management training is based on the view that conduct disorders are inadvertently developed and sustained in the home by maladaptive parent–child interactions (K. Baker, 2013). Parent management training teaches parents to pay attention to and reinforce desirable behaviors and to use strategies for dealing with unwanted responses. The characteristics of the child and family affect the outcomes of parent training programs. For example, boys, ages 4 to 9 with and without CU traits, responded equally well to the part of an intervention that focused on teaching parents methods of using positive reinforcement to encourage prosocial behavior, but only the group without CU traits showed added improvement with the part of the intervention that focused on teaching parents more effective discipline strategies (Hawes & Dadds, 2005). Comorbidity in the child, such as untreated ADHD, language disorders, and learning difficulties, may also reduce the efficacy of parent programs. Failure to benefit from parent training/ education programs is also associated with parental disadvantage, lack of parental perception of a need for an intervention, and parental mental health problems, especially alcohol and drug problems, personality difficulties and depression (K. Baker, 2013).

Child- and Adolescent-Centered Interventions

Child- and adolescent-centered interventions have been of two types, social skills training, and cognitive behavioral therapy (CBT), both of which are typically done with small groups of students. In school settings, these interventions are often conducted jointly by a counselor, a social worker, or a school psychologist, along with a speech-language pathologist. This collaboration is critical because students' ability to participate in these interventions is dependent upon adequate comprehension and use of the language of the curricula, and many students with DBD have significant language impairments that could compromise their ability to participate adequately.

Social skills and CBT interventions are typically conducted in groups. There is evidence, however, that placing aggressive or antisocial children and adolescents in group therapy may exacerbate the unwanted behaviors (Lochman & Pardini, 2008; Poulin, Dishion, & Burraston,

2001). When youngsters with conduct disorders are placed together, in the absence of children with prosocial behavior, that is, without conduct disorder, peer bonding to deviant group members may occur and reinforce antisocial attitudes, values, and behaviors.

Social Skills Programs

Observation of the behaviors of children and adolescents with ODD and CD might suggest that they have social skills deficits and that teaching social skills would result in improved behavior. Although it is likely that some children and adolescents with DBD do lack knowledge of social skills, this is far from true for all of them. Sanger, Coufal, Scheffler, and Searcy (2003) found no difference between incarcerated and non-incarcerated adolescent girls in their pragmatic knowledge of the rules governing conversational practices according to societal dictates. Being able to state the rules for polite conversations, however, did not ensure that they used their knowledge in interactions.

Social skills training and programs to improve problem-solving skills seem to have high face validity, but they have not been demonstrated to be effective in any age group as a stand-alone intervention for children and adults with DBD. Trials of social skills training in adolescents with antisocial behavior reveal no evidence that the skills are generalized beyond the treatment setting, and therefore, these have limited impact on the delinquent behavior (K. Baker, 2013). Social skills training can have a role in the treatment of students with DBD who do lack knowledge of the rules of social interaction, but it is not an effective use of time and resources for students who have the pragmatic knowledge but do not use it. Those students require a careful assessment to determine what contributes to their lack of use of social cognitive knowledge.

Although some children and adolescents with DBD do have knowledge of social rules, many with DBD have distorted perceptions of social events and the intents of others and they use these distorted perceptions to justify their inappropriate behaviors. They tend to see hostile intents in many interactions and they fail to consider multiple cues when interpreting the meaning of others' behavior. Improving ToM skills in these individuals could result in more appropriate behaviors. Programs that incorporate role-play and creative dramatics may have the potential to improve students' cognitive and affective ToM skills if attention is given to identifying body and facial cues of emotions, noting and discussing factors in the situations that trigger emotions, and discussing how characteristics of persons affect their thoughts, beliefs, and emotions. Children are taught to identify and label different emotions and the situations in which they occur. The therapist may model expression of feelings and empathizing with others in addition to using pictures and games to increase emotional understanding. Such interventions have had some success in improving cognitive ToM and cognitive affective ToM in persons with language impairments or autism spectrum disorders (Charlop-Christy & Daneshvar, 2003; Feng, Lo, Tsai, & Cartledge, 2008; Wolf et al., 2008). Developing cognitive and cognitive affective ToM has proved easier than cognitive empathy has. But a study that provided either supplemental creative dramatics or art/music to neurotypical elementary and high school students did find that participation in creative dramatics over an academic year resulted in significantly improved scores on measures of affective empathy (Goldstein & Winner, 2012). Educators and clinicians need to be careful in teaching ToM skills, however. Improving ToM skills in students with Machiavellian traits or bullying tendencies may increase their abilities to manipulate and use others for their own ends.

Cognitive-Behavioral Interventions

Social skills programs may be integrated with CBT, which is designed to improve the child's understanding not only of interpersonal situations but also of their own thoughts and emotions as a means to improving their problem-solving abilities. The underlying concept behind CBT is that our thoughts and feelings play a fundamental role in our behavior. CBT focuses on examining the relationships among thoughts, feelings, and behaviors; hence it is a method for developing intrapersonal cognitive and affective ToM. Intrapersonal ToM involves reflecting on one's own thoughts and emotions and using this knowledge to regulate, plan, and monitor one's behavior.

Many of the behaviors exhibited by children and adolescents with DBD indicate their need for improved intrapersonal ToM. They tend to underestimate their own level of aggression and responsibility in arguments. They have a positive view of aggression, believing it is a necessary, if not an appropriate, approach to social problem solving and reduction of negative consequences. Their use of aggressive behavior enhances their self-esteem, and they value social goals of dominance and revenge more than affiliation (Bailey, 1996). When highly aroused, upset, or in situations that might cause upset feelings, they have fewer feelings of fear or sadness and respond aggressively. When problem solving, children with CD generate fewer verbal assertive solutions and many more action-oriented and aggressive solutions to interpersonal problems (Dodge & Newman, 1981).

CBT requires verbal ability and some degree of insight or ToM. Given that many children and adolescents with ODD and CD have language impairments and ToM deficits, speech-language pathologists will likely need to modify CBT programs to include development of the language and ToM skills essential for participating. Although CBT programs often acknowledge a role for emotions in behavior, they have typically focused on employing cognitive factors (cognitive ToM—dealing with thoughts and beliefs) to problem solve. CBT components generally include the following (L. L. Baker & Scarth, 2002):

- Defining the problem
- Generating solutions to the problem
- Evaluating possible solutions and selecting one
- Implementing the solution
- Evaluating the outcome.

A combination of modeling and self-instructional language training are used to teach children to control their impulsive behaviors, problem solve, and deal with frustration and failure in goal-directed activities (Kendall & Braswell, 1993; Meichenbaum, 1977). Older students also are engaged in cognitive restructuring—rethinking their behavior, recognizing their thoughts that led to antisocial actions, and examining and changing those thoughts to minimize chances of future misconduct.

There has been an increasing recognition of the need to address emotional factors in treatment and include activities to promote recognition, understanding, and regulation of emotions (Committee for Children, 2011; Conduct Problems Prevention Research Group, 2010; Greenberg & Kusche, 2006; Southam-Gerow, 2013; Webster-Stratton, Reid, & Stoolmiller, 2008). Compared to children in control groups, children participating in these programs had improvements in social problem solving, emotional understanding and self-control and lower rates of conduct problems. Vaske, Galyean, and Cullen (2011) suggest that CBT programs incorporating affective components are more likely than other interventions to result in behavioral changes because tasks involving perspective taking, emotional understanding, and emotionally regulate activate areas of the brain shown to be dysfunctional in persons with antisocial behaviors.

A Language Intervention Approach to DBD

We tell ourselves stories, and we live by the stories we tell ourselves. Children and adolescents with DBD are not good at telling themselves stories. Noel (2011), a speech-language pathologist with extensive experience with children and adolescents with DBD and the intervention programs described in this chapter, has employed a narrative-based intervention to address the language and problem-solving needs of youth offenders. Narrative discourse is dependent on ToM skills. When relating personal narratives, one needs to be able to reflect on and evaluate past experiences, not just list the event or experience.

Reflection and evaluation require intrapersonal ToM when thinking about one's own intents and emotions and interpersonal ToM when thinking about the reasons for the behaviors of others. Noel explicitly has taught incarcerated adolescents the components of stories, using what she calls the SPACE storytelling strategy, and then has had them use these skills. When retelling stories they had read, listened to, or viewed, adolescents were taught to organize their stories with these components:

- Setting (S): Who is involved? When does it happen? What's going on?
- Problem (P): What is the problem? How do the characters feel? What do the characters need or want?
- Action (A): What did the characters do?
- Consequence (C): What was the result of the character's action
- End/evaluation (E): How did the story end? What was the lesson learned? How do you feel in response to the story?

Once students were able to retell stories using the SPACE storytelling strategy, they were instructed in the BEST PLANS social problem-solving strategy. Students were taught the components and process using the mnemonic BEST PLANS. This strategy has nine steps: (1) Be aware of the setting. (2) Examine the problem. (3) Set an end goal. (4) Think about what you could do. (5) Predict the possible consequences. (6) Label your decision. (7) Arrange a plan and take action. (8) Notice the consequences. (9) Study the end; did the plan work? These steps were taught embedded in a modified SPACE framework. The adolescents used the BEST PLANS framework to produce narratives of their own experiences. Compared to their preintervention language and problem-solving samples, the youth offenders who participated in this narrative language intervention produced structurally more complex narratives, greater inclusion of social problem-solving, and greater use of landscape of consciousness in their postintervention personal narratives; that is, they made more reference to the mental states and emotions of themselves.

MULTISYSTEMIC THERAPY

Multisystemic therapy (MST) is a multicomponent program for adolescents with serious conduct disorders that combines all the intervention elements already discussed. This approach recognizes the multidimensional nature of serious antisocial behavior, so it draws on a broad spectrum of techniques to address individual, parental, family, and peer relationship problems. The main treatment interventions include family therapy, parent training, marital therapy, and supportive psychotherapy related to interpersonal problems, social skills components, and cognitive behavioral therapy, as well as case management in which the therapist acts as an advocate to outside agencies for the young person and family. The main goal of MST is to give parents the skills and resources needed independently to address the difficulty of raising adolescents while also empowering the young person to cope with family, peer, and school problems. MST was more effective in reducing externalizing behavior in adolescents with lower CU or lower narcissism traits than in those with high CU or high narcissism (Henggeler, 2011; Manders, Dekovic, Asscher, van der Laan, & Prins, 2013). It was more effective than other methods in decreasing externalizing behaviors (including fewer arrests, less serious offenses, fewer weeks of incarceration) in adolescents, but not in reducing psychopathic traits per se.

The summer following sixth grade, Alec was enrolled in a 9-week summer language/literacy camp. Each daily session was divided into three components: decoding/orthographic skills, narrative comprehension/production, and science activities to build expository language skills and social skills through collaborative problem solving. Sentence frames were used to develop Alec's syntactic skills to express emotional relationships in narratives (**When** _____ [what happened] the character **felt** _____ [emotion], **because** _____ [reason for emotion]) or rationales for characters' intentional behaviors (The character **wanted** _____ [intent, goal, objective] **because** _____ [reason for goal] **but** _____ [obstacle to achieving goal], **so** _____ [what character did to overcome obstacle and achieve goal]). He watched videos of interactions, noting expressions and tone of voice of the characters to interpret characters' thoughts and feelings and to predict what characters would do. The clinician taught strategies for decision making and problem solving by using a framework proposed by Elias (2004) for students with social-emotional difficulties. Alec was asked to identify problems faced by characters in narratives, identify and evaluate their solutions to the problems, then apply the problem-solving strategies to his own experiences.

IMPLICATIONS

Children with DBD present with complex individual and environmental factors that affect their behavior and social interactions. Results of studies evaluating interventions suggest that attention to these multiple factors and the subtypes of aggressive children likely will enhance the effectiveness of interventions (Caldwell, Skeem, Salekin, & Van

Rybroek, 2006). CU traits are associated with poorer treatment outcomes in samples of antisocial youths (Frick & Dickens, 2006). Multicomponent programs that integrate or fuse programs into one coherent intervention have been shown to be the most effective for children and adolescents with DBD. Effects of most single intervention programs are modest. This may be due to equifinality; that is, different risk factors lead to the same behavioral problems. Consequently, treating only the observed behavior does not necessarily address the factors contributing to behavioral problems in a specific child.

Children with differing environmental influences, comorbid conditions, patterns of behavior, and psychopathic traits require differing approaches to interventions. School discipline for students with DBD typically employs punishments, for example, time-outs, denial of privileges, or suspensions. Children with CU traits, however, are not intrinsically motivated to "do the right thing" and tend to be reward oriented; punishments have little effect on changing their behaviors. These children tend to respond better to programs that provide clear, tangible external reinforcements for appropriate social behavior and teach empathy (Caldwell et al., 2006; Wong & Hare, 2005). Interventions for children with DBD and narcissistic traits might need to replace unconditional and excessive praise with tangible rewards and assistance in learning to cope with receiving negative feedback (Barry, Frick, & Killian, 2003). Interventions for students with DBD and Machiavellian traits might need to modify the larger social climate in which such behavior takes place. Students with Machiavellian traits obtain rewards through manipulating others, often in subtle ways that go unnoticed. Teachers and staff must be alert to manipulative behaviors if they are to reduce the social rewards students are achieving (Olweus, Limber, & Mihalic, 1999). Sutton and Keogh (2000) further suggest engaging the students in discussions about interpersonal trust and the values of cooperation, but caution that children with Machiavellian traits are less inclined to keep their side of behavioral contracts. If students with DBD are to be able to respond to the interventions described in this chapter, they must have adequate language and ToM skills. Because the majority of children and adolescents with DBD are at risk for impairments in these areas, speech-language pathologists need to be part of the teams that serve them.

DISCUSSION QUESTIONS

1. Discuss the ways that environmental conditions and individual (and genetic) characteristics interact in DBD.

2. Describe the patterns of behaviors you might see in children and adolescents with DBD. Why is it important to recognize the specific behavioral patterns exhibited by students with DBD?
3. How would you approach assessment of a student with DBD?
4. Many efficacy studies of interventions for DBD have shown only modest effects. Why might this be the case?
5. Develop a language-based intervention plan for a student with DBD with CU traits. Consider the vocabulary, syntactic patterns, discourse structures, and ToM concepts that would be addressed.

INSTRUCTIONAL RESOURCES

Baron Cohen, S. Zero Degrees of Empathy. Retrieved from www.youtube.com/watch?v=Aq_nCTGSfWE

Cognitive Behavioural Approaches to Treating Children & Adolescents with Conduct Disorder. Retrieved from www.kidsmentalhealth.ca/documents/Cognitive_Behavioural_Conduct_Disorder.pdf

Dennis Embry, How Are the Children?: www.youtube.com/watch?v=h7olxaYofdk

Emotion in Education: An Interview with Maurice Elias. Retrieved from www.edutopia.org/maurice-elias-sel-videoKids at Hope website. www.kidsathope.org/

Nelson Muntz—A Simpson's Case Study in Conduct Disorder. Retrieved from www.youtube.com/watch?v=lLU3agENOFc

Oppositional Defiance—Easy Strategies for Dealing with ODD Disorder: Smart Discipline: www.youtube.com/watch?v=EkJtcO8t_3E

Oppositional Defiant Disorder: www.youtube.com/watch?v=uoXBFOZml80

Positive Behavior Supports website: www.resa.net/curriculum/positivebehavior/

Second Step Program website: www.cfchildren.org/second-step.aspx

Stewie Griffin—A Case Study in Oppositional Defiant Disorder (more conduct disorders): www.youtube.com/watch?v=rdG_1_Pic8Y

TED Talks: The Challenge of Early Conduct Disorder, Derek Patton. The Virtues Project. Retrieved from www.youtube.com/watch?v=uptMwDiJn-I&list=PL2CBRa7760FwnN6kNh89e4rGhM8W6BcqL&index=8 Or www.virtuesproject.com/rfacilitators.html

REFERENCES

Adams, C., Lockton, E., Freed, J., Gaile, J., Earl, G., McBean, K., . . . Law, J. (2012). The Social Communication Intervention Project: A randomized controlled trial of the effectiveness of speech and language therapy for school-age children who have pragmatic and social communication problems with or without autism spectrum disorder. *International Journal of Language and Communication Disorders, 47,* 233–244.

American Psychiatric Association. (2013). *Diagnostic and statistical manual of mental disorders* (5th ed.). Arlington VA: Author.

Bailey, V. F. A. (1996). Intensive interventions in conduct disorders. *Archives of Disease in Childhood, 74,* 352–356.

Baker, K. (2013). Conduct disorder in children and adolescents. *Paediatrics and Child Health, 23,* 24–29.

Baker, L. L., & Scarth, K. (2002). *Cognitive behavioral approaches to treating children and adolescents with conduct disorders.* Toronto, ON: Children's Mental Health Ontario.

Barry, C. T., Frick, P. J., & Killian, A. L. (2003). The relation of narcissism to self-esteem and conduct problems in children: A preliminary investigation. *Journal of Clinical Child and Adolescent Psychology, 32,* 139–152.

Baron-Cohen, S. (2011). *The science of evil: On empathy and the origins of cruelty.* New York, NY: Basic Books.

Baughman, H. M., Dearing, S., Giammarco, E., & Vernon, P. A. (2012). Relationships between bullying behaviours and the dark triad: A study with adults. *Personality and Individual Differences, 52,* 571–575.

Benner, G. J., Nelson, J. R., & Epstein, M. H. (2002). Language skills of children with EBD: A literature review. *Journal of Emotional and Behavioral Disorders, 10,* 43–59.

Blair, R. J., Colledge, E., & Mitchell, D. G. (2001). A selective impairment in the processing of sad and fearful expressions in children with psychopathic tendencies. *Journal of Abnormal Child Psychology, 29,* 491–498.

Bradshaw, C. P., Mitchell, M. M., & Leaf, P. J. (2010). Examining the effects of schoolwide positive behavioral interventions and supports on student outcomes: Results from a randomized controlled effectiveness trial in elementary schools. *Journal of Positive Behavior Interventions, 3,* 133–148.

Brendtro, L., & Shahbazian, M. (2004). *Troubled children and youth: Turning problems into opportunities.* Champaign, IL: Research Press.

Bryan, K., Freer, J., & Furlong, C. (2007). Language and communication difficulties in juvenile offenders. *International Journal of Language and Communication Disorders, 42,* 505–520.

Buitelaar, J. K., Smeets, K. C., Herpers, P., Scheepers, F., Glennon, J., & Rommelse, N. N. (2013). Conduct disorders. *European Child Adolescence and Psychiatry, 22,* S49–S54.

Burke, J. D., Waldman, I., & Lahey, B. B. (2010). Predictive validity of childhood oppositional defiant disorder and conduct disorder: Implications for DSM-V. *Journal of Abnormal Psychology, 119,* 739–751.

Caldwell, M., Skeem, J., Salekin, R., & Van Rybroek, G. (2006). Treatment response of adolescent offenders with psychopathy features: A 2-year follow-up. *Criminal Justice and Behavior, 33,* 571–596.

Charlop-Christy, M. H., & Daneshvar, S. (2003). Using video modeling to teach perspective taking to children with autism. *Journal of Positive Behavior Interventions, 5,* 12–21.

Christie, R., & Geis, F. L. (1970). *Studies in Machiavellianism.* New York, NY: Academic Press.

Cohen, N. J., Davine, M., Horodezky, M. A., Lipsett, L., & Isaacson, L. (1993). Unsuspected language impairment in psychiatrically disturbed children: Prevalence and language and behavioral characteristics. *Journal of the American Academy of Child and Adolescent Psychiatry, 32,* 595–603.

Committee for Children. (2011). *Second Step: A violence prevention curriculum.* Seattle, WA: Author.

Conduct Problems Prevention Research Group. (2010). The effects of a multiyear universal social-emotional learning program: The role of student and school characteristics. *Journal of Consulting and Continuing Psychology, 78,* 156–168.

Davis, M. H. (1980). A multidimensional approach to individual differences in empathy. *JSAS Catalog of Selected Documents in Psychology, 10,* 1–19.

Dodge, K. A., & Newman, J. P. (1981). Biased decision-making processes in aggressive boys. *Journal of Abnormal Psychology, 90,* 375–390.

Donahue, M., Cole, D., & Hartas, D. (1994). Links between language and emotional/behavioral disorders. *Education and Treatment of Children, 17,* 244–254.

Donno, R., Parker, G., Gilmour, J., & Skuse, D. H. (2010). Social communication deficits in disruptive primary-school children. *British Journal of Psychiatry, 196,* 282–289.

Dunn, L. M., & Dunn, D. M. (2007). *Peabody Picture Vocabulary Test–4.* San Antonio, TX: Pearson.

Elias, M. J. (2004). Strategies to infuse social and emotional learning into academics. In J. E. Zins, R. P. Weissberg, M. C. Wang, & H. J. Wallberg (Eds.), *Building academic success on social and emotional learning* (pp. 113–134). New York, NY: Teachers College Press.

Fairchild, G., Van Goozen, S. H. M., Calder, A. J., Stollery, S. J., & Goodyer, I. M. (2009). Deficits in facial expression recognition in male adolescents with early-onset or adolescence-onset conduct disorder. *Journal of Child Psychology and Psychiatry, 50,* 627–636.

Fanti, K. A., & Kimonis, E. R. (2012). Bullying and victimization: The role of conduct problems and psychopathic traits. *Journal of Research on Adolescence, 22,* 617–631.

Feng, H., Lo, Y., Tsai, S., & Cartledge, G. (2008). The effects of theory-of-mind and social skill training on the social competence of a sixth-grade student with autism. *Journal of Positive Behavior Interventions, 10,* 228–242.

Frick, P. J., Cornell, A., Bodin, D., Dane, H., Barry, C. T., & Loney, B. R. (2003). Callous-unemotional traits and developmental pathways to severe conduct problems. *Developmental Psychology, 39,* 246–260.

Frick, P. J., & Dickens, C. (2006). Current perspectives on conduct disorder. *Current Psychiatry Reports, 8,* 59–72.

Frick, P. J., Kimonis, E. R., Dandreaux, D. M., & Farell, J. M. (2003). The 4 year stability of psychopathic traits in nonreferred youth. *Behavioral Sciences & the Law, 21,* 713–736.

Frick, P. J., & Nigg, J. T. (2011). Current issues in the diagnosis of attention deficit hyperactivity disorder, oppositional defiant disorder, and conduct disorder. *Annual Review of Clinical Psychology, 8,* 77–107.

Frick, P. J., & Viding, E. M. (2009). Antisocial behavior from a developmental psychopathology perspective. *Developmental Psychopathology, 21,* 1111–1131.

Gasser, L., & Keller, M. (2009). Are the competent the morally good? Perspective taking and moral motivation of children involved in bullying. *Social Development, 18,* 778–816.

Gini, G. (2006). Bullying as a social process: The role of group membership in students' perception of inter-group aggression at school. *Journal of School Psychology, 44,* 51–65.

Goh, A. E., & Bambara, L. M. (2012). Individualized positive behavior support in school settings: A meta-analysis. *Remedial & Special Education, 33,* 271–286.

Goldstein, T. R., & Winner, E., (2012). Enhancing empathy and theory of mind. *Journal of Cognition and Development, 13,* 19–37.

Greenberg, M. T., & Kusche, C. A. (2006). Building social and emotional competence: The PATHS curriculum. In S. R. Jimerson & M. Furlong (Eds.), *Handbook of school violence and school safety: From research to practice* (pp. 395–412). Mahwah, NJ: Erlbaum.

Hawes, D. J., & Dadds, M. R. (2005). The treatment of conduct problems in children with callous-unemotional traits. *Journal of Consulting and Clinical Psychology, 73,* 1–5.

Henggeler, S. W. (2011). Efficacy studies to large-scale transport: The development and validation of Multisystemic Therapy programs. *Annual Review of Clinical Psychology, 7,* 351–381.

Hollo, A., Wehby, J. H., & Oliver, R. M. (2014). Unidentified language deficits in children with emotional and behavioral disorders: A meta-analysis. *Exceptional Children, 80,* 169–186.

Jones, A. P., Laurens, K. L., Herba, C., Barker, G., & Viding, E. (2009). Amygdala hypoactivity to fearful faces in boys with conduct problems and callous–unemotional traits. *American Journal of Psychiatry, 166,* 95–102.

Kendall, P. C., & Braswell, L. (1993). *Cognitive-behavioral therapy for impulsive children* (2nd ed.). New York, NY: Guilford.

Kerig, P. K., & Sink, H. E. (2010). The new scoundrel on the schoolyard: Contributions of Machiavellianism to the understanding of youth aggression. In C. T. Barry, P. K. Kerig, & T. D. Barry (Eds.), *Narcissism and Machiavellianism in youth* (pp. 193–212). Washington, DC: APA Press.

Kerig, P. K., & Stellwagen, K. K. (2010). Roles of callous-unemotional traits, narcission, and Machiavellianism in childhood aggression. *Journal of Psychopathathology Behavior Assessment, 32,* 343–352.

Lochman, J. E., & Pardini, D. A. (2008). Cognitive behavioral therapies. In M. Rutter, D. Bishop, D. Pine, S. Scott, J. Stevenson, E. Taylor, & A. Thapar (Eds.), *Rutter's Child and Adolescent Psychiatry* (5th ed., pp. 1026–1045). London, UK: Blackwell.

Loney, B. R., Frick, P. J., Clements, C. B., Ellis, M. K., & Kerlin, K. (2003). Callous–unemotional traits, impulsivity, and emotional processing in adolescents with antisocial behavior problems. *Journal of Clinical Child and Adolescent Psychology, 32,* 66–80.

Manders, W. A., Dekovic, M., Asscher, J. J., van der Laan, P., & Prins, P. J. M. (2013). Psychopathy as predictor and moderator of multisystemic therapy outcome among adolescents treated for antisocial behavior. *Journal of Abnormal Child Psychology, 41,* 1121–1132.

Mandy, W., Skuse, D., Steer, C., St. Bourcain, B., & Oliver, B. R. (2013). Oppositionality and socioemotional competence: Interacting risk factors in the development of childhood conduct disorder symptoms. *Journal of the American Academy of Child & Adolescent Psychiatry, 52,* 718–727.

Marsh, A. A., Finger, E. C., Mitchell, D. G., Reid, M. E., Sims, C., Kosson, D. S., . . . Blair, R. J. (2008). Reduced amygdala response to fearful expressions in children and adolescents with callous–unemotional traits and disruptive behavior disorders. *American Journal of Psychiatry, 165,* 712–720.

Matthys, W., & Lochman, J. E. (2010). *Oppositional defiant disorder and conduct disorder in childhood.* Walden, MA: Wiley.

Maughan, B., Rowe, R., Messer, J., Goodman, R., & Meltzer, B. (2004). Conduct disorder and oppositional defiant disorder in a national sample: Developmental epidemiology. *Journal of Child Psychology and Psychiatry, 45,* 609–621.

McIlwain, D. (2003). Bypassing empathy: A Machiavellian theory of mind and sneaky power. In B. Repacholi & V. Slaughter (Eds.), *Individual differences in theory of mind: implications for typical and atypical development* (pp. 39–66). New York, NY: Psychology Press.

McMahan, R. J., & Frick, P. J. (2007). Conduct and oppositional disorders. In J. M. Mash & R. A. Barkley (Eds.), *Assessment of Childhood Disorders* (pp. 132–184). London, UK: Guilford Press.

Meichenbaum, D. (1977). *Cognitive-behavioral modification: An integrated approach.* New York, NY: Guilford.

Moffitt, T. E. (2006). Life-course persistent versus adolescence-limited antisocial behavior. In D. Cicchetti & D. J. Cohen (Eds.), *Developmental Psychopathology, Vol 3. Risk, disorder, and adaptation* (pp. 570–598). New York, NY: Wiley.

Moffitt, T. E., Arseneault, L., Jaffee, S. R., Kim-Cohen, J., & Koenen, K. C., Odgers, C. L., . . . Viding, E. (2008). Research review: DSM-V conduct disorder: research needs for an evidence base. *Journal of Child Psychology & Psychiatry, 49*, 3–33.

Monks, C., Smith, P., & Swettenham, J. (2003). Aggressors, victims, and defenders in preschool: Peer, self-, and teacher reports. *Merrill-Palmer Quarterly: Journal of Developmental Psychology, 49*, 453–469.

Muris, P., Meesters, C., & Timmermans, A. (2013). Some youths have a gloomy side: Correlates of the Dark Triad personality traits in non-clinical adolescents. *Children Psychiatry & Human Development, 44*, 658–665.

Nelson, K. E., Craven, P. L., Xuan, Y., & Arkenberg, M. E. (2004). Acquiring art, spoken language, sign language, text, and other symbolic systems: Developmental and evolutionary observations from a dynamic tricky mix theoretical perspective. In J. M. Lucariello, J. A. Hudson, R. Fivush, & P. J. Bauer (Eds.), *The development of the mediated mind: Sociocultural context and cognitive development* (pp. 175–222). Mahwah, NJ: Erlbaum.

Nelson, J. R., Martella, R. M., & Marchand-Martella, N. (2002). Maximizing student learning: The effects of a comprehensive school-based program for preventing problem behaviors. *Journal of Emotional & Behavioral Disorders, 10*, 136–148.

Noel, K. (2011). *The effects of a narrative-based social problem-solving intervention with high-risk adolescent males* (Unpublished doctoral dissertation). University of New Mexico, Albuquerque.

Offord, D. (1987). Prevention of behavioural and emotional disorders in children. *Journal of Child Psychology & Psychiatry, 28*, 9–19.

O'Hare, A. E., Bremner, L., Happé, F., & Pettigrew, L. M. (2009). A clinical assessment tool for advanced theory of mind performance in 5 to 12 year olds. *Journal of Autism and Developmental Disorders, 39*, 916–928. doi:10.1007/s10803-009-0699-2

Olson, S. L., Lopez-Duran, N., Lunkenheimer, E. S., Change, H., & Sameroff, A. J. (2011). Individual differences in the development of early peer aggression: Integrating contributions of self-regulation, theory of mind, and parenting. *Developmental Psychopathology, 23*, 253–266.

Olweus, D., Limber, S., & Mihalic, S. (1999). *The bullying prevention program: Blueprints for violence prevention*. Boulder, CO: Center for the Study and Prevention of Violence.

Paulhus, D. L., & Williams, K. M. (2002). The Dark Triad of personality: Narcissism, Machiavellianism, and psychopathy. *Journal of Research in Personality, 36*, 556–563.

Pons, R. Harris, P., & de Rosnay, M. (2004). Emotion comprehension between 3–11 years: Developmental periods and hierarchical organization. *European Journal of Developmental Psychology, 1*, 127–152.

Poulin, E., Dishion, T. J., & Burraston, B. (2001). 3-year iatrogenic effects associated with aggregating high-risk adolescents in cognitive-behavioral interventions. *Applied Developmental Sciences, 5,* 214–224.

Reid, C., Davis, H., Horlin, C., Anderson, M., Baughman, N., & Campbell, C. (2013). The Kids' Empathic Development Scale (KEDS): A multi-dimensional measure of empathy in primary school-aged children. *British Journal of Developmental Psychology, 31,* 231–256.

Repacholi, B., Slaughter, V., Pritchard, M., & Gibbs, V. (2003). Theory of mind, Machiavellianism, and social functioning in childhood. In B. Repacholi & V. Slaughter (Eds.), *Individual differences in theory of mind* (pp. 67–97). New York, NY: Psychology Press.

Robinson, R., Roberts, W. L., Strayer, J., & Koopman, R. (2007). Empathy and emotional responsiveness in delinquent and non-delinquent adolescents. *Social Development, 16,* 555–579.

Sanger, D. D., Coufal, K. L., Scheffler, M., & Searcey, R. (2003). Implications of the personal perceptions of incarcerated adolescents concerning their own communicative competence. *Communication Disorders Quarterly, 24,* 64–78.

Sanger, D. D., Moore-Brown, B., Magnusson, B., & Svoboda, N. (2001). Prevalence of language problems among adolescent delinquents: A closer look. *Communication Disorders Quarterly, 23,* 17–26.

Semel, E., Wiig, E., & Secord, W. (2003). *Clinical Evaluation of Language Fundamentals—4th edition (CELF-4).* San Antonio, TX: Harcourt Assessment.

Snow, P. C., & Powell, M. B. (2004). Developmental language disorders and adolescent risk: A public-health advocacy role for speech pathologists? *Advances in Speech-Language Pathology, 6,* 221–229.

Snow, P. C., & Powell, M. B. (2005). What's the story? An exploration of narrative language abilities in male juvenile offenders. *Psychology, Crime & Law, 11,* 239–253.

Southam-Gerow, M. A. (2013). *Emotion regulation in children and adolescents.* New York, NY: Guilford.

Stellwagen, K., & Kerig, P. (2013a). Dark triad personality traits and theory of mind among school-age children. *Personality and Individual Differences, 54,* 123–127.

Stellwagen, K., & Kerig, P. (2013b). Ringleader bullying: Association with psychopathic narcissism and theory of mind among child psychiatric inpatients. *Child Psychiatry & Human Development, 44,* 612–620.

Sutherland, K. S., & Morgan, P. L. (2003). Implications of transactional processes in classrooms for students with emotional/behavioral disorders. *Preventing School Failure, 48,* 32–37.

Sutton, J., & Keogh, E. (2000). Social competition in school: Relationships with bullying, Machiavellianism and personality. *British Journal of Educational Psychology, 70,* 443–456.

Sutton, J., Smith, P. K., & Swettenham, J. (1999). Social cognition and bullying: Social inadequacy or skilled manipulation. *British Journal of Developmental Psychology, 17*, 435–450.

Tobin, T. J., & Sugai, G. (2005). Preventing problem behaviors: Primary, secondary, and tertiary level prevention interventions for young children. *Journal of Early and Intensive Behavior Intervention, 2*, 125–144.

Vaske, J., Galyean, K., & Cullen, F. T. (2011). Toward a biosocial theory of offender rehabilitation: Why does cognitive-behavioral therapy work? *Journal of Criminal Justice, 39*, 90–102.

Viding, E., Jones, A. P., Paul, J. F., Moffitt, T. E., & Plomin, R. (2008). Heritability of antisocial behaviour at 9: Do callous-unemotional traits matter? *Developmental Science, 11*, 17–22.

Wainryb, C., & Brehl, B. (2006). I thought she knew that would hurt my feelings: Developing psychological knowledge and moral thinking. In R. Kail (Ed.), *Advances in child development and behavior* (Vol. 34, pp. 131–171). New York, NY: Academic Press.

Wainryb, C., Komolova, M., & Florsheim, P. (2010). How violent youth offenders and typically developing adolescents construct moral agency in narratives about doing harm. In K. C. McLean & M. Pasupathi (Eds.), *Narrative development adolescence* (pp. 185–206). New York, NY: Springer.

Webster-Stratton, C., Reid, M. J., & Stoolmiller, M. (2008). Preventing conduct problems and improving school readiness: Evaluation of the Incredible Years teacher and child training programs in high-risk schools. *Journal of Child Psychology and Psychiatry, 49*, 471–488.

Wellman, H. M., & Liu, D. (2004). Scaling of theory-of-mind tasks. *Child Development, 75*, 523–541.

Wolf, J. M., Tanaka, J. W., Klaiman, C., Cockburn, J. Herlihy, L., Brown, C., . . . Schultz, R. T. (2008). Specific impairment of face processing abilities in children with autism spectrum disorder using the Let's Face It! skills battery. *Autism Research, 1*, 329–340.

Wong, S., & Hare, R. D. (2005). *Guidelines for a psychopathy treatment program.* Toronto, ON: Multi-Health Systems.

Woodworth, M., & Waschbusch, D. (2008). Emotional processing in children with conduct problems and callous/unemotional traits. *Child: Care, Health & Development, 34*, 234–244.

INDEX

Note: Page numbers followed by *f* indicate a figure on the corresponding page. Page numbers followed by *t* indicate a table on the corresponding page.